Recent Advances in Computational Terminology

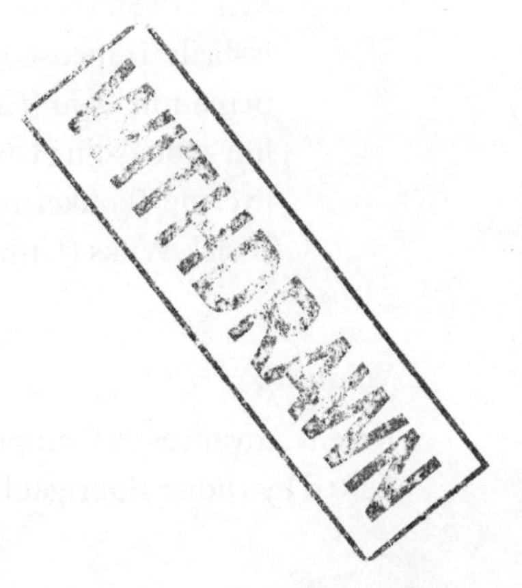

Natural Language Processing

Volume 2

Recent Advances in Computational Terminology
Edited by Didier Bourigault, Christian Jacquemin and Marie-Claude L'Homme

Recent Advances in Computational Terminology

Edited by

Didier Bourigault
CNRS, ERSS, Université Toulouse-le-Mirail

Christian Jacquemin
CNRS-LIMSI, Orsay

Marie-Claude L'Homme
Université de Montréal

John Benjamins Publishing Company
Amsterdam / Philadelphia

The paper used in this publication meets the minimum requirements of American National Standard for Information Sciences — Permanence of Paper for Printed Library Materials, ANSI Z39.48-1984.

Library of Congress Cataloging-in-Publication Data

Recent advances in computational terminology / edited by Didier Bourigault, Christian Jacquemin, Marie-Claude L'Homme.

p. cm. -- (Natural language processing, ISSN 1567-8202 ; v. 2)

Includes bibliographical references and index.

1. Terms and phrases--Data processing. I. Bourigault, Didier . II. Jacquemin, Christian. III. L'Homme, Marie-Claude. IV. Natural language processing ; 2.

P305.18.D38 R43 2001

401'.4'0285--dc21 00-051911

ISBN 90 272 4984 9 (Eur.) / 1 58811 016 8 (US) CIP

John Benjamins Publishing Co. • P.O.Box 36224 • 1020 ME Amsterdam • The Netherlands

John Benjamins North America • P.O.Box 27519 • Philadelphia PA 19118-0519 • USA

Scientific Committee

Sofia Ananiadou (Center for Computational Linguistics, UMIST, Manchester, U.K.)
Peter Anick (Altavista, Compaq)
Anne Condamines (ERSS, Université Toulouse-le-Mirail, Toulouse, France)
Bruce Croft (Computer Science, University of Massachussetts)
Béatrice Daille (IRIN, Nantes, France)
Eric Gaussier (Xerox Research Centre Europe, Grenoble, France)
Gregory Grefenstette (Xerox Research Centre Europe, Grenoble, France)
Benoît Habert (CNRS-LIMSI, Orsay, France)
Stephanie Haas (University of North Carolina, USA)
Ulrich Heid (University of Stuttgart, Germany)
Kyo Kageura (Japan, National Center for Science Information Systems, Tokyo, Japan)
Jian-Yun Nie (Département d'informatique et de recherche opérationnelle,
Université de Montréal, Montréal, Canada)
Padmini Srinivasan (The University of Iowa, USA)
Jennifer Pearson (Dublin City University, Dublin, Ireland)
Pierre Zweigenbaum (Université Paris VII, Paris, France)

Table of contents

Introduction

Didier Bourigault, Christian Jacquemin
and Marie-Claude L'Homme

1. Computational terminology

It is a well-known fact that terminology has attracted the interest of researchers with very different backgrounds and motivations. Information science specialists, lexicographers, translators, as well as other specialists, such as engineers, scientists, and technicians have experienced the need to improve communication, or to access subject specific information. Several types of terminological (or terminology-related) resources, such as specialized dictionaries, term banks, glossaries, and thesauri, have been built in order to satisfy these needs.

Although these motivations remain unchanged for the most part, the means to construct terminological resources on the other hand have evolved considerably. First, specialized texts in electronic form are easily accessible; their volume has also increased dramatically (due to the Internet). Secondly, several techniques borrowed from natural language processing, information retrieval, corpus linguistics, or artificial intelligence enable the extraction and representation of specialized knowledge in an efficient and often elegant manner. Efficient, since huge amounts of data can be rapidly processed and filtered (to extract terminological units, for example). Elegant, since these terminological units can be further analyzed and organized into sophisticated networks that reflect the knowledge structure of a specialized field. Methods and models have been developed by researchers, once again with different backgrounds: computational linguists, terminologists, and computer scientists.

In addition, specialists in natural language processing who were not primarily concerned with terminology have come to realize that the formalization of specialized texts is necessary in order to build useful applications. This is the case in machine translation, as well as in computer-aided translation, automatic or semi-automatic abstracting, text generation, etc.

Researchers in computational terminology face a number of problems requiring new insights from both theoretical and practical viewpoints. First, the automatic identification of terminological units in running text is a task that needs further refinement. Linguistic approaches as well as probabilistic methods provide lists of candidate terms, that still need to be filtered (with automatic or semi-automatic procedures) in order to be usable in everyday applications. Secondly, once the terms have been extracted, variants must be regrouped (synonyms, or morpho-syntactic variants) in order to give users an accurate picture of the content of a document. Finally, corpora used to extract terminological units can be further investigated to find semantic and conceptual information on terms or to represent conceptual relationships between terms.

Thus, there is a growing need to report on research and development in computational terminology. This book attempts to do so by presenting 17 articles written by experts in the field. The authors address specific problems related to computational terminology and propose innovative solutions.

This book follows the *First Workshop on Computational Terminology* which took place at COLING-ACL'98.[1] The goal of the workshop was to bring researchers from different scientific communities together, leading to the recognition of a field that can now be called "computational terminology". The book contains the extended and revised versions of the papers published in the proceedings. Furthermore, some members of the scientific committee have agreed to write a contribution on a fundamental aspect of the field. The contributions reflect the innovative and fruitful advances in computational terminology at the crossroads of terminology, linguistics and computer science.

2. Computational terminology for different purposes

Without covering all possible applications, the contributions reflect a wide range of fields for which computational terminology tools are developed. The following applications are covered in the book: information retrieval, the building of bilingual lexicons, terminography, and automatic abstracting.

2.1 Extracting terms for information retrieval and other applications

The role of terms in information retrieval is so important that word units or stems used to represent documents are misleadingly called "terms". The studies included in this volume go beyond the simplistic approach that would consider any descriptor as a valid term. They propose several techniques for the acquisition and filtering of terms for the purpose of information access.

Recent trends in information retrieval have stimulated the need for enriched terminological data and for their extraction from electronic corpora. The coarse extraction techniques tend to produce huge lists of undifferentiated terms that are of little or no use for efficient document indexing and retrieval. The article by *Peter Anick* (Chapter 2) proposes to select only facetted terms, that is to say terms that pertain to the domain of a query. A similar effort — with regards to terminological disambiguation — to avoid conflating morphologically related words with no semantic relationship is proposed by *Hongyan Jing* and *Evelyne Tzoukermann* (Chapter 12). These two studies lead to more accurate indexing of documents, and enhance precision in document retrieval without loss of recall.

Another means of enhancing term quality is to select specific zones in documents, such as parenthetical expressions, from which terms can be acquired in correlation with other terms. The article by *Toru Hisamitsu* (Chapter 10) focuses on such terms and provides a comprehensive study of various statistical criteria used to filter out relevant terms.

An important emergent issue in information retrieval is the so-called cross-language information retrieval. Its purpose is to allow users to access documents in one language through queries in another language. One of the requirements of these techniques is the access to multilingual terminological data with cross-language connections between terms and their equivalents in other languages. *Akiko Aizawa* and *Kyo Kageura* (Chapter 1) show how the bilingual keyword lists frequently found in scientific journal articles can be used to build multilingual keyword clusters. Such clusters can be used for query expansion in cross-lingual information access and even for monolingual query expansion.

Document abstracting is also an area of information access in which term acquisition needs more attention. As in the field of information extraction, terms and their contexts must be taken into consideration in order to provide tools for automatic abstracting information on the semantic role of terms. The article by *Michael Oakes* and *Chris Paice* (Chapter 17) offers a template-based technique for term extraction that instantiates semantic roles of contextual words during the extraction process.

2.2 Extracting terms from bilingual corpora for translation and other applications

The availability of bilingual corpora has increased with the development of electronic resources. The Internet itself is a good source of bilingual corpora because more and more sites offer multilingual versions of their pages. It is now a well-known fact that such bilingual corpora can be aligned at the paragraph or sentence level. More difficult is alignment at the term level since terms tend to span several words with no clear delimitation. The articles on bilingual term extraction by *Éric Gaussier* (Chapter 8) and *David Hull* (Chapter 11) propose techniques for automatically extracting pairs of bilingual terms that are plausible translations.

Other specific types of bilingual documents can also be used for producing bilingual term associations. In their study, *Akiko Aizawa* and *Kyo Kageura* (Chapter 1) use bilingual keyword lists found in Japanese scientific articles to produce valid bilingual clusters composed of informationally-related terms. Even though such bilingual lists are less frequent than traditional bilingual corpora, it is likely that more and more specific pairs of bilingual documents will be available in the future as a source of bilingual term associations.

The output of the applications for bilingual term extraction presented in this volume can be used in several areas of natural language processing and information retrieval. In particular, translation aid software is designed to provide translators with term equivalents in other languages.

2.3 Enriching term extraction (building concept hierarchies or networks, looking for semantic or conceptual information)

An increasing amount of research in computational terminology is devoted to extracting semantic information on terms from specialized texts. It is generally admitted that texts contain several clues as to the meaning of terminological units. These clues can be automatically or semi-automatically detected and/or extracted to provide a better understanding of what terms mean. They can also lead to the construction of conceptual hierarchies or networks in which terms are interrelated according to hypernymic/hyponymic, meronymic/holonymic, or synonymic/quasi-synonymic relationships. The conceptual hierarchies can afterwards be implemented in what have been called "terminological knowledge bases".

Anne Condamines and *Josette Rebeyrolles* (Chapter 6) show how conceptual information on terms can be found in corpora. The authors present different methods for extracting information that can later be used to build terminological knowledge bases based on corpora (as opposed to application-based terminological knowledge bases). Similarly, *Ingrid Meyer* (Chapter 14) has developed a method designed to extract information on terms from running text in order to assist terminographers in their everyday work. They can focus on knowledge-rich contexts, i.e. contexts that contain relevant information on terminological units that is signaled with specific patterns.

Thierry Hamon and *Adeline Nazarenko* (Chapter 9) focus on a specific semantic relationship: synonymy. The authors evaluate a method for detecting synonymy links between terminological units contained in a specialized corpus. This method makes use of machine-readable dictionaries (general-language dictionaries as well as specialized dictionaries) to infer synonymy relationships among the components of complex terms.

In a rather different study, *James Cimino* (Chapter 5) presents a specific knowledge base in the field of medicine and discusses the addition of new terminology to the existing semantic network. He provides useful insights on how to manage a knowledge base once it has been built.

2.4 Finding ways to improve term extraction

Term extraction is based on the detection of syntactic patterns, on statistical counts, or on a combination of both techniques. However, these techniques alone fail to deliver perfect results. Most papers included in this book propose different methods that can improve term extraction regardless of the application. The researchers resort to a variety of strategies.

Béatrice Daille (Chapter 7) relies on linguistic analysis, namely morphology, to find specific terms. *Diana Maynard* and *Sophia Ananiadou* (Chapter 13) integrate syntactic and semantic information to find, rank and disambiguate terminological units. With similar purposes in mind, *Hiroshi Nakagawa* (Chapter 15) proposes techniques for the ranking and the classification of candidate terms that rely on structural and statistical properties. In the article by *Hongyan Jing* and *Evelyne Tzoukermann* (Chapter 12), morphological properties are estimated using an external source, i.e. the CELEX database.

In fact, it is worth mentioning that the use of machine-readable resources (general language dictionaries, specialized dictionaries, etc.) appears well suited to the accomplishment of specific tasks. This is the case in work by *Thierry Hamon* and *Adeline Nazarenko* (Chapter 9) who aim to identify synonymy links between terms. *Adeline Nazarenko, Pierre Zweigenbaum, Benoît Habert* and *Jacques*

Bouaud (Chapter 16) use a medical nomenclature to infer the semantic classes of words from the semantic classes of their neighbors. *Diana Maynard and Sophia Ananiadou* (Chapter 13) use the representation provided by a thesaurus.

Another way of finding methods to improve term extraction is to examine the performance of current systems. This is done by *Teresa Cabré Castellvi, Rosa Estopà Bagot* and *Jordi Vivaldi Palatresi* (Chapter 3). They provide a thorough evaluation of term extraction systems and a discussion of their performance. *Lee-Feng Chien* and *Chun-Liang Chen* (Chapter 4) offer an efficient and effective computational framework for the acquisition of terms from very large corpora.

3. The notion of context

The studies included in this book, demonstrate that the field of computational terminology is heavily corpus-based, and that "context" is one of its central concepts. This section is structured according to the way a majority of the contributors define and exploit the notion of "context".

There are many ways of taking context into account in computational terminology. We suggest two main conceptions:

- **Textual context.** The classical conception views the *textual* context of a unit as the set of words, terms or candidate terms with which this unit co-occurs in the source text, either within sentences or fixed-length windows. Textual contexts gather words according to the syntagmatic axis.
- **Lexical Context.** Although not as common, the *lexical* context of a unit can be defined as the set of words, terms or candidate terms which appear in the same given dependency relation within a syntactic structure. For example, the lexical context of a noun could be defined as all the distinct nouns that adjoin onto it to make a compound noun. Lexical contexts gather words according to the paradigmatic axis.

When building a terminology, a tool with a specific task to perform exploits the context either to extract candidate terms, filter or rank them, or structure the set of terms obtained after the extraction.

3.1 Textual context

Most of the works included in this book adhere to the idea of *textual context.* The articles which refer most often to this notion of context are those by *Ingrid Meyer*

(Chapter 14) and *Anne Condamines* and *Josette Rebeyrolles* (Chapter 6). It is hardly surprising that these researchers are more directly specialized in terminology *per se* as well as linguistics. In lexicography and terminology, consulting texts written by experts is generally recognized as being one of the basic strategies for acquiring terminological knowledge, and linguistic contexts are the most valuable source of information. KWIC (key-words in context) tools are used most of the time, but for words or terms occurring hundreds of times, terminologists are faced with the problem of selecting relevant contexts from the glut.

To tackle this problem, both teams adopt a similar approach. They rely on the notion of "knowledge rich" contexts for a term, which is defined by Ingrid Meyer as "contexts which indicate important conceptual characteristics for the search term by expressing attributes or relations with other terms". The methods for searching such contexts are based on "knowledge patterns" or "linguistic patterns", which are groups of words likely to express a given relation. There are different kinds of patterns, mixing lexical, grammatical and paralinguistic formal clues. In both works, various experiments led to the conclusion that it is necessary to enrich patterns with "restrictions" (Ingrid Meyer) or "constraints" (Anne Condamines and Josette Rebeyrolles) to reduce noise while keeping a high level of recall. For example, for the hyperonymy relation; Ingrid Meyer analyzes the pattern "*x* + BE + article + *y*" for English, whereas Anne Condamines and Josette Rebeyrolles present the more constrained one "definite article + *x* + BE + undefinite article + *y* + relative clause" for French. These patterns are implemented in tools whose function is to compare the source text with the set of knowledge patterns. Even though considerable help is gained by these methods, a few problematic issues remain: e.g. building an inventory of linguistic patterns for a specific relation for a new corpus; finding patterns for a new relation; and extent to which theses patterns can be reused in new domains.

Michael Oakes and *Chris Paice* (Chapter 17) define "context" in a very similar way. Their so-called "contextual templates" are equivalent to the aforementioned "knowledge patterns" and are used to instantiate semantic frames, in which slots are associated with relevant semantic roles in the domain of crop husbandry. There are nevertheless two main differences. Firstly, Ingrid Meyer, as well as Anne Condamines and Josette Rebeyrolles exploit relevant contexts in an *term-oriented* approach as part of the task of structuring a set of terms, either by building definitions for a given term or by inserting conceptual links between a given term and other terms. Michael Oakes and Chris Paice adopt a *relation-oriented* approach for the task of extracting candidate terms. Candidate terms which occur in one of the contextual templates are extracted. Secondly, while Ingrid Meyer, Anne Condamines and Josette Rebeyrolles work on very "general" relations such as hypernymy or meronymy, Michael Oakes and Chris Paice adopt a very domain- and application-dependent approach. They focus on specific relations and contextual templates which are related with their application (concept-based abstracting) and to their domain of application (crop husbandry).

We now turn to the notion of *global* textual context. Instead of focusing on *individual* contexts for a given unit, some techniques exploit statistics calculated for all occurrences of a given term in the source text. *Diana Maynard* and *Sophia Ananiadou* (Chapter 13) claim context is the "key to understanding a term". They propose a method which exploits the notion of context in order to (re)*rank* candidate terms which were extracted using the NC-value measure by an automatic term recognition tool. This method relies on the hypothesis that terms tend to occur in groups, rather than singly or randomly, in other words that "terms are better indicators of other terms". The set of terms used as a bootstrap to initialize the process is the top list of terms extracted using the C-value approach. Each candidate term is assigned a context term weight which is computed as the number of times a term (i.e. a candidate term belonging to the bootstrap list) occurs in a fixed-size context window calculated from all the occurrences of the given candidate term. The way context is taken into account is twofold, since Diana Maynard and Sophia Ananiadou combine the context term weight with a semantic similarity weight. This weight is measured using the UMLS Metathesaurus, by combining the horizontal distance and the vertical distance between nodes in the UMLS network.

The work of *Hongyan Jing* and *Evelyne Tzoukermann* (Chapter 12) also adheres to the notion of global textual context. The goal is to integrate a context distance model with a morphological analysis in order to improve the average precision of an information retrieval task. The context distance is computed in three steps. Firstly, a context vector is computed for each word on the basis of *all* the occurrences of the word in the document. The context vector includes the 10 closest candidate words. A weight which measures the word's importance in the context vector is then assigned to each candidate. Secondly, a corpus relevance distance for each word pair is pre-computed before retrieval on the basis of Mutual Information. Thirdly, the context distance between words is computed by combining the corpus relevance distance between words pairs belonging to each of the context vectors. This is based on the observation that the semantic closeness of two words is not always demonstrated by the presence of the *same* words in the context vectors, but often by the presence of *related* words. This semantic-based context distance is integrated with morphological information, extracted from the CELEX lexical database.

3.2 Lexical context

One of the most salient characteristics of technical texts is the heavy use of complex terms that are often long. These complex terms are created by the combination of existing simple terms. Many researchers in the field of computational terminology exploit the fact that nouns or noun phrases are often part of larger noun phrases. A term which appears in many different lexical compounds should be considered as a key term or as a relevant term. This idea is implemented by using the notion of lexical context: the lexical context of a unit is the set of words which occur in the same dependency relation with it.

Hiroshi Nakagawa (Chapter 15) is one of the authors who delves the deepest into the notion of lexical context. He claims that the relationship between complex terms and the simple terms they include must be analyzed; according to the author, this is essential in estimating candidate term importance. In order to rank candidate terms a term extractor derives from a corpus, he extends the idea beyond the C-value used by *Diana Maynard* and *Sophia Ananiadou* (Chapter 13) in which the greater the number of candidate terms contained in a unit, the greater the unit's C-value. Hiroshi Nakagawa goes even further and defines a measure which does not take frequencies into account. He defines two values for a noun N: pre(N) is the number of distinct nouns with which N adjoins to make a compound, and post(N) is the number of distinct nouns that adjoin onto N to form a compound. This score method is extended to cover compounds nouns: the Imp coefficient is computed as the product of the factors (pre(N+1) * Post(N+1)) for each N in the compound. The measure is used to rank candidate terms.

In the field of information retrieval, *Peter Anick* (Chapter 2) considers the property that allows certain nouns to belong to many lexical units. The result is a system which dynamically generates a terminological feedback for query result sets. The result set of documents yielded by a given query is tagged and analyzed by a pattern matcher which extracts all phrases whose length is two or greater and who match the pattern {?adjective noun+}. Then the lexical "dispersion" of each noun is computed: the number of distinct phrases in which the given noun appears. Nouns with the highest dispersion are presented to the user together with the phrases in which they appear, and the user may select a phrase in order to focus his research on that topic.

Adeline Nazarenko, Pierre Zweigenbaum, Benoît Habert and *Jacques Bouaud* (Chapter 16) propose a method for adapting a terminological semantic lexicon to meet the requirements of new domains and corpora. The method calls upon lexical context extraction. Parse trees of complex terms retrieved by a noun phrase extractor are simplified and reduced to elementary binary dependency trees, whose leaves are single words. The lexical context of each word is then built by gathering all the words which modify it. A graph is computed by Zellig to exhibit salient similarities. The words constitute the nodes. An edge corresponds to a certain amount of shared contexts. Words are grouped in classes by computing the strongly connected components and the *k*-cliques in the graph. This classification is used to guess the semantic category of unknown words. The SNOMED tags are projected on the word nodes belonging to the SNOMED lexicon. Unknown words are semantically-tagged according to the class selected by the majority of its neighbors.

The notions of Association Norm Estimation, Left Context Dependency and Right Context Dependency proposed by *Lee-Feng Chien* and *Chun-Liang Chen* (Chapter 4) also rely on the notions of lexical context and lexical dispersion.

4. Conclusion

The preceding sections have highlighted a few similarities and many differences between the techniques and approaches computational terminologists make use of in order to improve term extraction or to assist terminology-related applications. Enriching statistical measures, implementing linguistic knowledge in extraction programs, accessing machine-readable resources are all means that are investigated by researchers and reflected the contributions included in this book.

It is also worth mentioning that researchers — while developing methods to improve computational applications — usually provide an evaluation of the strategy they put forward. This trend is also reflected in this book.

Finally, although the techniques developed by computational terminologists are strongly application-oriented, they also provide a better understanding of the behavior of terminological units in specialized texts.

Chapter 1

A graph-based approach to the automatic generation of multilingual keyword clusters*

Akiko Aizawa and Kyo Kageura
National Institute of Informatics

In this paper, we report an effective graph-theoretic method for generating Japanese and English *bilingual keyword clusters* using the keyword lists assigned to academic papers by the authors where each of the generated clusters contains keywords with similar meanings from both languages. The advantages of the method are that (i) various domain-dependent keyword pairs useful for IR can be automatically extracted and clustered, (ii) the computation cost is reasonable, and (iii) low-frequency keywords can be properly treated and maintained for later use in IR applications. We apply the method to a set of Japanese and English keywords extracted from academic conference papers in computer science, and show that our method gives a very promising result.

1. Introduction

In this paper, we introduce a graph-based approach to the automatic generation of *multilingual keyword clusters*, which we define here as a set of clusters, each of which consists of keywords with similar meanings from more than two languages. The keyword clusters generated by our method are useful as a domain-specific thesaurus for query translation or expansion in IR applications.

The graph-based method we propose here is fairly general and would be applicable to wide range of roughly aligned bilingual term pairs. Here, we make use of Japanese and English keyword pairs assigned by authors as the basic data, because we have specifically noted that keywords attached by the authors to scientific papers constitute an important and useful information source for the following reasons:

1. The majority of scientific papers published in Japan have, and are encouraged to have (to make the academic results available worldwide) both Japanese and English keywords given by the authors. Correspondingly, these bilingual keywords are included in databases and are thus readily available for a great many domains.
2. The correspondences between the Japanese and English keywords are sufficiently regular that a large number of bilingual pairs can be extracted mechanically, though there is some accompanying noise.
3. Various keyword pairs are found that may not be listed in the standard terminological dictionaries, but are nevertheless useful in IR; they may be a valuable complement to the existing terminological resources, if an appropriate noise detection method is applied.

In the following, we first summarize the basic nature of the Japanese and English keywords of the academic papers used in this study. Then we briefly review related work, most of which is statistically-oriented rather than graph-oriented, and examine the position of our approach. A detailed explanation of the graph-based method adopted in our study will be presented next, followed by a presentation and examination of our results.

2. Basic nature of the data

2.1 Extraction of keyword pairs

The basic data used in the current study are the Japanese and English keywords assigned by the authors to their papers, extracted from the NACSIS Academic Conference Database (NACSIS, 1997). Of the 28, 122 papers we selected from the field of computer science, 27, 399 (about 97.5%) have both Japanese and English keywords, and each paper typically has 4–6 keywords in each language. The following is an example:

Japanese: 遺伝アルゴリズム (*genetic algorithm*)/最適探索 (*optimal search*)/学習 (*learning*)[1]
English: Genetic Algorithms/Optimization/Machine Learning

Though authors are not explicitly required to provide precise conceptual correspondence between the keywords in the two languages, it is likely that semantically corresponding English and Japanese keywords are listed in order.

Thus we started our study by examining the *rough* correspondence of the lists. Of the 27, 399 papers, 1, 339 (about 5%) had different numbers of keywords in the two languages. The mismatch was caused by a variety of factors including one or more missing keywords in either of the languages, or noise in the database such as a single keyword being separated into two fields. These papers with mismatched keywords were considered to be too noisy and were not used in our method.

On the other hand, papers with the same number of Japanese and English keywords (about 95%) were expected to maintain a one-to-one correspondence to a large extent. To obtain a general idea of the nature of the data, we randomly extracted 1000 pairs from these papers and manually classified them into the following five types:

1. Semantically and terminologically correct pairs, e.g. ⟨情報検索 (*information retrieval*), information retrieval⟩.
2. Semantically correct pairs with minor spelling errors, e.g. ⟨情報検索 (*information retrieval*), information retreival⟩.
3. Semantically correct pairs with expressional variations, e.g. ⟨情報検索 (*information retrieval*), information retrieving⟩.
4. Pairs that are closely related in meaning, e.g. ⟨情報検索システム (*information retrieval system*), information retrieval⟩.
5. Non-corresponding pairs, e.g. ⟨キーワード (*keyword*), information retrieval⟩.

Table 1 shows the sample count of each error type among the 1000 pairs. The table shows that about 93% of the sample were semantically correct including 8% with spelling errors and expressional variations. Our analysis also showed that all the type (5) errors occurred only once in the corpus, indicating that the probability that semantically unlinked errors would be regenerated was negligible.

Table 1. Types of keyword pairs

Type of pair	Sample counts
Correct pairs	856
Spelling errors	25
Expressional variations	47
Related pairs	53
Obvious errors	19

From the above figures, we concluded that the bilingual keyword lists extracted from our database provided proper translation pairs with a high precision if we simply coupled them according to the listed order. Based on this assumption, we extracted a total of 112, 364 keyword pairs (60, 186 different ones) using only the papers with equal numbers of Japanese and English keywords, and used them as a bilingual keyword corpus throughout the paper.

Table 2 shows examples of the extracted pairs. For each Japanese keyword, the most standard or frequent English correspondence is marked with '*'.

Table 2. Example of keyword pairs

Japanese keywords		English keywords	Frequency
キーワード	(*keyword*)	information retrieval	1
キーワード	(*keyword*)	keyword	39*
テキスト検索	(*text retrieval*)	information retrieval	1
テキスト検索	(*text retrieval*)	text retrieval	6*
テキスト検索	(*text retrieval*)	text search	3
検索指示語	(*query term*)	keyword	1
広域情報検索	(*wide-area information retrieval*)	information retrieval	1
情報検索	(*information retrieval*)	information gathering	4
情報検索	(*information retrieval*)	information retreival	1
情報検索	(*information retrieval*)	information retrieval	320*
情報検索	(*information retrieval*)	information search	5
情報収集	(*information gathering*)	information gathering	6*
情報収集	(*information gathering*)	information retrieval	1
文献検索	(*bibliographic retrieval*)	bibliographic search	1*
文献検索	(*bibliographic retrieval*)	document retrieval	11
文書検索	(*document retrieval*)	document retrieval	19*
文書検索	(*document retrieval*)	text retrieval	1

2.2 Comparison with the standardized technical Dictionaries

Next, we compared the extracted keyword pairs with 22, 690 different term pairs obtained from four dictionaries and handbooks in computer science (Aiso 1993; Japan Society for Artificial Intelligence 1990; Ralston 1983; Shapiro 1987).

Table 3 shows that the number of common elements between the keyword data and the dictionaries is relatively small, i.e. many of the keyword pairs assigned by the data are not listed in the standard technical dictionaries. It can also be observed that the average number of translations is smaller in the dictionaries than in the keyword data.

This may be partly because the dictionaries are to some extent prescriptive

Table 3. Comparison of the technical dictionaries and the bilingual keyword data

	Dictionary terms	Corpus pairs	Common for both
Japanese words	20,636	37,170	3,966
English words	19,562	49,918	2,814
Different translation pairs	22,690	60,186	2,066
Average number of translations per word (J)	1.10	1.62	–
Average number of translations per word (E)	1.16	1.21	–
Maximum number of translations per word (J)	7	86	–
Maximum number of translations per word (E)	6	29	–
Number of English acronyms (J)	844	1,007	212
Number of English acronyms (E)	451	1,233	114
Identical Japanese and English pairs	57	1,336	18

while the keyword pairs reflect particular views and concepts of the authors. At the same time, it is also expected that the keyword data contain some noise due to simple input errors, errors of correspondence, related but improperly linked words, and so on. Because of these many-to-many bilingual correspondences, the overall set of keyword pairs constitutes a complex network with rich correspondences as well as noise.

In conclusion, it is expected that the keyword corpus reflects particular views and concepts of authors important for real-scale IR, which cannot be covered by standard dictionaries. Also, certain noise (e.g., spelling errors, variants) in the keyword corpus can be utilized in the IR task since they may also be found in queries. From the viewpoint of possible application to IR, the following points should be taken into consideration in the processing of keyword pairs:

1. In terms of the precision of the search, it is important to eliminate erroneous or improper translations.
2. In terms of the recall of the search, it is advantageous to maintain spelling errors, expressional variations and (to some extent) such minor errors as pairs whose meanings are related but different.

Recognizing that a considerable amount of information useful for IR is embedded in low frequency data, we have decided to adopt a graph theoretic method instead of the statistical approaches, which seem dominant in corpus-based studies today. The advantage of the graph theoretic view is that it provides us with a way to treat low frequency keyword pairs of different error types differently by utilizing topological information.

3. Related work

Let us briefly overview related work here, in order to locate our own approach within the background of current research in related topics.

3.1 Identification of bilingual lexical pairs

There have been many studies recently on the automatic identification of translation pairs in bilingual textual corpora. Methodologically, the studies can be categorized into two types. The first is based on summary/test statistic measures such as the Mutual Information or ϕ^2 (Gale and Church 1991; van der Eijk 1993; Fung 1995; Smadja, McKeown and Hatzivassiloglou 1996), and the second is based on some kinds of iterative optimizations (Kupiec 1993; Melamed 1996).

These techniques assume a bilingual textual corpus only loosely aligned (e.g. at sentence level), and use statistical measures to calculate the most plausible correspondences. As such, they can extract proper pairs only for lexical items with relatively high frequencies. Pairs with less significant occurrences, though they sometimes include useful information such as rare translation examples or allomorphs, are in general neglected. In case of a textual corpus, this is necessary to overcome the noise introduced by compound identification in each language, term-to-term alignment between languages, and, in the case of Japanese, morphological pre-processing, to fix word boundaries. In addition, the processing of a textual corpus needs much computation, even for such simple and easy-to-calculate summary statistic measures as ϕ^2 or Mutual Information.

In contrast, the method used in the present study, which is based on bilingual keyword lists with much less noise in their correspondences, is much easier and much less costly to execute. Though the types of pairs obtained from the textual and the keyword corpora do not exactly match, it can be assumed at least that the keywords given by the authors constitute the most important subset of the possible keyword pairs extractable from the corresponding textual data.

Note however that the core methodology we propose here, i.e. a graph-based method for keyword clustering, can also be applied to keyword pairs aligned and extracted from bilingual textual corpora by various existing methods. Methodologically, therefore, it is important to emphasize that what we propose here is *complementary* to these works, rather than *contrastive.*

3.2 Automatic thesaurus generation

Another important research area related to our study is automatic thesaurus generation. Many studies have been carried out recently on this subject, mainly using corpus-based statistical methods (Finch 1993; Grefenstette 1994; Hughes 1994; Schütze and Pedersen 1997; Strzalkowski 1994). One of the most widely known methods in IR is Latent Semantic Indexing (Deerwester et al. 1990) where Singular Value Decomposition is applied to a term by a document matrix extracted from a textual corpus in order to calculate the similarity between documents and documents, terms and terms, and also documents and terms.

The same idea can also be applied to the task of extracting term clusters from a bilingual textual corpus (Dumais, Landauer and Littman 1996). However, as in the statistical extraction of bilingual term pairs, the method totally depends on the frequency of co-occurrence of the terms and is thus unsuitable for treating low-frequency terms, which include minor but valuable translation examples, spelling errors that need to be retained for the purpose of IR, etc.

On the other hand, little work has been carried out which explicitly uses a graph-based method for thesaurus construction. The work by a French research group (Habert, Naulleau and Nazarenko 1996; Habert et al. 1998) comes somewhat close to our approach in that they look at the data as a graph. Their objective is to construct a domain-dependent terminological network or ontology and also to locate the position of new terms in the ontology. Using a text corpus, they define a graph of terms, regarding focus terms as nodes and shared context words obtained by syntactic analysis as the representation of edges. However, they pay more attention to defining the capacity of edges, introducing different methods for calculating capacities on the basis of shared context words. For manipulating the network, they use only the capacity of edges and their relations around a focus term, and do not use a graph-theoretic method in its technical sense.

4. Generation of multilingual keyword clusters

We have already mentioned informally that the bilingual keyword pairs constitute a tangled graph of Japanese and English keywords. As such, the problem of creating bilingual keyword clusters can be regarded as the detection of wrongly generated links of the graph, which is equivalent to the minimum cut problem in graph theory. In this section, the creation of the initial keyword graph, the detection of the error candidates, and the method of partitioning the graph are explained, followed by some clustering examples.

4.1 Generation of the initial keyword graph

The initial graph expression of a bilingual keyword corpus is easily derived by representing Japanese and English keywords as nodes and their translation pairs as links. The frequency of appearance of each keyword pair in the corpus is expressed as the capacity of the corresponding link. Figure 1 shows the initial keyword graph generated from the keyword pairs shown in Table 2.

The initial keyword graph is composed of a number of disjoint sub-graphs, which we define as *bilingual keyword clusters*. Based on this definition, every node connected to another is regarded as representing a similar meaning,

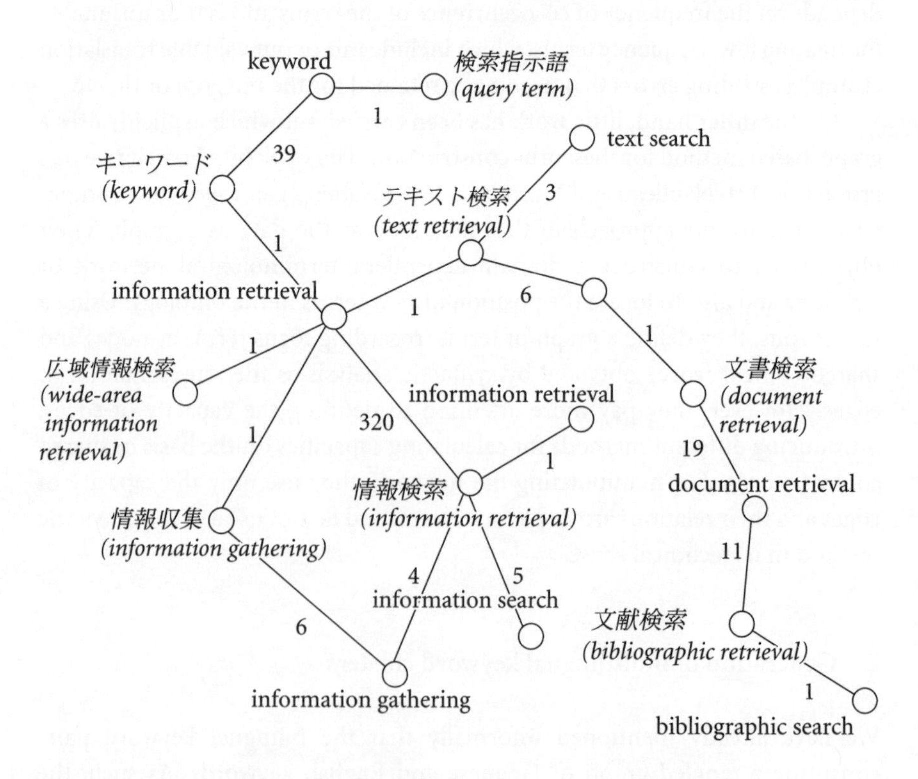

Figure 1. Example of initial keyword graph

regardless of the capacity of the connecting links. In the case of the example shown in Figure 1, whole nodes are connected to each other and considered to be semantically related.

The initial keyword graph constructed from our corpus of 60,186 different keyword pairs contains a huge sub-graph with 20,659 nodes, which means about 34% keywords are categorized into a single cluster at the initial stage. Since we restricted our subject to the field of *computer science*, the major cause for this happening is not the existence of homonymous words, as would be expected in more general cases. Instead, the problem is the existence of improper translation pairs, which connect otherwise disjoint keyword clusters into a single cluster. A typical example of such improper correspondence found in Figure 1 is the link ⟨キーワード (*keyword*), information retrieval⟩.

To summarize, our challenge in relation to this problem becomes how to detect and eliminate such improper translation links to obtain semantically meaningful clusters of synonyms.

4.2 A strategy for detecting possible correspondence errors

The detection algorithm proposed is based on the simple principle that

> *sets of links, which decompose a connected keyword cluster into disjoint sub-clusters when they are removed from the original cluster, are candidates for improper translations.*

In conventional graph theory, such a link set is called an *edge cut*, and an edge cut with the minimal total capacity among all the edge cuts obtained for a given graph is called a *minimum edge cut.*

The problem of identifying the minimum edge cut for a given graph is one of the principal problems in graph theory and has been studied quite extensively since the 1950's (Nagamochi 1993). The complexity of the simple Edmonds and Karp algorithm used in our current implementation is $O(m^2n)$ for the graph with n nodes and m edges, which guarantees sufficient performance for practical use.

Though the principle mentioned above is very simple, the following terminological issues should be taken into consideration when applying the graph theoretical view to error candidate detection. First, a minimum edge cut does not necessarily imply a single translation error. For example, in Figure 2, two links ⟨テキスト検索 (*text retrieval*), information retrieval⟩ and ⟨情報検索 (*information retrieval*), text retrieval⟩ must be removed simultaneously in order to divide the cluster into two disjoint sub-clusters.

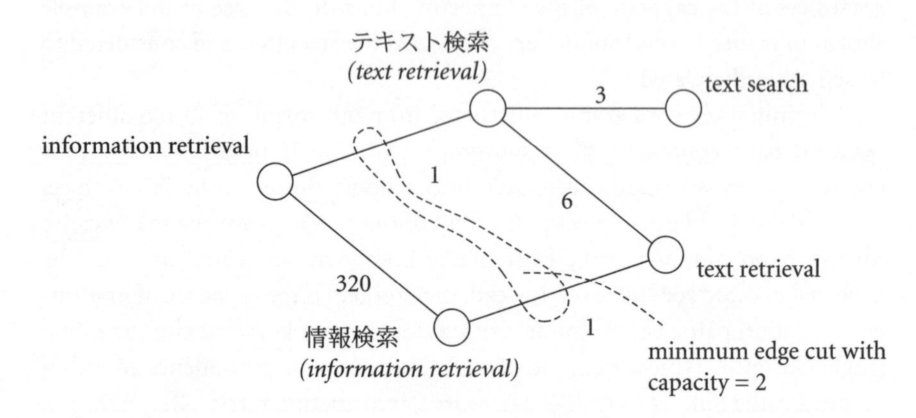

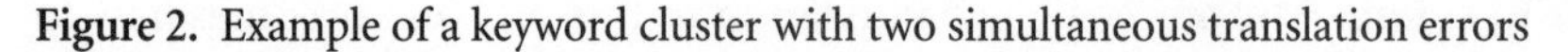

Figure 2. Example of a keyword cluster with two simultaneous translation errors

Second, there may exist more than one minimum edge cut. Particularly, disambiguation is needed when only one of them can be removed from the graph. For example, in Figure 3, either the link ⟨電子会議 (*electronic conference*), desktop conferencing⟩ or the link ⟨在席会議 (*desktop conference*), desktop conferencing⟩ can be removed together with ⟨電子会議 (*electronic conference*), desktop conference⟩. Our current implementation selects the most 'error-likely' cut among candidates using a similarity measure calculated based on histograms of characters. In Figure 3, for example, the link ⟨電子会議 (*electronic conference*), desktop conferencing⟩ is selected since the word 'desktop conferencing' is more similar to 'desk-top conference' than 'electronic meeting'.

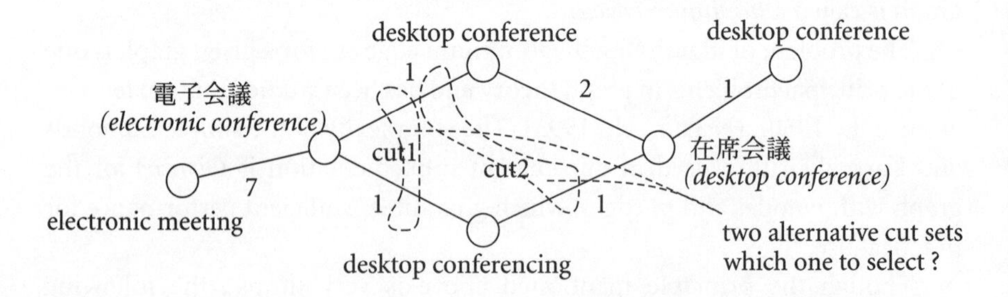

Figure 3. Example of a keyword cluster with two conflicting minimum edge cuts

Third, the minimum edge cut only shows the weakest connections within a given cluster. The edge cut is a candidate for, but does not always represent, imprecise translation. Removing correct pairs inevitably causes over-splitting, i.e. generating more than one cluster with similar meanings. It is very important to adopt appropriate criteria for stopping the partitioning process, which in our implementation is recursively applied for all the clusters in the graph. In the next section, we introduce three clustering parameters to avoid over-splitting.

4.3 Procedure for partitioning keyword clusters

Our analysis in Section 2 suggests that two different types of errors, namely, totally irrelevant and semantically associated (but non-corresponding) errors, need consideration. While the first type of error should be eliminated whenever detected, the treatment of the second type depends on the application. For example, the pair ⟨テキスト検索 (*text retrieval*), information retrieval⟩ may be improper in view of a strict terminological definition, but not necessarily incorrect for people searching academic paper databases.

The proposed procedure utilizes graph topological information as well as frequencies of the links to control the degree of cluster partitioning. The procedure is composed of the following steps:

- Step (1) Mark significant translation links which should not be eliminated.
- Step (2) Mark significant keywords which can support a separated new cluster.
- Step (3) Detect the removable minimum cut between two significant keywords.
- Step (4) Remove the minimum cut from the graph.
- Step (5) Repeat Steps (2)–(4) until no further partition is possible.

Steps (1), (2), and (3) are explained further below.

Step 1. Mark significant translation links

First, as a pre-processing step, links which should not be eliminated from the graph are checked. The *significant translation links* which we define here as non-removable are either (a) links whose Japanese and English notations are identical, or (b) links whose frequency is more than N_α. These conditions are easily tested at the pre-processing stage before the minimum-cut detection to save computation time, since links with at least $(N_\alpha + 1)$ frequency are maintained throughout the partitioning process.

Now, condition (a) mainly refers to proper nouns or acronyms. The presence of this condition is by no means trivial because for these proper nouns or acronyms, Japanese academic papers usually maintain the original English form. In our case, 1, 336 pairs out of 60, 186 (about 2%) matched this condition.

Condition (b) represents the minimum frequency for a translation pair to be considered correct and thus the value can be determined by analyzing the nature of the target corpus. By examining the type (4) and type (5) pairs sampled in Table 1, it turned out that all the irrelevant and about 85% of the associated had frequencies equal to or less than 3. Based on this observation, we fixed N_α at *3* for the target corpus. Amongst the 51, 062 pairs obtained by normalizing (see Section 6.1) the original 60, 186 pairs, a total of 3, 901 pairs (about 8%) satisfied this condition. Note that all the irrelevant errors we sampled occured only once in our data. Thus, reducing N_α does not have much effect on the detection of irrelevant errors.

Step 2. Mark significant keywords

In this step, nodes which occur frequently in the corpus are checked. Fixing the minimum cut detection for a graph is actually a problem of finding the smallest cut (i.e. maximum flow) of all possible cuts separating any two nodes on the graph. Thus it follows that we can control the degree of partitioning by imposing a restriction on the node pairs used in minimum cut detection.

The *significant keywords*, which are used for this purpose, are defined as keywords with (a) more than one translation link, and (b) at least one translation link whose frequency is more than N_β. These conditions need to be checked every time links are removed from the graph.

Here, condition (a) guarantees that every cluster generated contains at least one Japanese and one English keyword. Also, increasing N_β has the effect of suppressing cluster partitioning. $N_\beta = 1$ means (a) is the only restriction preventing over-splitting.

Step 3. Detect removable minimum cut

At this step, two significant keywords are selected to apply minimum cut detection algorithm. If a minimum cut, which (a) has a total capacity equal to or less than N_ε, and (b) generates clusters containing at least one Japanese and one English keyword, exists between the selected pairs (which do not include any significant links), the detected minimum cut can be eliminated from the graph. It is obvious that increasing N_β means more clusters are partitioned.

To summarize, N_α, N_β, and N_ε, are the three parameters used to control cluster partitioning. We are currently using the same parameter values for all the clusters (though these values might possibly depend upon cluster size; see the discussion in Section 5.2). The values for N_β and N_ε are determined heuristically. Their effect on resulting clusters is examined in detail in the next section

4.4 Clustering examples

Figure 4 shows the result of the partitioning of the keyword cluster given in Figure 1, where $N_\varepsilon = N_\alpha = N_\beta = 3$.

In step (1), such links as ⟨情報検索 *(information retrieval)*, information retrieval⟩ with more than N_α frequencies were marked as non-removable. In step (2), keywords such as 'information retrieval', 'information gathering', 'text retrieval', 'document retrieval', and 'keyword' were marked as significant. Only English keywords were highlighted in the figure because in most cases it is sufficient to check either of the languages. In step (3), the minimum edge cut algorithm was applied between nodes 'information retrieval' and 'text retrieval' and the link ⟨テキスト検索 *(text retrieval)*, information retrieval⟩ was detected as removable. These steps were repeated and eventually, three pairs, ⟨キーワード *(keyword)*, information retrieval⟩, ⟨テキスト検索 *(text retrieval)*, information retrieval⟩, ⟨文書検索 *(document retrieval)*, text retrieval⟩, were removed, resulting in the four clusters A, B, C, and D. It follows that such pairs as ⟨情報検索 *(information retrieval)*, information retreival⟩ (spelling error), ⟨検索指示語 *(query term)*, keyword⟩ (rare case), and ⟨広域情報検索 *(wide-area information retrieval)*, information retrieval⟩ (related but not equivalent pair) were retained even after the partitioning.

If we let $N_\beta = 10$, then only 'information retrieval', 'document retrieval', and 'keyword' would be marked as significant. Then, group B could not be an independent cluster, and would be merged either with group D or C. The ambiguity is caused by the existence of more than one minimum cut in the cluster, and by the fact that there is no topological cue for deciding which link is more plausible for deletion. As has been mentioned, which group B should belong to is currently determined by similarities of keywords.

Intuitively speaking, sub-graphs generated in step (1) using significant links work as *core clusters* and only errors across core clusters can be detected in the succeeding steps. If an initially generated sub-graph does not contain any significant link, no error detection is possible. An example of such a minor cluster is shown in Figure 5.

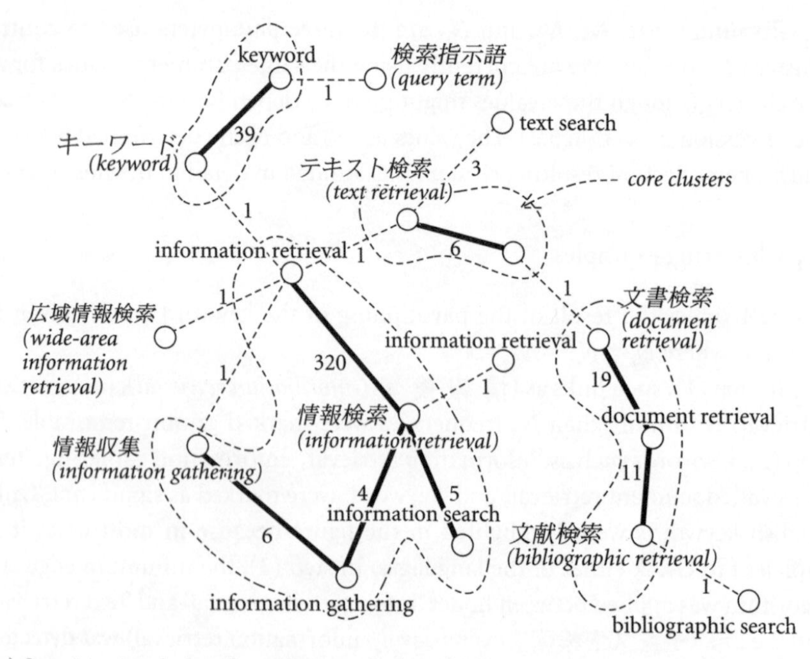

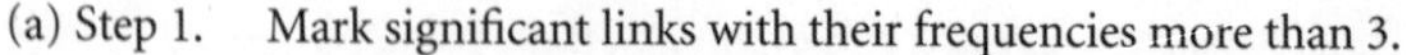
(a) Step 1. Mark significant links with their frequencies more than 3.

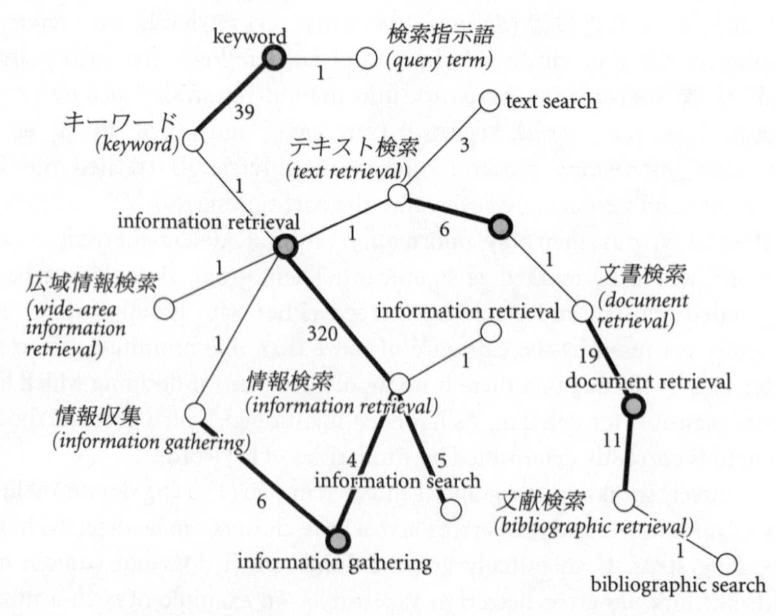

(b) Step 2. Mark significant keywords (only significant English keywords are highlighted in the figure).

Figure 4. Cluster partitioning procedure

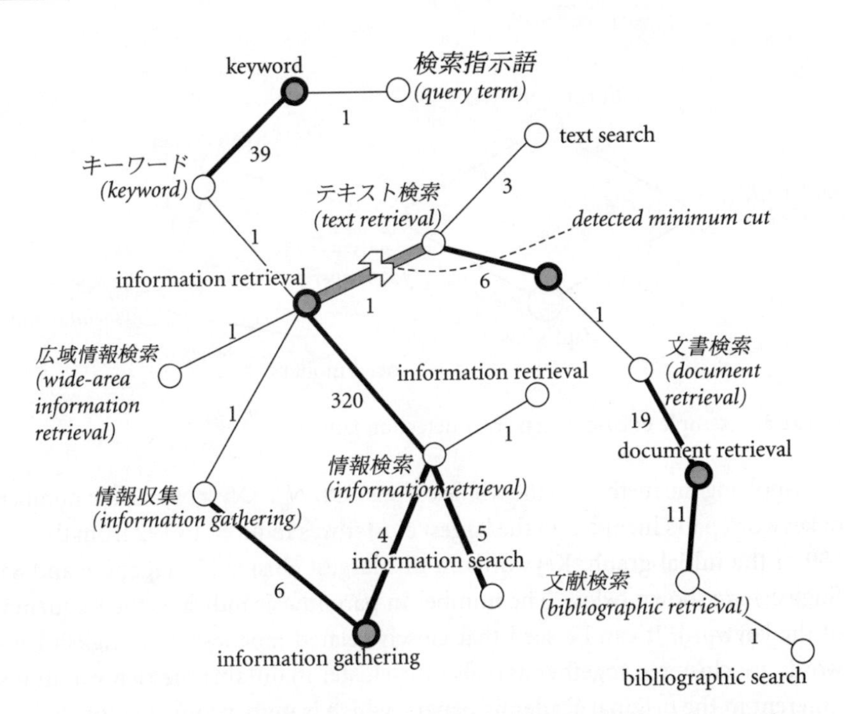

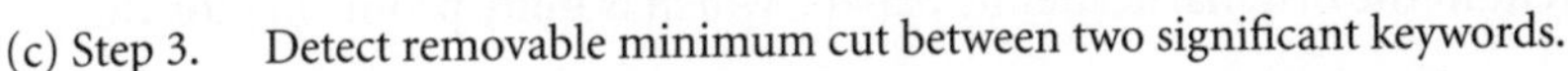
(c) Step 3. Detect removable minimum cut between two significant keywords.

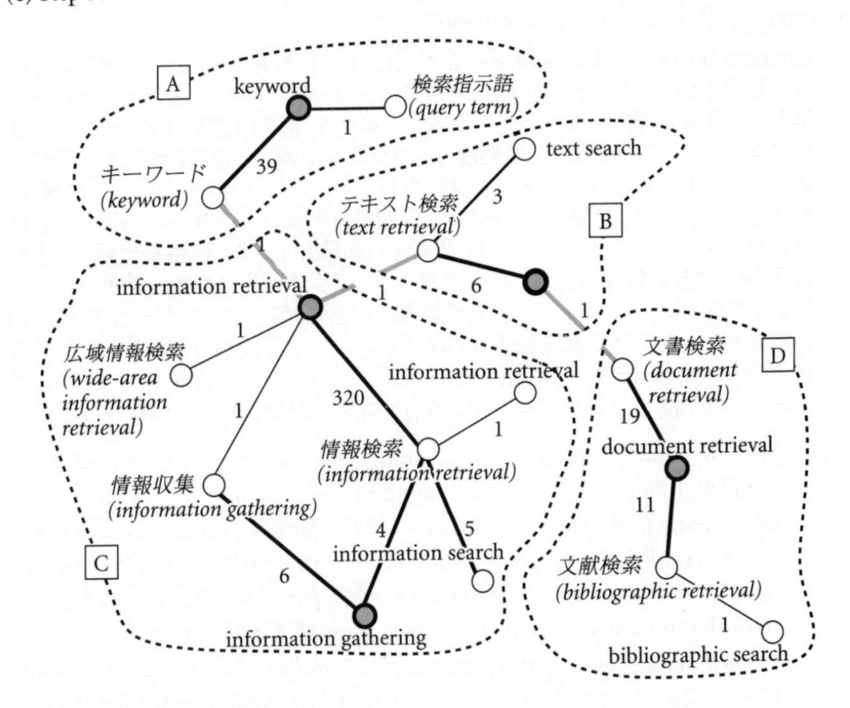

(d) Final clustering result

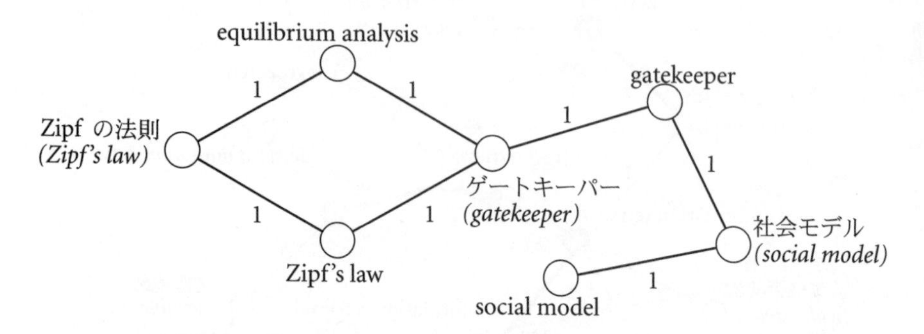

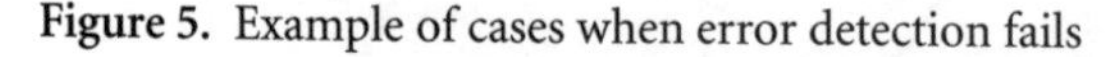
Figure 5. Example of cases when error detection fails

Applying the method to the whole corpus with $N_\alpha = N_\beta = N_\varepsilon = 3$, the number of keyword pairs included in the largest cluster was reduced to 192 from the 20, 659 of the initial graph. Keywords in this largest cluster (54 Japanese and 84 English) are shown below. The number in parenthesis indicates the frequency of the keyword. It can be seen that closely related Japanese and English keywords are clustered together and also the cluster maintains the rich variations inherent in the original academic papers, which is quite promising for IR.

Example 1. Keywords in the largest cluster

Japanese:並列処理(743), 並列(63), 並列化(56),並列計算(29), 並行 処理制御(24), 並行処理(23), 同時実行制御(16), 並列実行(15), 並列性 (10), 並行実行(8), 並行制御(6), 多重処理(6), マルチプロセス(5), 並行性 制御(4), 並列プロセス(4), 多重プロセス(3), 実行制御(3), 並列度(3), パラレル処理(3), 並列制御(3), 一貫性制御(3), マルチプロセッシング(3), コンカレント(2), フユ-チャ-(2), 並列演算(2), 並行化(2), 横型(2), 複数プ ロセス(2), 同時並行制御(1), 多重並行処理(1), 並列プロセッシング　　コ ンカレンシ-制御(1), 並列法(1), 並列化自動配線(1), 並列処理系(1), 実行 制御方式(1), 平行処理(1), パラレル(1), 命令内の並列性(1), パラレルコンピュ-ティング(1), 整合性制御(1), 並列プロセシング(1), 並行処理制御機能 (1), 2 次元熱伝導方程式(1), コンカレンシ-(1), 並列処理制御(1), 同時更新 制度(1), マ-カ-伝播(1), 並列作業(1), 並列図式(1), 並列性制御(1), 並列 コンピュ-ティング(1), パラレルプロセシング(1), コンカレンシ-コントロ- ル(1),

English: *Parallel Processing(670), parallel(74), concurrency control(62), Parallelization(44), parallel execution(23), Concurrent Processing(20), parallel computing(18), Parallel Computation(18), parallelism(15), parallel process(8), parallel processings(6), Multi Process(5), multiprocessing(5), concurrent(5), multiprocess(5), multi-processing(4), parallelize(3), Parallel Operation(3), consistency control(3), Multi-Process(3), Parallel Processes(3), Paralell Processing(3), multi processing(2), Parallell Processing(2), Execution Control(2), concurrent execution(2), parallelizing(2), Marker Passing(2), con-*

current Schema(2), parallel praessing(2), parallel scheduling(1), Concurrenly Control(1), concurrent problem(1), Pararell Process(1), Parallel Promcess(1), parallel degree(1), CONCURRENCE(1), quasi destructive(1), prallelism(1), Parallel Proceseing(1), Parallel Handling(1), decomposing(1), parallel procesing(1), paralled processing(1), parallel processing(1), concurrency contnol(1), prallel processing(1), Parallellism(1), 2D Heat propagation(1), parallel proeessing(1), Parallel Prosessing(1), concurency control(1), paralel prpcessing(1), Concunency(1), Parallel-Processing(1), Pravallel processing(1), Parallel processiry(1), Perallel Algorithm(1), Concurrent Computing(1), Multiple Processing(1), future(1), processing(1), Porallel Precessing(1), Parallel Execation(1), paralle(1), A Parallel Execution(1), Paralell Computing(1), VL2000(1), Parallel exection(1), A Parallel Processing(1), Comcurrency Control(1), Activity Control(1), Parallel exeoution(1), Parallele Processing(1), pararell processing(1), Parallel Prcessing(1), Parallel Phrase(1), Pararell Programing(1), paralle lism(1), PARALLEL PROmCESSING(1), Parallal Processing(1), concurrency contral(1), Darallel Processing(1), Parallel SA(1)

5. Analysis of results

In this section, the resulting clusters, as well as the detected errors, are analyzed and compared to see the effect of clustering parameters N_β and N_ε.

5.1 Analysis *of generated clusters*

Table 4 compares the size of clusters generated for $N_\beta = 1, 3, 10$ and $N_\varepsilon = 1, 3, 10$ where N_α is fixed at 3. Here, we define *the size of a cluster* as the number of different translation links contained. Since the majority of the generated clusters are of small size, averaged statistics such as the mean cluster size do not show much about the partitioning effect. Instead, we show the total number of clusters generated as well as the size of the largest cluster in the table. For comparison, the figures without sub-graph partitioning are also shown, indicating that the initial keyword graph contained 26, 983 clusters and the execution time needed to generate the initial keyword graph was 3 seconds.

From the figures in the table, it can be seen that the size of the maximum cluster is quite effectively reduced by removing improper links detected by the proposed method. In addition, the result consistently shows that a greater number of clusters are generated with a larger N_ε value and a smaller N_β value.

Table 4. Change of cluster sizes using different clustering parameters

N_β	N_ε	Total number of clusters	Size of the largest cluster	Number of removed links	Execution time (user/sec)
1	1	28067	5011	1415	242
1	3	27637	6067	887	179
1	10	27409	7708	612	144
3	1	29103	332	2567	244
3	3	28077	499	1437	192
3	10	27738	539	1035	231
10	1	28988	161	2837	251
10	3	27991	192	1672	199
10	10	27670	404	1223	237
no partitioning		26983	15409	0	3

execution time (obtained using the UNIX time command) is around 4 minutes user time on an Ultra 450 workstation with 300 MHz Ultra SPARC II, which shows the computational efficiency of our method.

5.2 Analysis of detected errors

In order to evaluate the performance of the graph-based method, we manually analyzed the links removed by our algorithm, using the link type categories introduced in Section 2.1, i.e. (1) links that connect semantically and terminologically correct pairs, (2) links that connect semantically correct pairs with minor spelling errors, (3) links that connect semantically correct pairs with expressional variations, (4) links that connect pairs which are related in meaning, (5) links that connect non-corresponding pairs, i.e. obvious errors.

Among those listed in Table 4, only the links removed without ambiguity are examined (see 4.2 for details about the ambiguity of minimum cut and disambiguation procedure we adopted).

When generating keyword clusters, it is advantageous to maintain (1), (2) and (3), while (5) should be eliminated. The treatment of related keywords depends on the database and also the context of the search, but in general, when smaller clusters are to be obtained, then related keyword pairs should be cut in addition to the obvious errors.

Therefore, a good algorithm should detect obvious errors first, and then eliminate related pairs. Table 5 shows the types of links removed by our algorithm, for each combination of parameters N_β and N_ε we tried.

Table 5. Types of removed links against different clustering parameters

N_β	N_ε	Obvious errors		Related pairs		Expression variations		Spelling errors		Correct pairs		Total
1	1	290	44.82%	306	47.30%	2	0.31%	2	0.31%	47	7.26%	647
1	3	233	51.89%	195	43.43%	0	0.00%	0	0.00%	21	4.68%	449
1	10	167	53.35%	138	44.09%	0	0.00%	0	0.00%	8	2.56%	313
3	1	355	38.34%	467	50.43%	15	1.62%	3	0.32%	86	9.29%	926
3	3	288	47.92%	278	46.26%	5	0.83%	0	0.00%	30	4.99%	601
3	10	240	52.29%	204	44.44%	3	0.65%	0	0.00%	12	2.61%	459
10	1	359	36.48%	492	50.00%	24	2.44%	6	0.61%	103	10.47%	984
10	3	291	45.26%	303	47.12%	8	1.24%	1	0.16%	40	6.22%	643
10	10	244	49.19%	229	46.17%	4	0.81%	1	0.20%	18	3.63%	496
Average			46.62%		46.58%		0.88%		0.18%		5.75%	

From Table 5, we can observe that on average 90 percent of the links removed were either obvious errors or related pairs, while the correct links wrongly removed constituted on average less than 6% and at most 10%. This is an outstanding performance, considering that more than 85% of all the pairs are correct pairs, while obvious errors and related pairs amount to only 2% and 5% respectively (see Table 1).

Observing the change of ratio of removed links with respect to the parameters, it is clear that the algorithm performs very well, i.e. when the parameters are set in such a way that the number of removed pairs are not large, then the algorithm tends to remove comparatively many obvious errors, while the relative number of obvious errors removed decreases as the number of removed links is increased.

Assuming that the ratio of obvious errors in the corpus is the same as the ratio in Table 1 (about 2 percent), the number of obvious errors is estimated to be 1, 200. If we assume that about 36.5% (see Table 5) of the total of 2, 837 (see Table 4) of links removed with $N_\beta = 10$ and $N_\varepsilon = 1$ are obvious errors, then more than 85% of all the obvious errors are estimated to have been removed.

Although we discussed how the treatment of related pairs probably depends on the situation, we found that in most cases the clusters produced by removing related pairs have internal consistencies, as shown in the following examples:

Example 2. Removal of hierarchically related link between ⟨グラフ (*graph*), directed graph⟩.

cluster 1: グラフ, グラブ, *graph, Graph, Graphs*

cluster 2: 有向グラフ, 有向グラブ, *Directed Graph, directed graph, Directed graph, directed graphs, acyclic digraph, Directed Path, directed path*

Example 3. Removal of semantically related link between ⟨立体画像 (*stereoscopic image*), 3d image⟩.

cluster 1: 立体画像, *stereoscopic picture, stereoscopic image, Stereo Imagery*

cluster 2: 次元画像, *3-dimensional image, 3DImages, 3D image, 3D Images, 3-D Image, 3-dimensional color image*

In order to examine problems concerning the correct pairs wrongly detected and removed, we further analyzed the wrongly detected correct pairs in the case where $N_\beta = 10$ and $N_\varepsilon = 1$, which has the largest number of wrong removal. 26 of the total 103 cases were caused by acronyms which were not treated properly, and 15 were caused by broad homonymous keywords such as 'estimation' or 'sense'. The other 62 cases were due to incorrect pairs occurring more frequently than correct pairs. Among these 62 cases, we noticed 27 cases where correct pairs were wrongly removed but the removal nevertheless contribute to improve the internal consistency of the clusters, as in the following examples:

Example 4. Removal of correct link between ⟨知覚 (*perception*), human perception⟩.

cluster 1: 知覚, *Perception, perception*

cluster 2: 視知覚, 視覚心理, 視認, 人間の視覚特性, *visual perception, human perception, Visual Perception, Vision Psychology, Human Visual Perception,*

Example 5: Removal of correct link between ⟨複製デタ (*replicated data*), replicated data⟩.

cluster 1: デ-タ複製, デタ複製, 複製デ-タ, *Data Replication, data replication,*

cluster 2: 重複デ-タ, 重複デタ, *Replicated Data, Replicated data, Duplicated Data, replicated data, duplicated data*

From these observations, it can be expected that a few additional routines would easily reduce the number of links removed wrongly, i.e. (i) full-scale processing of acronyms, (ii) homonym disambiguation by incorporating information for existing dictionaries, and (iii) use of morphological analysis to transfer individual keywords after clusters are partitioned.

Lastly, with respect to the main routine of graph-based methodology, we are currently using the same value regardless of the size of the cluster, but this might be changed from case to case. We have informally observed that bigger clusters tend to include heterogeneous keywords, so better results may be obtained by changing the value of parameters depending on the cluster size.

6. Discussions

6.1 Other incorporated features

So far, we have focused on the treatment of improper translations in bilingual keyword clusters. Other aspects of the issue are now also remarked upon.

6.1.1 *Normalization to deal with notation variation problem*

After the extraction of bilingual keyword pairs, simple normalization was applied to deal with the problem of notation variation such as *multi-lingual* and *Multi Lingual.* Also, acronyms were detected and marked so that they could be tested for homonyms at a later stage.

6.1.2 *Splitting homonymous acronyms*

Though homonyms do not seem to occur frequently in a specific scientific domain such as computer science, we still observed several cases as is shown Figure 6.

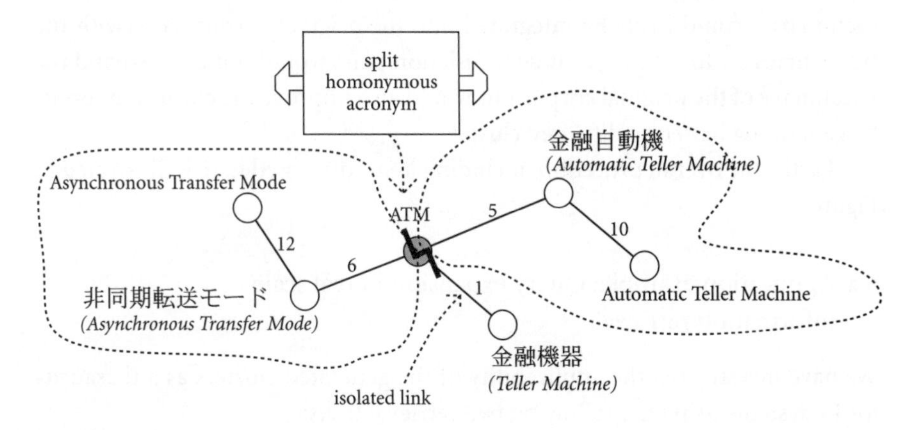

Figure 6. Example of a homonymous keyword.

The detection of possibly homonymous keywords can also be carried out utilizing topological features of the keyword cluster. It can be assumed that

> *homonymous nodes are the ones that decompose the cluster when the node and all the edges starting from the node are removed.*

Thus, the problem is transformed again into the well-known node cut problem of graph theory. Once a candidate node for a homonym is obtained using existing graph algorithms, partitioning is done by splitting the node into newly generated clusters as shown in Figure 6.

However, homonyms require extra considerations. First, we need deeper lexical knowledge to avoid over-splitting. Since most of the homonyms we have observed are acronyms, we are currently only considering keywords composed of English capital characters and symbols as candidates for node cuts, but this may be insufficient in some cases. Secondly, when a homonymous node is split, every edge starting from the node should be classified into one of the newly generated clusters. However, there exists no topological clue for an isolated edge like ⟨金融機器 (*teller machine*), ATM⟩ in Figure 6. Thus, the attribution of the isolated pairs must be decided by other means. For this purpose, we are currently using character-base similarity between keywords, but again, deeper lexical knowledge may be needed for better performance.

6.1.3 *Integrating standard technical dictionaries*

As can be seen from Table 2, the information source used in this study was triplets of a Japanese keyword, an English keyword, and a frequency count. Japanese and English translation pairs extracted from standard technical dictionaries could easily be integrated into the original corpus data (with the frequencies set to infinite). These translation pairs would not only expand the vocabulary of the original corpus but would also improve the clustering results by generating better quality core cluster.

Lastly, the overall procedure including items discussed here is illustrated in Figure 7.

6.2 Application example: Query expansion in real scale information retrieval

We have investigated the applicability of the generated clusters as a thesaurus for IR systems using the following two retrieval tasks:

1. Monolingual IR: Japanese queries retrieving documents from a Japanese collection (J-J task), and
2. Cross-lingual IR: Japanese queries retrieving documents from an English collection (J-E task).

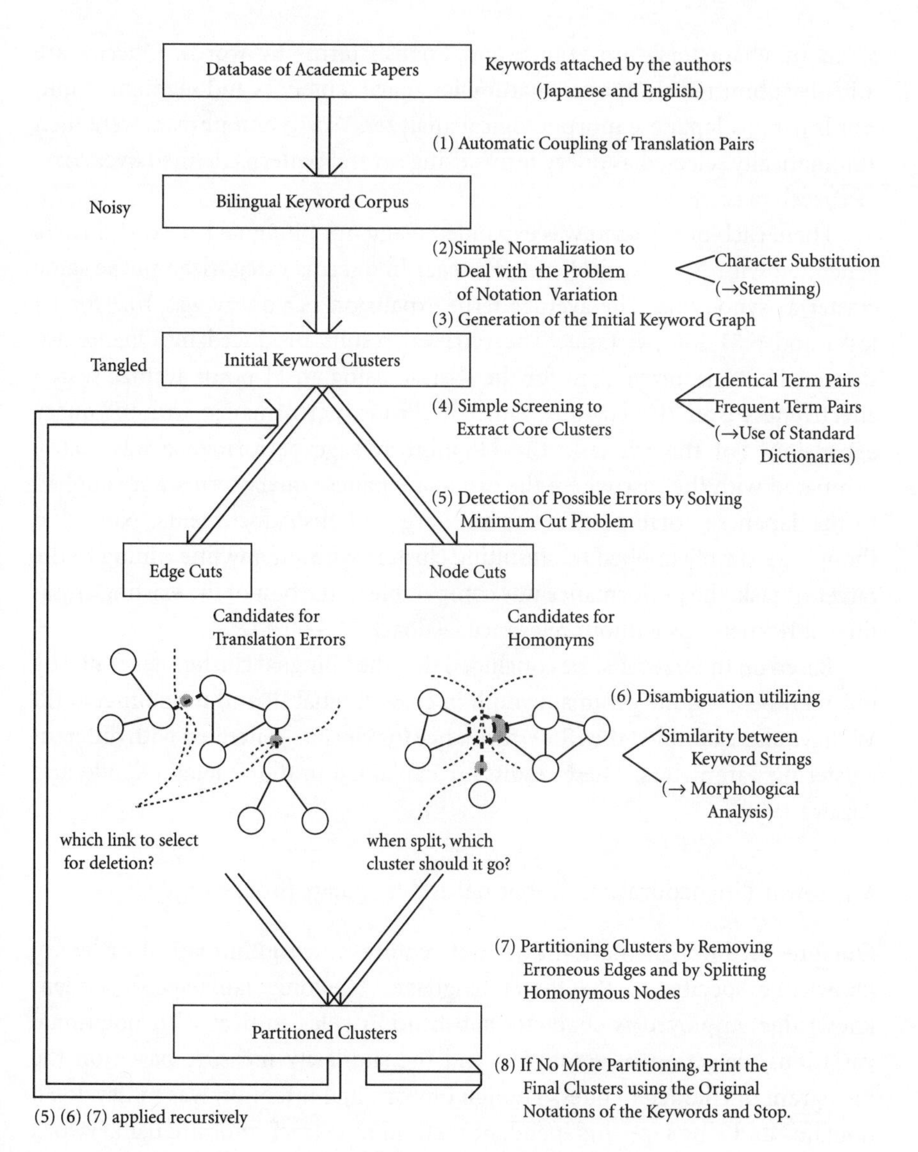

Figure 7. Overview of the proposed keyword clustering procedure

The search performance was tested against the test version of the NACSIS Test Collection 1 (Kageura et al. 1997; Kando and Aizawa 1998). For the J-E task, 'E collection', which contains 186, 809 English documents, and for the J-J task, 'J collection', which contains 338, 668 Japanese documents, were used.

In our IR system, all terms appearing in a document are indexed, Japanese terms by characters (uni-gram), and English terms by words. Queries are initially submitted as Japanese natural language sentences and segmented into words using a Japanese morphological analyzer. Words and phrases were then automatically selected as query terms using several patterns defined over part-of-speech tags.

Then, each query term was expanded using our bilingual keyword clusters generated with $N_\alpha = N_\beta = N_\varepsilon = 3$ and regarding terms categorized in the same cluster as synonyms. The average term expansion per query was 10.7 for J-J tasks and 6.81 for J-E tasks. The retrieval results produced by Opentext 6 showed 11.7% improvement for the J-J task using an 11 point average search effectiveness over the *baseline*, which indicates performance without query expansion. For the J-E task, the 11 point average performance was 46.6% compared with the case where the original Japanese query terms were applied to the Japanese corresponding to the target English documents. Note that though we simply applied the resulting clusters without any fine tuning to the target IR task, the performance was comparable to the best of the existing cross-lingual IR methods without relevance feedback (40–60%).

Based on these results, we concluded that the bilingual clusters generated by our method are quite promising both in cross-lingual IR and monolingual IR. We have also examined the IR performance for clusters generated with different clustering parameters. These results are explained in more detail (Kando and Aizawa 1998).

6.3 Toward incorporating deeper natural language processing

Our present implementation does not require much grammatical or lexical knowledge specific to the target language. The only language-dependent knowledge employed is character substitution rules to deal with notational variations, detection of acronyms, and the similarity measure based on the histogram of character codes. Though our original intention was to develop a domain- and language- independent method to extract multilingual keyword clusters automatically, the standard natural language processing techniques can also be incorporated easily.

We summarize in the following where and how such natural language processing can be employed.

1. (*At the normalization stage*) Detecting semantically identical notation variations. For example, stemming or approximate string matching using edition distance.

2. (*At the screening stage*) Discriminating between obvious errors and non-errors. Algorithms employed here should not be computation intensive since they are used only for preprocessing for later stages. For example, simple string matching with existing standard dictionaries would work well.

3. (*At the disambiguation stage*) Disambiguation includes (i) selecting an edge cut for deletion when more than one candidate exists, and (ii) determining the cluster for the isolated edge of the cluster size and the selected node cut. Though we are currently using only surface level information based on character histograms of the clusters, we can resort to more advanced language processing means including morphological analysis. Since the number of candidates is greatly reduced by the graph theoretic means, it is possible to use more time consuming processing mechanisms at this stage.

7. Conclusion

Starting from the Japanese and English keywords assigned to the papers by the authors and applying the graph theoretical method, we have successfully generated interesting clusters which consist of related bilingual keywords.

The major advantages of our methodology are that, unlike statistical methods, clusters can be properly generated for low frequency keywords as well as high frequency keywords, and computational costs are relatively low. Looking at the resultant clusters, we can observe that they include not only canonical and standard bilingual pairs of the type listed in dictionaries but also other pairs which are considered to be relevant.

With respect to the procedure for making keyword clusters, we are currently extending and refining our methods in the following directions:

1. Refinement of the basic methods used at each stage in Figure 7. For example, we have used only keyword-level correspondences so far, since Japanese does not have clear word boundaries. Given that many keywords are complex, we can expect more information by utilizing morpheme- (or word-) level correspondences.

2. Extracting representative bilingual pairs for a given cluster using graph topological information. We have so far emphasized that an interesting aspect of the clusters is that they include useful but non-standard pairs. In IR, this may well be an advantage, but at the same time, it may be quite useful if we can extract canonical bilingual pairs among the clustered data. The simple co-

occurrences already show interesting information, but this will be further refined by considering other factors.

At the same time, we are also carrying out experiments in which keyword pairs extracted from noisy parallel corpora are used as initial input, instead of author given keywords, to the clustering algorithms discussed here.

Notes

* This research is part of the research project "A Study on Ubiquitous Information Systems for Utilization of Highly Distributed Information Resources", funded by the Japan Society for the Promotion of Science.

1. English words in italics are added for the sake of explanation, and are not in the original data. Henceforth for Japanese examples, we add standard or literal English equivalents using the same convention.

References

Aiso, H. (ed) 1993. *Joho Syori Yogo Daijiten.* Tokyo: Ohm.

Deerwester, S., Dumais, S.T., Furnas, G.W., Landauer, T.K. and Harshman, R. 1990. "Indexing by latent semantic analysis." *JASIS* 41(6): 391–407.

Dumais, S.T., Landauer, T.K., and Littman. M.L. 1996. "Automatic cross-linguistic information retrieval using Latent Semantic Indexing." *SIGIR '96 Workshop on Cross-Linguistic Information Retrieval.* 16–23.

Eijk, van der P. 1993. "Automating the acquisition of bilingual terminology." *Proc. of the 6th EACL.* 113–119.

Finch, S.P. 1993. *Finding Structure in Language.* PhD Thesis. Edinbourgh: University of Edinbourgh.

Fung, P. 1995. "A pattern matching method for finding noun and proper noun translations from noisy parallel corpora." *Proc. of 33rd ACL.* 233–236.

Gale, W.A. and Church, K.W. 1991. "Identifying word correspondences in parallel texts." *Proc. of DARPA Speech and Natural Language Workshop.* 152–157.

Grefenstette, G. 1994. *Explorations in Automatic Thesaurus Discovery.* Boston: Kluwer Academic.

Habert, B., Naulleau, E. and Nazarenko, A. 1996. "Symbolic word clustering for medium-size corpora." *COLING '96.* 490–495.

Habert, B., Nazarenko, A., Zweigenbaum, P. and Bouaud, J. 1998. "Extending an Existing Specialized Semantic Lexicon." *First International Conference on Language Resources and Evaluation.* 663–668.

Hughes, J. 1994. *Automatically Acquiring a Classification of Words.* PhD Thesis. Leeds: University of Leeds.

Japan Society for Artificial Intelligence (ed) 1990. *Jinko Tinou Handobukku.* Tokyo: Ohm.

Kageura, K., Koyama, T., Yoshioka, M., Takasu, A., Nozue, T. and Tsuji, K. 1997. "NACSIS corpus project for IR and terminological research." *NLPRS '97.* 493–496.

Kando, N., Kuriyama, K., Nozue T., Eguchi, K., Kato, H., Hidaka, S. 1999. "Overview of IR tasks at the first NTCIR workshop." Proceedings of the First NTCIR Workshop on Research in Japanese Text Retrieval and Term Recognition. 11–44.

Kando, N. and Aizawa, A. 1998. "Cross-lingual information retrieval using automatically generated multilingual keyword clusters." The 3rd International Workshop on Information Retireval with Asian Languages at Singapore.

Kupiec, J. 1993. "An algorithm for finding noun phrase correspondences in bilingual corpora." *Proc. of 31st ACL.* 17–22.

Melamed, I.D. 1996. "Automatic construction of clean broad-coverage translation lexicons." *2nd Conference of the Association for Machine Translation in the Americas.*

NACSIS 1997. *Introduction to the National Center for Science Information Systems.* Tokyo: NACSIS.

Nagamochi, H 1993. "Minimum cut in a graph." In *Discrete Structure and Algorithms II*, S. Fujishige (ed), 155–202. Tokyo: Kindaikagakusha.

Ralston, A. (ed) 1983. *Encyclopedia of Computer Science and Engineering.* Amsterdam: Van Nostrand Reinhold. Toujou, A. (trans. ed.) 1987. *Compyu-ta Daihyakka.* Tokyo: Asakura.]

Schütze, H. and Pedersen, J.O. 1997. "A cooccurrence-based thesaurus and two applications to information retrieval." *Information Processing and Management* 33(3): 307–318.

Shapiro, S (ed) 1987. *Encyclopedia of Artificial Intelligence.* New York: John Wiley. [Ohsuga, S. (trans. ed.) 1991. *Jinko Tinou Daijiten.* Tokyo: Maruzen.]

Smadja, F., McKeown, K.R. and Hatzivassiloglou, V. 1996. "Translating collocations for bilingual lexicons: A statistical approach." *Computational Linguistics* 22(1): 1–38.

Strzalkowski, T. 1994. "Building a lexical domain map from text corpora." *COLING '94.* 604–610.

Chapter 2

The automatic construction of faceted terminological feedback for interactive document retrieval*

Peter G. Anick
AltaVista Company

We present a linguistic method for the automatic construction of terminological feedback for use in interactive information retrieval. The method exploits the tendency for key domain concepts within result sets to participate in families of semantically related lexical compounds. We show how lexical dispersion may be used to identify terms that can serve in the role of "facets", broad categories that organize domain concepts into separate hierarchies. The phrases in which these terms occur serve to provide a set of attributes, specializations, related concepts, etc., for the so-identified facet terms. We investigate the effect of a number of parameters on the output, with the aim of providing a relevant set of feedback categories while minimizing run-time overhead.

1. Introduction

1.1 Terminological feedback

The primary function of a textual information retrieval system is to match a representation of a user's information need with representations of target documents. In *full-text* indexing, a document is represented by the set of words it contains, while a user's need is a natural language search expression, often containing only one or two words. Given the many ways in which ideas can be expressed, it is unlikely that the terms in a user query will precisely match the vocabulary used in all relevant documents. Furthermore, thanks to rampant lexical and contextual ambiguity of natural language, query terms are likely to match many irrelevant documents. As a consequence, the typical result list is a mixture of relevant items with some surprisingly irrelevant ones. It is not uncommon to find oneself asking, "What does this article have to do with my query?" during an information seeking session.

This potential mismatch of query terms and document terms is not the only problem facing the online information seeker. The information need itself may be poorly defined in the user's mind. Through repeated interaction with the system, the user must define the need, assess the results returned, develop a sense of what material is likely to be in the database, etc.

One of the ways a system can aid the information seeker in both the formation of a problem statement and its evolution over the course of a retrieval session is to suggest terminology that is likely to be relevant. Perhaps the most common approach has been to employ a thesaurus to present terms related to words appearing in the user's query (e.g., Beaulieu et al. 1997; Srinivasan 1996). Presented with such feedback, the user may increase recall by adding synonyms, broaden the search by adding generalizations, and narrow it by using specializations and related terms.

Another related approach is to employ a *faceted* classification, which represents a subject area as a collection of separate hierarchies designed to capture alternative ways of structuring the domain. Consider, for example, the set of facets which might be identified for the field of Astronomy (from Vickery et al. 1958):

Celestial bodies (star, comet, planet, etc.)
Their parts (axis, tail, surface, etc.)
Systems of bodies (galaxy, constellation, etc.)
Properties of bodies (size, temperature, etc.)
Properties of systems (e.g. distribution of stars)
Motion of bodies (orbit, rotation, etc.)
Relations between bodies (perturbation, capture)
Operations (e.g. spectroscopic observation)
Tools (e.g. telescope)

Such a representation of a domain of discourse can be employed within a system/user dialog to help the user conceptualize the problem space, identify and focus on dimensions of interest, and create a search expression restricted to specific values along those dimensions. Several powerful interfaces have been constructed around faceted domain knowledge (e.g., Vickery et al. 1987; Pollitt 1997). The OAKASSIST interface (Meadow et al. 1989) breaks a user's query down into its major logical subdivisions and provides a separate window of potential search terms for each subdivision identified.

Unfortunately, for most databases the cost and intellectual effort required to construct and maintain thesauri or classification schemes prohibit their use. As a result, much research has focused on methods for acquiring terminological information automatically from corpora. It is possible, for example, to construct a "thesaurus" of statistically related terms using collocational patterns (SparckJones 1971) or mutual information measures (Church 1990). Such methods rely on the degree of co-occurrence of words within text windows such as sentence, paragraph, or document to suggest terms that are semantically related. By combining statistical with linguistic evidence across a large corpus, it is possible to heuristically construct synonym, related term, and even hierarchical links between many of the terms in a corpus (Ruge 1991; Pustejovksy et al. 1993; Strzalkowsi and Byrd 1994; Cooper 1997]). These methods employ a shallow syntactic parse of the corpus in order to identify sets of terms that share lexico-syntactic contexts. For example, nouns that appear as objects of the same set of verbs or occur with the same set of modifiers can often be assumed to share semantic features.

Phrases, long recognized as good candidates for narrowing a search expression (Salton 1986), can also be used directly within an interactive interface. The REALIST system (Ruge 1990) constructed a database of noun phrases through a syntactic analysis of its corpus, permitting users to review terms heading or modifying potential query terms before they actually entered and queried a commercial database. In a similar fashion, the AI-STARS system (Anick et al. 1990) allowed users to substitute phrases for initial query terms as part of its direct manipulation interface for query reformulation. SQLET (Grefenstette 1997) used a parsed corpus to provide users with an enumeration of all the phrasal contexts for a query term throughout a corpus.

There are many retrieval situations in which it is more appropriate to generate terms that are relevant to a query *as a whole*, rather than to the individual words making up the query. Given a query about "class action suits", for example, it would be inappropriate for a system to suggest terms relating to schools or tailors. One alternative to the corpus preprocessing methods described above is to use *relevance feedback* to identify additional potential search terms through user interaction at query time (e.g., Harman 1988). In this approach, user feedback is solicited to indicate which of the documents retrieved for a query are most relevant. Then terms from these documents are either automatically added to the query or else presented to the user as suggestions for augmenting the original query. This approach has been shown to be effective in laboratory settings, with evidence from recent studies suggesting that direct interaction with such terminological feedback improves not only actual retrieval performance but also perceived performance, trust in the system, and subjective usability (Koenemann and Belkin 1996). Unfortunately, many users appear reluctant or unable to make relevance judgments about documents (Croft 1995).

Another query-time approach is illustrated by Bruza's "Hyperindex" search engine (Bruza and Dennis 1997), which helps users make linguistically well-formed transformations to their queries. A hyperindex is constructed on the fly by executing a user's query, parsing the returned titles to extract noun phrases containing query terms, and assembling these structurally analyzed noun phrases into a tree structure capturing the full set of possible "enlargements" (generalizations) and "refinements" (specializations) for these terms. Starting at the query term *internet*, for example, one can navigate to the refinement *internet security*, and from there to *internet security software*. At this point, if the user finds the phrase to be too specific, it is possible to enlarge the search via the lattice to either *internet security* or *security software*.

2. Toward automatic faceted terminological feedback

Of all the techniques for generating terminological feedback for use in interactive query refinement, faceted feedback schemes are unique in providing users not only terminology but also an explicit framework for reasoning along the multiple dimensions that characterize a domain. Given that many users approach an information seeking session with only a vague idea of their needs and an even vaguer idea of what information actually resides in the database, the provision of such structured domain feedback provides a mechanism for the incremental development of a search formulation through high level system/user interaction (Belkin and Marchetti 1990). Unfortunately, as noted earlier, the human effort in constructing a faceted classification limits their practical use to a very small number of domains.

In this chapter, we describe a new linguistic approach to the automatic generation of terminological feedback which, like a faceted classification, structures terminology along salient dimensions. The approach is based on the observation that key domain concepts within databases and result sets tend to participate in families of semantically related lexical compounds. Section 2 motivates the "lexical dispersion hypothesis" and presents our algorithm for capturing a term's dispersion within nominal compounds. In Section 3, we analyze the overall degree of dispersion present within several topically distinct textual databases and consider the terms with highest dispersion within each corpus. Section 4 describes the application of the lexical dispersion hypothesis to the dynamic generation of terminological feedback for query result sets, showing sample output using different facet ranking heuristics. Section 5 reviews the advantages and drawbacks of this approach.

2.1 The lexical dispersion hypothesis

New concepts are often expressed in English not as new single words, but as concatenations of existing nouns and adjectives. This is especially noticeable in technical language, where long chains of nouns are not uncommon ("database management system", "byte code interpreter") and it appears to be one of the primary characteristics of sublanguages such as medical briefs and naval messages, which have domain specific grammars for combining terms into terse expressions of complex concepts (e.g., Jacquemin and Royauté 1994; Marsh 1984). Multi-word terms also permeate everyday language. Noun compounds are regularly used to encode ontological relationships — an "oak tree", for example, **isa** tree. They concisely encode many other kinds of relationships as well (Finin 1982). In "tree rings", rings are a property of the tree. In "tree roots", the roots are a part of the tree. One would therefore expect that documents dealing with trees would tend to contain many different collocations containing the word "tree", (e.g., tree diseases, tree bark, tree sap, tree roots, pine tree, coniferous tree) since such compounds linguistically serve to identify subordinate categories, attributes, and other relationships within the domain of trees. Similarly, other salient concepts related to trees would likely be expressed as nominal compounds within such a collection. For example, we might find compounds incorporating the concept "forest" (rain forest, forest fire) or specializations of types of trees (white birch, silver birch).

By applying abductive reasoning, it may be possible to exploit this linguistic tendency for the purpose of *diagnosing* key topical dimensions of document collections:

Given rule: Terms expressing key categories or dimensions of a topical domain often appear in many different lexical compounds within a collection relating to that domain.

And result: Term *x* appears in many compounds within collection *y*.

Hypothesize: Term *x* expresses a key category or dimension of the topical domain of collection *y*.

We will refer to the proposition that a word's *lexical dispersion* — the number of *different* compounds that a word appears in within a given document set — can be used as a diagnostic for automatically identifying key concepts of that document set as the *lexical dispersion hypothesis.*[1]

2.1.1 *Computing lexical dispersion*

In this section, we describe our algorithm for computing lexical dispersion. We will refer to the candidate thematic terms identified by our algorithm as *facets,* because of their superficial resemblance to the dimensions and categories of manually developed faceted feedback schemes, and to their associated compounds as *values.*

2.1.2 *Lexical contexts*

The linguistic unit we will use for measuring a term's dispersion is a noun compound composed of a string of contiguous nouns, optionally preceded by an adjective. As argued above, noun compounds are good candidates for our purposes for many reasons:

- Noun compounds are widely used across sublanguage domains for describing concepts succinctly.
- Because they are contiguous, they are relatively easy to detect and extract from text corpora.
- Unlike many phrasal constructions, which reflect transient relationships among objects, noun compounding is generally applied to express tighter, more "long-lived" relationships between concepts, thereby contributing less "noise."
- Most proper nouns are subsumed under this definition of noun compound.
- Nouns and noun compounds form the bulk of the terms that show up in actual queries.
- In most cases the relationship between a noun compound and the head noun of the compound is a strict conceptual specialization.

Since adjectives are also commonly used to specialize concepts, we found it valuable to include noun phrases preceded by an adjective modifier, such as "international law" or "ancient history." In this way, we can capture concepts which are formed with the adjectival form of a morphologically related noun, as in "French cuisine" or "literary criticism." Many of the nouns and adjectives that frequently occur in phrases have little value for information retrieval, however. To filter out candidate phrases of dubious worth, we have had to construct a large list of *noiseword* modifiers and head terms. These include quantitative nouns and adjectives, such as cardinal and ordinal numbers, words like "many", "some", "amount", temporal nouns like "year", and qualitative adjectives, such as "significant" and "reasonable."

2.1.3 *Extracting lexical contexts*

Our process for extracting a set of lexical contexts for a collection of documents consists of the following steps.

Each HTML page is parsed and tokenized. No further canonicalization is done in this phase. Next, a version of the Brill tagger (Brill 1995) is applied to associate each token with a part of speech tag and a pattern matcher is run over the tagged text to extract all phrases with length two or greater matching the pattern {?adjective noun+}. If a phrase so matched contains more than four tokens, it is truncated to the final four tokens.

The next step is to convert the collection of nominal compounds extracted for each document into a list of *lexical contexts.* We formally define a *lexical context* as a tuple of the form ⟨facet, value⟩ where the facet is one of the components of the phrase and the value is the entire phrase. For example, the compound "jazz band" generates two tuples: ⟨jazz, jazz band⟩ and ⟨band, jazz band⟩.

When we reviewed the lexical contexts produced in this manner, we found that the handling of proper nouns presented a dilemma. In databases containing many personal names, we noted that a term such as *David* or *Michael* tends to show up with many different last names, therefore giving it a high dispersion. Such terms are unlikely to serve as good facets for the collection, however, since people sharing a first name is not usually an interesting dimension for refining a query. On the other hand, many proper nouns are composed of common terms that are semantically informative when co-occurring within a name. For example, in company names such as "Western Mining Corporation", the terms within the name are often indicative of the nature of the company. The name "Boston Red Sox" relates a city to a team, etc. Therefore, filtering out all proper names would eliminate many useful relationships and potential search topics.

We settled on a heuristic to eliminate components of proper names as facets only under a restricted set of conditions: if the candidate phrase begins with a sequence of two capitalized words, no tuple is generated for the first term of the phrase. This heuristic has the effect of eliminating most lexical contexts in which a first name is the facet without eliminating many potentially useful facets and phrases from the ultimate set of lexical contexts.[2]

Another question that arose in the construction of lexical contexts was whether or not to morphologically canonicalize head nouns. Although this is often done (via "stemming") in information retrieval system indexes, there are cases in which the plural noun occurs in semantically different contexts than the singular noun. This is particularly so in the case of proper names, in which canonicalizing an inflected word form would actually change the name. After some experimentation, we chose to canonicalize common nouns (lowercased nouns) while leaving proper nouns (uppercased) unchanged.[3] This heuristic generally preserves the integrity of proper names while merging variants of common nouns. The facet term itself, however, (the first element in each tuple representing a lexical context) is always case-folded into lower case. In this way, uses of a term within a generic concept and within proper names are logically grouped together with the lowercased facet term.

This tuple format, composed of a facet/value pair, makes it easy to rank terms by lexical dispersion. One can concatenate the lexical contexts for all files of a corpus into a single file, remove duplicate entries, then count the number of occurrences of each facet to compute its dispersion. Likewise, one can use the *grep* utility to extract all entries for a given facet, apply the *uniq –c* utility to the results to get a count of occurrences of each value for the selected facet, then sort the results to create a frequency ordered list of lexical contexts for the facet.

3. Corpus-wide lexical dispersion

Using this process to extract lexical contexts, we analyzed lexical dispersion within a number of text corpora, including the Financial Times corpus used in TREC, a computer troubleshooting web site, a corporate newsfeed, and the results of a world wide web query on "jazz music." By computing the lexical dispersion for each term, then sorting the terms by their dispersion, we were able to plot the degree of dispersion by the rank of terms in this sorted list.

Figure 1 shows such a graph for the 210,000 article Financial Times database. This graph illustrates the effect of restricting dispersion to lexical

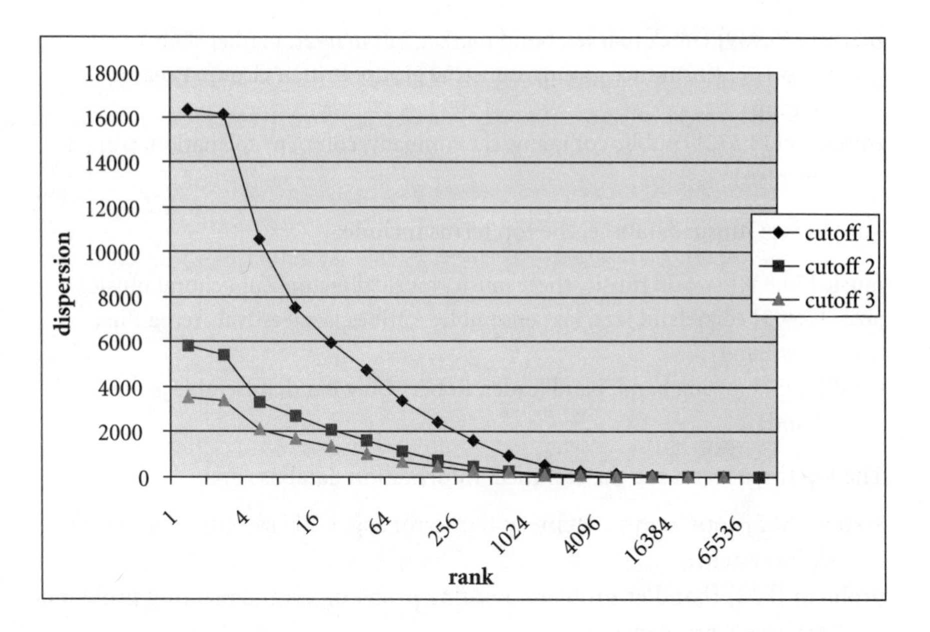

Figure 1. Lexical dispersion for terms in Financial Times database, ranked by degree of dispersion at three phrase occurrence cut-off levels.

contexts that occur a minimum of 1, 2 or 3 times in the corpus. Out of the total of 126,142 nouns and adjectives that participate in at least one lexical context, those terms ranked at the top appear in thousands of contexts. At a phrase occurrence cut-off of 1, over 4000 terms have a dispersion > 100 and over 32000 terms appear in at least 5 contexts. When dispersion is restricted to phrases occurring at least 3 times, there are still over 8000 terms that appear in 6 or more different contexts.

High levels of dispersion were also evident in the other corpora we studied. Even in the relatively small (2,000 article) technical information database, there were over 250 words with dispersion > 50 and over 2000 words with dispersion > 6.

As expected, the terms with highest lexical dispersion do represent key generic concepts for their respective domains. The top three terms for the Financial Times database, for example, are the following (shown with their dispersion and a sample of the compounds containing each term):

market [16,339] (stock market, bond market, gilt market, market share)
group [16,121] (insurance group, industrial group, Britten Group, Pegasus Group)
company [14,572] (public company, car company, company formation, company plan)

For the jazz music database, the top terms include:

music [20,826] (world music, sheet music, music director, Zulu choral music)
jazz [11,403] (dixieland jazz, jazz ensemble, Antibes Jazz Festival, Yerba Buena Jazz Band)
band [8,937] (swing band, band leader, Robert Cray Band, miserable garage rock band)

The top three terms for the technical information database are:

system [865] (operating system, system error log, CPU system configuration, Alpha system)
problem [682] (handler problem, booting problem, erratic printing problem, port access problem)
error [629] (memory parity error, fatal drive error, baduaf error message, error log)

The terms with the highest dispersion also tend to have very high document frequencies within their respective collections; therefore, their discrimination value as query terms is very low. The collocated terms contained within compounds, however, tend to be not only highly germane to the subject area but also much more discriminatory as search terms. These compounds provide a potpourri of attributes, specializations, related concepts, etc., for the more generic terms they contain.

The most encouraging result of this study of corpus-wide lexical dispersion was the finding that across a variety of databases, the number of terms with even a moderate degree of dispersion is very high. Our hope, therefore, was that the lexical dispersion hypothesis would also generate useful facet-like terms within the more constrained context of result lists for individual queries.

4. Extracting facets from result sets

In order to evaluate whether lexical dispersion might serve to identify facets on the fly appropriate for use in interactive query refinement, we prototyped a web application, the *Paraphrase Search Assistant*, which presents users with a list of 15–20 facet terms derived from their query result set. Figures 2–4 show snapshots of the user interface. Figure 2 shows the facets produced for the query "global warming" issued to the TREC Financial Times database. The facets, appearing in the lower left-hand frame, are presented as select boxes; a user may click on a facet name to view a list of compounds containing the facet term. As shown in Figure 3, a user may select a phrase in order to focus the search on that topic. When a phrase is selected, a new query is constructed composed of the original query and the selected focus phrase. A new result list is computed and displayed. However, the initial set of facets and the original query are retained to preserve the user's original context. A user is therefore free to choose other phrases as focus terms in order to explore different aspects of the original query in an iterative fashion. The user can also change contexts, either by drilling down (i.e., merging the query and focus phrase into a new query context) or by replacing the original query with the focus phrase alone. Each of these options results in the generation of a new set of facets, computed from the new result set (as illustrated in Figure 4.)[4]

Using the *Paraphrase* application as a testbed, we have begun to examine the effects of varying a number of parameters on the facets produced for various queries. Among the questions we addressed were the following:

- Should "facets" be ranked by dispersion alone or by other criteria as well?
- How many of the result set articles should be used to extract phrases?
- How frequently should a phrase be required to occur in a result list to include it in the computation?

In the sections that follow, we will describe some of the experiments conducted on the Financial Times database to help answer these questions. We used two sets of single word queries, a "broad" set (*finance, France, food, law, health*) whose members yielded result sets containing over 10,000 documents each, and a "narrow" set (*terrorism, movies, bicycle, jazz, virus*) whose members matched between 300 and 800 documents each. The underlying search engine used in the experiments was AltaVista (Altavista 1996), which takes queries in the form of natural language expressions and returns a ranked result list.

4.1 Facet ranking

The most straightforward method of applying the lexical dispersion hypothesis to the selection of facets is to rank all the terms appearing within a result set by

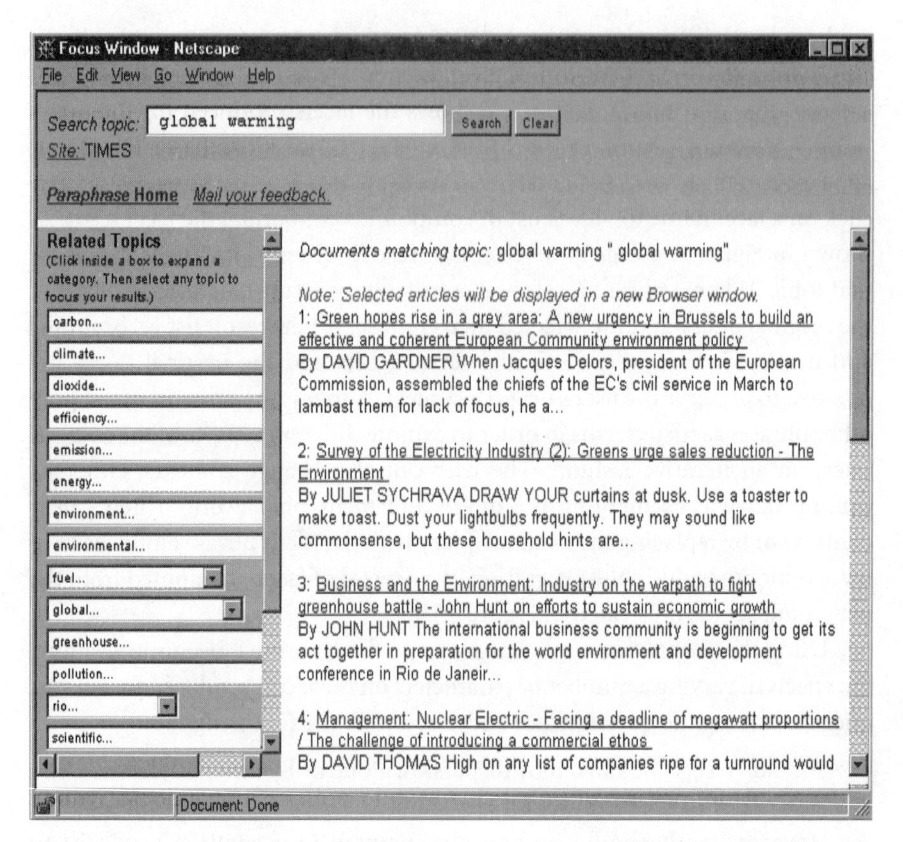

Facet terms appear as labels on select boxes in the lower left-hand frame (entitled "Related Topics").

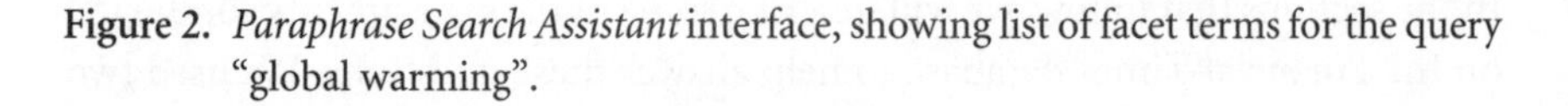

Figure 2. *Paraphrase Search Assistant* interface, showing list of facet terms for the query "global warming".

the number of different lexical contexts in which they occur and select the top *n* as facets. We found two drawbacks to this direct approach. First, it is possible for one or two long articles on a specific subject to contribute a large number of distinct phrases containing a specific term, even though the term may otherwise be relatively rare within the result set. Second, depending upon the subject matter of the database, there may be some terms that are likely to appear in many phrases within practically any result set within the database. For example, in our jazz music database of web articles, many queries resulted in the terms "jazz" and "music" showing up among the top ranked facets.

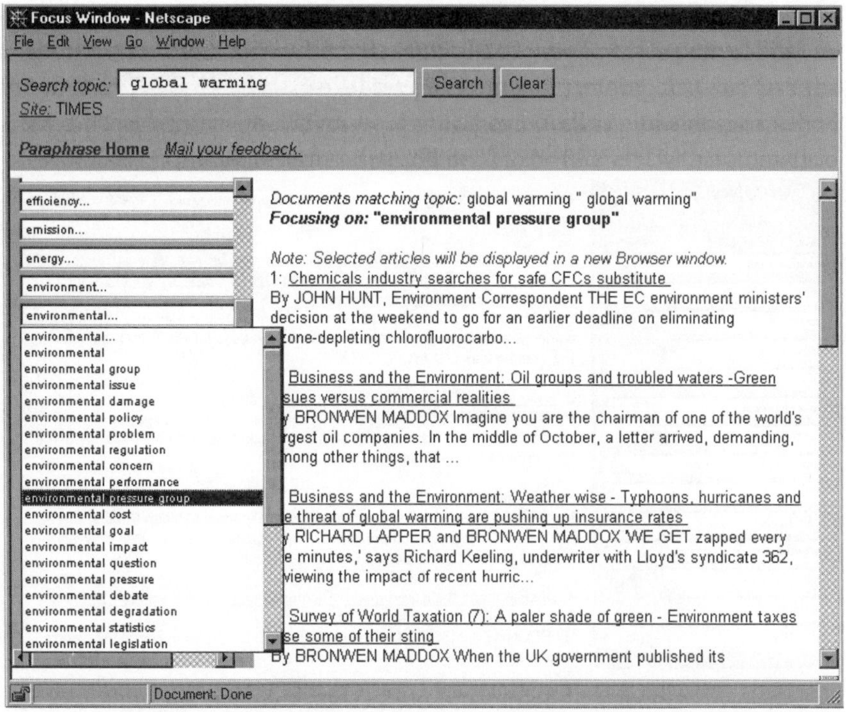

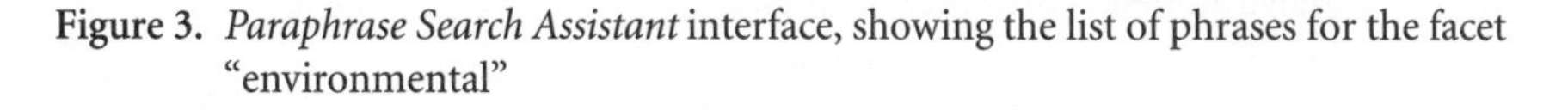

The user has selected the phrase "environmental pressure group" as a focus term and a new set of results has been generated.

Figure 3. *Paraphrase Search Assistant* interface, showing the list of phrases for the facet "environmental"

One way to reduce the effect of long articles on the results is to use only the first *n* phrases within each document. We also devised a two pass facet ranking algorithm, which first uses lexical dispersion to select a set of *m* candidate facets, then uses a second measure to rerank the candidates produced in the first pass. We implemented two reranking methods:

- **Spread** — Candidate facets are ranked according to the number of result set documents which contain at least one lexical context for the facet term. This approach favors facets which occur more widely throughout the result set.
- **Spread.icf** — Candidate facets are ranked by a variant of the tf.idf formula:[5] (w1 + log(100*spread(*f*)/result_set_size)) × (w2 + log(corpus_size/corpus_frequency(*f*))). This formula favors terms that occur widely throughout the result set but that are less common in the database as a whole.

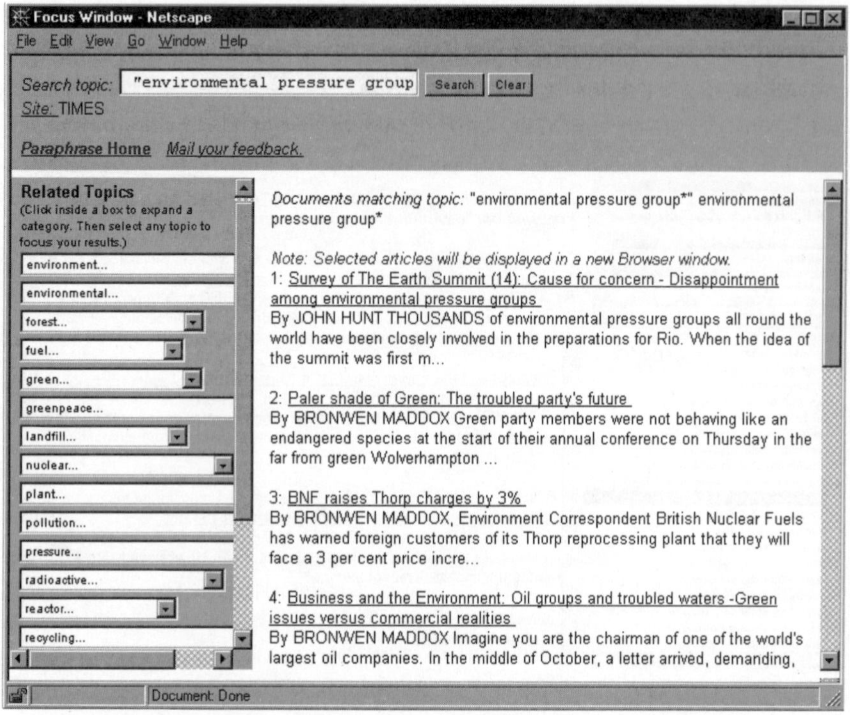

Figure 4. *Paraphrase Search Assistant* interface, showing the new list of facet terms generated after the user has replaced the initial query with the focus term "environmental pressure group".

Table 1 shows in column 2 the average number of values (phrases) generated by the three ranking strategies for our two sets of test queries (using phrases found in the top 100 ranked documents returned for each query). As would be expected, the total number of phrases associated with the top 15 facets decreases with both reranking strategies and is smallest for Spread.icf. In column 3, we show the average degree of overlap within the top 15 facets chosen by each ranking strategy. For example, the top cell shows that 10 of the top 15 facets chosen by dispersion alone also appear within the top 15 facets ranked by Spread. Six facets overlap with those produced by the Spread.icf ranking. Overall, of the top 15 facets chosen strictly by degree of dispersion, roughly two thirds of those terms also occur among the top 15 for the Spread strategy; roughly one third remain for the Spread.icf strategy.

To observe the specific effects of the reranking strategies on the utility of the facets produced, let us consider the results for two of our sample queries. Below

Table 1. Effect of ranking strategy on total number of facet values and number of facets shared between pairs of strategies. (phrase cutoff = 1, result subset size = 100)

Strategy	No. values	No. shared facets
Broad queries		
Dispersion	410	Spread: 10, Spread.icf: 6
Spread	388	Dispersion: 10, Spread.icf: 5
Spread.icf	320	Dispersion: 6, Spread: 5
Narrow queries		
Dispersion	350	Spread: 9, Spread.icf: 5
Spread	321	Dispersion: 9, Spread.icf: 5
Spread.icf	269	Dispersion: 5, Spread: 5

is the output produced for the query "food" for the three strategies, showing the top 15 sorted facet terms, each followed by its degree of dispersion and its spread (within the top 100 documents). We have bolded the terms in the output for the Dispersion strategy that do not appear in the output for Spread. Terms not appearing in Spread.icf are bolded in the Spread listing, and terms not appearing in Spread are bolded in Spread.icf.

Dispersion: food (110, 68) restaurant (24, 17) fish (24, 11) market (23, 20) **french** (22, 10) group (21, 16) industry (20, 22) **soup** (18, 7) product (18, 15) ec (19, 12) uk (17, 12) aid (16, 11) **sale** (14, 10) **british** (15, 10) price (14, 13)

Spread: food (110, 68) **industry** (20, 22) **market** (23, 20) restaurant (24, 17) **group** (21, 16) **product** (18, 15) **price** (14, 13) **minister** (12, 12) **company** (12, 12) **uk** (17, 12) **ec** (19, 12) **international** (10, 11) fresh (11, 11) aid (16, 11) fish (24, 11)

Spread.icf: restaurant (24, 17) **menu** (10, 8) **soup** (18, 7) fish (24, 11) **drink** (9, 9) food (110, 68) **supermarket** (10, 7) **vegetarian** (9, 2) **shop** (13, 9) aid (16, 11) fresh (11, 11) **wine** (12, 4) **russian** (12, 8) **hotel** (12, 6) **soviet** (10, 6)

Most of the facets shared by all strategies (*food, restaurant, fish*) are reasonable dimensions for this topic. Phrases associated with the food facet include *food manufacturer, European food industry, food credit, food import, food executive,* all suitable for focusing a query on the business aspects of food. The restaurant facet includes nationalities (*Thai, Irish*) and properties (*cost, menu, service*). Fish phrases include things made out of fish *(soup, cake, paste)* and types of fish (*white, parrot*). Overall, the particular facet terms selected by Spread.icf appear to be the most germane to the topic. However, the somewhat broader facets selected by Spread contain many food related terms among their facet values. Under the generic facet *industry*, for example, we find *food retailing industry, fishing industry, animal feed industry, food processing industry*. Likewise, under *product*, we find *dairy product, cereal product, baking product*, etc. For *UK*, phrases include *UK champagne market, UK grocery industry, UK poultry breeders*. Given the business perspective of the Financial Times, these facets are in many respects more relevant categories than the more specific food-related terms in Spread.icf. This apparent relevance is also consistent with the larger spread for these facets, compared to those returned by Spread.icf.

Our second example, for the query "virus", is particularly interesting because there are two distinct senses of the term represented in the database — the biological virus and the computer virus. In the top 100 documents returned by the search engine, 86 relate to the biological virus, the majority of these specifically dealing with HIV. This unbalance of senses within the result set is reflected in the facets produced, which primarily relate to the biological virus (*health, drug, medical*) and HIV in particular (*hiv, aids, blood, transfusion*). As in the previous example, generic terms not specifically associated with the query term, such as *research* and *UK*, turn out nevertheless to reflect potentially useful cuts of the domain. Under *research*, we find names of relevant research firms as well as types of research (*biological, transfusion*), while under *UK*, we find a range of concepts from *drug* and *pharmaceutical* to *health authority* and *accounting standard*. A number of concepts germane to computer viruses are captured under the *computer* facet in the Spread list, e.g., *computer hackers, abuse, fraud, security challenge* and *virus expert*.

Dispersion: computer (47, 16) virus (37, 49) health (22, 33) medical (22, 18) **security** (20, 11) company (20, 17) drug (18, 15) aids (19, 24) research (16, 15) system (15, 20) **genetic** (13, 7) **cell** (14, 12) uk (13, 14) **software** (13, 8) blood (13, 13)

Spread: virus (37, 49) **health** (22, 33) hiv (10, 31) aids (19, 24) **system** (15, 20) medical (22, 18) **company** (20, 17) cookson (6, 16) **computer** (47, 16) **product** (6, 15) **research** (16, 15) **drug** (18, 15) **uk** (13, 14) clinical (10, 13) blood (13, 13)

Spread.icf: virus (37, 49) hiv (10, 31) **cell** (14, 12) aids (19, 24) cookson (6, 16) clinical (10, 13) **transfusion** (6, 4) **genetic** (13, 7) **patient** (6, 9) blood (13, 13) **disease** (11, 9) **abrahams** (6, 7) **program** (8, 6) medical (22, 18) **user** (10, 9)

Comparing the output for the different strategies, we see a similar pattern to the previous example. The actual facet terms produced by the Spread.icf strategy have the most ostensible relationships to the query topic. Indeed, these are precisely the kinds of terms one might expect to find as related terms within a thesaurus. However, when taking into consideration the sets of values associated with each of the facet terms, the facets generated by Spread tend to more effectively serve as dimensions for conceptually subdividing the result set. Note that because of the relative frequency of the terms *computer* and *software* in the database as a whole,[6] the Spread.icf strategy fails to include any facets relating to the computer virus sense (with the exception of the term "virus" itself, which contains several values relating to computer viruses.)

Similar observations about the effects of the three ranking strategies were made for the other databases studied; as a result, we adopted the Spread strategy for the remainder of our experiments.

4.2 Result set size

The run-time speed of our facet extraction algorithm is primarily a function of the number of lexical contexts it must process, which in turn is a function of the number of documents which contribute to the list of lexical contexts. Because the analysis of result sets must be carried out during interactive retrieval sessions, we have a pragmatic incentive to minimize the number of result set documents included in our run-time dispersion analysis. As it turns out, there are other reasons not to base our analysis of dispersion on the entire result set for a query. First, result sets are ranked. Therefore articles at the beginning of a result set tend to be more relevant to the query than those appearing later in the list. Secondly, in search engines like AltaVista, search terms entered in natural language queries are ORed by default. Thus, the density of articles truly relevant to a multi-term query often falls off significantly after the top 20 or 30 articles. Consider, for example, the natural language query "cold fusion", applied to the Financial Times database. This query produces over 3000 hits, of which only ten actually contain the phrase "cold fusion". As a result, the facets generated from even the top 100 documents in the result set are more likely to reflect the more prevalent concepts of "cold war" and "ice cream", rather than the intended topic of "cold fusion."

To investigate the consequences of using smaller subsets of the result set for generating facets, we compared the facet sets produced for our ten sample queries while varying the number of result set documents used for extracting

Table 2. Cumulative number of facets with various degrees of dispersion, shown for different result subset sizes

Broad queries

Result set size	*Disp > 5*	*Disp > 10*	*Disp > 20*	*Disp > 30*	*Dsp > 40*
50	51	13	2	0	0
100	130	36	9	3	2
200	279	98	29	11	6
300	424	162	50	23	12
400	545	221	76	37	22

Narrow queries

Result set size	*Disp > 5*	*Disp > 10*	*Disp > 20*	*Disp > 30*	*Dsp > 40*
50	42	9	1	0	0
100	145	40	7	2	1
200	281	92	25	10	4
300	349	118	34	15	8
400	411	145	43	21	12

lexical contexts. As Table 2 shows, the cumulative number of facets with high degrees of dispersion increases dramatically as result set size is increased from 50 to 400 documents. Column 2 of Table 3, presenting the average total number of different values present for the top 15 facets for a range of result subset sizes, shows that this number grows by several hundred phrases for each additional 100 documents considered. Column 3 of Table 3 compares the number of top 15 facets generated for a particular result subset size with the set produced for the next smaller result set size in the table. We can see, for example, that 9 of the top 15 facets generated from a result subset size of 100 documents are also present in the set generated from the first 30 documents. Overall, we found that the set of 15 top ranked facets remains relatively stable across result subsets of different sizes.[7] This suggests that relatively small result subsets can be used to generate facet sets that are reasonably representative of much larger collections.

4.3 Phrase occurrence frequency

In many corpus linguistic applications, a phrase that occurs only once or twice in a collection might well be discarded as "noise". However, as noted in our study of dispersion within databases, the degree of dispersion falls off rapidly

Table 3. Average number of different values (phrases) extracted for the top 15 facets at each result set size; the average number of (top 15) facet terms that a particular result set size has in common with the set produced for the next smaller result set size in the table.

Broad queries

Result set size	*Total values*	*No. of shared facets*
10	51	0
30	149	5
100	388	9
200	665	12
300	932	12

Narrow queries

Result set size	*Total values*	*No. of shared facets*
10	39	0
30	119	5
100	306	9
200	557	12
300	754	13

when phrase occurrence constraints are applied. We have found this to be equally true within result sets. Using a result subset of only 30 articles, for example, and a requirement that facets have a dispersion of four or greater lexical contexts, our algorithm was on the average able to generate only 12 facets when restricted to contexts occurring at least twice and only three facets when using a cut-off of three occurrences. With no occurrence constraints, the algorithm is able to generate at least 15 facet terms for every one of our test queries. Thus, for small result subsets, using contexts with only one occurrence appears to be necessary.

When we compared the set of facets generated for a result subset of 30 documents using a cut-off of 1 with that generated for 500 documents using a cut-off of 3, we found that nearly half of top 15 facets were identical. Thus, facets chosen from a very small result subset using the most lax occurrence criteria appear to have a fair degree of overlap with facets chosen from a much larger subset with stricter conditions for computing dispersion.

From a linguistic perspective, using phrases with many singleton occurrences may be justified as well. A phrase that occurs many times in a text is likely to be a frozen lexicalization. The presence of a number of singleton phrases containing the same term, on the other hand, suggests a discourse need to coin new phrases using a particular discourse concept. We would expect facet terms to play such a generative role.

5. Discussion

Through experiments such as those described above, we have been able to tune the facet extraction algorithm used in the *Paraphrase Search Assistant* both to run efficiently and to generate reasonable output over a range of queries and databases. Our current run-time implementation uses a result subset size of 30–50 documents to generate a set of facets and then consults the first 100–200 documents in the result list to provide a larger set of values for those facets. Log data from two technical databases made available on the Compaq corporate intranet indicate that users do find the faceted feedback to be of practical value, employing it in over 40% of their information seeking sessions.

While it is true that values for the heuristically generated facets often contain a fair degree of noise as well as significant lexical gaps, when compared to a classification that might be constructed by hand, the majority of the automatically extracted "facets" do appear to represent useful dimensions for (1) reasoning about the domain topics(s), (2) assessing the contents of the result set, and (3) choosing a strategy for refining the search. The organization of terminology into categories allows the *Paraphrase* interface to display up to 40 values for each of the 15 themes presented to the user, yielding a possible total of 600 feedback terms. It would be daunting for a user to comb through an unstructured list containing so many items.[8] Although the "natural language" categories produced by our algorithm are rarely conceptually homogeneous sets, users are familiar enough with how phrases are constructed to understand why particular items appear in each list. Indeed, it is often possible to guess the meaning of an unknown term or proper name by its collocations within the phrase. We have found that browsing the categorized feedback is conducive to the serendipitous discovery of unanticipated relationships between query concepts and feedback terms.

The approach has its drawbacks as well. Since feedback terms are generated by an analysis of the result set, if the result set does not contain meaningful clusters of documents, the phrasal feedback is likely to be equally diffuse. In such cases, phrases associated with the query terms themselves are usually the only recourse, as they tend to reveal the set of possible interpretations for the query terms and therefore provide the best opportunity for focusing the query. Another drawback is the fact that certain kinds of terms relevant to a discourse topic may simply not often appear in lexical compounds. A query on "species extinction", for example, is more likely to return a list of animal subtypes (*wild animal, exotic animal, rare animal*) than a list of specific endangered species.

Indeed, in many respects, the lexical dispersion approach complements other methods of query reformulation, such as thesaurus feedback and relevance feedback. Thesauri, whether manually or automatically constructed, tend to reflect global static relationships among terms, as opposed to the context-sensitive relationships that are computed through run-time lexical dispersion analysis. Though lexical dispersion often manages to pick up useful morphological variants (e.g., "indonesia" and "indonesian"), it is not a device particularly suited for detecting synonyms, a forte of thesauri. For its part, interactive relevance feedback provides a focused, dynamic set of potential query expansion terms. However, these terms are typically based on the user's selection of one or two "relevant" articles and therefore do not reflect the contents of the result set as a whole. Thus one might use *Paraphrase*'s facet analysis to probe the database contents or browse along various conceptual dimensions; but if a particularly interesting article is encountered, relevance feedback may be the more appropriate strategy for finding similar documents. We therefore see lexical dispersion not as a substitute for these other techniques but rather as yet another device in the growing constellation of tools useful for the construction of the kind of multi-strategy interactive interface envisioned by Henninger and Belkin (Henninger 1996).

6. Conclusions

We have presented a new linguistic approach to the automatic construction of terminological feedback for use in interactive query refinement. Unlike most previous methods, which discard high frequency terms because of their poor discrimination power, we have found that many such terms provide value as "facets" through which families of related concepts may be identified, organized and presented to the end user. Such lexical families not only provide candidate search terms for refining a query; they also help a user to think about the domain and analyze the topical content of a result list, in ways that unstructured terminological feedback cannot do.

This feedback approach also requires a somewhat different approach to computational terminology. Since the corpus under study is a *dynamic* object (a result list) we must understand how families of terms are manifested under the wide range of conditions arising when users query textual databases. We must also understand the effects of various computational trade-offs made to permit interactive algorithms to run more efficiently. Future work will be directed at evaluating and improving the facet ranking algorithm, exploring a wider range of databases, studying user interaction with the feedback generated, as well as investigating how other lexical patterns might be exploited in a similar fashion.

Notes

* The author would like to thank Suresh Tipirneni for his assistance in the implementation of the *Paraphrase Search Assistant*, Bob Travis for his responsiveness in adding useful features to the AltaVista tcl API, and Donna Harman for her help in obtaining the Financial Times corpus.

1. Nakagawa 1997 and Nakagawa's chapter in this volume present evidence for this hypothesis based on studies attempting to identify good index terms in Japanese manuals.

2. An alternative approach would be to filter out such facets based on a list of common names.

3. Canonicalization was done by looking up terms in a 50,000 word on-line dictionary relating inflected forms to their uninflected forms. Terms not found in the dictionary were left as is; as a result, a small number of plural nouns remained in their uninflected form within the set of lexical contexts.

4. For further examples and discussion of a user study, see Anick (1999) and Anick and Tipirneni (1999).

5. Tf.idf is a term weighting formula commonly used in information retrieval (Salton 1989). Tf is a measure of the frequency of a term within a document while idf is the inverse of the number of documents in the collection that the term appears in. In our Spread.icf measure, spread reflects facet frequency within the result subset while icf (inverse corpus frequency) is based on the number of times the facet term appears within the corpus as a whole.

6. "computer", for example, occurs in 8933 documents, whereas "transfusion", by comparison, occurs in only 55.

7. Indeed, comparing the set of facets produced from a result subset of 300 documents with that produced from only 50 documents, we found that they shared an average of 9 facet terms.

8. Note that further structure could be derived from an analysis of multi-word conceptual subcomponents occurring within the sets of facet values. Indeed, there is no reason why facets themselves could not in certain cases be multi-word terms.

References

Altavista. 1996. *The AltaVista Search Revolution.* Digital Equipment Corp.

Anick, P.G. 1999. *Automatic Construction of Faceted Terminological Feedback for Context-Based Information Retrieval,* PhD Thesis, Brandeis University.

Anick, P. and Tipirneni, S. 1999. "The Paraphrase Search Assistant: Terminological Feedback for Iterative Information Seeking", in *Proceedings of SIGIR '99,* 153–159.

Anick, P.G., Brennan, J.D., Flynn, R.A., Hanssen, D.R., Alvey, B. and Robbins, J.M. 1990. "A Direct Manipulation Interface for Boolean Information Retrieval via Natural Language Query", in *Proceedings of SIGIR '90,* 135–150.

Beaulieu, M., Do, T., Payne, A. and Jones, S. 1997. "ENQUIRE Okapi Project", *British Library Research and Innovation Report 17.*

Belkin, N.J. and Marchetti, P.G. 1990. "Determining the Functionality and Features of an Intelligent Interface to an Information Retrieval System", in *Proceedings of SIGIR '90,* 151–177.

Brill, E. 1995. "Transformation-Based Error-Driven Learning and Natural Language Processing: A Case Study in Part of Speech Tagging," *Computational Linguistics.*

Bruza, P.D. and Dennis, S. 1997 "Query Reformulation on the Internet: Empirical Data and the Hyperindex Search Engine", in *RIAO '97,* 488–499.

Church, K.W. and Hanks, P. 1990 "Word Association Norms, Mutual Information, and Lexicography", *Computational Linguistics,* 16(1): 22–29.

Cooper, J.W. and Byrd, R.J. 1997. "Lexical navigation: Visually prompted query expansion and refinement", in *Digital Libraries '97.*

Croft, W.B. 1995. "What Do People Want from Information Retrieval? (The Top 10 Research Issues for Companies that Use and Sell IR Systems)", *D-Lib Magazine,* Nov, 1995.

Finin, T.W. 1982. "The Interpretation of Nominal Compounds in Discourse", *Technical Report MS-CIS-1982–3,* University of Pennsylvania.

Grefenstette, G., "Use of Syntactic Context to Produce Term Association Lists for Text Retrieval", in *Proceedings of SIGIR '92,* 89–97.

Harman, D. 1988. "Towards Interactive Query Expansion", in *Proceedings of SIGIR '88,* 321–331.

Henninger, S. and Belkin, N. 1996. "Interface Issues and Interaction Strategies for Information Retrieval Systems", in *Proceedings of the Human Factors in Computing Systems Conference (CHI '96),* ACM Press, New York.

Jacquemin, C. and Royaute, J. 1994. "Retrieving Terms and their Variants in a Lexicalized Unification-Based Framework", in *Proceedings of SIGIR '94,* 132–141.

Koenemann, J. and Belkin, N.J. 1996. "A Case for Interaction: a Study of Interactive Information Retrieval Behavior and Effectiveness", in *Proceedings of the Human Factors in Computing Systems Conference (CHI '96),* ACM Press, New York.

Marsh, E. 1984. "A Computational Analysis of Complex Noun Phrases in Navy Messages", in *Proceedings of COLING '84,* 505–508.

Meadow, C.T., Cerny, B.A., Borgman, C.L. and Case, D.O. 1989. "Online Access to Knowledge: System Design", *JASIS* 40(2): 86–98.

Nakagawa, H. 1997. "Extraction of Index Words from Manuals", in *Proceedings of RIAO '97*, 598–611.

Pollitt, S. A. 1997. The key role of classification and indexing in view-based searching. In *Proceedings of IFLA*, Copenhagen, Sept. 1997.

Pustejovsky, J., Bergler, S. and Anick, P. 1993. "Lexical Semantic Techniques for Corpus Analysis", *Computational Linguistics*, 19(2), 331–358.

Ruge, G, Schwarz, C. and Thurmair, G. 1990. "A Hyperterm System Based on Natural Language Processing", *International Forum on Information and Documentation*, 15(3): 3–8.

Ruge, G. 1991. "Experiments on Linguistically based Term Associations", in *Proceedings of RIAO '91*, 528–545.

Salton, G. 1986. "Another Look at Automatic Text-Retrieval Systems", *Communications of the ACM*, 29(7): 648–656.

Salton, G. 1989. *Automatic Text Processing — The Transformation, Analysis and Retrieval of Information by Computer*. Reading, MA: Addison-Wesley.

Spark Jones, K. 1971. *Automatic Keyword Classification for Information Retrieval.* London: Butterworths.

Srinivasan, P. 1996. "Query Expansion and MEDLINE", *Information Processing & Management*, vol. 32(4): 431–443.

Strzalkowsi, T. 1994. "Building a Lexical Domain Map from Text Corpora", in *Proceedings of COLING '94*, 604–610.

Vickery, A and Brooks, H. M. 1987. "PLEXUS — The Expert System for Referral", *Information Processing & Management*, 23(2): 99–117.

Vickery, B. C. 1958. *Classification and Indexing in Science*, London: Butterworths.

Chapter 3

Automatic term detection

A review of current systems*

M. Teresa Cabré Castellví, Rosa Estopà Bagot and
Jordi Vivaldi Palatresi
Universitat Pompeu Fabra

In this paper we account for the main characteristics and performance of a number of recently developed term extraction systems. The analysed tools represent the main strategies followed by researchers in this area. All systems are analysed and compared against a set of technically relevant characteristics.

1. Introduction

In the late 80s there was an acute need, from different disciplines and goals, to automatically extract terminological units from specialised texts. In the 90s large computerised textual corpora have been constructed resulting in the first programs for terminology extraction[1] (henceforth TE) which have showed encouraging results.

Throughout the current decade computational linguists, applied linguists, translators, interpreters, scientific journalists and computer engineers have been interested in automatically isolating terminology from texts. There are many goals that have led these different professional groups to design software tools so as to directly extract terminology from texts: building of glossaries, vocabularies and terminological dictionaries; text indexing; automatic translation; building of knowledge databases; construction of hypertext systems; construction of expert systems and corpus analysis.

From the appearance of TERMINO (the first broadly known term detector) in 1990 until today a number of projects to design different types of automatic terminology detectors have been carried out to assist terminological work. However, despite the large number of studies in progress, the automatisation of the terminological extraction phase is still fraught with problems. The main problems encountered by term extractors are: (1) identification of complex terms, that is, determining where a terminological phrase begins and ends; (2) recognition of complex terms, that is, deciding whether a discursive unit constitutes a terminological phrase or a free unit; (3) identification of the terminological nature of a lexical unit, that is, knowing whether in a specialised text a lexical unit has a terminological nature or belongs to general language and (4) appropriateness of a terminological unit to a given vocabulary (this has scarcely been addressed from the point of view of automatization).

Systems for TE are based on three types of knowledge: (a) linguistic; (b) statistical; (c) hybrid (statistical and linguistic). Hence, there are different approaches to automatic term detection. All systems analyse a corpus of specialised texts in electronic form and extract lists of word chunks (i.e. candidate terms) that are to be confirmed by the terminologist. To make the terminologist's task easier the candidate term is provided with its context and, when available, with any other further information (frequency, relationship between terms, etc.)

Two relevant aspects regarding the nature of terms are termhood and unithood[2]; TE systems may be designed based on only one of these two aspects. Some practical experiments following each scheme for ranking a set terms extracted from Japanese texts are presented in (Nakagawa and Mori 1998). They show that results in precision and recall are very close but the set of terms extracted are a somewhat different. This is still a research issue.

Alongside term detection we find the task of automatic document indexing (i.e. information retrieval, IR). This applied field of natural language processing (NLP) techniques has an interesting common point with automatic term detection, that is, word chunks that index a given document are often terminological units. This same goal explains why many extraction systems are rooted on IR as well as on the analysis of a specific IR system with no application whatsoever to TE.

The difference between these two approaches lies in the fact that a tool for TE should extract *all* terminological units from a text, whereas IR focuses on the extraction of only words or word sequences that better describe the contents of the document regardless of their grammatical features.

The standard approach to IR consists in processing documents so as to extract the so-called *indexing terms*. These terms are usually isolated words containing enough semantic load to provide information about its *goodness* when describing documents. Queries are processed in a similar fashion to extract *query terms*. With regard to queries the relevance of documents is based exclusively on their representing terms. This is the reason why their choice is crucial.

Often these indexing terms are single words although it is known that isolated words are seldom relevant enough to decide the semantic value of a document with regard to the query. This fact has given rise to the ever-growing appearance, in the TREC[3] assessments, of word and word-sequence indexing systems using NLP techniques.

Statistically based systems function by detecting two or more lexical units whose occurrence is higher than a given level. This is not a random situation, but it is related to a particular usage of these lexical units. This principle, called *Mutual Information*, also applies to other science domains such as telecommunications and physics. Term detectors based on hybrid knowledge tend to use this idea prior to a linguistic-based processing.

The problem with this kind of approach is that there are low-frequency terms difficult to be managed by extraction systems. Here it is important to note that these systems use basically numerical information and thus are prone to be language-independent. The two most frequently used measures in the assessment of these systems are found in IR: *recall* and *precision*. Recall is defined as the relationship between the sum of retrieved terms and the sum of existing terms in the document that is being explored. In contrast, precision accounts for the relationship between those extracted terms that are really terms and the aggregate of candidate terms that are found. These measures can be interpreted as the capacity of the detection system to extract all terms from a document (*recall*) and the capacity to discriminate between those units detected by the system which are terms and those which are not (*precision*). The fact that recall accounts for all terms from a document implies that it is a figure much more difficult to estimate and improve than precision.

In contrast with this traditional approach, other approaches attempt to solve the problem by using linguistic knowledge, which may include two types of information:

a. Term specific: it consists in the detection of the recurrent patterns from complex terminological units such as noun-adjective and noun-preposition-noun. This calls for the use of *regular expressions* and techniques of *finite state automata*.

b. Language generic: it consists in the use of more complex systems of NLP that start with the detection of more basic linguistic structures: noun phrase (NP), prepositional phrase (PP), etc.

In both approaches each word is associated to a morphological category. In order to do so different strategies are proposed: from coarse systems that do not make use of any dictionary to complex systems that have an extremely detailed morphological analysis and a final phase of disambiguation.

Systems that harness structural information resort to techniques of partial analysis to detect potentially terminological phrasal structures. There are also systems that benefit from their understanding of what is a non-term so they are at some point in between those systems already mentioned. Other systems try to reutilize current terminological databases to find terms, variants or new terms.

Systems based on linguistic knowledge tend to use *noise* and *silence* as a measure of its efficiency. Noise attempts to assess the rate between discarded candidates and accepted ones; silence attempts to assess those terms contained in an analysed text that are not detected by the system. Noise is the common problem of those systems using this approach. Errors in the assignation of morphological category are also shared by these systems.

The type of knowledge used leads to language-specific systems and therefore it requires a prior linguistic analysis and probably a redesign of many parts of the system. Knowledge in artificial intelligence has been traditionally obtained from experts in each domain. This has yielded several difficulties so that some scholars have focused on automatization and systematisation in knowledge acquisition. This strategy seems to show the benefits of a terminological approach. Thus some researchers (e.g. Condamines 1995) have proposed the construction of terminological knowledge databases so as to include linguistic knowledge in traditional databases. Although this is a recent approach, there is no database yet containing all the features that could be used in TE, i.e. there is hardly any semantic information. Thus closed lists of words containing sparse semantic information within a given specialised domain have been proposed.

In this paper we attempt to analyse the main systems of terminology extraction in order to describe its current status and thus be able to enrich them. This paper is divided up into two main parts: firstly, the largest part is devoted to describe various systems of terminology extraction together with a short evaluation in which weak and strong points have been outlined. Secondly, the terminology extraction systems have been classified according to some parameters.

2. Description of some terminology extraction systems

In the following sections we offer a critical description of number of semiautomatic terminology extraction systems. In all cases, the following information is given:

a. The reference data of the system, that is, the author and the publication where the tool is first mentioned and the system goal.
b. A brief description of the system.
c. A short evaluation of the most relevant aspects. This evaluation is mainly based on papers, oral presentations in congresses and working papers, etc.

2.1 ANA

Reference publication: Enguehard and Pantera (1994)
Main goal: Term extraction
ANA (Automatic Natural Acquisition) has been developed in accordance with the following design principles: non-utilisation of linguistic knowledge, dealing with written and oral texts (interview transcripts) and non-concern about syntactic errors.

According to the current trend of harnessing statistical techniques in the study of natural language, scholars use Mutual Information as a measure of lexical association.[4] In order to avoid the involvement of linguistic knowledge the concept of "flexible string recognition" is created, which generates a mathematical function so as to determine the degree of similarity between words. Thus, no tool for morphological analysis is needed. For instance, the string *colour of painting* represents other similar strings like: *colour of paintings, colour of this painting, colour of any painting,* etc. The system has neither a dictionary nor a grammar.

The architecture of ANA is composed of 2 modules: a familiarity module and a discovery module. The first module determines the following 3 groups of words, which constitute the only required knowledge for term detection:

a. function words (i.e. empty words): *a, any, for, in, is, of, to…*
b. scheme words (i.e. words establishing semantic relationships) such as *box of nails*, where the preposition shows some kind of relationship between *box* and *nails.*
c. bootstrap (i.e. set of terms that constitutes the kernel of the system and the starting point for term detection).

The second module consists in a gradual acquisition process of new terms from existing ones. Further, links between detected terms are automatically generated to build a semantic network. This module is based on word co-occurrence that can have 3 types of interpretations:

- *expression*: high-frequency existing terms appear frequently (T_{EXP}) in the same window. The new word is considered a new term and thus is included in the semantic network. For instance if the system has *diesel* and *engine* as known terms and finds sequences like: … *the diesel engine* is… or … *this diesel engine has*… Then the sequence *diesel engine* is accepted as a new term and is included in the semantic network as a new node with links to *diesel* and *engine* (see Figure 1 below).
- *candidate*: an existing term appears frequently (T_{CAND}) together with another word and a scheme word as in: … any *shade* of wood… or … this *shade* of colour… Here *shade* becomes a new term and is placed in a new node of the semantic network (see Figure 1 below).
- *expansion*: an existing term appears frequently (T_{EXPA}) in the same word sequence, without including any scheme word: … use any *soft* woods to… or … this *soft* woods or… As a result, *soft wood* is incorporated into the term list and the semantic network as a new node with a link to *woods* (see Figure 1 below).

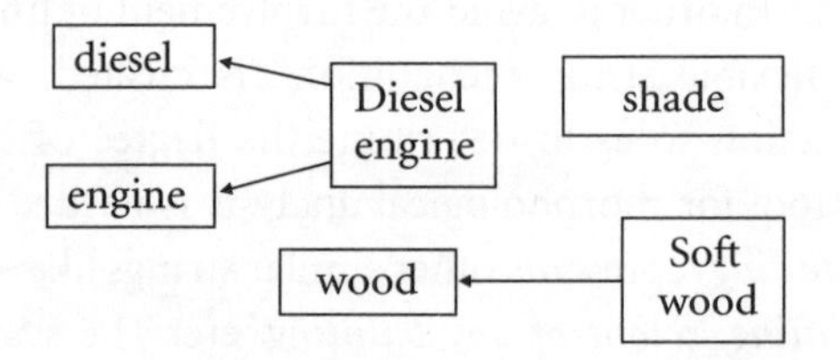

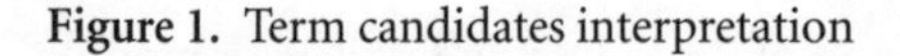
Figure 1. Term candidates interpretation

Evaluation

Minimising linguistic resources is an extremely interesting issue, since it is difficult to compile them. Likewise *flexible string recognition* may well apply to actual texts.

A negative aspect of the system is that those terminological units added to the list of valid terms after each cycle are not validated. Thus ANA allows for the inclusion of non-valid terms that add up to the term list. However, no data about the efficiency of this proposal are reported.

2.2 CLARIT[5]

Reference publication: Evans and Zhai (1996)
Main goal: Document indexing
Document indexing for IR is an important field of application of NLP techniques. This branch holds common points with term detection since the word sequences that help in document indexing are normally terminological units too.

CLARIT belongs to the group of systems that advocate an elaborated textual processing to detect complex terms in order to reach a more appropriate description of documents. This is the reason why we have included this system amongst terminology detectors.

Evans and Zhai (1996) propose the following kind of phrases for indexation purposes:

1. lexical atoms (*hot dog, stainless steel, data base, on line, …*)
2. head modifier pairs (*treated strip, …*)
3. subcompounds (*stainless steel strip, …*)
4. cross-preposition modification pairs (*quality surface* vs. *quality of surface*)

The methodology starts with the morphological analysis of words and the detection of noun phrases (NPs). The system distinguishes simplex noun phrases from cross-preposition simplex phrases.

What is behind this is the introduction of statistics to corpus linguistics. Statistics here focuses on documents, that is, there is no prior training corpus. Linguistic knowledge facilitates the calculation weeding out irrelevant structures, improves the reliability of statistical decisions and adjusts the statistical parameters.

The whole process is showed in Figure 2 below. First, the raw text is parsed so as to extract NPs. Then each NP is recursively parsed with the purpose of finding the most secure groupings. In this phase lexical atoms are also detected and NPs are structured. Finally at the generation phase the remaining compounds are obtained.

a. The words that constitute a lexical atom establish a close relationship and tend to lexicalise as if they were a single-word lexical unit.
b. When acting as NP, lexical atoms hardly allow the insertion of words.

The first condition takes place if the frequency of the target pair $W_1 W_2$ is higher than any other pair from the NP that is being processed. In the second condition the frequencies of grouped and separated occurrences are compared and

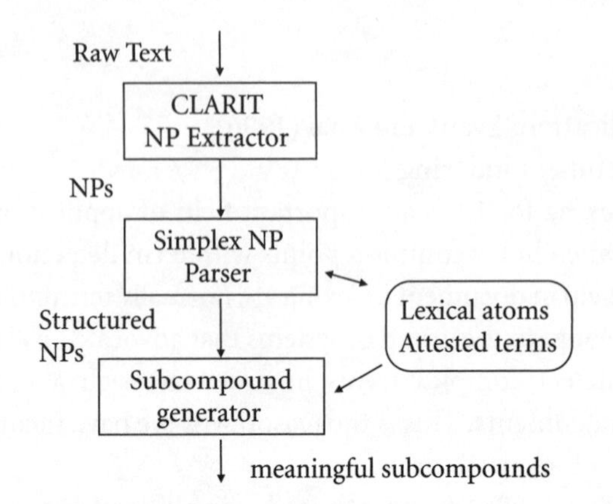

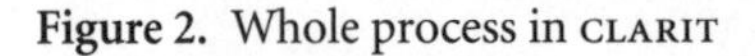

Figure 2. Whole process in CLARIT

there is a threshold beyond which the association is weeded out. This threshold is variable according to the function of sentence morphological category. In English texts, the most favoured sequence is that of noun-noun.

NP analysis is also a recursive process. At every new phase the most recent lexical atoms are used for finding new associations that will be used in the following phase. The process keeps going until the whole NP is analysed. Let us consider the example below:

general purpose high performance computer
*general purpose [**high performance**] computer*
*[**general purpose**] [high performance] computer*
*[general purpose] [[**high performance**] **computer**]*
*[[**general purpose**] [[**high performance**] **computer**]]*

The grouping order shows those sequences with a more reliable association score. In order to determine the association score a number of rules are taken into account:

- Lexical atoms are given score 0 as well as adverb combination with adjective, past participles and progressive verbs,
- Syntactically impossible pairs are given score 100 (noun-adjective, noun-adverb, adjective-adjective, etc.).
- As to the remaining pairs, there is a formula that account for the frequency of each word, the association score of this word with other words from the NP and of two random parameters.

To increase its reliability the association score is recomputed after every assignation association. The system has been tested in an actual retrieval task of document indexing substituting the default NLP module in the CLARIT system. The corpus and the queries were the standards used in the TREC conferences. There have been noticed some improvements in recall as well as in precision, which, in the author's opinion, justifies the use of these techniques. Then in the TREC-5 report a more detailed evaluation of the system is made (Zhai et al. 1996). All in all it is concluded that the use of these techniques is effective, which enforces the similarities between term indexing and terminology extraction.

Evaluation
This seems to be an interesting system and the applicability of some basic ideas to terminology detection appears to be feasible. Actually CLARIT holds similarities with the Daille's (1994) proposal (a linguistically-driven statistics).

It should be borne in mind, however, that problems of terminology extraction and document indexing are similar but no identical so that many decisions should be re-considered strictly from the point of view of term detection. It is also noteworthy that this system only extracts NP terminological units and the data provided about how this system works are related to the application for which it has been designed.

2.3 Daille-94 (ACABIT)

Reference publication: Daille (1994)
Main goal: Term extraction
The main idea behind this system is to combine linguistic knowledge with statistical measures. Here the corpus should contain all the morphological information. Then a list of candidate terms is created according to text sequences that provide syntactic patterns of term formation. This information uses statistical methods to filter out this list. This final process is different from other systems in that it only uses linguistic resources.

Assuming the fact that all terminological banks are basically composed of compound nouns, the program focuses on the detection of *binary compound nouns* and disregards other co-occurring categories. This assumption lies in the fact that there is a large number of this kind of nouns in specialised languages. Further, most of these compounds of 3 or more constituents can be treated in a binary form.

Those patterns considered relevant for French are N_1 Prep (Det) N_2 and N Adj Prep *à* (Det) N_2, together with right and left coordination. Statistical algorithms are applied to these patterns. The author is aware of the fact that the application of statistical measures leads to some noise rate, that is, low-frequency terms will not be recognised.

The technique used for pattern recognition is that of finite state automata. Automata are represented by a subset of grammatical tags to which some lemmas, inflected forms and a punctuation mark are added. Thus we can regard automata as linguistic filters that select defined patterns and also determine their occurrence frequency, distance and variation. Each morphosyntactic pattern is associated with a specific finite automaton.

The corpus is given a statistical treatment based on a large number of statistical measures, which are grouped in the following classes: frequency measures, association criteria, diversity criteria and distance measures. The starting point is considering the two lemmas that constitute a pair within a pattern as two variables on which the dependence degree is measured. Data are represented in a standard contingency table:

	L_2	L_n
L_1	A	b
L_m	C	d

where

a = L_1L_2 occurrences
b = L_1+L_n ($n \neq 2$) occurrences
c = L_m+L_2 ($m \neq 1$) occurrences
d = L_m+L_n ($m \neq 1$ and $n \neq 2$)

Eighteen measures are applied with the aim of establishing the degree of independence of the variables in the contingency table. The analysis of the results shows that only four of these measures are relevant to the purpose: frequency, cubed association criterion[6] (IM^3), likelihood criterion, Fager/MacGowan criterion.

Evaluation

Unlike in other systems, in ACABIT frequency has turned out to be one of the most important measures for term detection from a given area. However, the classification resulting from the application of this frequency shows an important number of frequent sequences that are not terms and, in contrast, does not suggest the low-frequency terms.

Daille (1994) believes that the best measure is the likelihood criterion, since it is a real statistical test, it proposes a classification that accounts for frequency, it behaves adequately with large and medium size corpora and it is not defined in those cases that are not to be considered. In any case, this measure yields some noise due to several reasons:

a. Errors in the morphological mark-up.
b. Some combinations that are never of a compounding nature: *ko bits* (kilobits), *à titre d'exemple* (as an example)… …
c. Combinations of 3 or more elements, related to the problems of composition and modification: *bande latérale -unique-* (-single- side band), *service fixe -par satellite-* (-satellite- fixed service), etc.

2.4 FASTR[7]

Reference publication: Jacquemin (1996)
Main goal: Term variation detection
The aim of this tool is to detect terms variants from a set of previously known terms. These terms may be available from a reference database or a term acquisition software. What is crucial in this system is that it is not needed to start from scratch every time. Optionally Fastr can also be used for TE.

The first step for applying Fastr is to obtain and analyse a set of existing terms and thus having a set of rules of a given grammar. The FASTR grammatical formalism is an extension of that of PATR-II (Shieber 1986). A partial parser based on the unification mechanism is responsible for the application of these rules. Term variants are obtained through a metarule mechanism that is dynamically calculated.

For instance, the term *serum albumin* corresponds to the Noun-Noun sequence and is associated with the following rule:

rule 1: $N_1 \rightarrow N_2\ N_3$
$\langle N_1$ lexicalization$\rangle$ = 'N_2'
$\langle N_2$ lemma$\rangle$ = serum
$\langle N_3$ lemma$\rangle$ = albumin.

The value indicated by the feature "lexicalization" will be used just before partial parsing to selectively activate the target rules. Thus the above rule is linked to the word *serum* and so is activated when this word occurs in the sentence that is being parsed.

At a different level several metarules generate new rules in order to describe all possible variations of each term from the reference list. Each metarule presents a particular structure and a specific pattern type. For instance, the following metarule can be applied to the previous rule:

$$\text{Metarule Coor}(X_1 \rightarrow X_2\, X_3) = X_1 \rightarrow X_2\, C_4\, X_5\, X_3$$

which leads to the new rule: $N_1 \rightarrow N_2\, C_4\, X_5\, N_3$
This latter rule allows new constructions that substitute C_4 for a conjunction and X_5 for an isolated word such as *serum and egg albumin.* The candidate term is not the whole new construction but the *coordinated* term (i.e., *egg albumin*). The words that have given way to the new rule (*egg* and *albumin*) maintain their function of constricted equations of the original rule. Further, they are the anchoring point for the application of the metarule. A metarule can be associated with specific restrictions, as for instance: $(\langle C_4\ lemma\rangle \neq but)$ or $(\langle X_5\ cat\rangle \neq Dd)$. In this way, those sequences with no lexical relationship such as *serum and the albumin* are rejected.

The above rule is a coordination rule and it should be noted that there are also other types of rules that account for different kinds of variations:

1. insertion rules: *medullary carcinoma* → *medullary thyroid carcinoma*
2. permutation rules: *control center* → *center for disease control*

The FASTR metagrammar for English contains 73 metarules altogether: 25 coordination rules, 17 insertion rules and 31 permutation rules. In any case, for efficiency reasons the new rules are dynamically generated. Each rule is linked to a pattern extractor that permits a very quick acquisition of information. As has been pointed out, the FASTR grammatical formalism is a PATR-II extension (Shieber 1986). This language allows to write grammars using feature structures. The rules describing terms are composed of a free-context part ($N_1 \rightarrow N_2\, N_3$) and a number of restriction equations (e.g. $\langle N_2$ lemma$\rangle$ = *serum*). First, the system filters the rules that are to be applied according to the given text and then an analysis take place.

When Fastr is applied for term acquisition the process is gradual: from a given set of terms the system detects new ones, which allows the beginning of a new cycle and the detection of new candidates. The loop goes on until new terms cannot be detected. The author presents an experiment carried out on a medicine corpus of 1,5 million words and a reference list of 70,000 terms from different specialised domains. After 15 cycles 17,000 terms were detected of which 5,000 were new. The text was processed at a 2,562 word/minute speed.

However, the number of recognised terms decreases when the reference list has fewer items. For instance, if the reference sublist of medicine drops to 6,000 terms, then only 3,800 new terms are recognized.

The author also postulates the existence of a conceptual relation. between the new terms and the term that has led to their recognition. This relationship is variable in accordance with the type of rule that is applied i.e., insertion or coordination rule. Permutation does not allow any relationship due to the phrasal nature of the relationship.

All the language dependent data used by Fastr is stored in separated text files. This feature facilitates the use of the system in other languages as showed by the recent application of Fastr to Japanese, German and Spanish/Catalan.

Recently Jacquemin has developed the detection of semantic variation using resources like WordNet or the Microsoft Word97 thesaurus (Jacquemin 1999).

Evaluation

The main characteristic of FASTR is its ability for detecting term variants, an aspect often not considered by other systems. The fact of using already recognised and accepted terms is very useful, although, as the author admits, it places restrictions on the acquisition of new terms that are not related to the source terms.

TE in Fastr implies that terms that are added to the list of valid terms after each cycle are not validated. Thus, a non-valid term may be added to the list so it is likely that in forecoming cycles more non-valid terms are added. Jacquemin (1996) believes that this is not an important error source because the system, in some way, corrects itself since "normally" non-correct candidates do not give way to new potential candidate terms.

Actually this technique should not be isolately applied. Rather, it should be coordinated with other strategies as in (Jacquin and Liscouet 1996) and (Daille 1998).

2.5 HEID

Reference publication: Heid et *al.* (1996)
Main goal: Term extraction
Heid et al. (1996) believe that automatic TE has various applications and dictionary or glossary construction would be the major one. In dictionary construction from computerized corpora two phases are distinguished: linguistic pre-analysis and a term identification tool. Each of these phases requires specific computer tools.

In the linguistic pre-processing phase the following processes are required:[8]

a. tokenizing, which identifies word and sentence boundaries.
b. morphosyntactic analysis, which identifies grammatical categories as well as distributional and morphosyntactic features.

c. POS tagging, which disambiguate morphosyntactic hypotheses.
d. lemmatization, which identifies the lemma candidates.

For term identification the system has a general corpus retrieval interface that includes a corpus query processor (CQP), a macroprocessor for the CQP query language and a key word in context (KWIC) program, to extract and sort concordances and lists of absolute and relative frequency of search items.

TE is linked to a complex query language. The queries will be different according to the types of candidate terms searched for. Thus, for instance, queries about single-word terms are made from morphemes or typical components of compound or derived words (derivatives). In these queries it is assumed that NP affixed terms from specialised languages use more specific affixes and/or prefixes than others. All the word sequence extracted (N-A, N-N, N-V), are based on POS patterns.

Heid et al. (1996) have applied these tools to technical texts on automobile engineering in German, which amounts to 35,000 words. The sample has been manually analysed before the application of the above procedures. The results are as follows:

- With regard to single-word terms, there has been found a 90% of candidate terms and a 10% of silence. This rate varies from one scheme to another.
- With regard to multiword terms, there are no concluding results. The results are less satisfactory and that the same problems as linguistic based are found: POS patterns do not constrain enough the context and produce too much noise. Heid et al. (1996) believe that by using a syntactic parser, as it is the case in English, noise would diminish.
- Finally, collocation extraction is shown to produce noise but not silence, since Heid et al. (1996) consider the frequency criterion.

The Ahmad's statistical measure (Ahmad et al., 1992) of relative frequency in corpora of specialised and general language is applied to this corpus of 35,000 words. They show that the results produced by linguistic corpus query are included in the output of statistical methods. However noise in statistical methods is higher than in linguistic methods.

Evaluation

To tackle this system it should be taken into account the morphosyntactic features of the German language. Unlike Romance languages, German prefers to form compounds in a synthesising manner. It means that what other languages express via terminological phrases in German is expressed with a single-word term (by word is meant any segment found between two blanks). Thus it can be seen that in German, automatic term detection does not depend much on term delimitation but on the terminological nature of a word. This is the reason why we need parameters to distinguish a term from a word of the general language, both having the same morphosyntactic structure.

Like most of the reviewed programs, Heid focuses on NP terms although it can also extract collocations combining nouns and verbs. In this case Heid et al. (1996) note that the results are much worse. We do not have specific data about the performance and the results of this system.

2.6 LEXTER

Reference publication: Bourigault (1994)
Main goal: Term extraction
This system has been developed in the need of the EDF (*Electricité de France*) society for improving their indexation system. LEXTER aims at locating boundaries among which potentially terminological NPs could be isolated. LEXTER carries a superficial analysis and makes use of the text heuristics in order to obtain those NPs of maximum length that it regards as candidate terms. The program is composed of several modules and works as follows:

1. Morphological analysis and disambiguation module. Texts receive information about the POS and the lemma assigned to every word.

2. Delimitation module. At this stage a local syntactic analysis is carried so as to split the text into maximal-length NPs. For example: *alimentation en eau* (water supply), *pompe d'extraction* (extraction pump), *alimentation electrique de la pompe de refoulement* (electric supply of the forcing back supply). Here the system takes advantage of the negative knowledge about the parts of complex terms. Thus those patterns of a potential term -finite verbs, pronouns and conjunctions- that will never become part of a term are identified and considered as boundaries. Some of these patterns are simple whereas others are complex (sequences of preposition + determiner).

A French example of the latter would be *SUR* (prep) + *LE* (definite article): the most common analysis is to propose that this sequence establishes a boundary between NPs as in: *on raccorde le câble d'alimentation du banc sur le coffret de décharge batterie.* However there is a rate (10%) in which this sequence is part of the term: *action sur le bouton poussoir de réarmement* or *action sur le systeme d'alimentation de secours.*

To solve this and other similar situations, the system uses an endogenous learning strategy of the patterns sub-categorisation. This strategy consists in looking at the corpus to find those sequences of *(noun)* + *sur* + *le* having different contexts on the right hand side. Then non-productive nouns are weeded out. Then sequences such as *sur* + *le* are considered sentence boundaries, except for those cases wherein sequences are preceded by the productive noun located in the learning phase. To see how this system works let us suppose that at a first analysis the sequences below are found.

Le protection ***contre*** *le gel est assurée par*
Protection ***contre*** *les grands froids*
il s'agit de maintenir la teneur en oxygène de cette eau
dans *les limites fixées*
on procède à l'injection d'eau ***dans*** *les générateurs de*
on procède à l'injection d'eau ***dans*** *vapeur*
le système permet l'aiguillage des automates ***sur*** *le prélèvement effectué*

Then productive sequences are not regarded as term boundaries whereas non-productive sequences are viewed as external boundaries of the candidate term. In the example above *protection contre* and *eau dans* do not become boundaries whereas *automates sur* does.

This strategy permits to detect a considerable amount of complex nouns which otherwise would have been lost. Unfortunately it also allows a great deal of undesirable material (between 10% and 50%).

3. Splitting module. NPs are analysed and their constituents are divided into head and expansion. For example the term candidate *pompe d'extraction* (extraction pump) is splitted into: *pompe* — head — (pump) + *extraction* — expansion — (extraction).

At this point the system may find ambiguous situations such as "Noun Adj_1 Adj_2" and "$Noun_1$ Prep $Noun_2$ Adj" whose analysis is uncertain. To solve these cases an endogenous learning process is followed which is similar to that presented in the delimitation module.

4. Structuring module. The list of term candidates is organised in a terminological network. This network can be produced only by looking at a list of candidate terms and recognising the different parts of each candidate term, like in the following example:

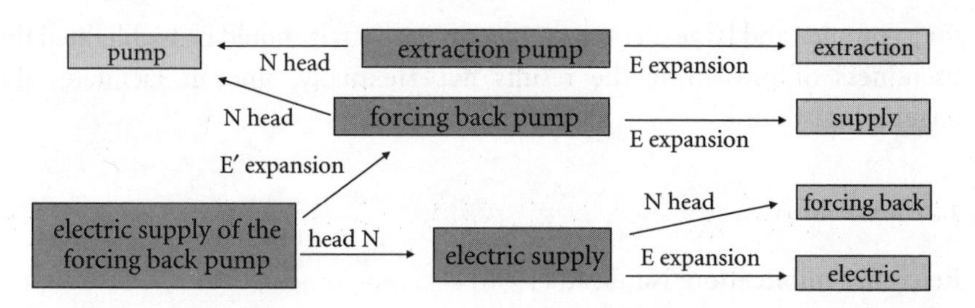

Additionally Lexter calculate some productivity figures based on links type occurrences. These coefficients do not become filters, but are passed on to the terminologist as a piece of data so as to facilitate the evaluation of candidate terms.

5. Navigation module. A consulting interface is built (called *terminological hypertext*) from the source corpus, the candidate term network and the above-mentioned coefficients and lists.

Although LEXTER is exclusively based on linguistic techniques it produces highly satisfying results and is currently used to exploit different corpora from EDF and different research projects. Besides it has been proved helpful in: text indexation, hypertextual consulting of technical documentation, knowledge acquisition and construction of terminological databases.

LEXTER is also used as a terminology extractor in the terminological knowledge base designed by the Terminologie et Intelligence Artificielle (Terminology & Artificial Intelligence) terminology group. SYCLADE (Habert 1996), a tool for word classification also makes use of LEXTER.

Evaluation

LEXTER was born in an industrial environment and from the very beginning it sought a robust, accurate and domain-independent tools. These objectives were basically attained although mark-up and disambiguation errors weaken the capacity of the system. Some scholars note that this system (like those which make use of symbolic techniques) produce a considerable amount of noise. Thus of a corpus of 200,000 words there are obtained 20,000 candidate terms which, after the validation stage, amount to 10,000. Also, Bourigault stresses the silence problem, which he estimated around 5% of the total valid terms. Like the vast majority of systems, LEXTER only focuses on NPs since verbs are believed to be term boundary and so they are never part of candidate terms.

One of the most remarkable achievements of this system is the endogenous learning mechanism that allow to work autonomously and so there is no need for a complex and large dictionary. In a similar vein it should be highlighted the usefulness of presenting the results hypertextually, since it facilitates the terminologist's task.

2.7 NAULLEAU

Reference publication: Naulleau (1998)
Main goal: Noun phrase filtering system
The model designed by Naulleau is a NP extraction system that proposes as term candidates those sequences that comply with certain user tailored profile. The whole process can be divided in two main stages: profile acquisition and profile application.

To define its own profile the user chooses the set of phrases that s/he considers relevant for his task and discards the ones that s/he does not consider useful at that time. The data collected in such way is generalised according to their morphological, syntactical and semantic characteristics dynamically creating a set of positive and negative filters. A simple example of positive and negative filters is the following:

1. positive filter: *metallic/automatic/nuclear/industrial taps*
2. negative filter: *important/recent/necessary/unreliable taps*

Then, those filters produced in the learning stage are applied to new sequences analysed. As a result, some noun arguments and/or PPs can be eliminated. Thus a NP can be divided or reduced and the resulting sequences are passed on to an expert to be evaluated.

In doing so the author acknowledges the sociolinguistic nature of the term. It implies that there is no linguistic model that can tell whether a NP is a term or not beyond the scope of a field or even the application. Also, this procedure introduces the idea of how relevant a phrase is in relation to the interest profile of the user and assumes that such relevance may be evaluated on linguistic grounds.

This is a fully symbolic approach that uses the AlethIP engine that produces sentences fully lemmatised, tagged and syntactically parsed. Then nouns and adjectives are semantically tagged according to both suffix information and semantic data from AlethIP and using a set of contextual rules for the more frequent and ambiguous words. The whole strategy is based on the evaluation of the relevance of simple syntactic dependencies. Such relevance is only based on the data provided by the user.

According to the author, the results are encouraging. However it is difficult to evaluate due to the practical problem posed by such a detailed evaluation. Some additional experiments are described in (Nalleau 1999).

Evaluation

This system may be considered the first one to use semantic data as a specific resource for proposing term candidates. Also, as far as we know, is the first time that the *user* and the *idea of relevance to an application* are taken into account since the very beginning in the design of a TE systems.

In this way the user may adapt the system to its specific needs but also its intervention may crucially affect the performance of the system. The loss of specific data makes difficult to evaluate the tool behaviour in an actual context.

2.8 NEURAL

Reference publication: Frantzi and Ananiadou (1995)
Main goal: Term extraction
Neural is a system for TE of a hybrid nature, that is it uses both linguistic (morphosyntactic patterns and a list of suffixes specific to the domain) and statistically knowledge (frequency and mutual information). Frantzi and Ananiadou (1995) pays special attention to two different problems: detection of nested terms and detection of low frequency terms using statistical methods. The test bench is a corpus of 55,000 words in the domain of medicine (ophthalmology). The structures analysed are Noun-Noun and Adjective-Noun that are identified using a standard tagger. The list of suffixes includes those frequently found in terminological units in the field of ophthalmology like *-oid*, *-oma*, *-ium*. The system is implemented using a Back-Propagation (BP) two layers neural network. The threshold has been set to .5 but this may vary. The BP neural network has been trained with a set of 300 compounds and the tests were made with another set of 300 words. It obtained a success rate of 70%.

The author and other scholars from the Manchester Metropolitan University have been active since 1995 developing specific statistical figures for TE. In this way it is necessary to mention those tasks related to the adding of context information (Frantzi 1997; Maynard and Ananiadou 1999). Usually the context is discarded or, alternatively, considered as a bag of words although its relevance is signalled by many scholars. Here the basic assumption is that terms tend to appear grouped in real text, so the termhood figure of a candidate would increase if there are other terms (or candidates highly ranked) in the context.

Both Frantzi 1997 and Maynard and Ananiadou 1999 propose a similarity figure based on the distance between the candidate and the context words (nouns, adjectives and verbs). This figure is calculated by Frantzi (1997) using statistical and syntactic information while Maynard and Ananiadou (1999) include also semantic information from a specialised thesaurus (UMLS semantic Network).

In Maynard and Ananiadou (1999) this similarity figure may also be used to take into account some kind of semantic disambiguation for the sense that gets a better value. A context factor (CF) is added to the figure already used to rank the candidates (Cvalue) and thus reordering the set of candidates as follows: SNCvalue(a)=0.8*Cvalue(a) + 0.2*CF(a). The authors report improvements in the ranking of term candidates from his eye pathology corpus.

Evaluation
The original system can be seen as a standard hybrid system. The linguistic knowledge includes Greek and Latin affixes and morphosyntactic patterns. The incorporation of this kind of suffixes should be highly productive. However the chosen patterns may well apply to English but not to Romance Languages.

The incorporation of the context as part of the data available for evaluating the termhood of a candidate is a very interesting contribution to the behaviour of terms in real texts. It should also serve to increase the relevance of low frequency candidates but no specific figure is given.

It is necessary to mention the use of semantic information as a kind of resource that is increasingly used in the TE field.

2.9 NODALIDA-95

Reference publication: Arppe (1995)
Main goal: Term extraction
NODALIDA, a product designed by the Lingsoft firm, is based on an enhanced version of NPtool that is a program developed at the Department of General Linguistics at the Helsinki University (Finland). NPtool (Voutilanen 1993) generates lists of NPs occurring in the sentences of a text and provides an assessment about whether these phrases are candidates terms or not (ok/?). From these lists all the acceptable sub-chains are obtained. Besides, the source list is multiplied. Let us see an actual example, for the sentence: "*exact form of the correct theory of quantum gravity*" NPtool proposes the following additional NPs:

form of the correct theory of quantum gravity form correct theory
exact form of the correct theory exact form gravity
form of the correct theory theory quantum gravity

Simultaneously there are a number of premises that become the first filter like in the following: "Those NPs preceded by a determiner, adjective or prefixed sentence (*kind of, some, one, …*) are weeded out."

As for the remaining NPs, their occurrence frequency is calculated. Further, they are ordered and grouped according to their grammatical head and are presented to the terminologist together with their context. The NPtool module (Voutilanen 1993) is at the heart of the system. It is a NP detector largely based on the *constraint grammar* formalism (Karlsson 1990). Its main features are: (1) Morphological/syntactical descriptions are based on a large set of hand-coded linguistic rules, (2) both the grammar and the lexicon allow a corpus analysis with non-controlled text and (3) disambiguation is made according to only linguistic criteria. As a result, between 3% and 6% of the words remain ambiguous.

The text goes through a previous process so as to determine sentence boundaries, idiomatic expressions, compound forms, typographical signs, etc. Then it is morphologically analysed and a result like this is obtained:[9]

```
("⟨*the⟩"         ("the" Det CENTRAL ART SG/PL (@>N)))
("⟨inlet⟩"        ("inlet" N NOM SG))
("⟨and⟩"          ("and" CC (@CC)))
("⟨exhaust⟩"      ("exhaust" ⟨SVO⟩ V SUBJUNCTIVE VFIN (@V))
                  ("exhaust" ⟨SVO⟩ V IMP VFIN (@V))
                  ("exhaust" ⟨SVO⟩ V INF)
                  ("exhaust" ⟨SVO⟩ V PRES -SG3 VFIN (@V))
                  ("exhaust" N NOM SG))
("⟨manifold⟩"     ("manifold" N NOM PL))
```

At this moment disambiguation takes place. For example in the sentence: "*The inlet and exhaust manifolds are mounted on opposite sides of the cylinder head*" two analyses are obtained:

(1) on/@AH opposite/@N sides/@NH of/@N⟨ the/@⟩N cylinder/@NH **head/@V**

(2) on/@AH opposite/@N sides/@NH of/@N⟨ the/@⟩N cylinder/@>N **head/@NH**

What distinguishes these two analyses is the consideration of whether the final sequence (*cylinder head*) is a NP or not. The ongoing process gives only two possible analyses for each sentence. First, those NPs of a maximal length are preferred (*NP-friendly*) and, second, those NPs of a minimal length are preferred (*NP-hostile*). Then the system compares both strategies and labels each NP as ok/? by considering whether the analysis is shared or not by both strategies. Thus the last sentence gets this analysis below:

(3) ok: *inlet and exhaust manifolds* ?: *opposite sides of the cylinder*
ok: *exhaust manifolds* ?: *opposite sides of the cylinder head*

In order to validate this additional information the terminologist is provided with a list of candidate terms. The results reported by the NPtool module are pretty good (precision=95–98% and recall=98.5–100%) with a text of about 20 Kwords.

Evaluation
NODALIDA is based on the use of linguistic knowledge through a structural approach (i.e., detection of phrasal structures and structural disambiguation). Arppe (1995) presents high-quality results. However, the corpus should be enlarged, since so far tests have been made on quite small corpora. It is not clear how precision and recall figures are calculated, particularly how to determine which terms are deemed to be correct (i.e., those which have the ok signal or all of them). Also it should be stressed that NODALIDA has not been tested using the NPtool enhanced version in an actual situation of terminology problems.

Taking into account that the disambiguator is one of the main error sources in this kind of systems, Arppe (1995) believes that a high-degree quality is achieved despite the fact that there are no data about terminology extraction in real situations. Besides, to achieve this quality NODALIDA proposes a great deal of rules, which yields management and control overhead.

The list that is passed on to the terminologist to be validated comprises those candidates signalled with **ok** and ?. The way in which potential NPs are obtained by the system leads us to suspect that there are many candidate terms in the validation list that the terminologist has to analyse.

2.10 TERMIGHT

Reference publication: Dagan and Church (1994)
Main goal: Translation aid
Termight is currently used by *A&T Business Translation Systems.* It was created

to be a tool for automating some stages of the professional translator terminological research.

To do so it starts with a tagged and disambiguated text as well as a list of predetermined syntactic patterns that could be adjusted to every document. Thus, a list of candidate terms is obtained comprising one or more words. Single-word candidates are defined as all those words that are not included in a previously determined list of empty words (i.e. stop list). Multiword terms are referred to one of the predetermined syntactic patterns via regular expressions. Dagan and Church (1994) considered only noun sequences patterns.
Candidate terms are grouped and classified according to their lemma (i.e. the right hand side noun) and frequency. Those candidates sharing the same lemma are classified alphabetically in accordance with the inverse order of their compounding words. Thus it is showed the order of changes of the English simple NPs.

For each candidate term the corresponding concordances are obtained, which are alphabetically classified according to their context. This information enables the terminologist to evaluate whether each candidate is appropriate or not.

Dagan and Church (1994) note that the rate of term list construction is of 150 and 200 terms per hour, which is twice faster than the average. As for the extraction quality, they state that, unlike exclusively statistical methods, Termight permits to extract low-frequency terms.

Moreover this system has a bilingual module which, via statistical methods, obtains a word-level alignment from texts. Thus terms found in language A are referred to their counterparts in language B. This well-ordered list of candidate terms is again passed on to the terminologist to be evaluated.

The Termight bilingual module does not seem to be developed and tested as the basic one. Tests have been made on 192 terms from a technical manual in English and German. The correct translation is found in the first suggested solution in 40% of the cases, whereas only 7% corresponds to the correct translation suggested in the second place. As for the remaining, the correct translation was in other places of the proposal list.

Evaluation

Termight is a remarkable system in that there is an accurate classification and presentation of candidate terms and it does not attempt to become an automatic system. Rather, it helps the translator.

However, it presents a number of shortcomings: (1) The only syntactic pattern considered is very simple: noun sequences. This pattern may well be valid for English but not for Romance languages and (2) no numerical information about the recognition quality is given. The type of pattern considered may suppose high precision but low recall

2.11 TERMINO

Reference publication: Plante and Dumas (1989)
Main goal: Facilitation of the term extraction terminographer's task.
The TERMINO program is composed of several tools to facilitate TE in French. It is a help for the terminologist insofar as the identification of those discourse units that denominate notions or objects. Besides it provides every unit with the immediate context from which data relevant to the notions denominated by theses units can be obtained. There are a number of TERMINO versions which improve in some ways previous ones.

This tool is based mainly on linguistic knowledge and it comprises 3 subsystems: a pre-editor, which separates texts into words and sentences and identifies proper nouns, a morphosyntactic parser and a record-drafting facility. The text does not get any special treatment: it is only required to be codified in ASCII form.

With regard to term delimitation and extraction the more interesting subsystem is the morphosyntactic parser. It consists of 3 modules: a morphological parser; a syntactic parser and a synapsy detector.

The morphological parser has two functions: (a) automatic categorisation; (b) lemma and tag identification. According to Plante and Dumas, 30% of words in French can be attributed to more than one category. This has led to the tagging of all the possible categories for each word. As a result, there is an overproduction of words with different tags. Categorisation and lemmatisation are obtained from the application of the LCML program, it is not a dictionary but a morphological parser of lexical forms so it can correctly lemmatise and tag new lexical forms.

The syntactic parser is responsible for weeding out the vast majority of ambiguities generated in previous stages. It is managed through the construction of a syntactic structure for each sentence.

Finally, the synapsy detector (MRSF) selects, among the syntactic units from the parser, those lexical noun units that are likely to be terms. S. David (David and Plante 1991) created MRSF especially for TERMINO. MRSF is based on principles of noun group construction. David's understanding of synapsy is that of a polylexical unit of a syntactic nature that is the head of the NP.

Thus, synapsies are only NPs groups: some of them will become terms and some of them will not. Further, some of them will only be "topics" that will enable the terminologist to know different concepts or grasp an overview of the text topics. The MRSF module comprises 5 sub-modules: (1) head hunter module; (2) expansion recogniser module; (3) categorisation module; (4) synapsy generator module and (5) representation and evaluation module.

TERMINO has a set of software tools, which is much larger and comprises different modules that allow to manipulate terminological data. These tools help the terminologist decide whether a synapsy is a term or not, elaborate terminological filing forms and create terminological databases.

TERMINO recognises between 70% and 74% of the complex terms. The fact that 30% of terms are not recognised by TERMINO can be explained by coordination (it is a signal of segment breaking), acronyms and common nouns in capital letters. Moreover, there is 28% of noise, of which 47% is due to a wrong mark-up and a 53% is due to synapsies belonging to general language.

Evaluation
TERMINO is one of the first candidate term extractors that worked and it is a linguistically-based extractor, composed of different independent modules. This system is based on the concept of *synapsy*. The synapsy detector is based on the establishment of a number of heuristic rules that may well be increased provided the corpus is delimited.

There is a need to improve this system taking into account that it is still too noisy (28%), which could be improved, for example, with a different treatment of capital letters and acronyms.

2.12 TERMS

Reference publication: Justeson and Katz (1995)
Main goal: Term extraction
Justeson and Katz (1995) hold the following views about terms:

a. Terminological noun phrases (TNP) are different from non-terminological noun phrases (nTNP) in that the modifiers of the first ones are much shorter than those of the second ones.
b. An entity introduced by a nTNP can be later referred to only by the head of the NP and often by other NP (synonyms, hyponyms, hyperonyms). By contrast, an entity introduced by a TNP is normally repeated identically in a

given document, as a single omission of a modifier could yield a change of the referred entity.
c. In technical texts lexical NPs are almost exclusively terminological.
d. Multiword technical terms are nearly always composed of nouns and adjectives (97%) and some prepositions (3%) between two NPs.
e. The average length of a TNP is of 1.91 words.

The proposed filter finds strings with a frequency equal or higher than two. These strings follow with this regular expression: ((A|N)+ | ((A|N)*(N P)?)(A|N)*N. Those candidate terms of a length of 2 (2 patterns: AN and NA) and 3 (5 patterns: AAN, ANN, NAN, NNN and NPN) are by far the most commonly encountered.

The purpose of this filter is to combine good coverage of the usual terminology from technical texts with high quality in the extraction phase. The filter prefers quality to coverage, since if it only made use of the grammatical constraints then the system would propose many irrelevant NPs. The vast majority of relevant NPs overcome the frequency constraint.

Selection of grammatical patterns also affects quality. If prepositions are admitted within the pattern many candidates are introduced, although few will be valid. As a result, quality decreases whereas quantity increases and, accordingly, Justeson and Katz (1995) prefer not to take prepositions into consideration.

The implementation of grammatical patterns also affects the quality/coverage trade-off. There are two ways in which a given linguistic unit is attributed to a grammatical category: disambiguation and filtering. The first one is rejected because disambiguators are not totally reliable yet.

Filtering consist in parsing and lemmatising each word of the text. Then those sequences following the pattern are considered. If a word is not identified as a noun, adjective or preposition, it is discarded. Thus each word maintains its nominal, adjectival and prepositional values and in this order. The chain is weeded out if more than one word can be identified as a preposition or if it does not follow the pattern (e.g. if the pattern ends with a noun and there is more than one preposition then the word following the preposition is not a noun).

Filtering has a coverage at least as good as what can be attained by a standard tagger. However, quality is not that good (e.g. *fixed* is only identified as an adjective — *bug fixed* — but it can also become a verb: *fixed disk drive*). In contrast, filtering is much faster than tagging.

In any case, Justeson and Katz (1995) suggest to control the patterns, the list of grammatical words and the frequency to adjust the performance of the system to each type of text.

This system has been applied to different domains (metallurgy, spatial engineering and nuclear energy) and it is used at IBM Translation Center. The TERMS results are presented on the basis of 3 technical texts (statistical classification of patterns, lexical semantics and chromatography). Coverage has only been estimated for one of the text and it is of 71%. Quality has been estimated between 77% and 96% of the instances.

Evaluation

Although Justeson and Katz (1995) present a detailed study on the performance of terminological units (wherein there are some overstatements), the proposed filter does not seem to take advantage of these previous analyses of terms. Further, it should be noted that this type of filtering based on quite simple patterns would not be so efficient if they were applied to languages other than English such as Romance languages. Also, this kind of patterns produces a lot of noise.

3. Contrastive analysis

Here we will contrast the systems' main features, according to six relevant aspects when designing a new detection system of terminological units: linguistic resources, strategies of term delimitation, strategies of term filtering, classification of recognised terms and obtained results. For some of these criteria we have created a table containing the most significant data so as to make the system comparison easier.

3.1 Linguistic resources

It has been observed that the vast majority of the reviewed systems make use of some sort of linguistic information, at least a list of empty words taken as boundaries. The standard process includes a morphological analysis followed by some kind of disambiguation system. The systems altering this procedure are the following:

a. ANA: does not use any linguistic resource, just a list of auxiliary words
b. TERMS: use its own disambiguation system: POS filtering
c. Naulleau: introduces semantic information

Additionally, for the systems that use an incremental strategy, like ANA and Fastr, it is necessary a set of initial terms to bootstrap the process.

3.2 Strategies of term delimitation

All systems of terminology extraction have to determine at some point the beginning and the end of the candidate term, that is, delimit the potential terminological unit. The reviewed programs have different strategies to delimit terms: word-boundary elements, structural patterns, syntactic parser, text distribution, typographical elements, term lists, structure disambiguation. Below we show a summary of the different options adopted by each system:

Table 1. Strategies of term telimitation

System	Term delimitation				Structure disambuguation	
Name/author	Boundaries	Patterns	Parser	Other	Learning	Other
1 ANA				x		–
2 CLARIT			x			statistical
3 Daille		x				–
4 FASTR		x	x	x		–
5 Heid		x				–
6 LEXTER	x				x	
7 Naulleau		x		x		–
8 NEURAL						–
9 NODALIDA-95		x	x	x		–
10 Termight						–
11 TERMINO		x				–
12 TERMS						–

3.3 Strategies of term filtering

Term filtering is a key stage of any term detection system. This means that the list of candidates is reduced as much as possible. Table 2 shows the strategies found in all the reviewed systems.

3.4 Classification of recognised terms

Some of the analysed systems classify recognised terms by grouping them

Table 2. Strategies of term filtering

System		Term filtering					
	Name/Author	Freq.[10]	Linguistic	Statistical + Linguistic	Linguistic + Statistical	Reference terms	User defined
1	ANA					x	
2	CLARIT			x	x		
3	Daille				x		
4	FASTR					x	
5	Heid		x				
6	LEXTER		x				
7	Naulleau						x
8	NEURAL				x		
9	NODALIDA-95		x				
10	Termight	x	x				
11	TERMINO		x				
12	TERMS	x	x				

according to some criteria. Thus, the related terms stay close to each other. Even FASTR attempts to infer an ontology from the recognised terms. Those systems which show some classification of recognised terms are the following:

a. ANA: it builds a semantic network from the detected terms.
b. FASTR: it builds a graph to relate recognised terms. Also it proposes the construction of partial ontologies for some terms.
c. LEXTER: it builds a terminological network splitting terms into head and expansion.

3.5 Results

Table 3 summarises for each system the type of corpus used for the tests and the results attained.

4. Conclusions

We can reach some conclusions after having analysed and evaluated some of the main systems of TE designed in the last decade:

Table 3. Results

System		Test corpora			Terms%	
	Name /Author	Domain	Language	Size.[Kw.]	precision	recall
1	ANA	Aviation engineering	French	120		?
		Acoustics	English	25	?	?
2	CLARIT[11]	News	English	240 Mb	–	81.6
3	Daille	Telecommunications	French	800	?	?
4	FASTR	Medicine (abstracts)	French	1.560	86.7	74.9
5	Heid	Engineering	German	35	?	?
6	LEXTER	Engineering	French	3.250	95	?
7	Naulleau	Technical	French	?	?	?
8	NEURAL	Medicine	English	55	?	70
9	NODALIDA-95	Cosmology Technical text	English	20	95–98	98.5–100
10	Termight	Computer science	English	?	?	?
11	TERMINO	Medicine	French	?	72	70–74
12	TERMS	Statistics	English	2.3	77	
		Semantics		6.3	86	
		Chromatography		14.9	96	

a. The efficiency of the extraction presents a high degree of variation from one to another. Broadly speaking, there is neither clear nor measurable explanation of the final results. Besides, we have to bear in mind that these systems are tested with small and highly specialised corpora. This lack of data makes it difficult to evaluate and compare them. However, it does not prevent pinpointing those solutions, which are considered valid to solve specific problems.

b. None of the systems is entirely satisfactory due to two main reasons. First, all systems produce too much silence, especially statistically-based systems. Second, all of them generate a great deal of noise, especially linguistically-based systems.

c. Taking into account the noise generated, all systems propose large lists of candidate terms, which at the end of the process have to be manually accepted or rejected.

d. Most of the TE systems are related to only one language: French or English. Usually the language specific data is embedded in the tool. This makes difficult to use the system in a language other than the original.

e. As has been already pointed out, training corpora tend to be small (from 2.3 to 12 Kwords) and highly specialised with regard to the topic as well as the specialisation degree. This allows for a quite precise patterns and lexico-semantic, formal and morphosyntactic heuristics albeit this only applies to highly specialised corpora.

f. All systems focus entirely on NPs and none of them deals with verbal phrases. This is because there is a high rate of terminological NPs in specialised texts. This rate can vary according to the topic and the specialisation degree. Despite what has just been noted, it is noteworthy that all specialised languages have their own verbs (or specific combinations of a verbal nature), no matter how low the ratio is in comparison with nouns.

g. As a result, none of the systems refers to the distinction between nominal collocations and nominal terminological units of a syntactic nature. Nor do they refer to phraseology.

h. Many of the systems make use of a number of morphosyntactic patterns to identify complex terms. However they account for most of the terminological units they are still too few and also not very constraining. Thus, for English are AN and NN, for French NA and N prep N. Some terms present structures other than these ones and they are never detected. Those systems based only on these types of linguistic techniques generate too much noise.

i. It is generally agreed that frequency is a good criterion to indicate that a candidate term is actually a terminological unit. However, frequency is not on its own a sufficient criterion, as it yields a great deal of noise.

j. Only a few recent systems use semantic information to recognise and delimit terminological units although its use takes place at different levels.

k. None of the systems uses extensively the combinatory features of terms from specialised languages in relation to a given domain. It is needed more studies about the type of constraints that terminological units present with regard to conceptual field and text type.

l. Only one of the analysed systems take profit of the possibilities given by the alignment of specialised text.

m. Most of the authors consider the POS disambiguation as one of the most important error sources. However, they do not provide exact figures about its incidence degree.

To improve these systems of terminology extraction and lessen the noise and silence that are generated, two type of studies should be encouraged. First, it is required more linguistic oriented studies on the semantic relationships among terms, the semantic relationships among constituents of a terminological unit, semantico-lexical representation, constraints of terminological units within a given specialised domain and in a given text type, all the grammatical categories that are likely to become terms in specialised domains, the influence of the syntactic function of terminological phrases on texts, the relationships between terms and their arrangement in texts.

Second, we should focus on software systems that: combine in a more active manner statistical and linguistic methods; improve statistical measures; combine more than one strategy; are easily applicable to more than one language; improve interfaces to facilitate the machine-user interaction. Also it should be very useful, as suggested in Kageura et al. (1998), the development of a common test bench for aiding the evaluation/comparison of extracting methods.

In sum, should we progress in the field of automatic terminology extraction, statistical and linguistic methods have to actively be combined. It means that they are not either-or approaches but complementary ones. The final goal is to reduce the amount of silence and noise so that the process of terminological extraction becomes as automatic and precise as possible. In the future, we believe that any current terminology extractor, apart from accounting for the morphological, syntactic and structural aspects of terminological units, has to necessarily include semantic aspects if the efficiency of the system is to be improved with regard to the existing ones.

Notes

* This paper has been written within the research project PB-96–0293, financially supported by the Spanish government.

We would like to thank Dr. H. Rodríguez (Universitat Politècnica de Catalunya), Dr. C. Jacquemin (Université de Nantes), Dr. L. de Yzaguirre and Mrs. J. Freixa (Universitat Pompeu Fabra) their valuable comments on preliminary versions of this paper. The remaining shortcomings are ours. We thank J. Morel for translating this paper from Catalan into English and C. Rodríguez its revision.

1. In order to give a broader view of TE we use both *extractor* and *detector* to refer to the same notion. However, we are aware of the fact that some scholars attribute different meanings to these words.

2. (Kageura and Umino 1996) refer to *unithood* as the degree of stability of syntagmatic combinations (collocations) and *termhood* as the degree in that a linguistic unit is related to a domain-specific concept.

3. TREC (*Text Retrieval Engineering Conference*) refers to a series of conferences supported by NIST and DARPA (U.S. agencies). Further information can be found at: *http://trec.nist.gov/*.

4. Remarkable examples of the use of these techniques are the works of Church and Hanks (1989) on word association and Smadja (1991) on collocation extraction from large corpora.

5. Further information can be found at: http://www.clarit.com.

6. The formula was experimentally obtained by the autor from the association number described in Brown et al. (1988) in the aim of favouring the most frequent pairs: $IM^3 = \log_2 (a^3/(a+b)(a-b))$

7. Further information can be obtained at http://www.limsi.fr/Individu/jacquemi/FASTR/index.html

8. Heid et al. (1996) note that a broad coverage morphosyntactic parser for German is not attained. Thus parser results are simulated using POS patterns.

9. The meaning of the syntactic function tags are: @>N = pre-modifier; @⟨N = post-modifier; @CC and @CS = coordination and subordination conjunction; @V = Verb; @NH = nominal head. Finally, "⟨" and "⟩" indicate the direction of the phrasal head.

10. The technique of term filtering through frequency terms has been considered something in between those methods based on linguistic knowledge and those methods based on extralinguistic knowledge.

11. The system has been intensively tested with regard to the indexing frequency, but not in relation to the quality of the extracted terms.

References

Arppe, A. 1995. "Term extraction from unrestricted text." *Lingsoft Web Site: http://www.lingsoft.com*

Ahmad, K., Davies, A., Fulford, H. and Rogers, M. 1992. "What is a term? The semiautomatic extraction of terms from text." *Translation Studies — an interdiscipline.* Amsterdam: John Benjamins.

Bourigault, D. 1994. *LEXTER, un Logiciel d'EXtraction de TERminologie. Application à l'acquisition des connaissances à partir de textes.* PhD Thesis. Paris: École des Hautes Études en Sciences Sociales.

Bourigault, D., Gonzalez-Mullier, I. and Gros, C. 1996. "LEXTER, a Natural Language Processing Tool for Terminology Extraction." *Proceedings of the 7th EURALEX International Congress.* Göteborg.

Brown, P.F., Cocke, F., Pietra, S., Felihek. F., Merces, R. and Rossin, P. (1988) A statistical approach to language translation. *Procedings of 12th International Conference of Computational Linguistic (Coling-88).* Budapest, Hungary.

Cabré, M.T. 1999. *Terminology. Theory, methods and applications.* Amsterdam: John Benjamins.

Church, K. 1989. "Word association norms, mutual information and lexicography." *Proceedings of the 27th annual meeting of the ACL.* Vancouver, 76–83.

Condamines, A. 1995. "Terminology: new needs, new perspectives." *Terminology,* 2, 2:219–238.

Dagan, I. and Church, K. 1994. "Termight: Identifying and translating technical terminology." *Proceedings of the Fourth Conference on Applied Natural Language Processing,* 34–40.

Daille, B. 1994. *Approche mixte pour l'extraction de terminologie: statistique lexicale et filtres linguistiques.* PhD dissertation. Paris: Université Paris VII.

Daille, B. and Jacquemin, C 1998. "Lexical database and information access: a fruitfull association?." *First International Conference on LREC.* Granada.

David, S. and Plante, P. 1991. "Le progiciel TERMINO: de la nécessité d'une analyse morphosyntaxique pour le dépouillement terminologique des textes." *Proceedings of the Montreal Colloquium Les industries de la langue: perspectives des années 1990,* 1:71–88.

Enguehard, C. and Pantera, L. 1994. "Automatic Natural Acquisition of a Terminology." *Journal of Quantitative Linguistics,* 2, 1:27–32.

Estopà, R. 1999. *Extracció de terminologia: elements per a la construcció d'un SEACUSE (Sistema d'extracció automàtica de candidats a unitats de significació especialitzada).* PhD thesis, Barcelona: Universitat Pompeu Fabra.

Estopà, R. and Vivaldi, J. 1998. "Systèmes de détection automatique de (candidats à) termes: vers une proposition intégratrice." *Actes des 7èmes Journées ERLA-GLAT, Brest,* 385–410

Evans, D.A. and Zhai, C. 1996. "Noun-phrase Analysis in Unrestricted Text for information retrieval." *Proceedings of ACL, Santa Cruz, University of California,* 17–24.

Frantzi, K. and Ananiadou, S. 1995. *Statistical measures for terminological extraction.* Working paper of the Department of Computing of Manchester Metropolitan University.

Frantzi, K.T. 1997. "Incorporating context information for extraction of terms." *Proceedings* of ACL/EACL, Madrid, 501–503.

Habert, B., Naulleau, E. and Nazarenko, A. 1996. "Symbolic word clustering for medium-size corpora." *Proceedings of Coling'96:* 490–495.

Heid, U., Jauss, S., Krüger, K. and Hohmann, A. 1996. "Term extraction with standard tools for corpus exploration. Experience from German." In: *TKE'96: Terminology and Knowledge Engineering,*, 139–150. Berlin: Indeks Verlag.

Jacquemin, C. 1994. "Recycling Terms into a Partial Parser." *Proceedings of ANLP'94,* 113–118.

Jacquemin, C. 1999. "Syntagmatic and paradigmatic representations of term variation." *Proceedings of* ACL'99, University of Maryland, 341–348.

Jacquin, C. and Liscouet, M. 1996. "Terminology extraction from texts corpora: application to document keeping via Internet." In: *TKE'96: Terminology and Knowledge Engineering, 74–83.* Berlin: Indeks Verlag.

Justeson, J. and Katz, S. 1995. "Technical terminology: some linguistic properties and an algorithm for identification in text." *Natural Language Engineering,* 1, 1:9–27.

Kageura, K. and Umino, B. 1996. "Methods of Automatic Term Recognition." Papers of the *National Center for Science Information Systems,* 1–22.

Kageura, K., Yoshioka, M., Koyama, T. and Nozue, T. 1998. "Towards a common testbed for corpus-based computational terminology." *Proceedings of Computerm '98*, Montreal, 81–85.

Karlsson, F. 1990. "Constraint grammar as a framework for parsing running text." *Proceedings of the 13th International conference on computational linguistic*, 3: 168–173.

Lauriston, A. 1994. "Automatic recognition of complex terms: Problems and the TERMINO solution." *Terminology*, 1, 1: 147–170.

Maynard, D. and Ananiadou, S. 1999. "Identifying contextual information for multi-word term extraction." In: *TKE '99: Terminology and Knowledge Engineering, 212–221.* Vienna: TermNet.

Nakagawa, H. and Mori, T. 1998. "Nested collocation and Compound Noun for Term Extraction." *Proceedings of Computerm '98*, Montreal, 64–70.

Naulleau, E 1998. *Apprentissage et filtrage syntaxico-sémantique de syntagmes nominaux pertinents pour la recherche documentaire.* PhD thesis. Paris: Université Paris 13.

Naulleau, E. 1999. "Profile-guided terminology extraction." In: *TKE '99: Terminology and Knowledge Engineering.* 222–240. Vienna: TermNet.

Plante, P. and Dumas, L. 1998. "Le Dépoulliment terminologique assisté par ordinateur." *Terminogramme*, 46, 24–28.

Shieber, S. N. 1986. "An Introduction to Unification-Based Approaches to grammar." *CSLI Lecture Notes of* University Press, 4.

Smadja, F. 1991. *Extracting collocations from text. An application: language generation.* Columbia: Columbia University. Department of Computer Science. [Unpublished doctoral dissertation]

Voutilainen, A. 1993. "NPtool, a detector of English noun phrases." *Proceedings of the Workshop on Very Large Corpora.*

Zhai, C., Tong, X., Milic-Frayling, N. and Evans, D. A. 1996. "Evaluation of syntactic phrase indexing CLARIT. NLP track report." *Proceedings of the TREC-5*. TREC Web Site: *http://trec.nist.gov/pubs/trec5/t5_proceedings.html*

CHAPTER 4

Incremental extraction of domain-specific terms from online text resources

Lee-Feng Chien and Chun-Liang Chen
Institute of Information Science, Academia Sinica / Dept. of CS and IE, National Taiwan University

Incremental extraction of domain-specific terms from online text resources is necessary in many information retrieval (IR) and natural language processing (NLP) applications. The purpose of this paper is to present an efficient approach which can classify online text collections from the Internet dynamically and extract domain-specific terms incrementally. This approach is developed through a successful integration of PAT-tree indexing, term extraction and document classification techniques.

1. Introduction

Many domain-specific terms, such as proper names, translated terms, technical terms, and even topic terms, which are often excluded from general dictionaries, must be efficiently extracted and collected in many IR and NLP applications (Lewis and Sparck Jones 1996). It is clear that a dictionary with a rigid terminological vocabulary can reduce the number of Out-Of-Vocabulary words (OOV's) in NLP (Wan et al. 1997) and perform precise term indexing and query expansion in IR (Salton 1989). Unfortunately, the number of online resources is increasing very fast. For many online NLP and IR systems, such as voice browsers, web-based machine translation systems, Internet searching engines etc., it is cost-ineffective and even unrealistic to manually construct a domain-specific dictionary for each service domain. To capture up-to-date information and reduce the amount of unknown vocabulary, automatic extraction of domain-specific terms from the increasing number of online resources is an attractive solution worth exploring.

The purpose of this paper is to address the significance of the above research problem and present an efficient approach for it. The approach is based on a *live dictionary* with online information systems on the Internet, in which most of the domain-specific terms can be incrementally extracted and adapted with changes in text collections. Such a live dictionary can reflect up-to-date information and will be very helpful in providing real-time information service; for example, it may make possible search engines with real-time term suggestion or event-detection capabilities. On the other hand, as unlimited number of corpus resources are available over the Internet, the proposed approach also attempts to find an automatic way to organize the text collections which are growing daily. So that many language processing applications will have sufficient corpora.

The proposed approach is an extension of a previous work (Chien 1997), which was originally designed to extract Chinese terms with correct lexical boundaries from a large but static text collection. The proposed approach extends the previous work in three ways. First, it enhances capability of the incremental extraction of new terms from online text resources. It is designed to monitor the change in significance of each candidate term (node of PAT trees) and extract the important terms as quickly as possible. Second, the proposed approach is also integrated with an efficient technique for online corpus storage and classification, so that terms specific to different subject domains can be extracted concurrently. Third, to allow online resources can be efficiently utilized as a corpus, the content of the online documents is completely indexed via PAT-tree indices (Gonnet et al. 1992), from which rigid linguistic information can be incrementally extracted.

The proposed approach was designed based on proper integration of linguistic knowledge acquisition (Zernik 1991) and IR technologies. Compared with conventional research on knowledge acquisition (Smadja 1993), the proposed approach carefully considers the dynamic characteristics of online information service. The developed techniques are capable of handling large and incremental texts and also can be easily integrated into IR and NLP systems. According to the obtained results for extracting domain-specific terms from online Chinese news incrementally, it is promising that a live dictionary can be, therefore, established. Online information systems based on the proposed techniques can perform much better in many aspects, such as online lexicon construction, term indexing, automatic term suggestion, cross-language information retrieval, information filtering, information extraction, etc. Although the proposed approach is mainly designed for Chinese and oriental language applications, some of the developed techniques are believed to be applicable to western languages.

2. The considered problem and an overview of the proposed approach

This section will define the considered problem and give an overview of the proposed approach to incremental extraction of domain-specific terms. A *domain-specific term* is defined as a string that consists of more than one successive character in Chinese (or words in English), which has a certain number of occurrences and is specific to a text collection with a distinct subject domain. Such a string should have a complete meaning and lexical boundaries in semantics; it might be a word, compound word, phrase or linguistic template.

Definition 1: The incremental term extraction problem
Given a new document D, a set of incremental and domain-specific text collections $C_{1\sim n}$ and corresponding term lexicons $T_{1\sim n}$, the goal of this problem is to determine the most promising collection C_i for D, extract new terms X from D and add them to T_i, where $X=\{x \mid x$ occurs in D; x can be a domain-specific term of C_i but is missing from T_i to date$\}$.

The above problem is meant to deal with the extraction of domain-specific terms with the increase of an online resource. The online resource can be divided into different text collections with specific subject domains in advance. Once a term is found to be specific to and important in a certain text collection, it is extracted as soon as possible. Such a domain-specific term often indicates the occurrences of a certain event. If it can be identified immediately, then different kinds of real-time response and information services, such as event detection in online news can be implemented.

It needs to note that the domain-specific terms to be extracted are which have certain occurrence to date and are expected to be used within a period of time in the corresponding text collections. Therefore, a term that is just a keyword of a single document but rarely occurs in other documents is not considered to be a domain-specific term. Many low-frequency proper names are, therefore, not taken into consideration for this reason.

To deal with the problem, several difficulties need to be overcome. *The first difficulty is to identify new and meaningful terms with document inputs as soon as possible.* It is known that to extract meaningful terms in an automatic way is still a challenging problem in western languages, but it is more critical in Chinese and oriental language processing because of difficulties in word segmentation and unknown word identification (Wu and Tseng 1995). Our idea is to develop an efficient algorithm and metric which is able to monitor the frequency change and usage freedom of each candidate term in a text collection, with the input of the new documents. The proposed completeness analysis technique that will be described in Section 5.1 was developed for this purpose. *The second difficulty is to estimate the significance of the candidate terms.* In our approach, each new document is classified into corresponding text collection(s), and the composed candidate terms of the document are checked by observing their distributions in different collections in the system. The candidates that are "non-specific" are removed. The corpus classification technique and the significance analysis technique that will be introduced in Sections 4 and 5.2 respectively were developed based on the above consideration. *The third difficulty is achieving satisfactory efficiency in handling large and dynamic texts.* Since real-time processing is required in many applications, the techniques used have to be efficient in execution. To deal with this difficulty, a PAT-tree-based working structure which will be introduced in Section 3 has therefore been developed.

The proposed approach, as shown in Fig. 1, combines three elementary modules: resource discovery, corpus storage and classification, and term extraction modules. The outputs obtained using the proposed approach will contain classified text collections, PAT-tree indices and the domain-specific term lexicons from the online text resources.

The resource discovery module contains an information spider that automatically extracts and organizes relevant resources from the Internet, such as newly-updated Web pages from similar Web sites and news documents from connected network news agencies. By searching and collecting information, the spider puts together a huge corpus that can be continuously updated. But the resources obtained by the spider are just raw data from the point of view of corpus linguistics, which need further processing and analysis, such as through duplicate document detection, title extraction, HTML tags deletion, etc., in the module.

So that domain-specific terms can be effectively extracted, each input document from online resources is classified into corresponding collection(s), which serve as a corpus for continued term extraction. To satisfy the demand for both corpus storage and classification, a method which employs *PAT trees* as the working structure is used in the corpus storage and classification module, as will be described in Section 4. This method utilizes the PAT-tree indices and/or the obtained domain-specific term lexicons as shown in Figure 1 to recognize key features for classification. Each classifying document generates a PAT tree

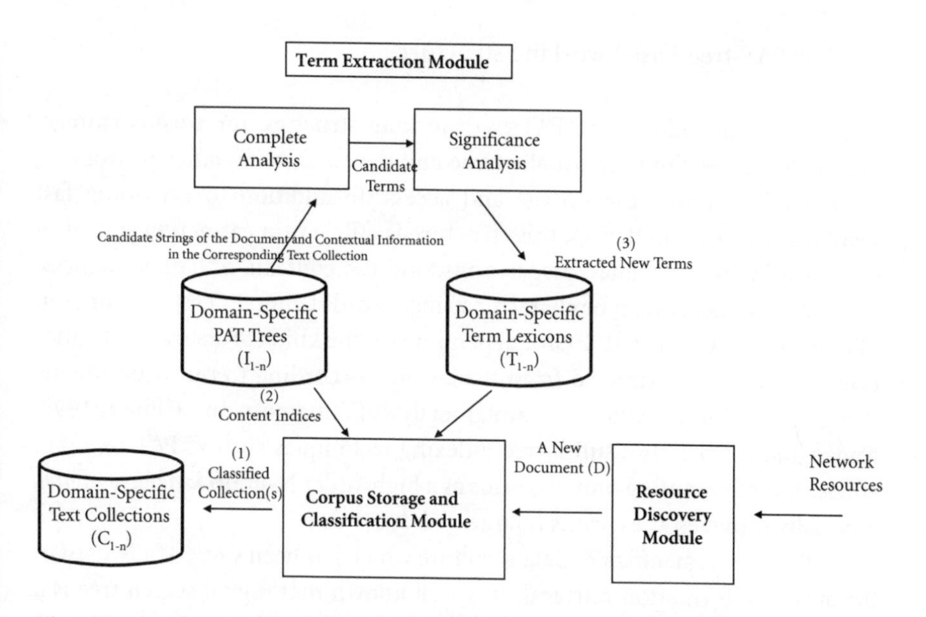

Figure 1. An abstract diagram showing the proposed approach to incremental extraction of domain-specific terms from online text resources

as the feature vector by its content, and compares them with the corresponding PAT-tree indices of each text collection in the system. By means of vector-space-based similarity estimation, the document then is classified and appended to a collection(s) and the corresponding PAT-tree indices are updated. The indices can efficiently record up-to-date information about the text collection(s), from which rigid linguistic information can be incrementally extracted.

When an input document has been classified (as seen in (1) of Figure 1) and indexed (as seen in (2) of Figure 1), the term extraction module goes to work. The module extracts possible new terms from the document content and add them to the corresponding term lexicon(s). It will estimate the significance of each complete composed strings of the document with the corresponding PAT tree(s). The underlying technique will be introduced in Section 5. As a consequence, the results obtained using the proposed approach contain the classified text collections, the corresponding PAT-tree full-text indices and domain-specific term lexicons, which can be updated based on the change in online resources and used to process incoming documents.

3. The PAT-tree-based working structure

This section introduces the PAT-tree working structure for corpus storage. Online text collections are usually large and dynamic, so an efficient working structure is required for storage and access. In addition to providing fast searching and easy updating, this structure is efficient in extracting statistical data, like frequency values, associations, and the contexts of data sequences. These data sequences can be character strings, word strings, POS strings or even phone strings (Chen et al. 1998), depending on the kinds of abstract information that are to be extracted from the corpus. According to our experiments (Chien 1998; Chien 1999) and similar analysis (Yamamoto and Church 1998; Nagao and Mori 1994), suffix-tree indexing techniques such as PAT trees are efficient in representing online corpus as a high-order N-gram *language model*, especially for when the corpus is large and dynamic.

A PAT tree is an efficient data structure which has been successfully used in the area of information retrieval. It is well known that digital search tree is a more natural data structure for digital search but wasteful in space and time because a lot of nodes (these nodes can be classified as branch nodes and leaf nodes as in Figure 2) need to be possessed and traversed during search process. To reduce such a complete digital binary search tree, compressed digital search tree usually utilizes comparison bit as the "CB" in Figure 3.

A PAT tree is conceptually equivalent to a compressed digital search tree but smaller. PAT tree was developed in 1987 by Gonnet based on PATRICIA

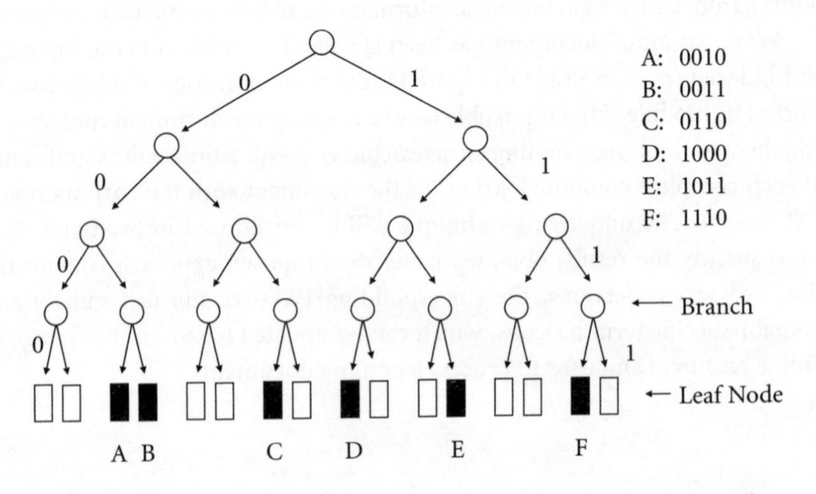

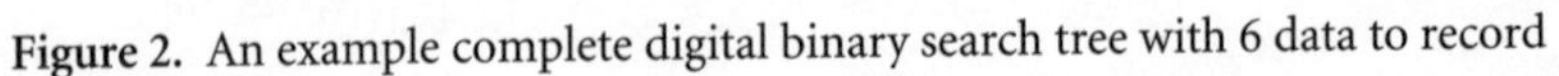
Figure 2. An example complete digital binary search tree with 6 data to record

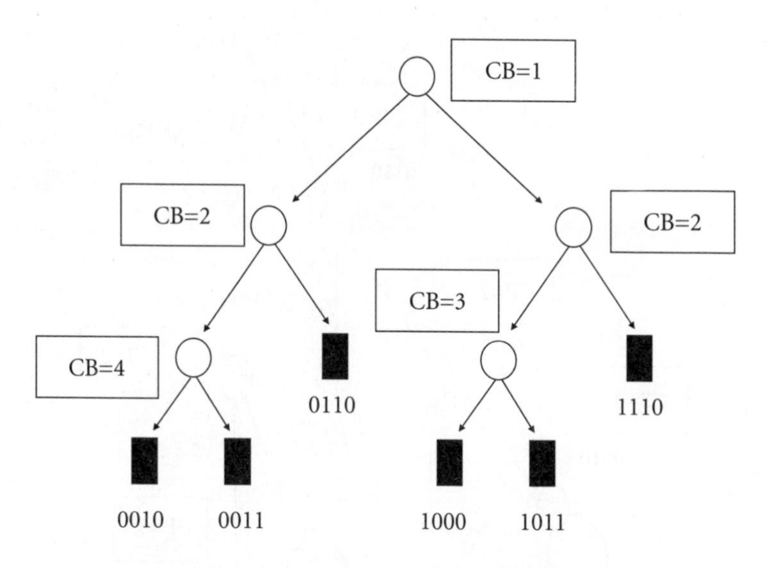

Figure 3. A compressed digital search tree of the example in Figure 2

algorithm (Gonnet et al. 1992) for indexing a continuous data stream. Instead of classifying the nodes into branch nodes and leaf nodes, PATRICIA uses an augmented branch node. For example, the compressed digital trie in Figure 3 has the equivalent PATRICIA in Figure 4. It is noted that each node in PATRICIA tree plays both roles of branch node and leaf node in digital search tree. It not only serves as branch node for branch decision making but also as leaf node for matching comparison. The key factor for differentiating them is by "UP" link or "DOWN" link. Simply speaking, the "UP" link points out from the node with small comparison bit to that with high comparison bit, while the "DOWN" link is on the contrary. The node pointed by arrowhead of an "UP" link is deemed leaf node while that pointed by "DOWN" link is deemed internal node. Another difference is the additional root node. This is because in the binary three the number of leaf node is always greater than that of internal nodes by one.

The superior features of PAT tree for indexing a continuous data stream result from the use of so-called *semi-infinite strings* (different suffixe strings). PAT tree is exactly like PATRICIA except that the indexing data elements are replaced by different suffix strings of the indexing data stream. Using this data structure to index the full-text content of document databases, all possible substrings of the full text data can be retrieved and updated in a very efficient way, but not every string of arbitrary length need to be stored. If fact, only different

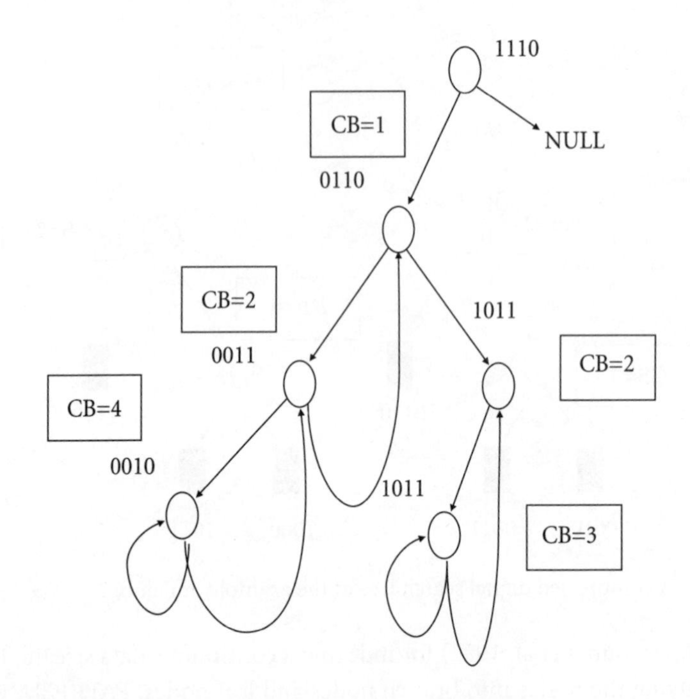

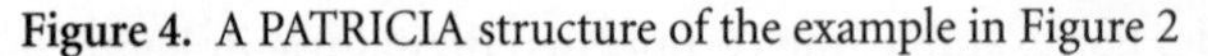

Figure 4. A PATRICIA structure of the example in Figure 2

suffix strings of the indexing data stream are stored in conventional applications. For example, the different suffixes generated for the string "αβγν" are "αβγν", "βγν", "γν", "ν". The existence of each composed sub-strings "α", "β", "γ", "ν", "αβ", "βγ", "γν", "αβγ", "βγν", "αβγν" can be easily detected if the searching string is exactly a prefix of one of the above suffix strings.

When we apply a PAT tree to record a Chinese corpus, there are several extensions. At first, we use punctuation marks such as "." and "," as delimiters to separate each indexing data stream of the indexing document. For example, string "αβγν, ωε" will be separated into two indexing strings, and the different suffixes to be recorded in the augmented PAT tree are only "αβγν", "βγν", "γν", "ν", "ωε", and "ε". This is based on an assumption that only the context within a certain logical segment is significant for determination of a candidate term.

During implementation, each distinct suffix string is represented as a node in the PAT tree, and only a pointer to its position is used in the document to save space. In the mean time, each node consists of three parameters: the comparison bit, the number of external nodes and the frequency count for the purpose of searching and information updating. The addition of the last two parameters is the second extension. The number of external nodes indicates the number of different suffix strings in the sub-trees, and the frequency count indicates the frequency of occurrence of the corresponding string in the data stream. Moreover, the comparison bit indicates the first different bit of the strings recorded in the sub-trees. The comparison bit is primarily used in each node to indicate which bit in the searching string is to be used for branching. By storing the frequency of the recorded string and the number of external nodes (those nodes which have comparison bits greater than their parents') of each node, we are able to determine the frequency of every string and even the occurrences of every string pair stored in the PAT tree. To illustrate, an example PAT tree is shown in Figure 5.

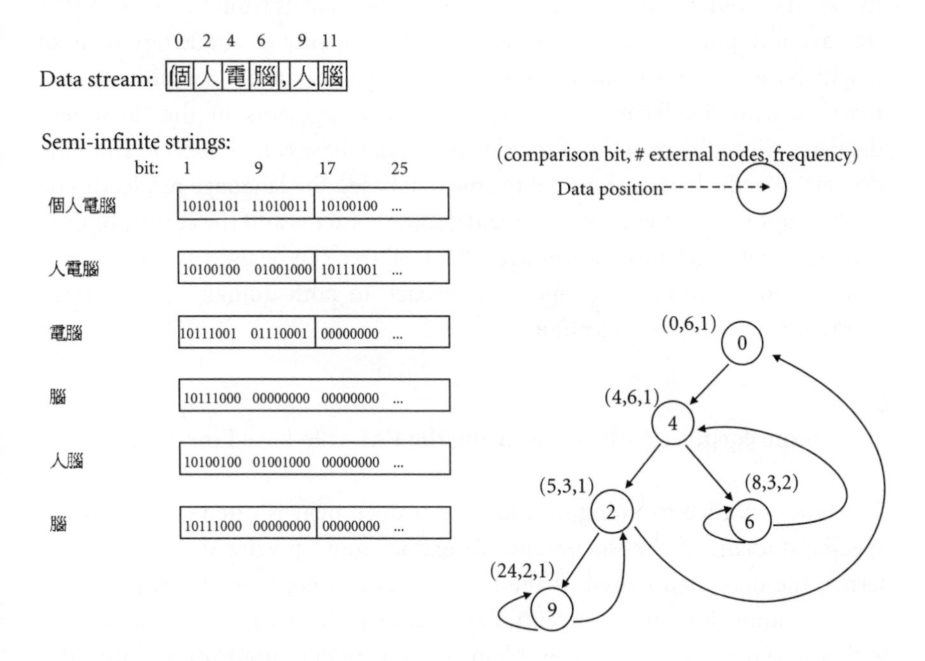

Figure 5. An example PAT tree

Considering the inherent difficulty of word segmentation and unknown proper noun extraction in Chinese (Wu and Tseng 1995), the indexing unit for Chinese documents is the character rather than the word for English documents in PAT trees (Kwok 1997; Chien 1997). Each distinct string (character or word string) of a document which occurs within sentence fragments is conceptually recorded. In fact, besides the original PAT tree for recording all different suffix sub-strings, for each text collection and examining document an additional

PAT tree is created for indexing all different prefix sub-strings. This is based on a consideration that efficient context analysis is required for each candidate term during the term extraction processing, especially for real-time applications.

In fact, the above data structure is especially useful in constructing a Chinese language model for modeling of domain-specific terms, which are often lexical patterns and proper nouns such as, names and locations that vary and change in different databases. This is because words are not easy to identify in Chinese, especially on patterns and proper nouns which are usually excluded from the lexicons. In order to avoid the loss of unknown proper nouns, in some applications, all of the character strings in Chinese texts must be assumed to be candidates of terms, and sophisticated context analysis is necessary to determine the word boundaries and to extract representative terms from the texts. A PAT tree actually provides indices to all possible segments of characters with an length N, where N can be arbitrary or just the maximum sentence length, together with the frequency counts for those segments in the document database. Since the content of the document database can be used to train the domain-specific language model for the databases, the language model can be easily adapted with the update of the database contents and the corresponding PAT tree. With the above advantages, the PAT-tree can be used as the primary working structure in the proposed approach to both domain-specific term extraction and corpus collection.

4. Online corpus classification using the PAT-tree-based method

The representative meaning of a term in a document is often subject to the specific domain of the document. To extract more precise domain-specific terms, the documents used as the training corpus need to be classified into corresponding domains. Conventional document classification normally deals with the static classification problem, i.e. documents used for training the feature values of each document category are static and have no change with the classification process. Different from conventional document classification, the problem to be dealt with the proposed approach is so-called online document classification. The documents to be classified are incremental and the classification result of the former documents in the classification process will influence the determination of the latter documents. At the same time, the proposed approach allows multiple classification of ambiguous documents, because a few documents miss-classified into wrong collections normally have little effect in many applications such as domain-specific term extraction.

The proposed PAT-tree-based method is not designed to be a specialized algorithm for classification but rather to be a flexible working structure for the purposes of both corpus classification and information extraction. There are two major steps: document similarity estimation and PAT-tree updating. Because words in common dictionaries are too general to be "key" words, it is necessary for the online corpus classification procedure to define a more proper feature set which can be easily adapted with the update of the text collections. With a suffix-tree-like data structure, it can generate a feature set dynamically (Chien 1997). As mentioned in Section 2, each text collection and classifying document has a PAT tree which represents its feature vector. With the PAT-tree indices, the feature set to be selected can be composed of variable length n-grams or extracted terms (Zamir and Etzioni 1998). Such a unique feature set enables the PAT tree to be efficient in performing *incremental classification* because each new document after classification can update the corresponding PAT tree(s). The feature set used for the classification process can be therefore dynamically changed and the obtained feature values can help for classifying incoming documents immediately. To study the performance, several different vector-space-model-based estimation methods have been implemented. A utilized estimation metric is defined below:

Let d be a document to be classified, c is an examining text collection, $T=(t_1,t_2,\ldots t_n)$ is a set of possible character variable n-grams in d where T can be accessed by the PAT tree of d. $Score_c(d)$ is a similarity estimation function illustrated and defined as follows.

$$Score_c(d)=\sum_i (L^2(t_i) * Tf(t_i;d)/N_c(t_i))$$

where $L(t_i)=0$ if $t_i \notin c$
$L(t_i)=stringlength$ if $t_i \in$

In the above equation, $L(t_i)$ is the string length of t_i while $Tf(t_i;d)$ is the term frequency of t_i in document d. $N_c(t_i)$ is the total number of distinct text collections where term t_i ever occurs. If the above formula is applied to bi-gram based estimation, the set T is all possible character bi-grams in d. Similarly, if it is applied to variable-n-gram based estimation, the set T is all possible character strings in d.

It is not hard to find that the required parameters with TF-IDF-based metrics such as term frequency values and document frequency values can be efficiently extracted using the PAT-tree indices. In the experiment introduced in Section 6, on average, the proposed method could index and classify more than ten news documents per second on a PC.

5. Incremental extraction of domain-specific terms

The proposed method for term extraction is a two-step automatic process as described below.

5.1 Completeness analysis

The first step is to extract complete terms from the examined document. Like the completeness analysis step in the previous approach, this step mainly checks if the strings of candidate terms are complete in lexical boundaries. But one difference is that the strings that need to be checked here are only those occurring in the new document *D*. These strings should a certain number of occurrences in the corresponding text collection C_i but are not found in the term lexicon T_i to date. For each string *X* in *D*, it will judge if *X* is complete in terms of semantics based on its distribution and context in the updated PAT tree I_i. *X* is defined as complete in terms of semantics iff its *association norm* of the composed sub-strings is strong enough and has no *left and right context dependency.* The estimations defined below are the same as those in previous works. This design really considers the characteristics of the Chinese language. To extract complete English terms, conventional tagging-based methods need to be included.

Definition 2: Association norm estimation
Association norm estimation *MI(X)* for each string *X* is defined below:

$$MI(X)=\frac{f(X)}{f(X_s)+f(X_e)-f(X)}$$

Here *MI(X)* is the mutual information of a target string *X*; X_s is the longest starting sub-string of *X*, i.e., the sub-string which is exactly *X* except that the last character of *X* is deleted; X_e is the longest ending sub-string of *X*, i.e., the sub-string which is exactly *X* except that the first character of *X* is deleted; and *f(X)*, $f(X_s)$ and $f(X_e)$are the frequency counts of *X*, X_s, and X_e, in the text collection, respectively. This definition is based on the efficiency of calculation in real-time applications. Character stings for which the above mutual information is below a threshold are considered to be incomplete.

Definition 3: Left Context Dependency (LCD)
Each string X has left context dependency if $|L| < t1$ or $MAX_{\alpha} f(\alpha X)/f(X) > t2$, where $t1$, $t2$ are threshold values, $f(.)$ is the frequency, L is the set of left adjacent strings of X, $\alpha \in L$ and $|L|$ is the number of unique left adjacent strings.

Definition 4: Right Context Dependency (RCD)
Each string X has right context dependency if $|R| < t1$ or $MAX_{\beta} f(X\beta)/f(X) > t2$, where $t1$, $t2$ are threshold values, $f(.)$ is the frequency, R is the set of right adjacent strings of X, $\beta \in R$ and $|R|$ is the number of unique right adjacent strings. Strings with either left or right context dependency are considered to be incomplete.

In fact, the above metrics are actually used to check if X contains highly associated composed strings and also has complete lexical boundaries by judging the usage freedom of X according to its contextual information. The basic assumption is that if X has few unique left or right adjacent strings, or if it frequently occurs together with certain adjacent strings, then it might be incomplete in terms of semantics. For clarity, an abstract diagram in Figure 6 shows the concept of completeness analysis based on such context dependency analysis. The biggest circle in the middle of the figure indicates the string (lexical pattern) to be estimated which is a node in the PAT tree. The remaining circles indicate the possible patterns which have occurred with the examining pattern either in the left context or right context, which could be searched with the PAT tree. For example, to search for all right context it only needs to check its descendant nodes with the PAT tree. On contrary, to search for all left context it is not easy with the original PAT tree. Considering the efficiency of the LCD estimation, it also creates a PAT tree for the reversed data streams. For example, for the string "αβγν", all different suffixes of its reversed string "νγβα" are also recorded. With the additional PAT tree, it is also easy to perform the LCD estimation process.

According to our observations from experiments, by using the above analysis, most incomplete Chinese character strings can be filtered out. For instance, the use of the character string "Lee Deng" in Chinese can be detected as being very limited by means of RCD checking. In fact, in a simple test on a news abstracts database of about 5MB, it was found that "Lee Deng" appeared 640 times and was always followed by "Hui", thus creating the personal name "Lee Deng-hui" (the president of the R.O.C.).

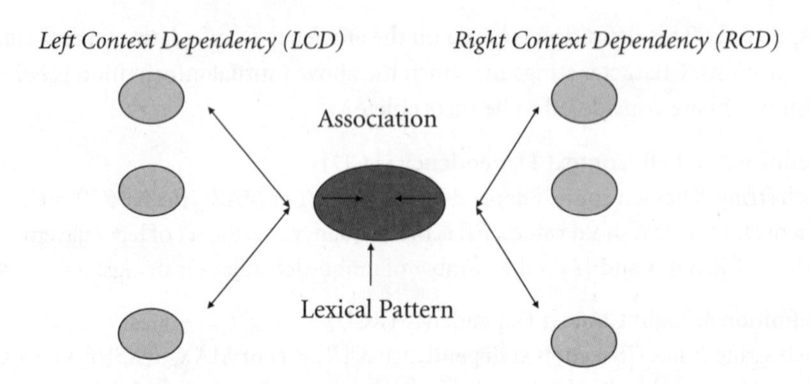

Figure 6. An abstract diagram showing the estimation of complete lexical patterns based on analysis of context dependency and association norm

The above estimations are easily implemented using PAT-tree indices. To find out if a candidate string in *D* is complete or not, it is only necessary to check its association norm of the composed sub-strings as well as left and right context dependency. All of these operations can be easily done with PAT-tree access.

5.2 Significance analysis

The second step is to find domain-specific new terms. As in the previous approach, the significance analysis step extracts specific and significant candidate strings as the domain-specific terms. Using the following procedure, all of the remaining candidates strings are checked using a common-word lexicon, a set of lexical rules and the analysis of the significance estimation function $S(Y)$ shown below (Schutze 1998). If a candidate string either appears in the common-word lexicon or can be formed using the lexical rules, it is treated as a non-significant candidate and is removed. The used lexical rules consist of non-significant numbers, times, adverb phrases etc. The remaining candidates are checked further by observing their frequencies and distributions between the corresponding and different PAT trees in the system. The candidates which also frequently appear in different PAT trees are treated as non-specific and are also removed. The remaining strings which satisfy the estimation (larger than a threshold value) are selected as new domain-specific terms.

Definition 5: The significance estimation function
$S(Y) = (f_i(Y)/f(T_i))/\ (f_g(Y)/f(T_g))$, where Y is a candidate term, $f_i(Y)$ is the frequency of Y in the collection T_i, $f(T_i)$ is the total number of strings in the collection T_i,

$f_g(Y)$ is the frequency of Y in the general collection, and $f(T_g)$ is total number of strings in the general collection.

The above estimation procedure compares the relative frequency in the text collection of interest with the relative frequency in a reference collection. The necessary parameters all are easily computed using the PAT-tree indices. Among them, $f_i(Y)$ and $f(T_i)$ can be obtained directly in PAT tree I_i. $f_g(Y)$ and $f(T_g)$ can be obtained by summing all of the domain-specific PAT trees in the system.

6. Experimental results

To test the performance of the proposed approach, extensive experiments were conducted. In the experiments, a Chinese online-news database from the Central News Agency (CNA) in Taiwan was used as the testing platform. This database was separated manually into eight sections, namely Section 1: congress/politics; Section 2: judiciary/transport; Section 3: business/finance; Section 4: education; Section 5: recreation; Section 6: local; Section 7: weather report; and Section 8: Misc. In terms of document classification, such a database is really not easy to correctly classify, because the news abstracts grouped in each section are not specific nor are balanced in size. Selection of the above database as a testing set is based on an integrated consideration that the database is a really natural, large, classified and incremental, and more importantly, information extracted from the resource is valuable and easily evaluated.

6.1 Corpus storage and classification

The first experiment was performed to study the flexibility of the proposed method for the considered problem rather than to develop a really efficient method for Chinese document classification at that point. The initial training documents were obtained from news abstracts in the eight sections published from January to May in 1997, and the testing documents were those published in June. Table 1 lists some of the detailed information about the testing database constructed for corpus classification. It is noted that the documents in the testing database were news abstracts. On average, a document contained about 150 Chinese characters.

In this example, each of the testing documents was incrementally classified and indexed in chronological order. The classified documents were immediately

Table 1. The testing database and some of the obtained processing results for corpus storage and classification, where the processing speed was estimated for classification using variable-n-gram features to store and classify the news abstracts published in June 1997.

Domain	PAT-tree size (KB)	Training size		Testing size		Processing speed (#Doc/sec on PC)
		Doc#	KB	Doc#	KB	
Congress/Politics	27,310	12,587	4,490	1,262	382.0	10.51
Judiciary/Transport	15,852	10,114	2,490	1,173	227.0	15.45
Business/Finance	7,071	7,337	1,800	1,082	219.0	15.03
Education	4,894	2,942	775	424	087.4	11.13
Recreation	2,571	1,626	413	248	049.3	13.47
Local	11,117	6,580	1,690	968	201.0	14.57
Weather	867	2,896	3,130	435	474.0	8.97
Misc.	5,844	989	1,690	132	193.0	3.80
Total/Avg.	75,526	45,071	16,478	5,724	1,832.7	12.07

Table 2. The recall and precision rates obtained in an experiment on incremental corpus classification

	With bi-gram features			With variable N-gram features		
	Top1 recall	Top2 recall	Precision	Top1 recall	Top2 recall	Precision
Congress/Politics	98.7%	99.8%	33.6%	96.8%	99.4%	45.1%
Judiciary/Transport	46.9%	87.1%	71.3%	60.0%	85.4%	74.6%
Business/Finance	20.8%	30.7%	99.6%	35.8%	54.9%	98.0%
Education	24.3%	71.0%	77.5%	50.7%	78.5%	72.4%
Recreation	59.3%	69.8%	97.4%	75.0%	82.7%	93.0%
Local	14.0%	47.3%	80.0%	42.9%	73.5%	80.0%
Weather	98.2%	100.0%	100.0%	100.0%	100.0%	99.8%
Misc.	38.6%	97.7%	38.9%	90.2%	98.5%	54.1%
AVG.	50.3%	71.7%	74.8%	64.3%	81.4%	77.1%

added into the corresponding text collection(s) for classification of subsequent documents. Several different VSM-based estimation metrics were implemented. The experimental results listed in Table 2 were those obtained using conventional TF-IDF-based metrics but with different features. The obtained results listed in Tables 1 and 2 show its feasibility in both corpus storage and classification. In terms of corpus storage, it performed efficiently especially in handling variable n-gram features. In fact, the proposed PAT-tree-based method was found to be able to handle several hundred megabytes of texts during extraction of linguistic information (Chen et al. 1998). On the other hand, from the viewpoint of corpus classification, the proposed method was satisfactory in our initial experiments though more sophisticated classification algorithms still can be developed. The results obtained actually depended on the grouping of each text collection. It was observed that the more precise the pre-divided text collection, the better were the results that could be obtained. The weather section (Section 7) is an example with very high precision and recall rates. In fact, in another test with different text collections the proposed method could achieve approximately 90% recall and precision rates.

6.2 Term extraction

The second experiment was performed to study the effectiveness of the proposed approach for incremental term extraction. First, a total of 1,872 political news abstracts published in July 1997 were tested based on the testing database and classification results obtained using variable N-gram features and top-2 recall. The testing database contained 5 months of manually classified documents and one month of automatically classified documents. In this experiment, the 1,872 news documents were added in chronological order for both corpus classification and term extraction. Only the new terms extracted from the politics collection were counted. Tables 3 and 4 show the results obtained. It should be pointed out that before the processing of term extraction the political text collection contained 5 months of manually classified, and one month of automatically classified news documents which have only 45.1% precision and 99.4% top 2 recall as in Table 2. Meanwhile, the corresponding term lexicon was empty at the initial stage.

Table 3 shows the recall and precision rates obtained using different threshold values in the significance analysis. The test was performed with changes of different threshold values, including *t1*, *t2* as in the definition of LCD and RCD, the threshold of *MI*, and the threshold of the significance estimation function. According to our previous work the obtained accuracy of completeness analysis can be very high if $t1=3$, $t2=0.75$, threshold of $MI=0.2$. Previous results show that most of incomplete character strings could be filtered out with the above parameters.

The correct domain-specific terms in the testing 1,872 documents were extracted manually in advance. The terms extracted using different threshold values were compared with the correct set. However, the determination of

Table 3. The testing results for incremental term extraction using different threshold values in the significance analysis; the results were obtained from a total of 1,872 political news abstracts published in July, 1997.

S(Y)	Total extracted terms (A)	No. of correct terms extracted (B)	No. of correct terms outside dictionary (C)	Precision (B/A)	Recall
>1.5	2,291	1,374	297	0.60	0.53
>2	1,455	1,135	258	0.78	0.44
>2.5	723	593	172	0.82	0.23
>3	214	184	66	0.86	0.07

Table 4. The detailed results for incremental term extraction when the threshold value was larger than 2 in the significance analysis; the results were obtained from a total of 1,872 political news abstracts published in July 1997.

Term length (character N-gram)	No. of extracted new terms	No. of documents with new terms extracted	Average no. of document inputs can find new terms (A)	Average freq. of the extracted new terms	Average freq. as the term can be extracted
2	776	515	3.93	34.22	9.37
3	416	325	6.04	24.60	9.09
4	171	157	12.16	19.22	8.97
5	51	49	37.28	20.35	9.18
6	17	17	109.81	27.00	8.65
7	15	15	123.60	27.40	11.20
8	6	6	274.67	13.00	9.83
9	3	3	205.67	18.00	11.33
Total N-grams	1,455	814	2.41	28.95	9.25

correct domain-specific terms is not natural even by human experts. This is why we selected political news abstracts for the test, because this kind of documents is relatively easy to judge. There were two librarians participated in determining the correct set of domain-specific terms. Only the terms simultaneously that were identified by the two librarians are taken as correct. It can be seen that the best performance in terms of both recall and precision rates was obtained using a threshold value of 2. In this case, 1,135 correct terms could be extracted, and the obtained precision and recall rates were 0.78 and 0.44, respectively. Such performance is satisfactory in many applications. It is worth noting that 258 of the extracted terms were not included in the KUH dictionary, the largest

Chinese dictionary we could find, which contains more than 160,000 word entries, and is believed to include many terms used in newspapers.

Besides the above effectiveness issues, there are other issues such as the average number of document inputs can find a new term, the average frequency as the new terms to be extracted, how often the extracted terms can be used, etc. For this reason, Table 4 shows the detailed results obtained when the threshold value was larger than 2. It is noted that in the table, "term length" is the number of characters of extracted terms. Since terms with different lengths behave differently (for example, three-character terms are very often personal names, and four-character or longer terms are very often compound words), the results are shown with the term length as a special parameter. From this table, it can be observed that, on average, every 2.41 document inputs (news abstracts) can find new terms. Also, each extracted new term occurred 28.95 times in the one-month testing documents and can be extracted at the 9.25 time on average. This indicates that most of the extracted terms are not too late to be extracted and many real-time response can be performed.

The proposed approach has been tested extensively and found to be very efficient in extracting terms from online text collections. For example, as shown in Table 5, more than ten thousand political terms could be extracted from a total of 13,849 political news abstracts published from August to Decemeber in 1997. The results obtained were found to be similar to those for extraction from one month of news abstracts. With the increasing number of documents, the frequency values of the extracted terms are obviously increased but the frequency the terms can be extracted are similar. Furthermore, different corpus sizes were tested and the space and time needed to perform term extraction are listed in Table 6, which shows that the proposed approach could process a short document, such as a news article, in real time.

However, there exist some difficulties which need to be addressed. Taking all the terms with different lengths into account, it can be found that the precision rate for three-character terms was relatively low because many frequently used single-character words and two-character words are easily combined to produce three-character terms, which are not necessarily key elements for most IR and NLP applications. Close examination of the extracted terms indicates that most of them are domain-specific terms, such as proper nouns and topic terms, which are often very important in IR applications. This phenomenon is especially significant for terms with three or more characters. It is also important to note that the proposed approach is weak in extracting low-frequency terms because the extracted terms should occur at least 9.25

Table 5. The detailed results for incremental term extraction when a threshold value larger than 2 was used in the significance analysis; the results were obtained from a total of 13,849 political news abstracts published from Aug. to Dec. in 1997.

Term length (character N-gram)	No. of extracted new terms	No. of documents with new terms extracted	Average no. of document inputs can find new terms (A)	Average freq. of the extracted new terms	Average freq. as the term can be extracted
2	3,376	2,502	5.75	72.12	11.41
3	4,274	3,056	4.69	31.15	9.51
4	2,408	2,021	7.10	22.23	9.17
5	694	642	21.89	25.02	9.40
6	303	295	47.20	26.25	10.29
7	145	145	95.17	33.23	14.59
8	87	87	156.90	25.08	11.86
9	52	51	265.65	24.33	13.54
Total N-grams	11,339	6,242			

Table 6. Space and time needed to perform term extraction with respect to the different corpus sizes

Corpus	Space			Time to construct the PAT tree and perform classification (sec)	Time to extract terms (sec)
	Corpus size (K Bytes)	PAT tree size (K Bytes)	PAT tree size/ Corpus size		
C1	12	77	6.42	0.19	0.01
C2	127	670	5.28	2.82	0.02
C3	1,033	4,687	4.54	25.52	1.62
C4	10,048	44,312	4.41	306.32	28.51
C5	107,333	439,087	4.09	2381.00	283.00

times and 10.12 times as shown in Tables 4 and 5 respectively. To perform the extraction of low-frequency but domain-specific terms, we are considering the possibility of combining linguistic analysis methods.

References

Chen, C., Bai, B., et al. 1998. "PAT-tree-based Language Modeling with Initial Application of Chinese Speech Recognition Output Verification." *Proceedings of the 1998 International Symposium on Chinese Spoken Language Processing (ISCSLP)*, Singapore.

Chien, L. F. 1997. "PAT-Tree-Based Keyword Extraction for Chinese Information Retrieval", *Proceedings of ACM SIGIR '97*, Philadelphia, USA, 50–58.

Chien, L. F. 1999. "PAT-Tree-Based Adaptive Keyphrase Extraction for Intelligent Chinese Information Retrieval." *Information Processing and Management*, Elsevier Press.

Gonnet, G. H., Baeza-yates, R. et al. 1992. "New Indices for Text: Pat Trees and Pat Arrays." In *Information Retrieval Data Structures & Algorithms*, 66–82, Prentice Hall.

Kwok, K. L. 1997. "Comparing Representations in Chinese Information Retrieval." *Proceedings of ACM SIGIR '97*, 34–41.

Lewis, D. and Sparck Jones, K. 1996. "Natural Language Processing for Information Retrieval." *Communications of the ACM*, 39 (1), 92–101.

Nagao, M. and Mori, S. 1994. "A New Method of N-gram Statistics for Large Number of N and Automatic Extraction of Words and Phrases from Large Text of Japanese." *Proceedings of COLING '94*, 611–615.

Salton, G. 1989. *Automatic Text Processing: the Transformation, Analysis and Retrieval of Information by Computer*, Addison-Wesley.

Schutze, H. 1998. "The Hypertext Concordance: A Better Back-of-the-Book Index." *Proceedings of the First Workshop on Computational Terminology (Computerm '98)*, 101–104.

Smadja, F., 1993. "Retrieving Collocations from Text: Xtract." *Computational Linguistics*, 19 (1), 143–177.

Wan, T. L., Evens, M. et al. 1997. "Experiments with Automatic Indexing and a Relational Thesaurus in a Chinese Information Retrieval System." *Journal of the American Society for Information Science*, 48(12), 1068–1096.

Wu, Z., Tseng, G. 1995. "ACTS: An Automatic Chinese Text Segmentation System for Full Text Retrieval." *Journal of the American Society for Information Science*, 46 (2), 83–96.

Yamamoto, M. and Church, K. 1998. "Using Suffix Arrays to Compute Term Frequency and Document Frequency for All Substrings in a Corpus." *Proceedings of the Sixth Workshop on Very Large Corpora*, Montreal, 28–37.

Zamir, O. and Etzioni, O. 1998. "Web Document Clustering: A Feasibility Demonstration." *Proceedings of ACM SIGIR '98*, 46–53.

Zernik, U. 1991. *Lexical Acquisition: Exploiting On-line Resources to Build a Lexicon*, Lawrence Erlbaum Associates, Publishers.

Chapter 5

Knowledge-based terminology management in medicine

James J. Cimino
Columbia University

Computer systems in clinical medicine are often integrated to facilitate data sharing, but the terminologies they use are typically not integrated. There is rarely any centralized repository of terms used in various systems, and no widely accepted standards exist. An exception is the Medical Entities Dictionary (MED) at the New York Presbyterian Hospital (NYPH) in New York. The NYPH clinical computing environment includes a centralized database of coded patient information collected from various ancillary sources and translated into codes provided by the MED. The MED includes all terms used in the ancillary departments and, as such, changes in the source terminologies must be maintained in the MED. In order to support the maintenance tasks, the MED includes knowledge about the terms themselves, arranged in a semantic network. This knowledge base is used to support sophisticated maintenance tools to facilitate additions and changes to the MED and verify their consistency and appropriateness. This chapter describes the design and development of the terminology and two case examples demonstrating some of the advantages to our approach: addition of a new terminology of laboratory terms and maintenance of an existing drug terminology.

1. Introduction

Clinical information systems make extensive use of controlled terminologies for coding data about patients. However, there are few widely accepted standard medical terminologies and, as a result, most systems make use of local, home-grown terminologies. This approach becomes problematic when attempts are made to pool data from various systems to create merged data sets and central repositories. The classic example of the central repository for medical data is the electronic medical record (EMR). In an EMR, ancillary systems such as laboratory, pharmacy and radiology systems provide details about patient test results and orders, while other applications such as physician workstations and billing systems reuse the data in multiple ways. The Tower of Babel that usually exists in such arrangements produces many complications. For example, every time an ancillary system adds a new term, the developers of other applications need to be aware in order to update their systems (Huff et al. 1987). This task is complicated not only by the need for close communication among disparate, widely dispersed personnel, but also by problems in the very nature of how terminologies are updated. For example, suppose a laboratory system is sending data to a central system and a researcher is aggregating these data for analysis. If the laboratory decides to change the name of the test, the implications of this to the researcher are unclear, especially if the researcher considers this name change to be a change in meaning (Cimino et al. 1996).

The National Library of Medicine has attempted to address some of the problems related to multiple diverse medical terminologies by creating the Unified Medical Language System (UMLS) (Lindberg et al. 1993). The UMLS brings together over fifty different terminologies and seeks to unify disparate terms into a single, concept-oriented "metathesaurus". This is accomplished by making use of a set of proprietary lexical matching techniques to identify terms that appear, at least based on their names, to have similar or identical meaning. Human reviewers then determine whether the terms are, in fact, synonymous. Synonymous terms are merged into concepts.

The usefulness of the UMLS approach is limited, however. First of all, the determination of synonymy is often subjective and arbitrary; as a result, many inconsistencies occur in mapping terms into concepts (Cimino 1998). Second, the UMLS lacks explicit relationships among similar terms; thus, mapping a term from one terminology into another becomes difficult or impossible if there is not an exact match. Third, the terminologies used by hospital information systems are typically "home grown" and therefore not included among the UMLS source terminologies.

New York Presbyterian Hospital (formerly Columbia-Presbyterian Medical Center) has great need for a unified terminology to support the encoding of data in its EMR (Clayton et al. 1992). The hospital's departmental systems (that generate the clinical data stored in the EMR) do not use standard terminologies (such as those found in the UMLS). It has not been possible to impose on all systems the requirement that they use a single standard terminology, such as the Systematized Nomenclature of Human and Veterinary Medicine (SNOMED

International) (Côté et al. 1993). The only practical (however tedious) solution has been to develop our own unified terminology. In order to reduce the manual effort required, and in an attempt to produce a more consistent and high-quality result, we have made use of a combination of automated lexical and knowledge-based approaches. This chapter describes the design and development of the terminology and two case examples demonstrating some of the advantages to our approach.

2. The New York Presbyterian Hospital Medical Entities Dictionary (MED)

The overall design of the unified terminology is relatively simple, yet flexible and expressive. We provide for the inclusion of all terms from various ancillary system terminologies, along with descriptive information that allows us to convey the meanings of the terms. Individual terms are referred to as "entities" and the repository as a whole is referred to as the Medical Entities Dictionary, or MED for short. Over the years, the actual environment used to create and maintain the MED has had a variety of incarnations, including a LISP knowledge structure, a MUMPS *global*, a DB2 relational database and, most recently, a C data structure. The actual implementation has been less important than the knowledge represented in it. In each instance, we have maintained a frame-based arrangement for the entities, with each entity being assigned a unique integer identifier (the MED Code). Each frame includes character string attributes and inter-entity relationships. The attributes include items such as the name of the entity, associated names from other terminologies, codes used for the entity by other systems, synonyms, and various other literal data. The relationships make use of the MED Codes as pointers to form a semantic network, linking each frame to one or more other frames. Included in these relationships are multiple hierarchical "is-a" links that, when taken together, form a directed acyclic graph. This structure (regardless of its actual physical implementation) has allowed us to represent all necessary information about the terminologies provided by the various ancillary systems, as well as additional knowledge we have added to support the creation and maintenance of the MED (Cimino et al. 1989).

2.1 Example entity: Serum glucose test

To understand how terms are actually represented, consider a laboratory term for a serum glucose test, identified in the laboratory system with the code "CC000006" and the name "GLUC". We added this term to the MED by creating an entity that we chose to name SERUM GLUCOSE MEASUREMENT. Initially, we created it with MED Code 1600 and made it a child of (that is, gave it an is-a relationship to) the entity LABORATORY TEST. This allowed it to inherit a number of attributes, for which we could assign values, including "Name" ("Serum Glucose Test"), "Laboratory Name" ("GLUC"), "Laboratory Code" ("CC000006"), "Units" ("mg/dl"), "Low Normal Value" ("50"), and "High Normal Value" ("110").

The new entity also inherited the ability to form relationships to other classes of entities. One such class is SPECIMEN. The laboratory system indicated that the specimen for GLUC was something called "SERUM". Once we added this term as an entity (with MED Code 169, named CLINICAL CHEMISTRY SERUM SPECIMEN, laboratory name "SERUM", and laboratory code "CC0002") we could link the two concepts with the relationship "Has Specimen".

We often need to provide additional information about terms, in order to represent their meaning. For example, SERUM GLUCOSE MEASUREMENT inherits the relationship "Substance Measured". We provide definitional information about the entity by instantiating this relationship with a link to the entity GLUCOSE (MED Code 31987). Taken together, we consider the knowledge included in the MED to form a definition of the entity, i.e. "SERUM GLUCOSE MEASUREMENT is a laboratory test that has specimen SERUM and measures GLUCOSE". Note that while the entity's name suggests this definition, the definition consists of semantic, not lexical, information.

2.2 Example class: Serum glucose tests

The laboratory system includes several codes for specific tests measuring glucose in serum, while another application, the clinical alerting system (that identifies potential problems to issue alerts and reminders), includes a more general term SERUM GLUCOSE. In the MED, the more specific entities are positioned as children of the more general entity. Thus, when the alerting system requests a "Serum Glucose", the MED can provide the codes for the more specific tests that actually appear in the patient database. It is therefore imperative that, when new test terms are added to the laboratory system, they also be added to the MED in the proper class. Because the MED allows multiple classification (arranged as a directed acyclic graph of "is a" relationships), the problem becomes making sure that new terms are added to *all* relevant classes and that newly added classes subsume all relevant terms.

We can make use of the definitional information in the MED to help with this classification task. If we identify an entity that we believe is a superclass of other entities, we can provide definitional information about the entity and then search the MED for entities with matching definitions. The general algorithm is:

For each entity in the MED not equal to the entity of interest
    Consider the entity to be a possible child
    For each definitional attribute of the entity of interest
        If the attribute has a value
            If the entity does not have the attribute **or**
                If the entity has a value that is not equal to the entity of interest's value **and**
                    the entity has a value that is not a descendant of the entity of interest's value
                Then the entity is not a possible child
    If the entity is still considered a possible child, make it a child of the entity of interest

Thus, when we added the term SERUM GLUCOSE TESTS from the decision support system, we created an entity (MED Code 32703) and gave a Substance-Measured relationship to Glucose and a Has-Specimen relationship to SERUM CHEMISTRY SPECIMEN (MED Code 2393). Because Entities 1600 and 32703 match on Substance-Measured (Glucose) and because 1600 is linked to a specimen term that is a child of SERUM CHEMISTRY SPECIMEN, 1600 qualifies as a child of 32703. Over all, four such children were found in the MED.

Over the years, the MED has continued to be constructed in this manner (Cimino et al. 1994). Today, the MED contains 60,000 terms from some twenty different systems. Each entity has from one to twelve is-a relationships (average, 1.4). There are over 140,000 string-valued attributes and over 180,000 non-hierarchical semantic relationships. As the MED has grown in size, its maintenance has become increasingly difficult. Tools that can take advantage of the knowledge in the MED are extremely useful for assisting with maintenance tasks. We will consider two such tasks here and show how the knowledge-based approach to terminology representation has proven beneficial.

3. Adding new laboratory terminologies

The first terms to be placed in the MED, in 1989, were those of the clinical laboratory system. This locally developed system included 2309 terms for individual tests, procedures (panels of tests), specimens and test results. As described in Section 2, each term was added to the MED along with attributes and relationship information. For the most part, this additional information was provided by the laboratory system. Additional descriptive information was added to provide what was empirically considered to constitute appropriate definitions for the terms. This information was used to automatically generate a hierarchy (Cimino et al. 1990). Over the subsequent 5 years, the laboratory terminology remained relatively stable, with the addition of 224 terms (less than a 10% increase).

3.1 Replacing a laboratory system

In 1994, a new commercial laboratory system was purchased. The new system provided a number of new capabilities for the laboratories, including opportunities to expand the coding of tests and results. As a consequence, the new terminology consisted of 5291 terms. Although there was some correspondence between the old and new terminologies, there were no formal translation capabilities, and due to some changes in the modeling of tests and results in the new system, one-to-one correspondence was rare. Therefore, it was necessary to place all of the terms from the new terminology into the MED as entirely new entities, requiring their own classification. Because the EMR still contained data encoded with the previous terminology, it was not possible to delete the old term set and replace it with the new term set; the two terminologies had to coexist in the MED. Simply adding the new terms was insufficient, however, because they needed to be classified properly among the old terms. For example, the new serum glucose test terms needed to be added as children of MED Code 32703 (see Section 2). The new terminology was not finalized until mid-June of 1994 with an expected go-live date of July 24, 1994. Given this time frame, attempting to add the 5291 new terms in a coordinated manner was not possible using manual methods.

The new terms were analyzed with a combination of automated lexical and knowledge-based approaches. Lexical methods included simple string matching using methods that ignore punctuation and case and allowed matching based on identical words and, if necessary, left stemming. Knowledge-based methods were used to restrict terms to specific classes. For example, when matching the new test term "GLUCOSE" (laboratory code "GLU"), 122 terms were found in the MED containing this word. Of these, 88 were in the class LABORATORY TEST.

Manual review of these 88 terms would identify the appropriate class for the new term. However, additional knowledge was used to restrict the match even further. Because the new test was known to have the specimen GOLD-TOP SERUM SPECIMEN, that has as its "Sampled Substance" the entity SERUM, the 88 terms could be further restricted to retain only those test terms for which the related specimen was related (in the MED) to SERUM. This reduced the selections to five, of which four were individual tests and only one was a test class. Thus, in this example, automated lexical and semantic matching identified a single likely class into which the new term could be placed.

Many of the test terms in the old terminology were "one of a kind" and so no specimen-and-measured-substance class had been created. In these cases, we took a different approach. The first step involved linking the test term to its measured substance. Next we looked for other test terms linked to that substance term. If the term was associated with a specimen term that matched the new term (based on the sampled substance, as in the previous example) we considered whether the new term and the old term(s) should be grouped into a new class. For example, when adding the new test term "Ceruloplasmin" (laboratory code "CERU"), we were able to link it (by name matching) to the substance term CERULOPLASMIN (MED Code 31936). This latter term was linked to a single old test term "CERULO" (MED Code 1831). Because the specimens of the old term (SPECIAL CHEMISTRY SERUM SPECIMEN) and the new term (GOLD-TOP SERUM SPECIMEN) were both linked to SERUM, we were able to create a new class of SERUM CERULOPLASMIN TESTS and add both terms to it as children. Figure 1 shows an example of this new class creation (in this case, for two tests that both measure Creatine Kinase).

As a result of this process, all of the new 5291 terms were added to the MED by the July 24 "go live" date. When the interface between the laboratory system and the central repository was activated, all laboratory data were successfully translated to MED codes for storage, and all programs that displayed, aggregated or otherwise reused these data continued to function without modification.

3.2 Adding a new laboratory system

Before 1997, the MED served as the terminology repository for Presbyterian Hospital (PH), the principal teaching hospital affiliated with Columbia University.

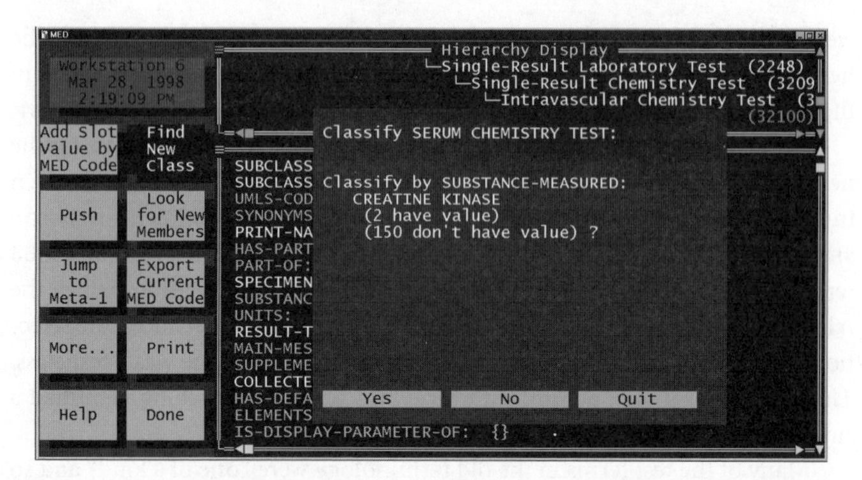

Figure 1. Example of new class discovery. The MED editor has been directed to find a new subclass of "Serum Chemistry Test", by finding concepts with the same value in their "Substance-Measured" slot. Here, it proposes grouping two tests that measure "Creatine Kinase".

In 1997, PH and New York Hospital (NYH) merged into New York Presbyterian Hospital (NYPH). Part of the merger agreement included a plan to consolidate clinical systems and their information. Although NYH had a repository for some data (including laboratory), there was no capability to expand to include PH data. It was therefore decided that the PH repository would be expanded to include NYH. A first step in this process was to include all NYH laboratory terms in the MED. The laboratory system was able to produce a list of test names and codes, but could produce no information about the associated specimen nor about the substances measured by the tests. In order to determine the specimen, we identified those tests with "serum", "plasma", "blood", "urine" and "CSF" (cerebrospinal fluid) in their names. We then manually matched the test names to substances already in the MED. Through this process, we were able to link 445 NYH laboratory terms to specimen terms and measured substance terms. Once this additional knowledge was in place, our tools were able to place the terms in their appropriate classes in a manner similar to the ones described in Section 3.1. As of this writing, we are waiting for the NYH laboratory personnel to provide additional information about their terminology. The addition of their terms to the MED has allowed successful testing of the storage of NYH data in the repository and its display by the clinical information system. In addition, the 445 terms that have been properly classified can be used by functions such as summary display, aggregation and automated decision support.

3.3 Linking the MED to LOINC

In the past two years, a new standard for laboratory terminology has been developed, called Logical Observations, Identifiers, Names and Codes (LOINC) (Forrey et al. 1996). The terms in LOINC contain explicit information about specimens, measured substances, units of measure, etc., similar to the MED model. LOINC is an emerging standard for exchanging health information across institutions and is being adopted for tasks such as reporting communicable diseases to the Centers for Disease Control. We therefore sought to develop techniques for mapping MED terms to LOINC and vice versa.

Each LOINC term has a numeric code, with a check digit, and a "fully specified name", containing the analyte (substance measured), the property of the substance measured (such as its concentration), the time course of the test measurement (such as a single point in time or 24 hours), the specimen, and method (quantitative or qualitative). For example, the LOINC term with code 6777–7 has the fully specified name "GLUCOSE|MCNC|PT|SER|QN", indicating that it is a quantitative measurement of the mass concentration of glucose in serum at a single time point.

We were easily able to adapt the MED model to accommodate the LOINC model, simply by adding attributes for the various parts of the LOINC names to existing concepts and then filling in the associated values. Analyte names were matched using lexical string matching, specimens were matched manually (there are only 50 in the MED), and the remainder of the attributes were assigned based on the "Units" attribute of the test terms. For example, if the units attribute for a test was "mg/dl" (milligrams per deciliter), the LOINC attributes are "mass concentration", "point", and "quantitative". If the value of the "Units" attribute was "mg/24hr" (milligrams per 24 hours), the LOINC attributes are "mass rate", "24 hour", and "quantitative".

Using the semantic information in the MED, it is possible to translate MED Codes to LOINC codes by selecting appropriate attributes from the test entities or other entities related to them. For example, MED Code 1600 is related to GLUCOSE and SERUM SPECIMEN (that provide "GLUCOSE" and "SER", respectively) and provides "MCNC", "PT" and "QN". Once assembled, this allows us to recognize that the LOINC code for MED Code 1600 is 6777–7.

Shortly after this work was done, although we did not anticipate it, NYPH had a sudden need to provide data coded in LOINC to a regulatory agency. We were able to provide a response in a matter of minutes. Without the MED, the task would have required laborious manual mapping. In addition, we have been exploring ways to pool data from multiple institutions for clinical research purposes and have had some success due to our ability to map from MED to LOINC (Baorto 1997).

4. Maintaining the pharmacy terminology

In 1993, Presbyterian Hospital purchased a commercial pharmacy system. This system contributed several new terminologies to the MED, including American Hospital Formulary System (AHFS) codes (American Society of Hospital Pharmacists, 1988), allergy classes, Drug Enforcement Agency (DEA) classes, and the drugs themselves. For the most part, these terminologies are stable. However, the hospital formulary is constantly changing and since the initial 2091 drug terms were placed in the MED, an additional 2510 have been added. These inclusions can occur on a daily basis and as soon as they occur, they may appear in drug order information that is transmitted from the pharmacy system to the central patient database. Therefore, it has become imperative that the MED updates occur in a timely manner.

4.1 Adding new terms automatically

In response to this need, an automated maintenance program was created. This program directly accesses, via a local area network, a formulary file on the pharmacy's computer and compares the information in this file with the information in the MED. When information about a drug has changed, the program calls the MED Editor functions needed to make the update. When a new drug is encountered, the program determines a likely position in the MED hierarchy for placing the new drug, based on information such as its AHFS code, generic ingredients, allergy codes, etc. In the fully automated mode, the program then adds the new drug to the MED. In the interactive mode, it suggests a position and allows the user to agree or to browse the MED and select a new position. The program uses several different techniques to carry out this task. We will describe one here to illustrate how knowledge in the MED is used to support maintenance tasks.

On March 28, 1998, a new drug ("Erythromycin Estolate 25mg/ml") was added to the hospital formulary. When the update program encountered it, it attempted to match the descriptive information provided by the pharmacy system with knowledge already in the MED. First, it identified the key ingredient of the drug to be the chemical "Erythromycin Estolate". The program was unable to find a chemical entity in the MED that matched this term. It was also unable to find a drug class that contained this string in its name. It then resorted to using the AHFS code for the drug term to find the corresponding

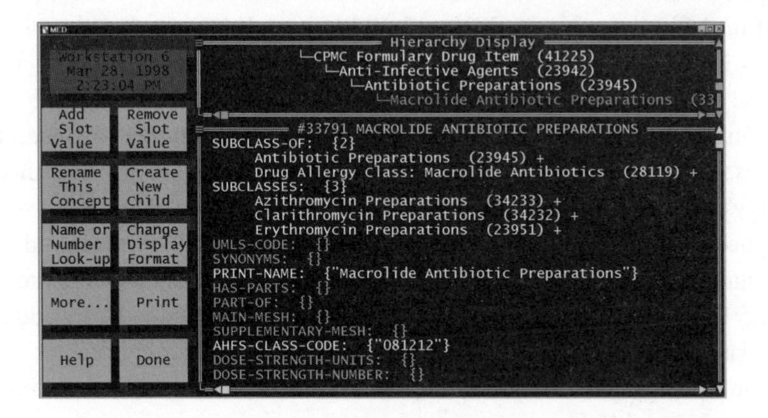

Figure 2. Helping the user find the right class in the MED. Here, the user is adding a new drug ("Erythromycin Estolate 25mg/ml"). The pharmacy system has not provided specific information about the ingredients (other than the name) but has indicated the drug is classified as a "Macrolide Antibiotic". The editor shows the user this class, and it can readily be seen that a better subclass, "Erythromycin Preparations" exists.

AHFS drug class. As shown in Figure 2, the program suggested adding it as a child of the class MACROLIDE ANTIBIOTIC PREPARATIONS. When the user examined this class in the MED, a better class was found (ERYTHROMYCIN PREPARATIONS) that was then used by the update program as the appropriate class for the new drug term. Note that the program did not attempt match the string "Erythromycin" alone. In our experience, using parts of the chemical name for lexical searching has not proven to be useful, because so many words in drug names appear in many unrelated chemical compound names. The program would not know, for example, whether to match on "Erythromycin" or on "Estolate". However, if the MED did contain the chemical entity ERYTHROMYCIN ESTOLATE and that entity was identified as a child of ERYTHROMYCIN, then the program would have been able to propose ERYTHROMYCIN PREPARATIONS as a possible appropriate class for the new drug term.

4.2 Auditing the knowledge in the MED

In addition to assisting with the addition of new drug terms, the update program performs a series of audits on the consistency of the knowledge in the MED. This can serve to catch errors that are introduced by the human participant in the update process. More often, however, it has succeeded in finding errors in the knowledge provided by the pharmacy system. Again, there are several different techniques used by the program; we will describe one here.

One of the ways drugs are added to the MED is as children of preparation classes, such as the erythromycin example above. Drugs are also classified by allergy classes. For example, each streptomycin drug in the pharmacy system is assigned (or supposed to be assigned) the allergy code "10", corresponding to "Aminoglycoside Allergy". The MED contains the corresponding entity for this allergy class and all drugs added to the MED with allergy code 10 are added to this class. Periodically, we review drug classes to see if their children are all in the same allergy class. As a result, the class STREPTOMYCIN PREPARATIONS has been made a child of AMINOGLYCOSIDE ALLERGY.

One day, the drug "Streptomycin 1 gm Vial" was added to the MED. Because of its ingredient, it was made a child of STREPTOMYCIN PREPARATIONS. At this point, the auditing program noticed that although the drug term was a descendant of STREPTOMYCIN ALLERGY, it did not have allergy code 10 and generated the message:

> Streptomycin 1 gm Vial in allergy class AMINOGLYCOSIDE ALLERGY but doesn't have code 10.

A message such as this could be generated if the preparation class has been placed in the wrong allergy class. Thus far, however, these messages are generated because of missing allergy codes in the pharmacy system. Such a situation can lead to the pharmacy allowing streptomycin to be prescribed to a patient with an allergy to that drug. When such information is discovered during MED editing, it is provided to the pharmacy so that the formulary database can be corrected. The pharmacy, in turn, provides this information to the database vendor who, in turn can correct the information provided to thousands of pharmacies throughout the United States.

5. Discussion

Since its inception, the MED has been growing at a fairly constant rate of 6000 terms per year and now contains 60,000 entities. MED concepts are used to encode patient data, provide aggregation classes and high-level concepts for applications as mundane as billing and as exotic as natural language processing and automated decision support. The maintenance of such a resource obviously requires a huge effort and the inclusion of knowledge about terms only adds to the work.

There are no clear guidelines regarding the appropriate degree of knowledge needed for entity "definitions". The attributes we chose to include were selected empirically, based on our experience with terminology maintenance. Cogent arguments can be made for providing sufficient information to allow the differentiation, on a semantic basis, of each entity in the MED from every other entity (Campbell et al. 1998). In some cases, this is possible; for example, each drug term can be differentiated based on its form, strength and manufacturer. In other cases, however, it is impractical; for example, the laboratory system may arbitrarily add (for administrative reasons) new test terms that are identical to existing ones. In still other cases, we lack sufficient resources to provide full descriptions; for example, we simply cannot create descriptions for the 25,000 disease terms in the MED. However, full specification for many terms may be available from other sources that are now under development from standards organizations (Spackman et al. 1998).

There may be some domains within the MED that simply will not lend themselves to clear descriptions, using the knowledge representation techniques we have chosen. For example, we cannot provide formal definitions for chemical terms because we have no mechanism for explicating chemical formulae through semantic net (simply linking DEXTROSE to CARBON, HYDROGEN, and OXYGEN would not allow us to differentiate it from FRUCTOSE, let alone its stereoisomer LEVULOSE).

The domains in the MED that lend themselves well to formal definitions tend to be the man-made artifacts, such as drugs and tests. In these cases, because people create them, they can be enumerated and their meaning can be stated unequivocally. For terms derived from our observations of the natural world, however, there is much disagreement about how to describe them appropriately. There are many different naming systems for leukemias, for example.

Despite these challenges to our approach, the use of knowledge to describe entities in a controlled terminology has proven to be manageable and practical in several well-defined situations, including laboratory tests and drugs. The original argument in favor of this additional knowledge was that sophisticated terminology maintenance tools could be created that would permit automation of some of the work and yield a more consistent, higher quality terminology. Experience to date has substantiated this claim. New terminologies are added much sooner than would be possible with manual methods and the quality has been higher than that of the original source terminologies. As an additional benefit, the MED has been able to serve as a knowledge base for nonmaintenance functions, such as automated transfer of patient data to a diagnostic expert system (Elhanan et al. 1996) and linking medical records to relevant online medical information resources (Cimino et al. 1997).

Other approaches to the creation and maintenance of large-scale controlled medical terminologies have largely ignored knowledge-based approaches. The UMLS is the foremost example, with its huge Metathesaurus created using pure lexical matching techniques, followed by human review. The decision to follow a lexical rather than semantic model was made consciously and with good reason (Humphreys et al. 1998). Nevertheless, the UMLS has very limited ability to support some of the intelligent functions capable with the MED, such as editing, auditing, and information interchange. Other developers have recently embraced the knowledge-based approach in order to achieve more consistent, high-quality, and ultimately more maintainable terminologies (Spackman et al. 1998).

6. Conclusion

The addition of formal descriptive knowledge to a controlled medical terminology has supported a wide variety of capabilities, including the ability to carry out large maintenance tasks with relative ease. The use of the knowledge in an "introspective" manner has led directly to improvements in the quality of the MED and thereby ultimately to improved patient care.

References

American Society of Hospital Pharmacists. 1988. *American Hospital Formulary Service Drug Information.* Bethesda (MD), 1988.

Baorto D.M., Cimino J.J., Parvin C.A. and Kahn M.G. 1997. "Using Logical Observation Identifier Names and Codes (LOINC) to exchange laboratory data among three academic hospitals." *Journal of the American Medical Informatics Association*; 4(Suppl): 96–100.

Campbell K.E., Cohn S.P., Chute C.G., Shortliffe E.H. and Rennels G. 1998. "Scalable methodologies for distributed development of logic-based convergent medical terminology." In *Methods of Information in Medicine* 37 (4–5): 426–439.

Cimino J.J., Hripcsak G., Johnson S.B. and Clayton P.D. 1989. "Designing an introspective, controlled medical vocabulary." In *Proceedings of the Thirteenth Annual Symposium on Computer Applications in Medical Care*, Kingsland L.W. (ed.), 513–518. New York, NY: IEEE Computer Society Press.

Cimino J.J., Hripcsak G., Johnson S.B., Friedman C., Fink D.J. and Clayton P.D. 1990. "UMLS as knowledge base — a rule-based expert system approach to controlled medical vocabulary management." In *Proceedings of the Fourteenth Annual Symposium on Computer Applications in Medical Care*, Miller R.A. (ed.), 175–180. New York, NY: IEEE Computer Society Press.

Cimino J.J., Clayton P.D., Hripcsak G. and Johnson S.B. 1994. "Knowledge-based approaches to the maintenance of a large controlled medical terminology." *Journal of the American Medical Informatics Association* 1 (1): 35–50.

Cimino J.J. 1996. "Formal descriptions and adaptive mechanisms for changes in controlled medical vocabularies." *Methods of Information in Medicine* 35 (3): 202–210.

Cimino J.J., Elhanan G. and Zeng Q. 1997. "Supporting Infobuttons with Terminological Knowledge." *Journal of the American Medical Informatics Association* 4 (Suppl): 528–532.

Cimino J.J. 1998. "Auditing the Unified Medical Language System with semantic methods." *Journal of the American Medical Informatics Association* 4 (1): 41–51.

Clayton P.D., Sideli R.V. and Sengupta S. 1992. "Open architecture and integrated information at Columbia-Presbyterian Medical Center" *MD Computing* 9 (5): 297–303.

Côté R.A., Rothwell D.J., Beckett R.S., Palotay J.L. and Brochu L. (eds). 1993. *The Systematized Nomenclature of Human and Veterinary Medicine: SNOMED International.* Northfield, IL: College of American Pathologists.

Elhanan G., Socratous S.A. and Cimino J.J. 1996. 'Integrating DXplain into a Clinical Information System using the World Wide Web." In *Proceedings of the American Medical Informatics Association Annual Fall Symposium (formerly SCAMC)*, Cimino J.J. (ed.), 348–352. Philadelphia, PA: Hanley & Belfus.

Forrey A.W., McDonald C.J., DeMoor G., Huff S.M., Leaville D., Leland D., Fiers T., Charles L., Griffin B., Stalling F., Tullis A., Hutchins K. and Baenziger J. 1996. "Logical observation identifier names and codes (LOINC) database: a public use set of codes and names for electronic reporting of clinical laboratory test results." *Clinical Chemistry* 42: 81–90.

Huff S.M., Craig R.B., Gould B.L., Castagno D.L. and Smilan R.E. 1987. "Medical data dictionary for decision support applications." In *Proceedings of the Eleventh Annual*

Symposium on Computer Applications in Medical Care, Stead W. W. (ed.), 310–317. New York, NY: IEEE Computer Society Press.

Humphreys B. L., Lindberg D. A., Schoolman H. M. and Barnett G. O. 1998. "The Unified Medical Language System: an informatics research collaboration." *Journal of the American Medical Informatics Association* 5 (1): 1–11.

Lindberg D. A. B., Humphreys B. L. and McCray A. T. 1993. "The Unified Medical Language System." *Methods of Information in Medicine* 32 (4): 281–291.

Spackman, K.A and Campbell, K. E. 1998. "Compositional concept representation using SNOMED: towards further convergence of clinical terminologies." *Journal of the American Medical Informatics Association*; 5(Suppl): 740–744.

Chapter 6

Searching for and identifying conceptual relationships via a corpus-based approach to a Terminological Knowledge Base (CTKB)

Method and Results*

Anne Condamines and Josette Rebeyrolle
CNRS / Université Toulouse-le Mirail

The aim of this paper is to provide an effective method for constructing a Corpus-based Terminological Knowledge Base — CTKB. The two stages of the method based on linguistic knowledge are outlined: the identification of candidate-terms and the identification of conceptual relationships. This method is applied to a French corpus and the results are assessed from the point of view of various applications.

Introduction

Ever since the concept of a Terminological Knowledge Base (TKB) was first created (Meyer et al. 1992), a number of teams have worked on defining models, methods and formalisms associated with this new concept. Research is now directed into two distinct fields depending on the interests of the research teams. Those with a background in Artificial Intelligence have worked on issues related to the formalization of terminological data, which has resulted in modeling experiments using conceptual graphs (Gillam and Ahmad 1996) or using descriptive logic (Biébow and Szulman 1997). Research teams, including our own, with a background in linguistics or terminology have been more interested in the extraction of data from texts. The concept of the TKB has now been revised and re-examined according to our aims to such an extent that it has become justified to re-organize the work into two categories. This is our conclusion after taking part in a number of multi-disciplinary projects.[1] In this paper, we describe the construction and validation of a TKB as a corpus-based approach to a terminological knowledge base (the CTKB), as opposed to an application-based and formalized TKB (ATKB). The main point of this paper is the presentation of the method for searching for and identifying conceptual relationships which play a very important role both in selecting terms and in constructing a model of corpus.

The results presented here aim to show the feasibility of constructing a CTKB. We show that it is possible, with appropriate systems and linguistic interpretation, to model a text, particularly the conceptual relationships contained in it. This demonstration is based on our most recent experiments, which have been carried out using a corpus supplied by the EDF (French State Electricity Board). However, our involvement with this type of work dates from around five years ago with corpora from Matra Marconi Space (Condamines and Amsili 1993), Aérospatiale, and the Centre National d'Etudes Spatiales. We firstly describe the CTKB model that we have set up and we outline a data constitution method. Finally, we will demonstrate the validity of the CTKB concept, both as a corpus model, as well as in its use in a number of different applications.

1. The CTKB

This section presents the main characteristics of a CTKB and the data model that we have proposed.

1.1 CTKB characteristics

Our experience in constructing terminological knowledge bases from corpora enables us to list the following characteristics for a CTKB:

- The construction of the CTKB is not dependent on a given application. Any choice can be justified according to the text studied (cf. 3.), using linguistic analyses.
- Such a CTKB is not formalized. There are no coherence or completeness calculations, although such calculations could be envisaged to assist the linguist/terminologist to design the CTKB.
- Experts, if required at all, are only brought in for the final stage to guarantee the validity of the CTKB concerning the textual content (and not with respect to their knowledge of either the domain or of a particular field of application).

This CTKB is conceived as a kind of text modeling (which we here contrast with formalization), a kind of pre-processing which can be used by anyone having to read the text for a specific application. The CTKB must be usable in a variety of applications, to create an index or to rewrite the text (as planned in the GIS project) or again to create a knowledge base system for a specific application. The CTKB data can be modified and adapted as required, such modifications being justified by the application and/or the formalization.

We also describe how this CTKB has been used for different applications (cf. 4.).

1.2 The CTKB model

In the last few years, we have developed a methodology for defining a CTKB model which would allow us to understand the functioning of terms and concepts in a given corpus. The four fields in this model contain the following information:

- The "terms" contains strictly linguistic data (type and gender, form variants, acronyms, abbreviations, etc.).
- The "concepts" contains data concerning the concept denoted by the term in the form of a definition and of explicit conceptual relationships. The choice of relationships is not restricted, but they are strictly defined.
- The "term/concept link" contains information on how valid the term is for the description of a particular concept, that is, its use in a given sub-domain or company, for example.

The "corpus" is used to establish the links between a term and its occurrences in the text which the CTKB models. For example, the text is also used to illustrate each Term — Conceptual relationship — Term triple.

The specification and development of a management and consultation tool (GEDITERM, cf. Aussenac 1999) based on this model has been carried out by our colleagues at the 'Institut de Recherche en Informatique de Toulouse', Nathalie Aussenac's team.

2. Method for constructing a CTKB

The method we propose for constructing a CTKB is intended to meet the following requirements:

To automate each stage of the research using corpus-processing systems.

To define systematic criteria in order to evaluate, interpret and organize the results provided by these systems.

This method is based on the same assumption as in Pearson (1998). Pearson's goal is to discover explanations of terms as input for the formulations of specialized definitions. Meyer and her team (Meyer this volume) have exactly the same goal when they identify knowledge-rich contexts in order to develop knowledge-extractions tools. As far as we are concerned, our aim is to build a model of the text, i.e., a CTKB.

We describe here the method for identifying the CTKB model's data. It consists of two major steps:

Identifying Candidate Terms (2.1).

Identifying conceptual relationships. This main step will be described in details below (2.2).

2.1 Identifying Candidate Terms

This involves establishing a list of Candidate Terms which will then be used for the identification of conceptual relationships on the basis of the results yielded by the terminological extraction systems.

2.1.1 *Noun and adjective Candidate Terms*

The tools for identifying noun and adjective phrases (cf. Daille et al. 1994; Bourigault et al. 1996; Enguehard and Pantéra 1995) are used both to identify phrasal variants and to establish an initial list of terms. However, the lists of phrases provided by these systems contain certain word groups which are not real terms such as, *complément du paragraphe (addition to paragraph), mise à jour du présent document* (*update of current document)*, etc. We have therefore defined a set of relatively stable criteria for removing this type of phrase and for delimiting a relevant sub-set of Candidate Terms. To this list are added the term variants, ellipsis and acronyms which are also provided by some terminology extraction systems, in order to search all the conceptual relationships. During the search for conceptual relationships, acronyms and variants are considered as denoting the same concept and can be substituted for the Candidate Terms in order to increase the search coverage.

2.1.2 *Verb Candidate Terms*

The majority of Candidate Terms Extraction Systems only selects noun phrases and sometimes a few adjectives. It is nevertheless possible to identify verb phrases from the noun phrases (for example, *gestion de configuration (configuration management)/gérer la configuration (managing the configuration)*). It is then necessary to manually look for those effectively used in the corpus. This initial list of verbs is then expanded by studying the conceptual relationships.

2.2 Searching for and identifying conceptual relationships

The search for conceptual relationships plays an important role in building a CTKB as long as it is mainly a model of the text content. From this point of view, the most important knowledge within the text is conveyed by conceptual (or semantic) relationships. Conceptual relationships are provided by some parts of the text, by means of certain linguistic patterns, to which we can associate a non-ambiguous interpretation. This interpretation consists in a binary relationship between two elements. We are particularly interested in identifying linguistic patterns to which we can associate a non-ambiguous interpretation, it means to which all the linguistic constraints are described.
Searching for conceptual relationships consists in two complementary steps: searching for taxonomies and searching for syntagmatic relationships.

2.2.1 *Searching for taxonomies*

This first step aims at building classes, i.e. hierarchies of concepts characterized by the same inherited feature(s). Two kinds of linguistics patterns are used for searching concepts:

- those used for expressing hyponymy relationships,
- others used for expressing meronymic relationships. These linguistic patterns are the same as for meronymic relationships but with the additional constraint that the heads of the related Candidate Terms have to be the same.[2] This is exemplified by the relationship between *departmental road network, national road network* and *communal road network.* These noun phrases may be considered as meronyms of *national network.* They have the same head: *road network* and they occur with meronymic patterns: *A road network is composed of a national road network, and a regional road network.* Note that hyperonymic contexts may also be used: *the national road network is the road network managed by national organisms.* Such hyperonymic contexts are possible because all the features of the national network are inherited by the other kinds of road network.

So when either hyperonymic patterns or meronymic patterns with repeated heads occur, we consider that the connected Candidate Terms may constitute a taxonomy. We start with these patterns for two main reasons.

a. These patterns are well known. We can think that most of them are context-free and may be used in any corpus (even if they are not always used). We derived this assumption from the experiment proposed by Morin (1999) for French patterns. By searching automatically recurrent contexts combined with pairs of hyperonym terms in an agricultural corpus, he identified almost the same patterns as the ones identified by Borillo (1996) intuitively. So, we can conclude that, for the two relationships, some specific patterns may appear in some corpora but the core set of patterns is stable and can be used as a starting point. We have compiled and used hyperonymic and meronymic French linguistic patterns proposed by Borillo (1996) and Jackiewicz (1996).

b. The taxonomies we obtain by using theses patterns are characterized by the fact that all members have one or more shared features. So, we think that, in some contexts, these members are substitutable. In the second part of the research (Section 3), we will show how we exploit this paradigmatic characteristic in order to identify syntagmatic relationships.

Taxonomies are built following two steps:

1. Looking in the corpus for contexts where one of the patterns appears in association with two Candidate Terms, for example:

a CT1 is a CT2 which
a CT1 is split into CT2 and CT3 (CT1, CT2 and CT3 have the same head).

Several types of results are obtained:

– bad contexts; i.e. contexts not showing the expected relationship or showing the good relationship but within a specific or subjective point of view, as in the following example: *Le plan de développement est le document le plus difficile à réaliser (The development plan is the most difficult document to write)*. Such contexts are abandoned.

– good contexts, i.e. contexts showing the expected relationship with a generic point of view. In this case, lists of term pairs are created.

2. Building taxonomies: term pairs are combined in order to build hierarchies. All pairs of terms that share a common term may be combined.
If we have T1 R T2, T2 R T3, T4 R T3, we can build the following hierarchy:

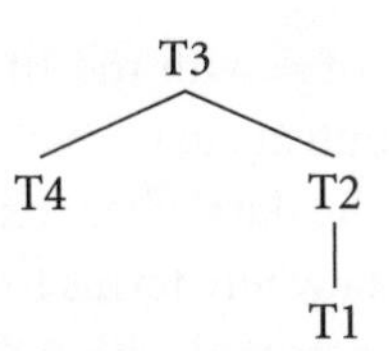

Then, we build several taxonomies with at least one common feature (see below examples of such taxonomies).

Note that when a Candidate Term has been identified, combined with a linguistic pattern, it becomes a term.

2.2.2 *Searching for syntagmatic relationships*

In order to search for syntagmatic relationships, we start from the hypothesis that in corpora, these relations may be identified by means of linguistic patterns including elements belonging to taxonomies. So, we try to identify syntagmatic relationships from paradigmatic relationships; these paradigmatic relationships are the ones used for building taxonomies in the previous step. Then, the aim is to identify both conceptual relationships and their associated linguistic patterns; the method consists in combining taxonomies two by two.

1. In the corpus, each Candidate Term is marked up with the feature(s) of the taxonomy to which it belongs.
2. An extract of each taxonomy is combined with an extract of all the other taxonomies in order to bring out contexts where the same relationship is potentially expressed. Consider the following taxonomies A and B and their members $CT^3{}_1A$ to CT_nA, for the first one and CT_1B to CT_mB, for the other one. Data to be analyzed would be all the combinations between all the CT of the A taxonymy with all the CT of the second (B).

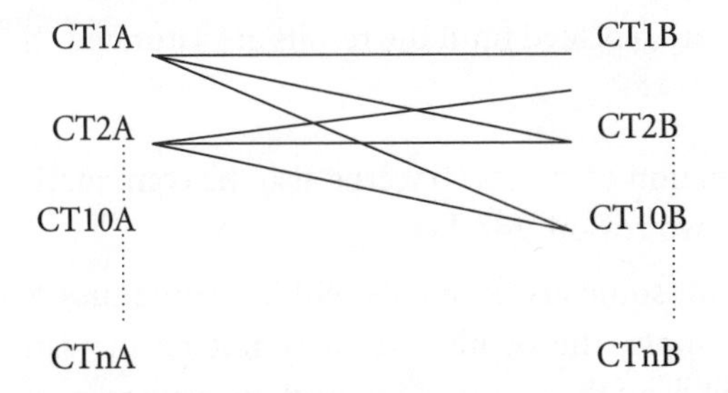

Note that for each combination, several contexts may be provided. Finally, contexts to be analyze may be very numerous. So, we reduce the number of the examined combinations by choosing arbitrarily to analyze only the combinations between the 10 first members of A with the 10 first members of B. Even with this selection the number of contexts to be analyzed may be very high. If this is the case, we can first examine the data where terms from A are combined with terms from B and then, the data where terms from B occur with terms from A. Actually, the combinations are oriented within the sentence, they are not always reversible. In some cases (but not all), the reversible combination corresponds to the passive voice and there is only one triple CT_1 R CT_2, but in other cases, there are two triples CT_1 R_1 CT_2 and CT_2 R_2 CT_1.

The aim of the analysis is to identify recurrent contexts that may be interpreted as referring to the same relationship. At this point we use our linguistic knowledge allowing us to interpret these contexts as referring to the same relationship. These contexts may either be equal, contain similar elements, or be completely different. What is important is that they can refer to the same relationship.

With such an approach, we get a lot of noise because it is not frequent that the context between two terms, even if they potentially label connected concepts, refers to the concerned relationship.

3. For each relationship, all the linguistic patterns are strictly specified with all the restrictions (morphologic, semantic and syntactic) in order that by applying them, we get as little noise as possible.

4. The linguistic patterns identified are projected onto the corpus, with all the Candidate Terms (not just with the CT from the classes concerned). The aim is to identify new pairs of terms. At the same time, each term is added to the relevant taxonomy.

5. These new pairs of terms are projected onto the corpus so as to bring out new patterns.

Steps 3, 4 and 5 are repeated until the results are saturated.

Notes:

a. The combination of classes concerns also the combination within a single class. There are two reasons for this:

On the one hand, some artificial cuts within taxonomies may appear in the corpus. For example, the depth level may not be the same within all the taxonomies built from the corpus. Moreover, in some cases, just one taxonomy is extracted from the corpus whereas it seems that it could be split up into two or more sub-taxonomies. In some other cases, it seems that taxonomies could be combined, even if no superordinate concept appears in the corpus.

On the other hand, the unity of each taxonomy is very often given just by one feature (see 3.3 for examples). It is possible for elements having just one common feature to be linked by a conceptual relationship. Take the case of the human taxonomy. It is very common to meet nouns with human feature linked by a conceptual relationship within corpora. For example, a *human may (cure, be in charge of, communicate with...) an other human.* So, the fact that two Candidate Terms may be in the same taxonomy does not prevent themselves from being linked by a relationship other than the hyperonymic one.

b. In the case of a small corpus, the second stage may be applied to all the elements of the classes, not just to a subset of them. In such case, steps 4- and 5- are omitted.

c. One of our aims is to amass linguistic patterns associated both with relationships and corpus type (domain, text genre). So, in the future, the second step will begin with the application of known linguistic patterns in order to accelerate the identification of conceptual relationships. Pairs of identified terms will then be used for bringing out new linguistic patterns either generic, or specific to the corpus.

This could be the case here with meronymic patterns. While we used them (with the constraint on heads) for searching for hyperonymic relationships, we could use them for identifying meronymic relationships; however, in order to avoid complicating the presentation, we have not developed this stage.

2.2.3 *Knowledge-extraction tools*

A new generation of tools are devoted to identifying relationships in French corpora; they use either a top-down or a bottom-up method. The former apply predefined linguistic patterns. This is the case for Seek for hyperonymic relationships (Jouis 1994), Coatis for causal relationships (Garcia 1997). The latter help in the search for and identification of relationships in texts, without any *a priori* linguistic knowledge. This is the case for Mantex (Rousselot et al. 1996) and Prométhée (Morin 1999). Some tools combine top-down and bottom-up methods such as Caméléon (Séguéla 1999). But, our work has a more linguistic aim on the one hand, and a more application-oriented aim on the other hand (we build CTKB for firms). Our main linguistic issues are the following:

What does one mean by linguistic patterns for relationships?

What are the links between a corpus (domain and genre) and some linguistic patterns?

Is the hypothesis that it is possible to build just one model from the corpus valid?

We think that, in order to re-use linguistic patterns, it is necessary to specify as much as possible two kinds of elements:

which linguistic constraints are necessary so that the linguistic patterns bring out only good contexts — that is to say contexts associated with just one relationship, without ambiguity.

which characterizations of corpora must be added to combine with the description of linguistic patterns in order to use only the good ones according to the nature of the corpus studied.

Then, any kind of tools helping us in our plan is welcome but all of these tools can only propose candidates (terms or relationships); none of them can interpret the output results. However, interpreting the output is time consuming and requires detailed analysis of contexts; these results may just constitute a starting point for us.

2.3 Results obtained

As a result of the 5-step procedure described in 2.2.2, the following data are available and accessible by means of the CTKB system:

the list of terms finally selected;

the list of pairs related by a given conceptual relationship;

for each conceptual relationship, its characteristic patterns;

for each "term-relationship-term" triple, the section(s) in the corpus which contains it.

3. Experiment on a French corpus

The experiment was carried out on a French handbook for software engineering specification (478 KB) used by EDF (Electricité De France). Note that this corpus is highly descriptive and explanatory because its main aim is to provide recommendations. Our hypothesis was that this corpus, relatively to its genre, includes a large number of knowledge rich-contexts.

Our aim here was twofold: first, to provide some quantified data using a corpus; second, to illustrate how we carried out the different steps of the method for constructing a CTKB.

3.1 Identifying Candidate Terms

To this end, we used the LEXTER (Logiciel d'EXtraction de TERminologies) software, developed at the EDF by Didier Bourigault (Bourigault 1996). A set of linguistic criteria was applied to reduce the 5878 Candidate Terms proposed by LEXTER to 1516 Candidate Terms, that is 22% of the initial list, which were to be included for the identification of conceptual relationships (Condamines and Rebeyrolle 1997).

The identification of verbs is not discussed here at any length. We just stress that we have identified 27 verbs, as *to distribute, to develop, to modify, to test* from noun phrase such as: *distribution activity, development activity, modification activity, test activity.*

We are therefore concerned here with the method used for searching conceptual relationships.

3.2 Searching for conceptual relationships

In our experiment, we used the "Système d'Analyse de Textes par Ordinateur" (SATO) developed at the ATO center in Montreal[4] because it has a number of interesting functions for implementing our method. The most significant one is enables the user to characterize text elements (from the morpheme to the textual segments) in order to search for structures indicating conceptual relationships in the corpus. This function compensates for the absence of syntactic categorization. Moreover, consulting the text is a very flexible process that makes it possible to modify or add structures to take into account linguistic knowledge which is specific to a sub-domain and/or a text genre.
The application of the method described in 2.2. led to the following results: 404 concepts and 455 C-terms. The difference between these two figures can be explained by the fact that 51 of the terms are synonymous, that is to say, that two or more terms can denote the same concept.

Table 1 summarizes the main types of conceptual relationships found in the corpus.

It is not surprising that for the most specific structures we only have a single characteristic structure, because even if there are several verbs, the structure itself is unchanged (except where a transitive verb becomes an intransitive verb,

Table 1. Number of patterns and pairs connected by each of the CTKB conceptual relationships

Conceptual relationships	Number of markers	Number of related pairs
is a	21	204
is composed of	41	128
occurs in	1	8
occurs during	1	59
starts during	1	5
ends during	1	8
precedes	1	16
conditions the start of	1	11
conditions the end of	1	14
is the result of	1	8
is updated during	1	7
is responsible for	1	3
has responsibility for	2	50
plays the role of	1	5

for example). Furthermore, the total number of concepts greatly exceeds the 404 specified since a given concept has relationships with many other concepts in the corpus.

Hitherto, we have concentrated on describing the linguistic patterns of the different kinds of relationships. The next section details with examples the steps described in 2.2.

3.3 Searching for taxonomies

The hyponymy relationship is marked by generic phrases such as: *Le/un/les* $N_{hyponyme}$ *est un/des* $N_{hyperonyme}$. However, these phrases are not precise enough to relate only hyperonymic pairs. Therefore, we think that some constraints can play an essential role in their identification. We have proposed a broader conception of marker, in terms of configurations of lexical, syntactic, typographical and layout features (Péry-Woodley and Rebeyrolle 1998).

From the 21 structures indicating hyperonymy, we can bring out:

§[5] + def_det + CT1 + Vtobe (present) + undef_det + {kind, type, etc. of} CT2 + {relative clause, past participle, present participle, adjective}

To quote an example from this structure:

(1) § *Le guide d'élaboration de la documentation de spécification est un guide méthodologique pour la production des documents de spécification des logiciels scientifiques. (The handbook of specification documentation development is a methodological handbook for specification documents of scientific software production).*

§ + def_det + CT1 + Vtobe (present) + undef_det + CT2 + {relative clause, past participle, present participle, adjective}

For example:

(2) § *La documentation de spécification est un des documents essentiels d'un projet (The specification documentation is one of the essential documents of a project).*

By applying the hyperonymic structures in our corpus, we found 199 pairs of concepts. It must be stressed that the hyperonymic relationship is also established using morphological criteria. Consider the following noun phrases: *dossier de conception, dossier de test, dossier de modification.* It is possible to say that *dossier* is the hyperonym of these noun phrases.

It will be repeated that certain linguistic patterns may denote hyponymy or meronymy as well. However, in the case of meronymy, the heads of the related Candidate Terms must be the same. In this study, we have identified only five pairs using to this pattern. It is exemplified by the relationship between *dossier de conception* (*conception document*) and *dossier de conception générale* (*general conception document*), *dossier de conception détaillée* (*specific conception document*) where *dossier de conception* (*conception document*) is the hyperonym of *dossier de conception générale* (*general conception document*) et *dossier de conception détaillée* (*specific conception document*).

The semantic analysis of the 204 pairs identified with relevant linguistic patterns enables us to grade these concepts according to their semantic features. We have distinguished four classes:

- a class of activity noun (classA) as *specific conception*
- a class of document noun (classD) as *specific conception document*
- a class of human noun (classH) as *project leader*
- a class of time section noun (classT) as *conception stage*

3.4 Searching for syntagmatic relationships

As seen in 2.2.1, non-taxonomic relationships have been identified by combining taxonomies. 16 combinations have been examined, as classA {context} classD, classA {context} classH, etc. and their reverse.

In the following paragraphs, we firstly present the syntagmatic relationships (3.4.1), and secondly we take an example of the different steps of the method, (3.4.2).

3.4.1 *Presentation of syntagmatic relationships*

Our linguistic analysis of combinations has shown that half of them (eight combinations) are particularly interesting.

1– $\text{classD}_{(\text{document})}$ {context} $\text{classD}_{(\text{document})}$

The relationship identified is "**is composed of**", a well known type of meronymic relationship. In order to analyze results and identify linguistic patterns, we have used our knowledge of French, on the one hand, and the results of work carried out on meronymic patterns (such as that of Jackiewicz 1996) on the other hand. We have described a set of lexico-syntactic patterns for this relationship, including:

CT2 + Vtobe (present) + undef_det {group, family, etc.} + of + CT1

Here is an example of this pattern:

(3) *Un Etat de Configuration est une famille de fichiers sources (A configuration state is a family of source files).*
CT2 + {contains, encompasses, includes, etc.} + CT1

For example:

(4) *Les unités documentaires sont constituées des documents de spécification et de conception (The documentary units include specification documents and design documents).*

This relationship connects 133 pairs of concepts in our corpus.

2– $\text{classA}_{(\text{activity})}$ {context} $\text{classA}_{(\text{activity})}$

The relationship identified is "**precedes**". We have called this relationship "precedes" because it stresses firstly how activities are linked together, and secondly how time sections are related (see below).

3– $\text{classT}_{(\text{time})}$ {context} $\text{classT}_{(\text{time})}$

The "precedes" relationship also holds between time sections. Another relationship identified by this combination is "**occurs during**". The following sentence provides an example:

(5) *Le cycle de développement Composant se déroule pendant la phase de réalisation Produit (The Component development cycle takes place during the product realisation phase).*

4– $\text{classA}_{(\text{activity})}$ {context} $\text{classT}_{(\text{time})}$

This combination is the most frequent one. The principal differences between the five relationships identified stem from their semantic significance.
The first two relationships identified are: "**starts during**" and "**ends during**". In this type of combination, the verbs which hold between the terms are *to conclude, to terminate, to finish, to start, to begin*, for example.
We have added the "**occurs during**" relationship which can also stress how activities are organized within a time frame. Here is an example:

(6) *Les vérifications qualité doivent être réalisées au cours de la phase de conception générale composant (The quality checks must be done during the general component design stage).*

Two other relationships have been identified: "**conditions the start of**" and "**conditions the end of**". They have been described thoroughly in another paper (Condamines and Rebeyrolle 2000).

5– $\text{classD}_{(\text{document})}$ {context} $\text{classT}_{(\text{time})}$

The relationship identified is "**updated during**" which indicates at which point of a process a document is modified, as shown in the following example:

(7) *Le plan de validation produit est mis à jour au cours de la phase d'intégration produit (The product validation plan is updated during the product integration stage).*

6– $\text{classD}_{(\text{document})}$ {context} $\text{classA}_{(\text{activity})}$

This combination provides the relationship labeled "**is the result of**". In fact, closer examination of contexts showing a precedence relationship as opposed to one of succession has allowed us to identify pairs which are related by this relationship. It indicates which document is the product of an activity. The characteristic patterns of this relationship are *is followed by, results in, is the consequence of*, for example. As shown in Table 1, only 8 pairs of concepts are linked by this relationship which is illustrated in the following example:

(8) *Le Dossier de Spécification Logiciel est le résultat de la phase de spécification composant (The Software Specification File is the result of the component specification phase).*

7– $\text{classH}_{(\text{human})}$ {context} $\text{classH}_{(\text{human})}$

The two relationships concerned with this combination are "**is responsible for**" and "**plays the role of**".

This combination is established between a few pairs of concepts (cf. Table 1). The first one is exemplified by the following sentence:

(9) Le chef de projet est le seul responsable de l'ensemble de l'équipe de projet (*Only the project leader is accountable for the project group).*

The second one in fact connects two human nouns when one human plays a different hierarchical function than the usual one, as in this example:

(10) *L'ingénieur qualité joue le rôle du responsable qualité.*

8– $\text{classH}_{(\text{human})}$ {context} $\text{classA}_{(\text{activity})}$

This is the relationship labeled "**has responsibility for**" as it occurs in this example:

(11) *Pour un projet donné, le chef de projet a la responsabilité des activités de gestion de projet (For a given project, the project leader is in charge of the projet management).*

We give a specific description of this relationship below.

Notes:

a. We have added another relationship which is not expressed by linguistic patterns in the corpus but occurs implicitly in schemata: "**occurs in**". It holds between activities such as *test validation activity, test qualification activity,* etc. and location concepts such as *space of delivery, space of receipt*, etc.

b. We had to deal with several case of ellipsis. In some cases, using ellipses entails a wrong interpretation, as in this sentence:

(12) Le chef de projet a la responsabilité du plan de développement (*The project leader is responsible for the development plan)*

where *plan de développement* (*development plan*) is an ellipsis of *rédaction du plan de développement* (*drafting of development plan*). So the relationship does not hold between a human and a document, as it seems, but between a human and an activity. This example is to be classified together with the "has responsibility for" relationship.

3.4.2 *Example of the process*

This section focuses on the "has responsibility for" relationship. The five steps described in 2.2 are applied as follows for this relationship.

1. We start the analysis by labeling (using SATO) all the CT belonging to the same class (either human, activity, time or document) on the one hand, and on the other hand, all the parts of the text containing a hyperonymic linguistic pattern. The point is that when we combine the members of our taxonomies, we do not want to reexamine the contexts found during the first steps — that is to say hyponymy pairs.
2. We examine more closely the distribution of the most frequent term of the human class — here it is *chef de projet* (*project leader*) — with all the terms of the activity noun class.
3. It shows some stable verb phrases. The linguistic analysis of the occurrences enables us to bring out a sub-class of verbs phrases as *has the responsibility for, is entrusted with, is responsible for*, as shown in the following example:

(13) *L'ingénieur qualité a la charge du contrôle qualité (The quality engineer is entrusted with the quality check).*

Then if we look for reverse combinations where an activity noun occurs with a human noun, we obtain verb phrases, such as *to be in charge of, to be within the competence of*, which correspond to the same relationship. All these verb phrases are linguistic patterns of the "has responsibility for" relationship. They are labeled as such in the corpus.

4. The next step of the method consists in finding places in the corpus where these patterns occur with a CT. We have to note here that we have not specified the noun class (all the CT are used) which can occur with the pattern because we hope to discover nouns which have not been identified in the first step of the method. That is to say that they did not occur in a hierarchical relationship. In the case of the "has responsibility for" relationship, we found no more term by this way.

In this section, the main steps of the method have been described and applied to a corpus: searching for conceptual relationships, identifying linguistic patterns and finally giving the term status to some Candidate Terms (that are the ones) linked by linguistic patterns.

Up to now the discussion is centered on the applicability of the method.

4. Evaluation

This section deals with two types of evaluation of the CTKB, one viewing the CTKB as a corpus model and the other evaluating the possibilities of using a CTKB for various applications.

4.1 CTKB as corpus model

As previously stated, the presence of a conceptual relationship is systematically justified by a reference to those parts of the corpus which support it. This allows us both to evaluate manually what proportion of text has been used to identify conceptual relationships, as well as to examine the passages which have not been used. To this end, we have kept in our study the division into Textual Units (TU), which roughly correspond to sentences, made by LEXTER. Out of the 4832 initial TUs, 1216 contain a concept pair linked by a linguistic pattern of one of the 14 conceptual relationships of the corpus. Note that certain "term-relationship-term" triples can be extended over several TUs, mostly due to anaphora.

A close examination of the remaining TUs has not led us to retain any relationship other than the 14 identified. We hesitated over one or two relationships (for example, "has the function of") but did not retain them in the end as there is no real linguistic pattern but only several lexical elements distributed in a paragraph: this kind of limit is also mentioned by (Davidson et al 1998).

We can thus conclude that about a quarter of the corpus contains defining elements. Recall that this text provides recommendations, that is, the more or less normative defining elements of the concepts belong to the genre of the text. These results seem to confirm the relevance of our hypothesis: in corpora which can be characterized as belonging to the expository-genre, it is possible to use linguistic patterns in order to identify relationships.

4.2 CTKB as a prerequisite to applications

Our hypothesis is that a CTKB is a first model for different kinds of application, so that it can be consulted, added to or even modified by any user who needs to use a corpus to access the knowledge it contains.

In the GIS project, we have been able to evaluate the possibilities of using the CTKB that we built for two different tasks aiming to improve access to the text:

construction of a task model for writing software engineering specifications;

construction of an index for consulting the handbook.

In the first case, the contents of the CTKB were shown to be very useful. In fact, several sections of the conceptual network could be used directly to model the user's task, that is, an engineer having to write software engineering specifications. This relies on the genre of the corpus which describes the normative linking between the stages of software engineering point by point, and which are modeled in the CTKB. The description of this linking is the basis of the task modeling which has been carried out by the project's ergonomists.
In the second case, the experiment has been a little bit less conclusive. This is not surprising insofar as an index contains descriptors which are not necessarily (in fact, rarely) terms from the corpus, but rather meta-terms, which encompass several terms. Many meta-terms have been added while several C-terms have been removed.

Another experiment is currently being carried out. It sets out to formalize the results of the CTKB, so that it can be used in a knowledge base system. Finally, an experiment should soon be started at the EDF. It involves rewriting the text so as to remove linguistic and conceptual inconsistencies (both of which have been revealed by our study).

These experiments will provide us with a better evaluation of the relevance of the CTKB, that is, the relevance of a corpus-based modeling which contains only a few formalized elements.

Conclusion

The main aim of this study was to evaluate a new form of TKB which we have called CTKB. It is application-independent and is defined as a corpus model. At the same time, we have tried to outline the stages in the method for constructing the CTKB, focussing on identifying conceptual relationships. We have thus been faced with the problem of identifying patterns which signal these relationships in the texts.

At the present time, it would be useful to evaluate, using new corpora, the relevance of the patterns modeled during the experiment, so as to test the hypotheses of stability versus variability of linked structures in the domain and/or text genre.

The real usability of a CTKB to create a ATKB is currently being evaluated.

This experiment will also allow to integrate a more advanced formalism in the CTKB in the form of proposals concerning conceptual relations made to the linguist/terminologist on the basis of calculations of completeness and coherence, for example.

The initial evaluation of the usability of the CTKB that we have made seems to suggest the relevance of this concept and the interest of the corpus-based approach that we have presented.

Notes

* We wish to thank Nathalie Aussenac for her helpful comments on an earlier version of this paper.

1. In the "Terminology and Artificial Intelligence" group as well as in a close collaboration with researchers from IRIT (Institut de Recherche en Informatique de Toulouse) on a Cognitive Sciences GIS project (Groupement d'Intérêt Scientifique), which aimed to evaluate the possibilities of using a TKB for various applications including the constitution of a Knowledge Base System.

2. When the heads of the related terms are different, there is no automatic way to decide if it is a meronymic or a hyponymic relationship while no formal mark appears. Nevertheless, with human interpretation, it is possible to take into account general linguistic competence to conclude that there is a common feature between the related terms.

3. where CT = Candidate Term

4. http://www.ling.uqam.ca/sato/outils/sato.htm

5. Insofar as the typographical and dispositional markings are concerned, we simply note here that three constraints appear to be sufficient for an exclusively hyponymy pattern: the fact that the structure is located at the start of a paragraph (shown by the symbol §), that the CT2 is typographically marked (by a bold or italic font, for example). The CT1 is a definite noun phrase (notated def_det). The CT2 is always an indefinite noun phrase (notated undef_det).

References

Aussenac, N. 1999. "GEDITERM: Un logiciel pour gérer des bases de connaissances terminologiques." *Terminologies Nouvelles* (proceedings of TIA'99, Terminologie et Intelligence Artificielle) 19: 111–123.

Aussenac, N., Bourigault, D., Condamines, A., Gros, C. 1995. "How can Knowledge Acquisition benefit From Terminology." In *Proceedings of 9th Knowledge Acquisition Workshop*, Banff (Canada).

Biébow, B., Szulman, S. 1997. "Méthodologie de création d'un noyau de base de connaissances en logique terminologique à partir de textes." In *Actes des Deuxièmes rencontres de Terminologie et Intelligence Artificielle*, Toulouse (3–4 avril, 1997), 69–84.

Borillo, A. 1996. "Exploration automatisée de textes de spécialité: repérage et identification automatique de la relation lexicale d'hyperonymie." *LINX*, 34–35: 113–121.

Bourigault, D., Gonzalez-Mullier, I, Gros, C. 1996. "LEXTER, A Natural Language Processing Tool for Terminology Extraction." In *Proceedings EURALEX'96*, Göteborg, 771–779.

Condamines, A., Amsili, P. 1993. "Terminology between Language and Knowledge: An example of Terminological Knowledge Base." In *TKE'93: Terminology and Knowledge Engineering*, Frankfurt: Indeks Verlags, 316–323.

Condamines, A., Rebeyrolle, J. 1997. "Utilisation d'outils dans la constitution de bases de connaissances terminologiques: expérimentations, limites, définition d'une méthodologie." In *Premières Journées Scientifiques et Techniques de l'AUPELF-UREF*, Avignon (15–16 avril 1997), 529–535.

Condamines, A., Rebeyrolle, J. 2000. "Construction d'une base de connaissances terminologiques à partir de textes: expérimentation et définition d'une méthode." In *Ingénierie des connaissances*, J. Charlet, M. Zacklad, G. Kassel, D. Bourigault (eds), 225–241. Paris: Eyrolle.

Daille, B., Gaussier, E., Langé, J. 1994. "Towards automatic extraction of monolingual and bilingual terminology." In *Proceedings of COLING'94*, 515–521.

Enguehard, C., Pantéra, L. 1995. "Automatic natural acquisition of a terminology", *Journal of Quantitative Linguistics* 2 (1): 27–32.

Garcia, D. 1997. "Structuration du lexique de la causalité et réalisation d'un outil d'aide au repérage de l'action dans les textes." In *Actes des Deuxièmes rencontres de Terminologie et Intelligence Artificielle, Toulouse (3–4 avril, 1997)*, 7–26.

Gillam, L., Ahmad, K. 1996. "Knowledge-engineered terminology (data)bases." In *TKE'96: Terminology and Knowledge Engineering*, Frankfurt: Indeks-Verlag, 205–214.

Hearst, M.A. 1992. "Automatic Acquisition of Hyponyms From Large Text Corpora." In *Proccedings, 14th International Conference on Computational Linguistics*, Nantes, France, 539–545.

Jackiewicz, A. 1996. "L'expression lexicale de la relation d'ingrédience (partie-tout)." *Faits de Langues* 7: 53–62. Paris: Ophrys.

Jouis, C. 1994. "Contextual approach: SEEK, a linguistic and computational tool for use in knowledge acquisition." In *University of Luxembourg, Proceedings of the first European Conference Cognitive Science in Industry*, Luxembourg (28th-30th september 1994), 259–274.

Meyer, I., 2000. "Extracting Knowledge — rich Contexts for Terminography: A Conceptual and Methodological Framework", this volume.

Meyer, I., Douglas, S., Bowker, L., Eck, K. 1992. "Towards a new generation of terminological resources: An experiment in building a terminological knowledge base." In *Proceedings 16th International Conference on Computational Linguistics*, Nantes, 956–957.

Morin, E. 1999. "Acquisition de patrons lexico-syntaxiques caractéristiques d'une relation sémantique", *TAL (Traitement Automatique des Langues)* 40 (1): 143–166. Paris: Université Paris VII.

Pearson, J. 1998. *Terms in Context.* Amsterdam and Philadelphia: John Benjamins.

Chapter 7

Qualitative terminology extraction

Identifying relational adjectives

Béatrice Daille
IRIN

This paper presents the identification in corpora of relational adjectives in French, phenomena considered by linguists as highly informative. The approach uses a termer which is applied on a tagged and lemmatized corpus. Relational adjectives and compound nouns which include a relational adjective are then quantified and their informative status is evaluated thanks to a thesaurus of the domain. We conclude with a discussion of the interesting status of such adjectives and compound nouns for terminology extraction and other automatic terminology tasks.

1. Introduction

Identifying relational adjectives such as *malarial*, and noun phrases in which they appear such as *malarial mosquitoes*, could be interesting in several fields of NLP, such as terminology acquisition, topic detection, updating of thesauri, because they hold a naming function acknowledged by linguists (Bartning 1976; Levi 1978; Mélis-Puchulu 1991, etc.). The use of relational adjectives are particularly frequent in scientific fields (Monceaux 1993).

Paradoxically, terminology acquisition systems such as TERMINO (David and Plante 1990), LEXTER (Bourigault 1994), TERMS (Justeson and Katz 1995), have not been concerned with relational adjectives.

Even if the relational adjectives hold an important naming function, they remain ambiguous in the same way as uniterms because of their possible migration from one scientific domain to another: the adjective *planetary* employed with the noun *right* belongs to legal domain, with the noun *system* to astronomy, with the noun *electron* to chemistry, etc. This ambiguity is raised only when the noun which goes along the adjective is identified. A noun phrase including a relational adjective is interpreted by Lerat (1995) as:

> (…) a way to condense information under a justifiable form rather than an explicit one.

The relational adjective, even inside a noun phrase, remains ambiguous as long as the prepositional phrase with which it could be paraphrased is not clearly enounced: does the noun phrase *animal flour* mean flour for animals or flour made with animals?
Our concern is:

1. To identify noun phrases in which relational adjectives appear, as well as the prepositional phrases by which they could be paraphrased. We will see through another source presented in Section 2 that this property of paraphrase can be used to identify these adjectives.
2. To check the naming character of these adjectives and to evaluate the naming character of the noun phrases in which they appear.

Identifying both the adjective and the prepositional phrase could be useful in several types of NLP applications and allow us:

– In the field of terminology acquisition, to group synonym forms referring to an unique concept such *produit laitier* 'dairy product' and, *produit au lait* 'product with milk', *produit de lait* 'product of milk', *produit issu du lait* 'product made of milk', etc. Assadi and Bourigault (1995) have proposed a clustering model for the grouping of adjectives inside noun phrases extracted by LEXTER (Bourigault 1994) in order to help terminology validation. In contrast to our approach, their objective was to group adjectives appearing in the same context, and more precisely those which share the same head nouns such as the class composed of the adjectives *annuel* 'yearly', *correspondant* 'corresponding', *total, réel* 'real' that appears with the noun *coût* 'cost';

– In the field of thesaurus updating, to replace the noun phrase with a prepositional phrase by one with a relational adjective, the latter being more characteristic of a scientific denomination;

– In the field of monolingual or bilingual dictionary, to disambiguate the meaning of the relational adjective thanks to its prepositional form.

To carry out this identification, we use shallow parsing (Abney 1991), and then, for morphological processing, a dynamic method which takes as input a corpus labeled with part-of-speech and lemma tags. This method does not use a lexical database, and, no derivational information is provided. This is because, for French, there is not as yet either a derivational morphology tagger, or a lexical database such CELEX for English[4] where to each lemma is attached its derivational morphological structure. Without derivational information, neither relational adjectives built from non autonomous bases of noun classes such as *cœur/card* 'heart/card', nor from Latin noun bases such as *père/pater* 'father/pater', *ville/urb* 'town/urb' will be identified. However, a dynamic approach for identifying derivational links of terms by stemming does give good results for document retrieval (Daille et Jacquemin 1998), even if these results are not as good as those obtained with a lexical database.

In this study, we first define, and give some linguistic properties of, relational adjectives (AdjR). We then present the termer and the modifications that we carried out in order to allow the identification of AdjR in texts. We quantify the results obtained from a technical corpus in the field of agriculture [AGRO] and compare the AdjR and the compound nouns in which they appear with the terms of a thesaurus in the same field. We conclude by the effective informative character of such adjectives for terminology extraction and also other NLP fields.

2. Definition and Linguistic properties of relational adjectives

According to linguistic and grammatical tradition, there are two main categories among adjectives: epithetic such as *important* 'significant' and relational adjectives such as *laitier* 'dairy'. The first ones cannot have an agentive interpretation in contrast to the second: the adjective *laitier* 'dairy' within the noun phrase *production laitière* 'dairy production' is an argument to the valent noun *production* 'production' and this is not the case for the adjective *important* 'significant' within the phrase *production importante* 'significant production'. The term of "adjective of relation" or "relational adjective" was introduced by (Bally 1965) and conveys this idea of "relation" usually expressed by a preposition. These adjectives are so-called "pseudo-adjective" by Government-Binding and Transformational linguistic schools (Postal 1969), (Zribi-Hertz 1972), (Bartning 1976). Epithetic adjectives (AdjE) and relational adjectives (AdjR) share the properties of agreement in number and gender with the accompanying noun and the possibility to be in an attributive position. However, these two categories differ as regards morphological, paraphrastic, syntactic and semantic properties which apply either to the adjective alone or to the noun phrase within which it appears.

2.1 Morphological properties

Relational adjectives are either denominal adjectives — morphologically derived from a noun thanks to suffix — or adjectives having a noun usage such as *mathématique* 'mathematical/mathematics'. For the former, not all the adjective-forming suffixes lead to relational adjectives. The following suffixes are considered by (Dubois 1962) as appropriate: *-ain, -aire, -al, -el, -estre, -ien, -ier, -il(e), -in, -ique.* These favorable suffixes attach themselves either to a noun: *cellule* 'cell' → *cellulaire* 'cellular', or a scientific noun root: *hôpital* 'hospital (noun)' → *hospitalier* 'hospital (adjective)'.

However, (Guyon 1993) remarks that a suffix, even the most appropriate, is never necessary nor sufficient. Several adjectives carrying a favorable suffix are not relational: this is the case with the adjectives ending with *-ique*, which characterize chemistry and which are not derived from a noun, such as *désoxyribonucléique* 'deoxyribonucleic', *dodecanoique* 'dodecanoic', etc. Other suffixes inappropriate are sometimes used such as the suffixes *-é* and *-eux*:
carbone 'carbon' → *carboné* 'carbonaceous', *cancer* 'cancer' → *cancéreux* 'cancerous', etc.

2.2 Paraphrastic properties

A relational adjective is usually paraphrasable by a prepositional phrase. The preposition employed, as well as the presence or not of a determiner, depends on the head noun of the noun phrase:

acidité sanguine 'blood acidity' ≈ *acidité du sang* 'acidity of the blood'
conquête spatiale 'space conquest' ≈ *conquête de l'espace* 'conquest of space',
débit horaire 'hourly rate' ≈ *débit par heure* 'rate per hour',
expérimentations animales 'animal experimentation' ≈ *expérimentations sur les animaux* 'experimentation on animals'.

2.3 Syntactic properties

Relational adjectives are subject to syntactic constraints mentioned in (Monceaux 1997) contrary to epithetic adjectives. These properties apply to the noun phrase formed by the noun and the relational adjective:

– Non-predicativity, saying the impossibility of predicative position, apart from in specific conditions where there is a particular interpretation:

AdjE: *cette production est importante* 'this production is significant'
AdjR: ?*cette production est laitière* '?this production is dairy' (strictly)
cette production est laitière 'this production is dairy' (typically)

– The incompatibility with a degree adverbial modification, including in predicative sentences with a particular interpretation:
AdjE: *une production très importante* 'a very significant production'
AdjR: **une production très laitière* '*a very dairy production'
**cette production est très laitière* '*this production is very dairy'
– The non-fronting position, saying the impossibility to encounter relational adjectives in a pre-noun attributive position:
AdjE: *une importante production*
AdjR: **une laitière production*

Other properties are also mentioned such as the non-coordination, neither between relational adjectives nor with epithetic adjectives (Guyon 1993), the direct contact with the head noun in a sequence of post-noun adjectives (Melis-Puchulu 1991), etc.

These syntactic properties should be handled carefully. Indeed, the relational adjective, when it reflects a "typological" or a "typical" property, accepts the predicative position: *une pollution agricole* 'an agricultural pollution'/*cette pollution est agricole* 'this pollution is agricultural', *un problème mathématique* 'a mathematical problem'/*ce problème est mathématique* 'this problem is mathematical', detachment, modification and enumeration: *les réformes politiques et économiques* 'the political and economical reforms', *une production surtout céréalière* 'a mainly cereal production', etc.

2.4 Semantic properties

By definition (Bally 1965), relational adjectives express a link of "relation" whereas the epithetic adjective gives a link of "inherence". For Kleiber (1990), the relational adjective contains a "categorematic" notion — which builds its own reference — contrary to the epithetic adjective which contains a "syncategorematic" notion — which is referentially dependent. For Tamba-Mecz (1980), the relational adjective reveals a "external-global" vision although the epithetic adjective reveals a "internal-partial" one. In short, relational adjectives point to notions with a defined reference and enable a relation between two independent notions inside the noun phrase: one carried by the head noun and the other contained in the relational adjective.

3. Identifying relational adjectives

Among all the linguistic criteria that we have presented, few operate on automatic identification: this is the case of semantic criteria, but also of negative syntactic criteria. Indeed, the fact that a predicative construction between the noun and the adjective is not encountered in the corpus, does not allow to deduce that the construction is impossible. The presence of a forbidden construction could allow us to refuse the relational status to an adjective. But, these constructions being possible in some semantic interpretations of the adjective, we prefer, initially, not to reject adjectives which accept them. We study in Section 5.3 the syntactic constructions encountered and see how they could be exploited. The morphological criterion is not sufficient and, to use it alone would induce noise (see Section 2.1) and might distort our study.

Syntactic and semantic properties being rejected, the morphological property being insufficient alone, we use their paraphrastic property which includes the morphological property. This paraphrastic criterion is a strong one, which will produce little noise, but which will not allow exhaustive identification of relational adjectives on account of:

- The absence of paraphrases in the corpus;
- A non-paraphrasability or a complex paraphrasability;
- The large derivational distance between the adjective and the noun, in particular for all adjectives built from non autonomous bases.

We will see in Section 5.3 how acquiring still with reliable criteria other relational adjectives.

Identifying Noun Adj sequences characterized by the paraphrastic criterion requires a program able to extract all noun phrases from a corpus. First, we present the termer chosen then, the modifications performed to enable the identification of relational adjectives.

3.1 Terminology Extraction Program

ACABIT (Daille 1996), the termer used for this experiment, eases the task of the terminologist by proposing, for a given corpus, a list of candidate terms ranked from the most representative of the domain to the least by using a statistical score. Candidate terms extracted from the corpus belong to a special type of cooccurrence:

- the cooccurrence is oriented and follows the linear order of the text;
- it is composed of two lexical units which do not belong to the class of functional words such as prepositions, articles, etc.;
- it matches one of the morphosyntactic patterns of what we will call "base terms", or one of their possible variations.

The patterns for base terms are:

[Noun1 Adj] *emballage biodégradable* 'biodegradable package'

[Noun1 (Prep (Det)) Noun2] *ions calcium* 'calcium ion', *protéine de poissons* 'fish protein', *chimioprophylaxie au rifampine* 'rifampicin chemoprophylaxis'

[Noun1 à Vinf] *viandes à griller* 'grill meat'

These base structures are not frozen structures and do accept several variations. Those which are taken into account are:

1. Flexional and Internal morphosyntactic variants:
   - graphic and orthographic variants which gather together predictable flexional variants: *conservation de produit* 'product preservation', *conservations de produit* 'product preservations', or not: *conservation de produits* 'products preservation' and case differences.
   - variations of the preposition: *chromatographie en* colonne 'column chromatography', *chromatographie sur colonne* 'chromatography on column';
   - optional character of the preposition and of the article: *fixation azote* 'nitrogen fixation', *fixation d'azote* 'fixation of nitrogen', *fixation de l'azote* 'fixation of the nitrogen';
2. Internal modification variants: insertion inside the base-term structure of a modifier such as the adjective inside the Noun1 (Prep (Det)) Noun2 structure: *lait de chèvre* 'goat's milk', *lait cru de chèvre* 'milk straight from the goat';
3. Coordinational variants: coordination of base term structures: *alimentation humaine* 'human diet', *alimentation animale et humaine* 'human and animal diet';
4. Predicative variants: the predicative role of the adjective: *pectine méthylée* 'methylate pectin', *ces pectines sont méthylées* 'these pectins are metylated'.

The corpus is tagged and lemmatized. The program scans the corpus, counts and extracts collocations whose syntax characterizes base-terms or one of their variants. This is done with shallow parsing using local grammars based on regular expressions (Silberztein 1994); (Basili et al. 1993). These grammars use the morphosyntactic information associated with the words of the corpus by the tagger. The different occurrences are grouped as pairs formed by lemmas of the candidate term.

Figure 1 demonstrates the output for a candidate term: the first line indicates the base structure of the candidate, a numerical identifier (13375), the lemmas of which the pair is composed (*produit, surgeler*) '(product, deep-frozen)', its frequency (frq=4), the value of the statistical score (stat=29.16) and a summary of the variations encountered (VAR=1110). The variation summary is a string of four characters, each character receiving a value of 1 if the variation has been encountered, 0 if not. The first character represents flexional and internal morphosyntactic variants, the second internal modification variants, the third coordination variants and the last, predicative adjective variants. Next, for each type of variation, we find the rules which have been used (for example b007), the number of occurrences recognized by the rule, the initial text.

```
Na 13375 produit surgeler frq=4 stat=29.16 VAR=1110 Flexion
    b007      nbr=1
    text1=produits surgelés
Modification
    i001      nbr=2
    text1=produits alimentaires surgelés nbo1=1
    text2=produits halieutiques surgelés nbo2=1
Coordination
    c001      nbr=1
    text1=produits congelés ou surgelés nbo1=1
```

Figure 1. Example of a candidate associated to a base structure

The candidate term proposed to the expert is by default the most frequent base form between the inventoried occurrences, *produits surgelés* 'deep-frozen products' for the example in Figure 1.

3.2 Modification of the termer

To identify relational adjectives, we use their paraphrastic property. We group base-terms of Noun1 Prep (Det) Noun2 structure with terms of Noun1 Adj structure where either, Adj is derived from Noun2, such as *production de céréales* 'cereal production', *production céréalière* 'cereal production', or Adj owns a noun use, such as *muscle bovin* 'bovine muscle', *muscle de bovin* 'muscle of the bovine'.

The identification of relational adjective takes place after extraction of the occurrences of the candidate terms and their syntactic variations. Each candidate comes with its base structure and a summary of different variations encountered. It would have been possible to check that the relational adjective is not used in a predicative position, or with a degree modification if (Monceaux 1997) had not demonstrated that these properties are not always true.

Each candidate sharing a Noun Adj structure is examined thanks to its ending, relational adjectives having determined endings.

The most common suffixes in French applying to relational adjectives have been enumerated by (Guyon 1993): the favorable suffixes are: *-ain, -aire, -al, -el, -estre, -ien, -ier, -il, -in, -ique*, and the non-favorable ones are: *-esque, -eux, -é, -if, -oire*. We have left aside the suffixes: *-ain, -il, -in, -esque*.

Table 1. Number and example of transformational rules by suffix

Suffix	Number of rules	Example of rule		
-al	5	-al/	*national/nation*	
-aire	8	-aire/	*dentaire/dent*	'dental/tooth'
-atif	2	-atif/+e	*normatif/norme*	'normative/norm'
-é	2	-é/+e	*carboné/carbone*	'carbonaceous/carbon'
-el	2	-el/+e	*industriel/industrie*	'industrial/industry'
-er	1	-er//+e	*paysager/paysage*	'landscaped/landscape'
-eux	3	-eux/+e	*veineux/veine*	'venous/vein'
-ien	1	-ien/+ie	*bactérien/bactérie*	'bacterial/bacterium'
-ier	2	-ier/	*fruitier/fruit*	'fruit'
-if	2	-if/	*sportif/sport*	'sport'
-in	1	-in/	*porcin/porc*	'porcine/pork'
-ique	15	-ique/+ie	*graphique/graphie*	'graphic/written form'
-iste	1	-iste/+isme	*nationalisme/nationaliste*	
-oire	1	-oire/+ion	*inflammatoire/inflammation*	'inflammatory'

The suffixe *-ain* characterizes adjectives derived from proper nouns such as *toulousain* 'native of Toulouse'; *-il* and *-estre* are rare; *-esque* carries a disparaging sense such as *livre* 'book', *livresque* 'bookish'.

For each suffix, we created transformational rules in order to generate the most predictable forms of the base noun from the adjective. These rules have been established by hand thanks to examples of compound nouns of structure

Noun AdjR found in (Guyon 1993) and (Monceaux 1993), and other readings. We do not pretend that they cover all the existing derivational forms, only the most frequent ones. Table 1 shows the number of rules written for each suffix and an example of one of the rules. These rules generate one or several possible base nouns for a given adjective. This overgeneration method used in information retrieval by (Jacquemin and Tzoukermann 1999) gives low noise because the base noun must not only be an attested for in the corpus, but must also appear as an extension of a head noun. For example, with the adjective *ionique* 'ionic', we generate both *ionie* 'ionia' and *ion* 'ion', but only *ion* is an attested form; with the adjective *gazeux* 'gaseous', the noun forms *gaz* 'gas' and *gaze* 'gauze' are generated and the two of them are attested; but, the adjective *gazeux* 'gaseous' appears with the noun *échange* 'exchange' which is paraphrased in the corpus by *échange de gaz* 'gas exchange' and not by *échange de gaze* 'gauze exchange'.

```
3076 BASE=0101 nbcand=16 stat=32.36
npn 1693 fibre aliment frq=1 VAR=1000
Flexion
b014      nbr=1
text1=fibres dans les aliments nbo1=1
nar 1826 fibre alimentaire frq=15 VAR=1000
Flexion
b007 nbr=15
text1=fibres alimentaires nbo1=14
text2=Fibres alimentaires nbo2=1
```

Figure 2. Example of a candidate associated to several base structures

The algorithm below resumes the successive steps for identifying relational adjectives:

1. Examine each candidate of Noun Adj structure;
2. Check that the adjective ends with one of the listed suffixes, with added constraints for some suffixes, such as for the suffix — *er*, that the identified adjective is not a past-participle;
3. Apply a transformational rule in order to generate all the possible corresponding base nouns;
4. Search the set of candidate terms for a pair formed with Noun1 (identical between a Noun1 (Prep (Det)) Noun2 and a Noun1 Adj structures) and Noun2 generated from step 3.

5. If step 4 succeeds, group the two base structures under a new candidate term. Take out all the Noun Adj structures owing this adjective from the set of Noun Adj candidates and rename them as a Noun AdjR structure.

For non-ethnical adjectives with a noun function, as for example *problème technique* 'technical problem' and *problème de technique* 'problem of techniques', we have accepted that a candidate term could share several base structures: one of type Noun1 (Prep (Det)) Noun2 and another of type Noun1 Adj. No computation is needed to see that Noun2 as Noun2 and Adj share the same lemma.

An example of the grouping of two base structures is given in Figure 2. The first line identifies the candidate thanks to an unique numerical identifier (3076), a summary of the encountered base structures (BASE=0101), its frequency (nbcand=16) and its statistical score value (stat=32.36).

Table 2. Number of base structures extracted from the [AGRO]

Number of occurrences of base structures	1	≥ 2	Total
Noun1 (Prep (Det)) Noun2	17 232	5 949	23 181
Noun Adj	12 344	4 778	17 122
Noun à Vinf	203	16	219
Total	29 779	10 743	40 522

The base structure summary is a string of four characters, each receiving a value of 1 if the base structure has been encountered, or 0 if not. The first character represents the Noun Adj structure, the second the Noun1 (Prep (Det)) Noun2 structure, the third the Noun Prep Vinf structure and the last one the Noun AdjR structure. The other lines supply the same information as before (cf. Fig 1 and Section 2.1) with the difference that the statistical score now applies to the grouping rather than the base structure.

4. Results and evaluation

Our corpus, called [AGRO], is made up of 7272 abstracts (2.5 Mbytes) from French texts in the agriculture domain and extracted from PASCAL.[5] We used the Brill part-of-Speech Tagger (Brill 1992) trained for French by (Lecomte and

Paroubek 1996) and the lemmatizer developed by F. Namer (Toussaint et al. 1998). This chain of corpus treatments is satisfactory, except for the treatment of agreements inside the sentence or the sentence phrases. It is impossible to check the agreement between the noun and the adjective and this leads to the extraction of erroneous candidate terms.

4.1 Quantitative results

Table 2 resumes the number of base structures extracted from [AGRO]. From these base structures, 395 groupings were identified. The linked presence of noun phrases of which the extension is fulfilled either by a relational adjective, or be a prepositional phrase the number is rare — a little bit more than 1% of the total of occurrences — . But, these groupings allow us to extract from the numerous hapax — more than 70% of the total of occurrences — candidates which, we presume, will be highly denominative.

The number of relational adjectives which have been identified is 129: *agronomique* 'agronomic', *alimentaire* 'alimentary', *arachidier* 'groundnut', *aromatique* 'aromatic', etc.

4.2 Qualitative results

We checked the linguistic accuracy of the 395 structural variations which group a Noun1 Prep (Det) Noun2 structure and a Noun1 AdjR structure. Reported errors are the following:

- Generation of a "monster": *évolution normale* 'normal evolution' linked to *évolution des normes* 'standard evolution' (1 grouping);
- Three incorrect groupings due to the homography, and the non homonymy, of the adjective and the noun: *fin* 'thin (Adj)/end (Noun)', *courant* 'ordinary (adjective)/current (noun)', *potentiel* 'potential'.
- Three incorrect groupings due to tagging errors where the frozen preposition *en fin de* has not been identified: *populations finales* linked to *population atteinte en fin (de)*, prepositional phrase which means 'at end of'.

This lead us to a linguistic precision of 98% in the identification of relational adjectives.

5. Evaluation with AGROVOC

The thesaurus AGROVOC,[6] is a taxonomy of about 15,000 terms associated with synonyms in a SGML format, which leads to 25,964 different terms. The thesaurus AGOVOC is used for indexing with data fitting agricultural retrieval systems and indexing systems.

We made two comparisons with AGROVOC: we first checked whether these relational adjectives were really part of terms of the thesaurus and second, we compared the candidate terms extracted with a relational adjective with the terms and the thesaurus. We consider that the presence of the relational adjective in AGROVOC confirms its informative character, and that the presence of a candidate term attests its terminological value.

5.1 Relational adjectives alone

From the 124 correct relational adjectives, 68 appear inside terms of the thesaurus in epithetic position, such as *continu* 'continuous', *dynamique* 'dynamic', *enzymatique* 'enzymatic', *fruitier* 'fruit', *gazeux* 'gaseous', and 15 only under their noun form in an extension position, for example the relational adjective *arachidier* 'groundnut' does not appear but *arachide* is used in an extension position. Moreover, among the 124 adjectives, 73 appear in AGROVOC under their noun term as uniterms. Among these 73 uniterms, 43 of them, such as *texture*, share a relational use, such as *textural*; the other 30, such as *estérase* 'esterase' do not have a relational use.

The adjectives which are not present in the thesaurus in an extension position under either their adjectival or noun form are 11 in number: *bibliographique* 'bibliographic', *compartimental* 'compartment', *coûteux* 'costly', *haplotypique* 'haplotypic', *logarithmique* 'logarithmic', *miscellaire, neuronal* 'neuronic', *opératoire* 'operating', *photonique* 'photon', *polyphénoloxydasique,* and *transmembranaire* 'transmembrane'. So 93% of them are indeed highly informative.

This first result corroborates the assumption of the linguists that relational adjectives possess a denominative character.

5.2 Candidate term with a relational adjective

If relational adjective are indeed highly informative, we still have to demonstrate that the noun phrases in which they appear are informative too.

For 9 relational adjectives, we have compared the noun phrases in which they appear with terms of the thesaurus AGROVOC. We have also carried out this comparison for the noun phrases with a prepositional extension including a noun from which a relational adjective has been derived. Pour each adjective, we compute the following indexes:

T_A the number of terms in AGROVOC in which the relational adjective appears in an epithetic position, i.e. the terms of Noun AdjR structure. For example $T_A = 15$ for the adjective *cellulaire* 'cellular' because it appears in 15 terms of AGROVOC such as *différenciation cellulaire* 'cellular differentiation', *division cellulaire* 'cellular division', etc.

T_N the number of terms in AGROVOC in which the noun from which has been derived the relational adjective appears inside a prepositional phrase, i.e. the terms of Noun1 Prep (Det) $Noun_{AdjR}$ structure. For example $T_A =$ 4 for the noun *cellule* 'cell' because it appears in 4 terms of AGROVOC such as *banque de cellules* 'cell bank', culture de cellules 'culture of cells', etc.

C_A the number of candidate terms of Noun AdjR structure. For example $C_A =$ 61 for the adjective *cellulaire* 'cellular' because it appears in 61candidate terms such as *acide cellulaire* 'cellular acid', *activité cellulaire* 'cellular activity', *agrégat cellulaire* 'cellular aggregate', etc.

C_N the number of candidate terms of Noun1 Prep (Det) $Noun_{AdjR}$ structure. For example $C_N = 58$ for the noun *cellule* 'cell' because it appears in 58 candidate terms such as *ADN de cellule* 'cell DNA', *addition de cellules* 'cell addition', etc.

Table 3. Averages of precisions and recalls

	Noun AdjR	**Noun1 Prep (Det) $Noun_{AdjR}$**
Precision	0,34	0,04
Recall	0,46	0,14

Then, for each candidate term of C_A and C_N, we checked for their presence in AGROVOC. The only matches that we have accepted are exact matches. With this comparison, we obtained the following indexes:

a. the number of candidate terms of Noun AdjR structure found in AGROVOC under the Noun AdjR structure.
b. the number of candidate terms of Noun AdjR structure found in AGROVOC under the Noun1 Prep (Det) $Noun_{AdjR}$ structure.

c. the number of candidate terms of Noun1 Prep (Det) $Noun_{AdjR}$ structure found in AGROVOC under the Noun AdjR structure.
d. the number of candidate terms of Noun1 Prep (Det) $Noun_{AdjR}$ structure found in AGROVOC under the Noun1 Prep (Det) $Noun_{AdjR}$ structure.

These indexes allow us to compute precision P and recall R for each Noun AdjR structure and each Noun1 Prep (Det) $Noun_{AdjR}$ structure with the help of the following formula:

$P_{\text{Noun AdjR}} = (a+b)/C_A$ $R_{\text{Noun AdjR}} = (a+b)/T_A$
$P_{\text{Noun1 Prep (Det) NounAdjR}} = (c+d)/C_N$ $R_{\text{Noun1 Prep (Det) NounAdjR}} = (c+d)/T_N$

The averages of precision and recall for the two structures are summarized in Table 3. This comparison of the average of precision computed shows that candidate terms with a Noun AdjR structure are 10 times more likely to be terms than their equivalent in Noun1 Prep (Det) $Noun_{AdjR}$. The analysis of the average of recall is also impressive: it is generally difficult to obtain a recall superior to 25% when comparing candidate terms extracted from a corpus and a thesaurus of the same domain (Daille et al. 1998). The average of recalls obtained thanks to the identification of relational adjective shows that nearly half of the terms built with the defined relational adjectives are identified. These good values of precision and recall have been obtained on linguistic criteria only without taking into account frequency.

Moreover, we notice that even if AGROVOC contains virtually the same number of terms of Noun Adj structure and of Noun1 Prep (Det) $Noun_{AdjR}$ structure, there is no real coherence in the thesaurus encoding; for example, we find *métabolisme protéique* 'proteinic metabolism', but not *métabolisme glucidique* 'carbohydrate metabolism', the term *métabolisme des glucides* 'metabolism of carbohydrate' being preferred. Our results could be used to update the thesaurus when the form Noun AdjR has been encountered in a corpus.

5.3 Analysis of syntactical variations

The Noun AdjR structures rarely undergo syntactic variations contrary to their equivalent in Noun1 Prep (Det) $Noun_{AdjR}$ structures, when they exist: only 10% of Noun AdjR structures accept variations and these are mainly coordinations such as *produit alimentaire/produits agricoles et* alimentaire 'food product/ agricultural and food product' and some modifications such as *composition lipidique cellulaire* 'cellular lipid composition'. We have examined all the coordinations and we found that they involve other relational adjectives. This result could be used to identify new relational adjectives, in the same way as (Jacquemin 1996) did for term acquisition through indexing. Modifications are more difficult to exploit in the case of an inserted adjective: either the adjective is indeed relational such as *lipidique* 'lipid' in *composition lipidique cellulaire* 'cellular lipid composition', or, the adjective is part of a compound such as *gras* 'fat' in *matière grasse industrielle* 'industrial fat content'. No predicative variants have been encountered. An interpretation could be that such structures are little used in technical domains.

On the other hand, 60% of the Noun1 Prep (Det) Noun2 structures grouped to a Noun AdjR structure accept syntactic variations, mainly modifications, as *filtration membranaire* 'membrane filtering'/*filtration frontale sur membrane* 'frontal filtering on membrane'. Some groupings are of particular interest: those where the Noun AdjR structure has been identified, but which lacks the Noun1 Prep Noun2 base form. For example, whereas *acide vinique* 'vinic acid' is attested, only syntactic variations of *acide* 'acid' Prep (Det) *vin* 'wine' are identified: *acides organiques du vin* 'organic acids of the wine', *acide malique dans le vin* 'malic acid of the wines', *acides aminés des vins* 'amino-acids of the wines', *acide tartrique dans les vin* 'tartaric acid in the wines', *acide salicylique dans les vins* 'salicyclic acid in the wines'. The term *acide vinique* 'vinic acid' groups all these different acids as *acides organiques, maliques, aminés, tartriques et salicyliques* 'organic, malic, amino-, tartaric, and salicylic acids' which are all kinds of acids existing in AGROVOC. These groupings constitute a first step in knowledge acquisition from texts, and could, for example, be used as the bootstrap in a system for acquiring semantic relations, such as PROMETHEE (Morin 1998).

6. Conclusion

We succeeded in the identification of relational adjectives by finding both Noun1 (Prep (Det)) Noun2 and Noun1 AdjR structures in texts. This experiment corroborates the linguistic studies and their intuition about the informative character of the relational adjectives. Identifying relational adjectives could be used to recover uniterms from corpora. We have also proved that noun phrases including a relational adjective are far more informative than their equivalent in Noun1 Prep (Det) $\text{Noun}_{\text{AdjR}}$ structure. The method presented is robust even if it does not allow us to identify exhaustively all relational adjectives appearing in a corpus, but it could be improved by exploiting coordination variants. Taking into account such lexical units is interesting for terminology extraction, but also for updating thesauri or for technological development where the occurrence of a relational adjective represents a stabilization of an emerging scientific concept.

Notes

1. A derivational lexical database is being built for French inside the FRANLEX project (http://www.limsi.fr/Individu/jacquemi/FRANLEX) (Dal et al. 1999)

2. A multilingual thesaurus developed by AGRIS (International Information System for Agricultural Sciences and Technology)

3. PASCAL is the Scientific Documentary Database maintained by INIST-CNRS, France.

4. A derivational lexical database is being built for French inside the FRANLEX project (http://www.limsi.fr/Individu/jacquemi/FRANLEX) (Dal et al. 1999)

5. A multilingual thesaurus developed by AGRIS (International Information System for Agricultural Sciences and Technology)

6. PASCAL is the Scientific Documentary Database maintained by INIST-CNRS, France.

References

Abney, S. 1991, "Parsing with Chunks." *Principle-Base Parsing.* Berwick, R. and Tenny, C. (eds), 257–278. Kluwer Academic Publishers.

Assadi, S. and Bourigault, D. 1995. "Classification d'adjectifs extraits d'un corpus pour l'aide à la modélisation de connaissances." In *Troisièmes Journées Internationales d'Analyse Statistique de Données Textuelles*: 313–320.

Bally, C. 1965. *Linguistique générale et linguistique française.* Berne:Francke Verlag, 4th edition.

Bartning, I. 1976. *Remarque sur la syntaxe et la sémantique des pseudo-adjectifs dénominaux en français.* Ph.D. thesis, University of Stockholm.

Basili, R., Pazienza, M.T. and Velardi, P. 1993. "Acquisition of Selectional Patterns in Sublanguages", *Machine Translation* 8: 175–201.

Bourigault, D. 1994. *LEXTER, un Logiciel d'Extraction de TERminologie. Application à l'acquisition des connaissances à partir de textes.* Ph.D. thesis, EHESS, Paris, France.

Brill, E. 1992. "A simple rule-based part of speech tagger." In *Third Conference on Applied Natural Language Processing (ANLP'92)*: 152–155.

Daille, B., Gaussier, E. and Langé, J.M. 1998. "An evaluation of Statistical Scores for Word Association." *The Tbilisi Symposium on Logic, Language and Computation: Selected Papers*, 177–188. CSLI Publications.

Daille, B. and Jacquemin, C. 1998. "Lexical database and information access: a fruitful association." In *LREC'98:*669–673.

Dal, G., Hathout, N. and Namer, F. 1999. "Construire un lexique dérivationnel: théorie et réalisations." In *TALN'99:* 115–124.

David, S. and Plante, P. 1990. "Le progiciel TERMINO: de la nécessité d'une analyse morphosyntaxique pour le dépouillement terminologique des textes." In *ICO,* vol. 2(3): 140–155.

Dubois, J. 1962. *Etude sur la dérivation suffixale en Français moderne et contemporain,* Paris, Larousse.

Guyon, A. 1993. *Les adjectifs relationnels arguments de noms prédicatifs,* PhD thesis, University Paris 7.

Jacquemin, C. 1996. "A symbolic and surgical acquisition of terms through variaition", In *Connectionist, Statistical and Symbolic Approaches to Learning for Natural Language Processing,* 425–438. Heidelberg, Springer,.

Jacquemin, C. and Tzoukermann, E. 1999. "NPL for term variant extraction: Synergy between morphology, lexicon and syntax", *Natural Langague Information Retrieval,* T. Strzalkowski (eds.), Kluwer Academic Publishers, Dordrecht.

Justeson, J. and Katz, S. 1995. "Technical terminology: Some linguistic properties and an algorithm for identification in text." In *Journal of Linguistic Engineering,* vol. 1(1), Cambrigde University Press.

Kleiber, G. 1990. *La sémantique du prototype — Catégories et sens lexical.* PUF, Linguistique nouvelle.

Lecomte, J. and Paroubek, P. 1996. *Le catégoriseur d'Eric Brill. Mise en œuvre de la version entraînée à l'INALF.* Technical report. CNRS-INALF.

Lerat, P. 1995. *Les langues spécialisées.* Paris, PUF

Levi, J. 1978. *The syntax and the semantics of complex nominals.* Academic Press, London.

Mélis-Puchulu, A. 1991. "Les adjectifs dénominaux: des adjectifs de "relation"." *Lexique,* 10: 33–60.

Monceaux, A. 1993. *La formation des noms composés de structure NOM ADJECTIF.* PhD. Thesis, University of Marne la Vallée, France.

Monceaux, A. 1997. "Adjectif de relation, complémentation et sous-classification." *Langages,* 126: 39–59.

Morin, E. 1998. "PROMETHEE: un outil d'aide à l'acquisition de relations sémantiques entre termes." In *TALN'98:* 172–181.

Postal, P.M. 1969. "Anaphoric island." In *Fifth Regional Meeting of the Chicago Linguistic Society.* R.B. et al. (eds.), University of Chigago.

Silberztein, M. 1994. "Intex: a corpus processing system." In *COLING'94:* 579–583.

Tamba-Mecz, I. 1980. "Sur quelques propriétés de l'adjectif de relation." *Travaux de Linguistique et de Littérature,* 18–1: 119–132.

Toussaint, Y., Namer, F., Daille B., Jacquemin, C. Royauté, J. Hathout, N. 1998. "Une approche linguistique et statistique pour l'analyse de l'information en corpus." In *TALN'98:* 182–191.

Zribi-Hertz, A. 1972. "Sur un cas de construction pseudo-predicative", *Recherches Linguistiques,* 1: 159–168.

Chapter 8

General considerations on bilingual terminology extraction

Eric Gaussier
Xerox Research Centre Europe

We want to present here general problems encountered in bilingual terminology extraction. Using French and English as the language pair to illustrate our discussion, we will first try to show how the specifications of terms in two different languages impact the alignment process. This will lead us to review three methods we believe to be well adapted to bilingual terminology extraction. Lastly, we discuss parameters a bilingual alignment model should integrate.

1. Introduction

Facing the world wide increase in the production of technical documentation, terminologists look for ways to extract terminological knowledge from documents. Furthermore, the rising demand for translations of technical documents, often in more than twenty or thirty different languages, calls for specialised bilingual dictionaries, which, when they exist, are generally not up to date with respect to the recent developments of a domain. These factors, when combined, demonstrate a need, which is more and more recognised by various actors, for methods for extraction of bilingual lexicons of terms from documents. The most useful documents one can think of for this task are bilingual corpora, i.e. corpora made of documents in one language, and their translation in another language.

Several works have focused on the extraction of knowledge from bilingual corpora. All these works address the problem of aligning units (smaller than the whole document) across languages. If very successful methods have been designed to align paragraphs and sentences in two different languages, aligning units smaller than a sentence raises a real challenge. We are going to describe some characteristics of the methods used to extract bilingual lexicons of terms from parallel corpora, this latter term referring to bilingual corpora aligned at the sentence level.

All the methods for bilingual terminology alignment share at some point a characterization of the terms of a given language. This characterization is important to focus on terms, but also has some impact on the type of procedures one can implement to align candidate terms across languages.

In the first part of this chapter, we present a standard characterization of terms based on morpho-syntactic patterns. We consider English and French as our two working languages, but the conclusions we will draw from a comparative study of English and French terms apply to other language pairs as well (note that all the examples we use to make our argument more explicit are taken from the domain of telecommunication satellites). In the second part, we will briefly review several methods we believe to be well adapted to bilingual terminology alignment, and present the parameters these methods can rely on.

2. Characterizing French and English terms

There is no fully operational definition of terms. Similarly to compounds, a term represents a lexicalized entity, at least when it is used within its technical context. Classical definitions for compounds integrate syntactic, semantic and referential criteria. If a term univoquely refers to a concept (or class of concepts), in general, the sense of a multi-word term can be derived, through composition, from the sense of the words it contains. The first syntactic criteria used to determine whether an entity was a compound or not reflected the fact that the structure of a compound was believed to be frozen. Most recent studies, e.g. (Gross 1988), have shown that the syntactic structure of compounds are nonetheless subject to variations, introducing the idea of a continuum between frozen and non-frozen entities. As we will see, most terms undergo such variations, with insertions of adjectives and/or adverbs. Computational studies on compounds and terms have then tried to characterize elementary structures of compounds and terms, as well as the modifications such structures can support (see (Mathieu-Colas 1988; Jacquemin 1997; Daille 1994) on French, and (Nkwenthi-Azeh 1992; Justeson and Katz 1995) on English). Such structures for characterizing French and English terms are the basis of the vast majority of monolingual term extractors (sometimes coupled with statistical information), and we first give an overview of these structures and their modifications, for terms of length 2, i.e. composed of two lexical (as opposed to grammatical) words. The restriction to terms of length 2 is justified by the central role they play in terminology: (a) they are by far the most frequent type of terms, (b) terms of length 3 and more are usually derived from terms of length 2 by various operations that we describe hereafter. Furthermore, all our examples are taken from a corpus on telecommunication satellites, provided by the EEC within the framework of the European Project ET-10/63. Lastly, the structures we are going to present are derived from the examination of terminology lists and dictionaries, as well as from corpus studies.

2.1 Syntactic patterns for French terms

All the syntactic patterns we are considering correspond to noun phrases (not all noun phrases are covered by these patterns). A short form, summarizing all the relevant patterns, is given below, where E corresponds to the empty string, N(1,2) to a noun, and Adj to an adjective:

N1 Prep Det E2

with:

Prep={de} Det={E,le,la,l',les}, E2=N2 (1)
Prep={à} Det={E,le,la,l'}, E2=N2 (2)
Prep={en,sur} Det={E}, E2=N2 (3)
Prep={dans,par} Det={le,la,l',les}, E2=N2 (4)
Prep={E} Det={E}, E2=N2 (5)
Prep={E} Det={E}, E2=Adj (6)

These patterns make use of definite articles, but not of indefinite articles. Even though some terms may integrate indefinite articles, as *mouvement d'une orbite*, most sequences containing indefinite articles are not terms. Moreover, the terms with indefinite articles often have a correspondent with definite articles. We face here the problem of recall versus precision. If recall is privileged, then one should consider both definite and indefinite articles. If, on the contrary, the emphasis is put on precision, then one should focus on candidates with definite articles. But, since the vast majority of candidates with indefinite articles are not valid terms, relying only on definite articles also represents a good trade-off between recall and precision. The same remarks apply for the selection of the articles, among the set of definite articles, with respect to the preposition used. The pattern **Adj N**, where the adjective appears before the noun, is not retained, since most candidates of this form are not terms. The criterion here is anyway indirect, since it is the type of adjective which mainly determines the terminological status of the unit. In French, only certain classes of adjectives can appear before the noun they modify. These adjectives are, in general, not used to form terms. However, most of these adjectives can also appear after the noun. We thus see that we could refine, if this information is present in our lexicons, the pattern **N Adj**, by **N Adjna**, where *Adjna* represents an adjective that cannot appear before the noun.

Here are examples of terms for each of the preceding patterns (we provide their English translation in parentheses):

(1) durée de vie (lifetime); vitesse du faisceau (beam velocity)
(2) trafic a l'émission (transmit traffic)
(3) répartition en fréquence (frequency division)
(4) répartition dans le temps (time division)
(5) diode tunnel (tunnel diode)
(6) lobe latéral (side lobe)

2.2 Syntactic patterns for English terms

The syntactic patterns for English are less numerous, since English relies on a composition of Germanic type, without prepositions, to produce compounds, and of Romance type, with prepositions, to produce free noun phrases, as in *examples of calculations*, whereas French relies on Romance type for both, as described in (Chuquet and Paillard 1989). Only two patterns are retained: **N N** and **Adj N**. Examples of Adj N compounds are *hot stand-by* (*secours permanent*) and *orthogonal polarization* (*polarisation orthogonale*). Examples of N N compounds are *frequency band* (*bande de fréquence*) and *telephone channel* (*voie téléphonique*).

However, two remarks need to be done concerning the use of the Saxon genitive in certain compounds, and the modifiation of an N N sequence into an N of N sequence.

The Saxon genitive (N1's N2) can be used to specify to which category N2 belongs to, as in *a man's job* (*un metier d'homme*), which could be considered as a term. Nevertheless, most studies reject this pattern insofar as such a use of the Saxon genitive is rare. The only example of Saxon genitive we found in our corpus, occurring only once, is *earth's curvature* (*courbure de la terre*). Furthermore, all the dictionaries we looked at propose *curvature of the earth*, and not *earth's curvature.*

There are very few terms in English corresponding to the pattern **N Prep N**. Our corpus contains 4300 candidates of the form **N N** or **Adj N** occurring at least twice, whereas only 530 candidates of the form **N Prep N**, occurring at least twice, are encountered. Among these candidates, 360 contain the preposition *of*.

The construction **N1 of N2** is usually used when the two nouns are considered independently of one another, when it is not possible to form, through composition, a new concept. Furthermore, the sequence **N1 of N2** is also used to translate the French sequence **N1 de N2** when the first noun is a quantifier or a classifier, as *type d'antenne* (*type of antenna*). Such French candidates are not valid terms, and if the pattern **N1 of N2** is not retained, we might expect these French candidates to be eliminated during the alignment process since their translation is not taken into account.

However, there are cases where syntactic constraints may force the use of **N1 of N2** instead of **N2 N1**. This is the case when one wants to unambiguously qualify, with an adjective, the noun *N2*. A sequence **Adj N2 N1** is ambiguous with respect to which noun is qualified by the adjective, whereas the sequence **N1 of Adj N2** is not. Such a process is illustrated in the following example, where *N1* and *N2* usually appear as **N2 N1**, and where the qualification of *N2* by an adjective yields the sequence **N1 of Adj N2** (the French translations are given in parentheses):

interference levels (niveaux de brouillage)
levels of permissible interference (niveaux de brouillage admissible).

Thus, certain term variants are to be found in sequences with preposition *of*. However, such variants are of length greater than 2, and should be recovered from the underlying term of length 2, as is done in (Jacquemin 1997). Furthermore, terms (of length 2 and more) with preposition *of* are not frequent. This explains why they are not retained in most studies. Lastly, in a bilingual environment, as argued before, not retaining English patterns with prepositions may act as an additional filter for French candidate terms.

2.3 Operations to form longer terms

Three types of operations are generally used to form longer terms from terms of length 2: composition, modification and coordination.

Composition forms new terms from existing ones, either by juxtaposition of the existing terms, or by substituting one component of an existing term by a term the head of which is the substituted component. Here is an example of juxtaposition, both in French and English:

temps de propagation → temps de propagation par satellite (Fr)
propagation delay → satellite propagation delay (En)

An example of substitution is:

densité de bruit → densité spectrale de bruit (Fr)
noise density → noise spectral density (En)

Modification creates new terms through an adjectival or adverbial modification of existing ones. The adjective/adverb can be inserted within a given term, or after or before a given term (in French (English), only adjectives post(pre)-modifying a term are considered). Here are some examples, in which the modifying elements appear in italics:

polarisation *quasi* circulaire (Fr)
nearly circular polarization (En)

réseaux par satellites *distincts* (Fr)
distinct satellite networks (En)

Lastly, coordination groups existing terms into a coordinated form:

répartition en fréquences, répartition dans le temps
→ répartition en fréquence ou dans le temps (Fr)

time division, frequency division
→ time or frequency division (En).

A sequence of the form **N1 Prep N2 Prep N3** in French can thus be obtained either by juxtaposition of *N1* to **N2 Prep N3** or *N3* to **N1 Prep N2**, or by substitution of **N1 Prep N2** in **N1 Prep N3** or **N2 Prep N3** in **N1 Prep N2**. Similarly, a sequence **N1 Adj Prep N2** can be *a priori* interpreted in terms of substitution or modification. The same remarks hold for English.
We can however draw a line between juxtaposition and substitution on the one hand, and substitution and modification on the other hand, by imposing what we call a non-overlapping constraint in juxtaposition and modification. The non-overlapping constraint states that the only sub-term of length 2 a sequence formed by juxtaposition or modification contains is the original term used as support of juxtaposition and/or modification. Thus, for a sequence **N1 Prep N2 Prep N3** to be a juxtaposition of *N1* to the sequence **N2 Prep N3**, neither **N1 Prep N2** nor **N1 Prep N3** must be terms of length 2.

The use of the non-overlapping constraint implies the knowledge of all the terms of length 2, not only the ones present in the corpus under study, but also the ones assumed within a certain domain. It is difficult to precisely establish this knowledge. However, once it has been established, it can be adequately used for analyzing longer terms into sub-terms, following for example the approach described in (Bourigault 1994).

2.4 Correspondences and non-correspondences across languages

In an ideal world, the English and French patterns cover exactly the same units, i.e. French terms following French patterns are translated into English terms following English patterns. (Maxwell 1992) speaks of "regularities" in rendering certain English patterns into certain French patterns.

On a small portion of our corpus, we have looked at which structures were used in English (French) to translate French (English) candidates following the above patterns. Considering each candidate only once, we obtained the following results (we do not claim that the figures we obtained are representative of the phenomena taken into account. They mainly serve as an illustration of our discussion):

Table 1. Pattern correspondences and non-correspondences

	N N	Adj N	N of N	N's N	N
N de N	122	15	2	1	8
N prep N	28	9	–	–	2
N Adj	23	63	–	–	1
N N	11	–	–	–	–
N	1	1	–	–	–

The preceding results can also be seen in the graphs in Figures 1 and 2 below, which show how the different patterns we have considered in one language are realized in the other one.

The numbering indicates the correspondence between elements of English and French terms. **N1 Prep N2** represents all the French patterns formed with two nouns.

The differences between the two graphs show that we should extract more French candidates than English ones. It is the case since we obtain a set of 2,235 English candidates occurring at least twice, against 3,205 French candidates occurring at least twice. Furthermore, we see that relying on patterns in both English and French should act as a filter for French candidate terms. As we

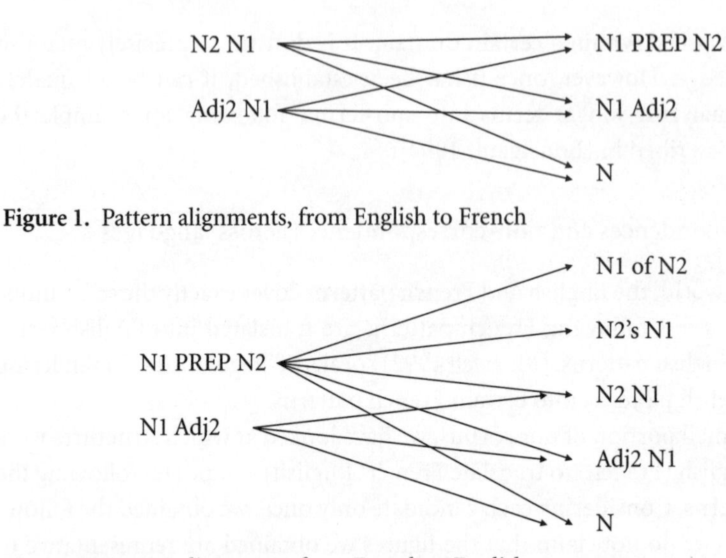

Figure 1. Pattern alignments, from English to French

Figure 2. Pattern alignments, from French to English

already mentioned, French candidate terms translated as an **N of N** sequence are not usually terms. Thus, the bilingual dimension could serve as a refinement for monolingual terminology extraction. However, if valid for French, this remark is not true for English, since most of the structures used to translate English candidate terms are retained in French.

The correspondences and non-correspondences between patterns across languages show that it is not possible to come up with patterns which cover exactly the same phenomena in both languages. We are thus bound to face non-correspondences between a set of candidate terms extracted following some patterns in one language and other patterns in another language. Different strategies can be envisaged to cope with this problem, as we see in next section.

3. Bilingual term alignment

3.1 Avoiding parse-parse match procedures

Several methods have been proposed to align noun phrases and/or terms within parallel corpora. These methods usually rely on the following steps: extraction of candidate terms (or NPs) in each language, and alignment of the extracted units, assuming that monolingually extracted units correpond to each other cross-lingually (see Kupiec 1993; Gaussier 1995, for example). Unfortunately, this is not always the case, and the above methodology suffers from the weaknesses pointed out by (Wu 1997) concerning parse-parse match procedures:

1. appropriate, robust, monolingual grammars may not be available,
2. grammars may be incompatible across languages,
3. selection between multiple possible arrangements may be arbitrary.

If the first point above concerns more particularly the grammatical analysis of complete sentences, the last two ones have a direct impact on bilingual terminology extraction, as we have seen in previous section. Three main solutions have been proposed to overcome these problems.

Extended parse-parse method

The first solution can be viewed as an extended parse-parse match procedure, and can be summarized as follows: starting with word alignments, use syntactic dependencies and contiguity constraints to derive unit alignments. As an example, consider the French and English terms *largeur de bande admissible* and *permissible bandwidth*, and let us assume that our word-to-word alignment produces a correspondence between *admissible* and *permissible*, *largeur* and *bandwidth*, and *bande* and *bandwidth*. Then, we can rely on a syntactic parser to extract the dependencies *permissible* → *bandwidth*, and *admissible* → (*largeur de bande*). In the latter case, a syntactic parser would most likely produce either *admissible* → *largeur* or *admissible* → *bande*. However, in both cases, we are able to derive the association *largeur de bande admissible* ↔ *permissible bandwidth*, based on the correspondences across languages, the dependency relations between words and the contiguity of the sequences considered. Of course, for bilingual terminology alignment, only certain dependency relations have to be taken into account, namely the ones corresponding to the patterns given in previous section.

(Debili and Zribi 1996) are the first ones, to our knowledge, to have proposed this method. (Hull 1998) uses a variant of this method, based on the following sequence: sort candidate term associations in descending order of a score based on the word alignments they contain (this step produces a sorted list of (Ts ↔ Tc) pairs, where Ts (Tc) is a candidate term in the source (target) language), take the largest association and align the associated terms, unless both are already aligned. If, for example, the source term Ts is already aligned with another term Tc1, then the target term Tc is concatenated to Tc1 if there is a dependency relation between head words of Tc and Tc1 or Tc and Tc1 are contiguous (i.e. there is no unit between Tc and Tc1 which is aligned elsewhere).

The method used by Hull differs from the method proposed by Debili, inasmuch as candidate terms are extracted in both languages, and so the first list of term associations built suffers from the problems associated with parse-parse match procedures. Furthermore, it is not possible, with this method, to recover the translation of a source term when this translation is a subpart of a target candidate term. Since there is no restriction on the length of candidate terms, such a case will happen.

Crucial for Debili's method is the word alignment algorithm used. If a type (1,1) alignment is used, that is each English (French) word is associated to one and only one French (English) word, then, in the preceding example, either *largeur* or *bande,* but not both, will be associated with *bandwidth,* and the correspondence between *largeur de bande admissible* and *permissible bandwidth* may not be recovered. Less restrictive alignment types can be used, but they may lead to less precise results, and thus endanger the whole procedure.

One way parsing

An alternative solution to the problems of parse-parse match methods for bilingual terminology extraction can be found in (Gaussier 1998), where candidate terms are extracted in one language (English), and guessed, through the alignment process, in the other language (French). The method is based on flow network models for aligning units within aligned sentences. An English sentence is represented by a set of vertices corresponding to the different candidate terms and words in the English sentence. In order to take into account contiguity constraints, the French sentence is represented as a set of layers of vertices, the lowest layer being associated with the French words themselves, and each vertex in any upper layer being linked to two consecutive vertices of the layer below. The uppermost layer contains only one vertex and can be seen as representing the whole French sentence. Capacity values can also be used to control the length of a French unit a given English unit can be aligned to. A minimum cost flow algorithm is then run between the English and French vertices to discover translations of English candidate terms.

Such a procedure allows one to discover translation of English terms which are subparts of French candidate terms, without suffering from parse-parse match procedure problems. Furthermore, the associations between words do not serve as a starting point from which larger associations are derived, but are rather used to define a score between English and French units. A possible extension of this approach is to replace the vertices corresponding to contiguous units with vertices corresponding to dependency relations between units. However, for terminology extraction purposes, since terms are usually made up of contiguous elements, it is not clear that there will be much difference between the two approaches, if one restricts oneself to dependency relations present in terms. Nevertheless, we can expect that with larger grammars, i.e. not restricted to term identification, we will have a better disambiguation of different relations, since the context is no more local to a term. We could thus take advantage of the dependency relations in this case.

Parallel parsing

Lastly, a third solution can be envisaged along the lines given by (Wu 1997). In this work, an inversion transduction bilingual grammar is built to parse in parallel aligned sentences, based on word alignments. Once the grammatical analyses have been built for each sentence, we can, for example, select the units corresponding to candidate terms in the English parse and associate them with their corresponding units in the French parse. This method is thus general enough to accommodate our needs for bilingual terminology extraction. Nevertheless, since this method aims at finding parallel parses for complete sentences, it is more subject to errors than a method restricted to term alignments, and may miss correct associations or yield incorrect ones that the methods restricted to terminology alignment will not miss or yield.

In light of the problems described in previous section for bilingual terminology alignment, we believe it is important to design an alignment method which alleviates the problem of parse-parse match procedures. We have described three such methods, trying to outline their strengths and weaknesses. We now want to turn to the problem of which parameters should be taken into account in a bilingual term alignment program.

3.2 Which parameters for bilingual terminology alignment

3.2.1 *Standard parameters*

A parameter common to all the methods is the set of word associations. Word associations, which roughly correspond to probabilities of associating two

English and French candidate terms, can be refined using positional information, leading for example to the distortion model used in (Brown et al., 1993), and/or part-of-speech information. Positional information allows one to distinguish different identical words in a given sentence, and to search for the translation of two contiguous source words in the same window of the target sentence. This latter requirement reflects the fact that words are not translated independently of each other, but, since they are part of larger units, their translation is part of the translation of the whole unit, and is thus close to the translation of other words in the unit. The identification of terms in one language is precisely a way to extract larger units. Furthermore, the contiguity constraints used in certain methods to discover terms represent a strong form of positional information. Thus, it is not necessary to include the position of candidate terms within their sentence to look for term alignments. However, if the procedure to establish the set of word associations does include positional information, then this information will be adequately used by the term alignment procedure.

Following the presentation we made of the French and English patterns, and their association across languages, a natural question which comes to mind is whether or not pattern affinities can be used to help align terms. This is what we are going to investigate.

3.2.2 *Pattern affinities*

By *pattern affinities*, we mean that French (English) candidate terms following certain patterns seem more likely to be rendered in English (French) into certain patterns, as can be seen in Table 1.

Pattern affinities may thus impact the search for the translation of a given term of length 2. In the case of terms of length 3 or more, the use of pattern affinities is less clear. However, if one disposes of a grammatical analysis of each term, then one can introduce pattern affinities based on the terms of length 2 present in the longer term. We will thus focus here on terms of length 2, assuming that the conclusions we can draw from the study of pattern affinities on these terms can be interpolated to longer terms.

To test the influence of pattern affinities on term alignment, we conducted two experiments, with and without pattern affinities. In each experiment, we used a version of model 1 of (Brown et al., 1993). This model assumes that a given French unit can be aligned with one and only one English unit, whereas a given English unit can be aligned with several French units. Since the set of French candidate terms is much larger than the set of English candidate terms, this assumption seems reasonable. Furthermore, the use of the EM algorithm within this model allows us to estimate probabilities of associating patterns across languages in a natural way.

Let *m* (*n*) be the number of candidate terms in the French (English) sentence *Fs* (*Es*). Let *A* design an alignment between candidate terms of *Fs* and *Es*. *A* is uniquely determined by the values it can take, *A*=(*a1*, …, *am*), where *ai* can take any value between 1 and n. We can then write the probability of associating the two sentences Fs and Es as:

(1) $P(Fs,Es)=C\ Sum_A\ p(A,Fs,Es)=Sum_A\ Prod_j\ p(Fs_j, Es_{aj})$

where *C* is a constant, *aj* is the position, in the English sentence, of the candidate to which the French candidate Fs_j is associated to in alignment *A*. Using the EM algorithm, as defined in (Demspter et al., 1977), one arrives at the following reestimation formula (see (Gaussier 1995) for more details):

(2) $P^{(t+1)}(Tf,Te)=Sum_s\ cs(Tf)\ cs(Te)\ (\ P^{(t)}(Tf,Te)/Sum_{e'}P^{(t)}(Tf,Te'))$

where *cs*() represents the number of occurrences in the current pair, *s*, of aligned sentences, and $P^{(t)}$ is the current estimation of probabilities.

The introduction of pattern affinities implies a modification of equation (1), and suggests writing the probability of associating two candidate terms *Tf* and *Te* as the product of two independent probabilities, one based only on lexical affinities (as above), and one involving pattern affinities:

(3) P(Tf,Te)=Plex(Tf,Te) * Ppat(pat(Tf),pat(Te))

where *pat(Tf)* is the pattern of the candidate term *Tf*. The reestimation of lexical affinities (*Plex*) leads to a reestimation formula similar to (2) with pattern affinities (we do not provide reestimation formulas based on equation (3) since they are not necessary for the rest of the discussion. The interesting reader is referred to (Gaussier 1995)).

Interestingly, from formula (3), we can use either a fixed set of probabilities based on pattern affinities (derived for example from a portion of our corpus), or reestimate them. The reestimation of these probabilities gives us a better view of how patterns are connected across languages in our corpus.

We tested the two models, with and without pattern affinities, on our bilingual corpus. We first present the results evaluated against a reference list, based on *Eurodicautom*, and provided within the framework of the European Project, ET-10/63. For each experiment, the results are sorted according to the score they received. The first hundred associations were then evaluated, then the first two hundred, … For each set of association (up to 1000 associations), we provide precision and recall in parentheses.

Table 2. Influence of pattern affinities on bilingual terminology extraction

Number of associations	Without pattern affin.	With pattern affinities
100	0.89 (0.07)	0.9 (0.07)
200	0.86 (0.134)	0.855 (0.14)
300	0.84 (0.2)	0.83 (0.20)
400	0.827 (0.267)	0.8025 (0.26)
500	0.796 (0.32)	0.796 (0.32)
600	0.77 (0.32)	0.776 (0.376)
700	0.758 (0.43)	0.77 (0.435)
800	0.752 (0.486)	0.7575 (0.49)
900	0.73 (0.53)	0.742 (0.54)
1000	0.707 (0.57)	0.711 (0.574)

As we can see from Table 2, pattern affinities do not provide any significant change on the results obtained without taking them into account. One may think that, based on the figures given in Table 1, we failed, in our experiment, to make substantial use of pattern affinities. From Table 1, we can derive the following set of probabilities between French and English patterns (the following figures correspond to the probability of translating a particular English pattern into French).

Table 3. Pattern affinities, *a priori* probabilities

	N de N	N prep N	N N	N Adj
N N	0.79	0.15	0.04	0.02
Adj N	0.13	0.02	0.01	0.84

However, these figures are based on counting only once any candidate terms, regardless of their number of occurrences. While reestimating pattern affinities using the EM algorithm, we make use of the number of occurrences of each term. This leads us to a very different set of probabilities, namely the one in Table 4.

We now see that the English pattern **Adj N** can be almost equally translated into French as **N de N** or **N Adj**. A more precise study of English **Adj N** candidate terms shows that almost all the candidates in which the adjective is a verbal

Table 4. Pattern affinities, reestimated probabilities

	N de N	N prep N	N N	N Adj
N N	0.57	0.10	0.01	0.32
Adj N	0.41	0.095	0.005	0.49

adjective of the form *-ing* (and was tagged *Adj* by our POS-tagger) are translated into French as a sequence **N1 de N2**, in which *N2* is the translation of the English *-ing* form and modifies *N1*, translation of the English noun, as in *signalling system* (*système de signalisation*) or *switching equipment* (*équipement de commutation*).

Another phenomenon we encountered is related to adjectives derived from nouns as *convolution*→*convolutional*. When such adjectives are used in one language, the translation of their associated noun may be used in the other language. This is typically the case for the English adjective *terrestrial*, which is translated (in all cases but one) as the French prepositional phrase *de terre*.

We thus see that, without consideration of the particular terms, pattern affinities are not relevant for bilingual terminology extraction. However, the preceding remarks suggest that we should modify our model and make pattern affinities dependent on the particular terms involved. This would lead to a significant increase in the number of parameters our alignment model uses, and would imply the use of very large corpora on a particular technical domain. Simplifications may however come from the above considerations. In particular, one could treat all the English sequences *-ing N*, where the *-ing* form is tagged as an adjective, in the same manner, privileging **N de N** translations. Similarly, we can envisage a special treatment for **Adj N** sequences where the adjective derives from a noun. This shows that precise knowledge of how terms behave monolingually (e.g. which form, adjective or noun, is preferred in one language for a given concept) is necessary to build a program for bilingual terminology extraction. We have not modified our model in order to take into account fine-grained distinctions between candidate terms, but hope to do it in a near future.

4. Conclusion

We have presented general considerations on bilingual terminology extraction, based on a case study of English-French terminology. This study showed that, in order to account for the differences that exist between two languages, the alignment methods must be very flexible. In particular, we believe it is important not to rely only on parse-parse match procedures. Lastly, we have discussed the use of (terminology) pattern affinities across languages during the alignment process, showing that those affinities should not be used independently of the current terms under consideration.

References

Bourigault, D. 1994. *LEXTER, un Logiciel d'Extraction de TERminologie. Application à l'acquisition de connaissances à partir de textes.* PhD Thesis. Paris: École des Hautes Études en Sciences Sociales.

Brown, P., Della Pietra, S., Della Pietra, V. and Mercer, R. 1993. "The Mathematics of Statistical Machine Translation: Parameter Estimation." *Computational Linguistics*, 19(2).

Chuquet, H. and Paillard, M. 1989. *Approche linguistique des problèmes de traduction anglais-français.* Ophrys.

Daille, B. 1994. *Approche mixte pour l'extraction de terminologie: statistique lexicale et filtres linguistiques.* PhD Thesis. Paris: Univ. Paris 7.

Debili, F. and Zribi, A. 1996. "Les dépendances syntaxiques au service de l'appariement des mots." In *Proceedings of 10ième Congrès Reconnaissance des Formes et Intelligence Artificielle.*

Dempster, A., Laird, N. and Rubin, D. 1977. "Maximum likelihood from incomplete data via the EM algorithm." *Journal of the Royal Statistical Society*, 34(B).

Gaussier, E. 1995. *Modèles statistiques et patrons morphosyntaxiques pour l'extraction de lexiques bilingues de termes.* PhD Thesis. Paris: Univ. Paris 7.

Gaussier, E. 1998. "Flow Network Model for Bilingual Lexicon Extraction." In *Proceedings of the joint COLING-ACL Conference.*

Gross, G. 1988. "Degré de figement des noms composés." *Langages*, vol. 90.

Hull, D. 1998. "A practical approach to teminology alignment." In *Proceedings of the First Workshop on Computational Terminology.* Montreal, 1998.

Jacquemin, C. 1997. *Variation terminologique: reconnaissance et acquisition automatique de termes et de leurs variantes en corpus.* Habilitation à diriger des recherches, IRIN, Univ. de Nantes.

Justeson, J. and Katz, S. 1995. "Technical terminology: some linguistic properties and an algorithm for identification in text." *Natural Language Engineering*, 1(1).

Kupiec, J. 1993. "An algorithm for finding noun phrase correspondences in bilingual corpora." In *Proceedings of the 31st Annual Meeting of the Association for Computational Linguistics.*

Mathieu-Colas, M. 1988. *Typologie des noms composés.* Rapport technique. Univ. Paris 13.

Maxwell, K. 1992. *Automatic translation of English compounds: problems and prospects.* Rapport technique Working Papers in Language Processing, 39, University of Essex.
Nkwenti-Azeh, B. 1992. Positional and Combinational characteristics of Satellite Communications terms. Technical Report, CCl-UMIST, Manchester.
Wu, D. 1997. "Stochastic inversion transduction grammars and bilingual parsing of parallel corpora." *Computational Linguistics*, 23(3).

CHAPTER 9

Detection of synonymy links between terms

Experiment and results*

Thierry Hamon and Adeline Nazarenko
LIPN — UPRES-A 7030 & Université Paris-Nord

This paper presents a new approach for the evaluation of the detection of synonymy relations between terms. Our goal is to help the terminology structuring. This approach exploits the synonymy relationships which have been extracted from lexical resources to infer synonymy links between complex terms. The inferred links are then validated by an human expert in the context of a terminological application. In a previous evaluation on documents dealing with electric power plant, the expert has underlined that the most important point is to increase the recall even if the precision is low and if some links are mistyped. This paper reports new experiments which help to understand how this synonymy detection approach is to be used. Various lexical resources — from general language dictionary to very specialized semantic information — are exploited and compared as bootstrapping knowledge. Results show the complementary of the different sources.

The first evaluation relied on traditional recall and precision measures. However, those scores do not reflect the usefulness of the inferred links for the terminology structuring. From the terminologist's point of view, erroneous links are quick to eliminated. They may even suggest good ones. Above all, the system points out relations between terms which are generally not found manually. We thus aim at proposing a new evaluation criteria which better reflects the expert's and terminologist's point of view in the application context. This score points out the quality of the results and the validation cost rather than the proportion of validated links. We have designed an evaluation score which takes into account the productivity of the dictionary links. It can be viewed as a normalized precision.

1. Introduction

Document Consulting Systems require a terminology to help the user's navigation through the document. Structured terminologies enhance the document access by providing information about the terms and their semantic links. For instance, it is useful to know that the terms *matériel électrique* (electric equipment)[1] and *équipement électrique* (electrical fittings) or *marche normale* (normal running) and *bon fonctionnement* (right working) are synonymous if one wants to identify the various sections of the document that deal with electric equipment.

Several tools are available to help terminologists in the terminology structuring tasks. We focus on the detection of synonymy links between terms. We rely on a rule-based approach using general lexical resources, *i.e.* synonymy links between words extracted from a general language dictionary. The rules have been tested and tuned on different corpora of various size and domain.

We report here a new experiment which results from a collaboration with French electricity company (EDF). This industrial context and the interaction with users helped us to understand how the acquisition process should be bootstrapped and evaluated in the context of realistic terminological applications.

The results have been analyzed by the terminologist in charge of the terminology construction process. Various lexical resources have been exploited as bootstrapping knowledge from general language dictionary to very specialized semantic information. Results show the complementarity and the usefulness of the different sources. The evaluation phase showed that the traditional precision and recall are difficult to measure and do not take into account the terminologist's usefulness judgment. We propose a new evaluation measure for terminology structuring tasks.

The following section presents the terminology building process in the context of a Consulting System and describes our approach for the detection of synonymy links. The acquisition of synonymy links using a general dictionary is first tested. The Section 3 reports this experiment and analyses the results. This experiment then leads us to study the contribution of various lexical sources to the terminology structuring (Section 4). The Section 5 addresses the evaluation problem. A new evaluation measure is proposed, which better reflects the help of our system and of terminological tools to the terminology structuring.

2. Enhancing a Document Consulting System with a structured terminology

2.1 The Document Consulting task

The increase of technical documentation leads companies to build document navigation systems. The Technical Documentation Consulting System (TDCS) developed at the French electricity company Electricité de France (EDF) by Gros and Assadi (1997) provides an hypertextual access to information contained into technical documents. It offers various access modes:

- a traditional table of content;
- a full-text keyword access as in information retrieval systems;
- an index of the activity modeling the user's task;
- an index of the domain with synonymy and hyponymy links between entries and sub-entries (the part of the terminology of the domain which is relevant for the document).

The indexes are also used to expand or specify the user queries.

Consultation systems differ from hypertextual systems such as SNITCH (Mayfield and Nicholas 1992) which deals with a document base composed of short texts. SNITCH automatically and dynamically generates a semantic representation of a document in the form of a semantic network whose nodes are the document terms. Consultation systems do not process the whole document, they rather focus on the queries, helping the users to expand or specify their keyword list and proposing various access modes. This latter approach, which is not as costly as the former one and which is less sensitive to errors is well-suited for large technical documents such as a technical service manual.

Whereas information retrieval systems aim at finding relevant documents from a large corpus of various theme for a given query, consultation systems usually deal with a single document of few hundreds of pages (less than one million words). In the former systems, the relevancy of documents is based on statistical scores or general semantic networks such as WordNet (Richardson et al. 1994) whereas consulting systems use terminologies *i.e.* domain dependent resources, to compute relevancy measures.

2.2 Terminology structuring

The integration of a new document in a consultation system is efficient if there exists a terminology of the corresponding domain. As such terminologies are seldom available for specific technical domains, they must be built automatically.

However, the terminology building process cannot be fully automated. Identifying the terms of a technical domain is a matter of word usage and expert agreement. The detection of term links requires a thorough knowledge of the underlying concepts. There also exists various types of terminologies (Srinivasan

1992). The aim of the French electricity company EDF is therefore to develop a tool that helps the terminology building task. The system suggests a first selection of terms and term relations. The terminologists then correct and/or extends this sketch. Even if they have to go back to the document to check some specific points, they can avoid reading the full document.

The overall architecture of such terminology building tools is usually divided in two subsystems. The terminology extraction tools acquire terms from a corpus and build a term list. The structuring tools build a semantic network out of this list, by adding semantic links between the terms. Both the terms and the term relations require to be controlled by the expert. This two-step computer-aided process is adopted in Termight (Dagan and Church 1994) in the case of multilingual terminologies, for instance. The architecture of the Technical Document Consulting System is similar. A terminology extraction software (LEXTER (Bourigault 1992)) first automatically extracts candidate terms from documents. The terms are either simple or complex if they are composed of several words. The terms form a syntactic network which is then enriched with semantic relations during the structuring phase.

Traditionally, a terminology has different types of semantic relations (Srinivasan 1992: 162): hierarchical relations (is-a) which link a term to a more specific/generic one, equivalence relations (synonymy) and non-hierarchical relations (see-also), among which are the preference relations connecting a controlled term to its less accepted variants. The accuracy and the number of these relations vary from a terminology to another.

There is no general method for terminology structuring. Several complementary tools have been designed, each one dealing with a specific type of semantic relations. They respectively provide the terminologist with

- hyperonymy, the hierarchical relation that traditionally structures the terminologies and allows for generalization inferences (Hearst 1992; Morin 1998): *substances* > *bromine*; *substances* > *hydrogen* or *cation* > *calcium* (were > stands for "is the hyperonym of");
- term variants, the phrases that are semantically equivalent to a term (Jacquemin 1996): knowing these variants helps the terminologist to choose the controlled term: *gene expression vs. expression of gene*;
- conceptual word classes or groupings (Habert et al. 1996; Assadi 1997; Pereira et al. 1993), sets of words which require to be hierarchically organized: {*225 kV double circuit line, overhead line, 225 kV underground line*};
- causal relations, which are especially important in technical domains where diagnosis, repair, planning, physical action are involved (Garcia 1998):

to_create(*electric charging increase, electric network expansion*);
- theme and domain clues, which are also used to disambiguate terms: in the EDF Thesaurus, the entry *behavior* is tagged [psychology];
- etc.

2.3 Acquisition of synonymy links between terms

Our synonymy definition is close to that of WordNet (Miller et al. 1993). It is a simplified one. We consider synonymy as a Boolean rather than as a scaling property as in Cruse (1986). We define a "contextual synonymy": two terms X and Y are synonymous relatively to a context C if both terms are syntactically identical and semantically substitutable in the context C.
We assume that the semantics and the synonymy of the complex candidate terms are compositional. This working hypothesis is discussed in Hamon and Nazarenko (2000). We assume that complex terms are composed of a head and an expansion. Two terms are considered as synonymous if their components are identical or synonymous.

We designed three rules to detect synonymy relations between candidate terms. Given the complex candidate terms $CCT_1 = (T_1, E_1)$ and $CCT_2 = (T_2, E_2)$, and $syn(CT_1, CT_2)$ a synonymy relation between the candidate terms CT_1 and CT_2, following inference rules are used:

$$R_1: T_1 = T_2 \wedge syn(E_1, E_2) \supset syn(CCT_1, CCT_2)$$
$$R_2: E_1 = E_2 \wedge syn(T_1, T_2) \supset syn(CCT_1, CCT_2)$$
$$R_3: syn(T_1, T_2) \wedge syn(E_1, E_2) \supset syn(CCT_1, CCT_2)$$

This means that, considering two candidate terms, if one of the following conditions is met, a synonymy link is added to the terminological network:

- the heads are identical and the expansions are synonymous (*collecteur général* (general collector)/*collecteur commun* (common collector)), (R_1);
- the heads are synonymous and the expansions are identical (*matériel électrique* (electric equipment)/*équipement électrique* (electrical fittings)), (R_2);
- the heads are synonymous and the expansions are synonymous (*marche normale* (normal running)/*bon fonctionnement* (right working)), (R_3);

We first use the dictionary links as a bootstrap to detect synonymy links between complex candidate terms. Then, we iterate the process by including the newly detected links in our base to infer links between more complex candidate terms. The iteration process stops when no new link can be found.

3. Experiment

3.1 Experimental data

3.1.1 *Working corpora*

In the context of our collaboration with EDF, we applied the proposed rules on the DSE corpus (DSE_2 in the following). This 160,000 words corpus is composed of Elementary System Files (*Dossiers de Système Elémentaire*, henceforth DSE) and deals with the operations on nuclear power plants. This corpus has been analyzed by LEXTER (Bourigault 1992) which extracts 17,675 candidate terms: 4,171 simple candidate terms (2,865 nouns and 1,306 adjectives) and 13,504 complex candidate terms *i.e.* noun phrases. Each complex candidate term (*ligne d'alimentation*, supply line) is analyzed into a head (*ligne*, line) and an expansion (*alimentation*, supply). It is part of a syntactic network (cf. Figure 1).

Reported results are compared with a first DSE corpus (DSE_1 in the following) on which we initially tuned the rules (Hamon et al. 1998). This 200,000 word corpus deals with the same domain. It has been analyzed by LEXTER: 12,043 candidate terms have been extracted: 3,428 simple candidate terms (2,831 nouns and 597 adjectives) and 8,615 complex candidate terms.

The synonymy detection process has also been applied on the Menelas corpus (Zweigenbaum 1994), a collection of documents[2] dealing with coronary diseases. LEXTER analyzed this 85,000 words corpus and 13,233 candidate terms have been extracted (2,675 nouns, 1,006 adjectives and 9,552 noun phrases).

Results of the term extraction for three different corpora are summarized in the Table 1.

Table 1. Results of the candidate term extraction

Corpus	DSE_1	DSE_2	Menelas
Candidate terms	12 047	17 675	13 233
Simple candidate terms	3 428	4 171	3 681
Nouns	2 831	2 865	2 675
Adjectives	597	1 306	1 006
Complex candidate terms	8 615	13 504	9 552

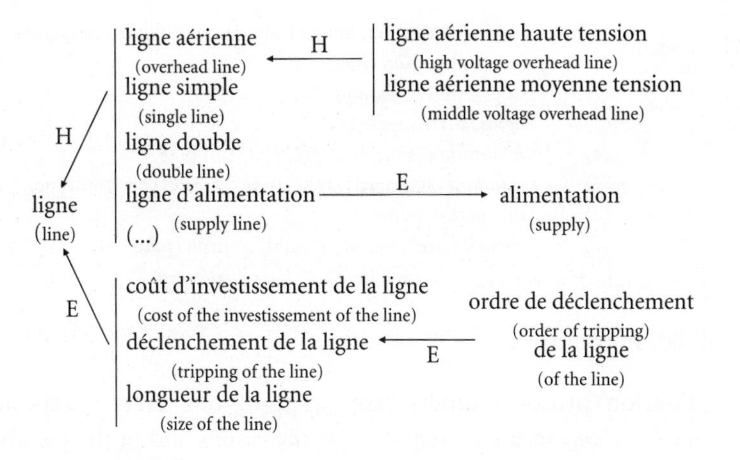

Figure 1. Part of the LEXTER syntactic network

3.1.2 *General language dictionary*

For the reported experiment, we used a French general dictionary *Le Robert* supplied by the *Institut National de la Langue Française (INaLF)*. The dictionary provides synonyms distributed among the different senses of each word entry (see Figure 2). It is exploited as a synonym dictionary. We choose a standard and widely available — although imperfect — dictionary so as to carry out our experiment in realistic conditions. The semantics of the extracted relations is often fuzzy and sometimes reflects mere see-also relations that one would hardly consider as synonymy. For instance, our dictionary extraction gives *temps* (time)/*température* (temperature) as a synonymous pair whereas the synonymy holds for a very specific meaning of both words (in the meteorological context). As we will see below, such weak dictionary relations generate erroneous links in the final terminology. This is partly due to the fact that we do not take into account the various sense distinctions of the dictionary entries, as in Ploux and Victorri (1998).

Although "contextual synonymy" is a transitive relation, we cannot consider the transitivity property, because the dictionary synonymy relations are context-free. The application of this property would produce a great deal of errors. However, most of the relevant links which can be inferred by transitivity already exist in the dictionary.

modèle (model)	⟨1⟩	*canon* (canon), *étalon* (standard), *exemplaire* (copy), *exemple* (example), *plan* (plan)
	⟨2⟩	*sujet* (subject), *maquette* (maquette)
	⟨3⟩	*héros* (hero), *type* (type)
	⟨4⟩	*échantillon* (sample), *spécimen* (sample)
	⟨5⟩	*standard* (standard), *type* (type), *prototype* (prototype)
	⟨6⟩	*maquette* (model)
	⟨7⟩	*gabarit* (size), *moule* (mould), *patron* (pattern)

Figure 2. Example of a word entry from the *Le Robert dictionary*

3.2 Validation protocole

The validation protocol differs from that of our former experiment (Hamon et al. 1998) in the presentation of the results and in the possibilities given to the expert.

A domain expert who is also a terminologist has validated the inferred links in the context of an access to the information contained in documents.

The interface allows to modify the relation type of each link. Although we aim at detecting synonymy relations between terms, other relations are inferred. Moreover, whereas the rules are applied on lemmatized terms, we choose to present the term inflected forms of the terms for the sake of validation comfort. Two presentations have been used for the validation of the inferred links. Besides the connected components[3] which give an overall view of the links, we propose to structure the results in families.

Indeed, we have noted in the validation of the DSE_1 corpus (Hamon et al. 1998) that all the links inferred from some dictionary word couple are rejected. This is the case for *capacité* (capacity)/*puissance* (power):

capacité maximale (maximal capacity)	*puissance maximale* (maximal power)
capacité faible (low capacity)	*puissance faible* (low power)
capacité nulle (null capacity)	*puissance nulle* (null power)
capacité petite (small capacity)	*puissance faible* (low power)

We chose to group inferred links in families. A family is a set of links inferred from the same dictionary link. The links inferred with the third rule belong to two families corresponding to two initial links. For instance, the link *capacité faible* (low capacity)/*volume petit* (small volume) belongs the families inferred from *capacité* (capacity)/*volume* (volume) and from *faible* (low)/*petit* (small).

This results presentation therefore helps the validation phase. The terminologists can easily reject a whole family if they consider that the dictionary link is erroneous for a given corpus.

3.3 Results

3.3.1 *Overall results*

We applied the rules on the DSE_2 corpus. The inferred links have been validated by an expert of the domain according to the protocol presented above. 590 links have been inferred between complex candidate terms. The expert agreed on 33.72% of these links *i.e.* 199 links (cf. Table 2). Synonymy links represent 50.75% (*i.e.* 101 links) of the validated links: *catégorie sismique* (seismic category)/*classe sismique* (seismic class).

As expected, see-also relations are numerous. They represent 42.22% of the links (*i.e.* 84 links): *échelle logarithmique* (logarithmic scale)/*gamme logarithmique* (logarithmic range) (cf. Table 3).

The expert identified hyponymy relations: *phénomène naturel* (natural phenomenon)/*phénomène physique* (physical phenomenon) or meronymy relations: *équipement REA* (REA fittings)/*matériel* REA (REA equipment).

The links validated as antonymy relations are often due to biases of lemmatization and presentation. The term lemmatization modifies some terms with negation mark. For instance, *matériels non statiques* (non-static equipment) is lemmatized as *matériel statique* (static equipment). Therefore, we infer the antonymy link *matériels non statiques* (non-static equipment)/*équipement statique* (static fittings).

Table 2. Results and validation of the links

	Number	Percentage
Validated links	199	33.72%
Invalidated links	391	66.28%
Total	590	100%

The distribution of the links varies from a rule to another (cf. Table 4). The inference rule 2 is the most productive whatever the relation, except for the hyperonymy. This shows the complementarity of our approach compared with the terminologist work. 67% of the synonymy links proposed by our approach have synonymous head while terminologists generally build links corresponding to the two other rules. The rule 3 is the less productive rule as we have already noted in Hamon et al. (1998). However, the resulting links are generally not found by the terminologists.

Table 3. Type of the validated links

Type of relation	Number of links	Percentage
Synonymy	101	50.75%
See-Also	84	42.22%
Hyperonymy	11	5.53%
Meronymy	1	0.5%
Antonymy	2	1%
Total	199	100%

Table 4. Distribution of the links according to the inference rules

Type of relation	Synonymy	See-Also	Hyperonymy	Meronymy	Antonymy	Total
Rule 1	28	17	7	0	1	53
Rule 2	67	61	4	1	1	134
Rule 3	6	6	0	0	0	12

3.3.2 *Analysis of the result structure*

The distribution of the family size is similar for the three corpora (cf. Table 5). Most of the families are composed of one link (more than 2/3). The families with more than two links represent less than 1/10 of the families.

Table 5. Distribution of the families according to their size

Size	DSE_1 corpus	DSE_2 corpus	Menelas corpus
1	179 (67.29%)	314 (67.38%)	286 (71.5%)
2	40 (15.03%)	84 (18.03%)	60 (15%)
3	19 (7.14%)	32 (6.87%)	20 (5%)
4	13 (4.88%)	16 (3.43%)	7 (1.75%)
5	1 (0.38%)	6 (1.3%)	11 (2.75%)
6	7 (2.64%)	7 (1.5%)	4 (1%)
7	3 (1.12%)	2 (0.43%)	5 (1.25%)
8–21	4 (1.52%)	5 (1.06%)	7 (1.75%)
Total	266 (100%)	466 (100%)	400 (100%)

We compute the homogeneity of each family *i* which is defined as:

$$Homogeneity_i = \frac{|NbVal_i - NBErrors_i|}{NbLinks_i}$$

where $NbLinks_i$ is the size of the family, $NbVal_i$ is the number of validated links and $NbErrors_i$ is the number of erroneous links.

The homogeneity of a family is 1 if all the links are either validated or invalidated. The ratio is null when half of links are validated.

Analysis of the results of the DSE_2 corpus shows that the validation is homogeneous for 90% of the families (cf. Table 6): 69.52% of the families have been entirely rejected while 21.67% have been entirely accepted (cf. Table 7). We note a similar distribution for the DSE_1 corpus.

Table 6. Homogeneity of the families according to their validation

	DSE_1 corpus		DSE_2 corpus	
Homogeneity	**Number of families**	**Percentage**	**Number of families**	**Percentage**
0	9	3.38	17	3.65
0.14	1	0.38	-	-
0.2	-	-	2	0.43
0.333	6	2.25	016	3.44
0.42	1	0.38	1	0.21
0.5	4	1.5	3	0.65
0.66	2	0.75	-	-
0.75	1	0.38	1	0.21
0.82	-	-	1	0.21
1	242	90.98	425	91.2
Total	266	100	466	100

3.3.3 *Limits of the evaluation with recall and precision rates*

The validation of the results shows that the rules infer not only synonymy links, but also other types of semantic relations such as hyperonymy and see-also relations. Although the precision is low (33% of the links have been validated), results are interesting for the terminology structuring. Indeed, while the

Table 7. Distribution of the family validation according to the precision rate

	DSE_1 corpus		DSE_2 corpus	
Precision	Number of families	Percentage	Number of families	Percentage
0	169	63.53	324	69.52
0.12	1	0.38	-	-
0.16	2	0.75	-	-
0.25	3	1.12	1	0.22
0.285	-	-	1	0.22
0.333	5	1.88	11	2.36
0.42	1	0.38	-	-
0.5	9	3.38	17	3.64
0.6	-	-	2	0.43
0.66	1	0.38	5	1.07
0.71	1	0.38	-	-
0.75	1	0.38	2	0.43
0.875	-	-	1	0.22
0.909	-	-	1	0.22
1	73	27.44	101	21.67
Total	266	100	466	100

acquisition of links by an expert would take tens of hours, the validation of the links automatically inferred on the DSE_2 corpus took three hours.[4]

The recall rate seems very moderate. It is difficult to evaluate. There is no golden standard which would give the relevant relations of the document. The comparison with links manually detected by an expert is biased as manual detection is subjective. It is well-known that various experts give different results depending on their various backgrounds (Szpakowicz et al. 1996). Moreover, building a consensual terminology from several ones is a real problem because the terminology structuring itself varies from one terminologist to another (Roulin and Cooper 1993; Srinivasan 1992).

However, from the terminologist's point of view, recall rate must be increased, even at the precision's expense. As opposed to information retrieval systems, the precision rate is less important than the recall in terminological tools (Jacquemin 1994). One way to increase recall is to combine various resources. The collaboration with EDF allows to evaluate the complementarity of different resources. Specialized lexical resources are available for the DSE corpora. We report results of the semantic links detection using these various sources (Section 4).

On the other hand, we note that the precision rate does not reflect the help to the terminology building. Results point out unobvious semantic relations between the terms of a document and suggest new links. Semantic links are generally different from those found by the experts: terminologists rather focus on specialized terms already attested. This contrast between the helpfulness of our algorithmic approach and the interpretation of the precision rate raises the problem of the evaluation of our tools. We propose a new measure to evaluate results in the context of a terminology structuring tool (Section 5).

4. Which lexical source for which corpus?

4.1 Using lexical sources with technical corpora

Endogenous approaches are insufficient for terminology building. The acquisition of specialized knowledge from technical documents requires methods which combine existing knowledge sources and specialized corpora. Various lexical sources can be used.

Resources are generally specific for the domain of the working corpus. In the context of a document filtering tool, Naulleau (1998) builds semantic classes starting with information extracted from the EDF Thesaurus. Acquisition of new hyperonymic links from an agronomy corpus is bootstrapped with relations provided by a thesaurus of the domain (Morin 1998). Habert et al. (1998) aim at extending and adapting a medical nomenclature with the Menelas corpus which deals with coronary diseases. Term disambiguation method proposed by Maynard and Ananiadou (1998) is based on a corpus word distribution and on UMLS thesaurus.

As general semantic information has often been considered as irrelevant for specialized language, it has rarely been used for knowledge acquisition from technical corpora. However, Basili et al. (1997) and Basili et al. (1998) show how WordNet and LDOCE can be tuned and specialized for technical corpora. We adopted a similar approach for terminology structuring by combining a candidate term list extracted from a corpus and the synonymy links of a general language dictionary (Hamon et al. 1998).

However, few works have studied the respective contribution of these two types of resources (general and specialized) for terminology building. The reported study tries to draw light on their respective usefulness.

In the context of our collaboration with EDF, we tried to identify the best way to bootstrap our semantic links acquisition. We therefore tested our approach with various lexical sources from the most to the least general ones: *Le Robert* dictionary, a technical thesaurus, and some very specific hand built semantic classes. The following sections describe these experiments.

4.2 Using manually built semantic class as a bootstrap

For the DSE_2 corpus, synonymy classes manually built by a terminologist are available. Terms extracted from a different corpus of the same domain have been studied. The terminologist regrouped 1,335 terms in 500 classes. We have considered those classes as equivalence classes. 3,456 synonymy links have been extracted. Those links are morpho-syntactic relations *appoint en acide borique* (supplement in boric acid)/*appoint en bore* (boron supplement) or semantic relations *eau de refroidissement* (cooling water)/*fluide réfrigérant* (cooling fluid). Contrary to *Le Robert*'s synonyms, links may hold between two complex terms or between a simple and a complex terms: *appareil de mesure* (measuring device)/*capteur* (sensor). Such specialized resources are important in terminology structuring. Unfortunately, they are rare and time-consuming to build.

We applied the inference rules on the DSE_2 corpus starting with the links provided by the semantic classes. Among the 3,456 links, only 281 links are used by the rules to infer 169 links between complex terms. The expert validated 115 of the links (68%).

We also tried to combine these two different sources. This help to understand the respective contribution of each source type. Besides the 590 links inferred from the dictionary and the 169 links inferred from the classes, 44 new links are detected thanks to the third rule (which takes advantage of both lexical sources jointly). Indeed, links such as *tronçon du circuit de réfrigération intermédiaire* (section of the intermediate cooling circuit)/*portion du circuit RRI* (portion of the RRI circuit) need two initial links issued from the different sources. The dictionary provides the links *tronçon* (section)/*portion* (portion) while *circuit de réfrigération intermédiaire* (intermediate cooling circuit)/*circuit RRI* (RRI circuit) belongs to a semantic class. Among the links inferred from the dictionary and the semantic classes, 266 links (39%) have been validated by the expert.

4.3 Inferring links from a thesaurus

We also attempted to infer links from the EDF thesaurus (EDFDOC). This thesaurus is composed of 20,000 simple or complex terms. Terms are laid out into 330 semantic fields which are grouped into 45 points of view. These are general classes which can be viewed as the top of an ontology. Terms are linked with three types of relations: hierarchical one (hyperonymy), associative one (see-also) and synonymy one (is used for). We exploited all the semantic links *i.e.* 25,000 links.

Although most of the thesaurus links are morpho-syntactic or semantic relations between complex terms, we attempted to saturate the terminological network as for the semantic classes. The rules used only 389 links of the thesaurus and inferred 55 links. The expert validated 36 of the links (65.45%). As thesaurus initial terms are already complex, only few links between more complex terms can be inferred.

4.4 Comparison of the results

4.4.1 *Global comparison*

Table 8 summarizes results obtained from the three sources. We define the *initial links* as the links resulting of the filtering step *i.e.* the links provided by a lexical resources for which both linked words are present in the corpus. *Inferred links* are defined as the links proposed by the inference rules.
The ratio of inferred links according to the links used by the rules varies from one source to another: 3/5 for the semantic classes and only 1/5 for the dictionary. Nevertheless, 78% of the links are inferred from the dictionary while only 22% for the semantic classes. This is due to the dictionary large coverage. It must be noted that using semantic information from the dictionary is far less time-consuming than the building and the use of semantic classes. The thesaurus stands in the worst position. Both its inferred links ratio (1/7) and its coverage are low. The distribution of the links according to the rules are identical whatever the lexical source: 62% of the links have been inferred with the rule 2. The rule 3 is the less productive.

We characterized the ratio of morpho-syntactic links found with our approach. Three types of relation are considered: derivation, ellipsis and etymology.[5] Only 28 validated links are morpho-syntactic: 16 links are derivational relations (*ligne des drains* (line of drain)/*ligne de drainage* (draining line)), 4 links are ellipsis relations (*dégazage du circuit TEP* (outgassing of the TEP circuit)/*dégazage du TEP* (outgassing of the TEP)) and 8 links are etymological relations (*refroidissement des pompes primaires* (cooling of the primary pumps)/*réfrigération des pompes primaires* (cooling of the primary pumps)). We compare these results with the links that FASTER analysis (Jacquemin96)

Table 8. Results of the detection of semantic links

	Link filtering	Inference of links on the DSE corpus		
	Number of initial links	Number of terms	Number of inferred links	Validation
Dictionary	3 129	1 299	590	199 (33.72%)
Semantic classes	281	344	169	115 (68%)
EDF Thesaurus	389	478	55	36 (65.45%)
Dictionary then classes	3 376	1 547	689	266 (39%)

proposes (this tool designed to detect morpho-syntactic variants of terms is available for our experiments): only 4 derivational links are common (*classement sismique* (seismic classification)/*classification sismique* (seismic classification)). Although no definitive answer can be given from the few examples, they suggest that our dictionary-based approach is complementary to methods which have been specifically design for the detection of morpho-syntactic variants. It proposes relations that tools as FASTER do not detect (ellipsis and etymological relations).

4.4.2 *Complementarity of the semantic classes and the dictionary*

The semantic classes are not only used as a lexical resource. They reflect a manual terminological work to which the results obtained through automatic detection can be compared. The Table 9 presents the results according to the number of inferred links present in the semantic classes *i.e.* the inferred links already built by the expert.

Table 9. Distribution of the links built by the expert among the inferred links

	Number of inferred links built by the expert	Number of links which are not built by the expert
Semantic classes	25	144
Dictionary	23	567
Dictionary then classes	38	720

One interesting fact is that new links can be inferred from the semantic classes: this shows that the expert did not saturate the classes. Only few links built by the terminologist have also been automatically inferred. For instance, the link *condition de fonctionnement* (condition of running)/*régime de fonctionnement* (running activity) exists in a semantic class and is inferred from the link (*condition* condition/*régime* activity) given by the terminologist. 144 links are inferred form the semantic classes and only 25 out of 144 links are already present in the semantic classes. It seems that while building the classes, the terminologist focuses on their consistency rather than their inferential enclosure. This shows that the human and algorithmic approaches are complementary for the detection of synonymy links.

Moreover, few links inferred from the dictionary are given by the terminologist in the semantic classes (23 out of 590 links). The expert seems to focus on the technical language. For him, the detection of links between terms existing in the general language is time-consuming. Nevertheless, during the validation, he considered those links as useful for a document consulting system.

4.4.3 *The thesaurus: A weaker aid*

Similarly, the overlap of links inferred from the dictionary or the semantic classes and the links provided by the thesaurus is low. Only two links are common to the links inferred from the dictionary and the thesaurus while one link is both inferred from the semantic classes and provided by the thesaurus (see Table 10).

Table 10. Distribution of the thesaurus links among the inferred links

	Number of links occurring in the thesaurus	Number of links not occurring in the thesaurus
Dictionary	2	588
Semantic classes	1	168
Dictionary then classes	2	756

The domain of the corpus is partially covered by the thesaurus. Only 28 links are common to the thesaurus and the semantic classes which are built from a different corpus of the same domain.

It seems that the thesaurus stands in an intermediate position between the general language dictionary and specialized resources such as semantic classes. However, as mentioned above, it combines the weaknesses of both.

This comparison of the semantic links inferred from various lexical sources shows the usefulness of the general language dictionaries to process specialized corpora. When they exist and even if they have been built for similar corpora,

$$WeightedPrecision = 1 - \sum_{i=1}^{Nf} (NdErrors_i \times W_i) / (\sum_{i=1}^{N} NbLinks_i)$$

where N_f is the number of families.

The factor W_i is used to minimize the weight of each error in the families where most of the links are invalidated, for instance *temps* (time)/*température* (temperature). Compared with the classical precision, the weighted precision better reflects the terminologist's point of view and the usefulness of the inferred links for the terminology structuring.

5.2.2 *Evaluation of the results on the working corpora*

We compute the weighted precision on two corpora. The Table 11 summarizes the results according to this measure on the DSE_1 corpus and the DSE_2 corpus. The weighted precision is 49.58% for the former corpus and 47.89% for the latter one while the classical precision is 37% on the DSE_1 corpus and 33.72% on the DSE_2 corpus.

Table 11. Comparison of the weighted and classical precision

	DSE_1 corpus	DSE_2 corpus
Weighted precision	49.58%	47.89%
Classical precision	37%	33.72%

5.3 Discussion

It is difficult to appreciate the relevancy of such an evaluation measure. Other experimentation in various application contexts would be required to get a better idea. One difficulty is that formally evaluating the cognitive cost of the validation process for the expert would call for specific psychological and ergonomic tests.

However, it is well-known that the way the terminological results are presented affects the validation. This presentation varies with the system and the application. Thus, the results of the LEXTER corpus analysis are presented as a hypertextual syntactic network. Assadi (1997) also tries to take these ergonomic aspects into account. We propose two representations of the results:

classes built by transitive enclosure[7] and families. The above weighted precision is therefore a first attempt to take the structure and the presentation of the results into account for their evaluation.

The way the results are presented may also make the terminologist think of new links. This suggestion process is an important one. We noted in a first experiment that the expert considered half of the links as interesting even if he validated only 37% of them as real synonyms. Morin (1998) makes similar observation for experiments with PROMETHÉE. Contrary to him, we choose to retain these links as good ones.

Wrong links such as *groupe froid* (cold group)/*groupe frigorifique* (refrigerating group) and *groupe froid* (cold group)/*unité de refroidissement* (cooling unit) may also suggest a good one: *groupe frigorifique* (refrigerating group)/ *unité de refroidissement* (cooling unit). The expert underlined himself that correcting links is far less difficult than finding new links spontaneously. Unfortunately, up to now, this last property has not been properly evaluated. This remains to be done.

6. Conclusion

The collaboration with EDF lead us to experiment our synonymy detection system in a realistic context. By interacting with a terminologist who makes use of the resulting terminology, we got an expert feedback which helps us to understand the usefulness of our approach and the best way to handle it.
Globally the results on the DSE_2 corpus confirms our previous experimental observations. The traditional precision measure and the distribution of detected links among families of different size are close.

The present experiment helps to understand the contribution of a general language dictionary for technical text processing. We carried out experiments to compare the synonymy links inferred from *Le Robert* dictionary with the semantic information given by two specialized hand built lexical resources. It appears that general language dictionary represents a useful knowledge source which is complementary to specialized ones.

The industrial collaboration also enabled a better evaluation of the resulting structured terminology in the context of a document consulting task. The precision and recall measures are difficult to appreciate and do not appear as very relevant from the terminologist's point of view. We therefore proposed a weighted precision measure which better reflects the practical usefulness of the results.

However several evaluation problems remain to be solved. As in several terminological works, we have underlined that errors may nevertheless be suggestive and thus interesting for the terminologists. This property is difficult to take into account for evaluation. On the other hand, as there is no golden standard to which the results can be compared, it is difficult to measure the silence of terminological tools. Recall is however an important piece of information for evaluation. In order to reduce erroneous links, we plan to test various relevance measures based on contextual distance and information extracted from the resources.

Notes

* This work results from a collaboration with the Direction des Etudes et Recherche (DER) d'Electricité de France (EDF). We thank Henry Boccon-Gibod, Yasmina Abbas, Marie-Luce Picard (DER-EDF), Didier Bourigault (CNRS). The discussions we had with them as well as Christian Jacquemin (LIMSI), Benoît Habert (LIMSI), Christophe Fouqueré (LIPN) have contributed to this work.

1. As the terms used in this paper have been extracted from French documents, their translation, especially for the synonymy, does not always express the same nuance than originally.

2. Coronarogaphy manual, physician letters, Patient Discharge Summaries.

3. A connected component is a graph such from a node, one can access to any other.

4. The validation included not only the links inferred from the general language dictionary, but also links inferred from other resources (see below).

5. One can argue that an etymology relation is not a morpho-syntactic relation. For a sake of simplicity, we group etymology with other morpho-syntactic relations.

6. *ligne* refers to the device and *tuyauterie* to the object. Accroding to the expert, the meaning of these words is not equivalent in the domain even if they are often used as if they were.

7. For instance, the two following links form a class: *échelle logarithmique* (logarithmic scale)/*gamme logarithmique* (logarithmic range) and *échelle logarithmique* (logarithmic scale)/*mesure logarithmique* (logarithmic measure).

References

Assadi, H. 1997. "Knowledge Acquisition From Texts: Using an Automatic Clustering Method Based on Noun-Modifier Relationship." In *Proceedings of The 35th Annual Meeting of the Association for Computational Linguistic (ACL'97), Student Session.* Madrid, Spain.

Basili, R., Rocca, M.D. and Pazienza, M.-T. 1997. "Contextual Word Sense Tuning and Disambiguation." *Applied Artificial Intelligence* 11:235–262.

Basili, R., Pazienza, M.-T., Stevenson, M., Velardi, P., Vindigni, M. and Wilks Y. 1998. "An Empirical Approach to Lexical Tuning." In *Proceedings of the Workshop on Adaptating Lexical and Corpus Ressources to Sublanguages and Applications (First International Conference on Language Resources and Evaluation)*. Grenada, Spain.

Bourigault, D. 1992. "Surface Grammatical Analysis for the Extraction of Terminological Noun Phrases." In *Proceedings of the 14th International Conference on Computational Linguistics (Coling'92)*, 977–981. Nantes, France.

Bourigault, D. and Habert, B. 1998 "Evaluation of Terminology Extractors: Principles And Experimentation." In *Proceedings of the First International Language Resources and Evaluation (LREC'98)*, 299–305. Grenada, Spain.

Cruse, D.A. 1986. *Lexical Semantics.* Cambridge University Press.

Dagan, I. and Church, K. 1994. "*Termight*: Identifying and Translating Technical Terminology." In *Proceedings of the Fourth Conference on Applied Natural Language Processing (ANLP'94)*, 34–40. University Of Stuttgart, Germany.

El-Hadi, W.M. and Jouis, C. 1998. "Terminology Extraction and Acquisition from Textual Data: Criteria for Evaluating Tools and Methods." In *Proceedings of the First International Conference on Language Resources and Evaluation (LREC'98) — Poster Session*, 1175–1178. Granada, Spain, 1998.

Garcia., D. 1998. *Analyse automatique des textes pour l'organisation causale des actions. Réalisation du système informatique COATIS.* Thèse de Doctorat Nouveau Régime en Informatique, Université Paris-Sorbone (Paris IV), Paris, France.

Gros, C. and Assadi, H. 1997. "Intégration de connaissances dans un système de consultation de documentation technique." In *Actes des Premières Rencontres du Chapitre Français de l'ISKO (ISKO'97)*. Presses Universitaire du Septentrion.

Habert, B., Naulleau, E. and Nazarenko, A. 1996. "Symbolic Word Clustering for Medium-Size Corpora." In *Proceedings of the 16th International Conference on Computational Linguistics (Coling'96)*, 490–495. Copenhagen, Danmark.

Habert, B., Nazarenko, A., Zweigenbaum, P. and Bouaud, J. 1998. "Extending an Existing Specialized Semantic Lexicon." In *Proceedings of the First International Conference on Language Resources and Evaluation (LREC'98)*, 663–668. Granada, Spain.

Hamon, T. and Nazarenko, A. 2000. "Dictionary-based detection of term semantic variation." *Meaning and Computation.* Linguistic Contributions from the Scuola Normale Superiore Editore Dell' Orso in Alessandria (Italy).

Hamon, T., Nazarenko, A., and Gros, C. 1998. "A Step Towards the Detection of Semantic Variants of Terms in Technical Documents." In *Proceedings of 17th International Conference on Computational Linguistics (Coling-ACL'98)*, 498–504. Université de Montréal, Montréal, Quebec, Canada.

Hearst, M.A. 1992. "Automatic Acquisition of Hyponyms from Large Text Corpora." In *Proceedings of Coling'92*, 539–545. Nantes, France.

Jacquemin, C. 1994 "Recycling Terms Into a Partial Parser." In *Proceedings of the 4th Conference on Applied Natural Language Processing (ANLP'94)*, 113–118. Stuttgart, Germany.

Jacquemin, C. 1996. "A Symbolic and Surgical Acquisition of Terms Through Variation." In *Connectionist, Statistical and Symbolic Approaches to Learning for Natural Language Processing*, S. Wermter, E. Riloff and G. Scheler, 425–438. Springer.

L'Homme, M.-C., Benali, L., Bertrand, C. and Lauduique, P. 1996. "Definition of an Evaluation Grid for Term-Extraction Software." *Terminology* 3 (2): 291–312.

Mayfield, J. and Nicholas, C. 1992. "SNITCH: Augmenting Hypertexts Documents with a Semantic Net." In *Proceedings of the Conference on Information and Knowledge Management (CIKM-92)*, 146–152. Baltimore, USA.

Maynard, D. and Ananiadou, S. 1998. "Acquiring Contextual Information for Term Disambiguation." In *Proceedings of COMPUTERM'98 (First Workshop on Computational Terminology) — Coling-ACL'98*, 86–90. Université de Montréal, Montréal, Quebec, Canada.

Miller, G. A., Beckwith, R., Fellbaum, C., Gross, D. and Miller, K. 1993. *Introduction to Wordnet: an On-Line Lexical Database.* Technical Report CSL Report 43, Princeton, Cognitive Science Laboratory.

Morin, E. 1998. "PROMÉTHÉE: un outil d'aide à l'acquisition de relations sémantiques entre termes." In *Actes de la Conférence TALN 1998.* Paris, France.

Naulleau, E. 1998. *Apprentissage et filtrage syntaxico-sémantique de syntagmes nominaux pertinents pour la recherche documentaire.* Thèse en Informatique, Université Paris 13, Paris, France.

Pereira, F., Tishbi, N. and Lee, G. 1993. "Distributional Clustering of English Words." In *Proceedings of the ACL'93*, 183–190. Columbus, Ohio, USA.

Ploux, S. and Victorri, B. 1998. "Constructions d'espaces sémantiques à l'aide de dictionnaires de synonymes." *Traitement Automatique des Langues* 39 (1): 161–182.

Resnik, P., and Yarowsky, D. 1997. "A Perspective on Word Sense Disambiguation Methods and their Evaluation." In *Proceedings of the SIGLEX'97.* Washington, DC.

Richardson, R., Smeaton, A. F. and Murphy, J. 1994. *Using Wordnet as a Knowledge Base for Measuring Semantic Similarity Between Words.* Working Paper CA-1294. School of Computer Applications, Dublin City University, Belfield, Dublin, Ireland.

Roulin, C. and Cooper, C. 1993. "Bringing Thesauri Together: Terminological Problems And Interests." In *Proceedings of TKE'93: Terminology and Knowledge Engineering*, Indeks-Verlag, 251–259. Frankfurt.

Spark-Jones, K. and Galliers, J. R. 1996. "Evaluating Natural Language Processing Systems." *Lecture Notes In Artificial Intelligence.* Springer.

Srinivasan, P. 1992. "Thesaurus Construction". In *Information Retrieval: Data Structures and Algorithms*, W. B. Frakes and R. Baeza-Yates, Chap. 9. New Jersey, Prentice Hall.

Szpakowicz, S., Matwin, S. and Barker, K. 1996. *Wordnet-Based Word Sense Disambiguation that Works for Short Texts.* Technical Report TR-96–03. Department of Computer Science, University of Ottawa, Ontario, Canada.

Zweigenbaum, P. 1994. "Menelas: an Access System for Medical Records using Natural Language." *Computer Methods and Programs in Biomedicine*, 45: 117–120.

Chapter 10

Extracting useful terms from parenthetical expressions by combining simple rules and statistical measures

A comparative evaluation of bigram statistics

Toru Hisamitsu and Yoshiki Niwa
Central Research Laboratory, Hitachi, Ltd.

One year's worth of Japanese newspaper articles contains about 300,000 'parenthetical expressions (PEs)', pairs of character strings *A* and *B* related to each other by parentheses as in *A*(*B*). These expressions contain a large number of important terms, such as organization names, company names, and their abbreviations, and are easily extracted by pattern matching.

We have developed a simple and accurate method for collecting unregistered terms from PEs which identified two types of PEs by using pattern matching, bigram statistics, and entropy, and collected about 17,000 terms with over 97% precision.

Bigram statistics, combined with a small number of rules, identified 'pairs of exchangeable terms' (PET) in PEs, such as 国際通貨基金(IMF), which mostly contained important terms and their abbreviations. Entropy worked to highlight inner PE terms (such as 会社人事, which means corporate personnel affair), that were clues useful for acquiring proper nouns such as company names, organization names, and person names.

Identification of PETs provided the opportunity to evaluate the usefulness of various bigram co-occurrence statistics. Seven statistical measures (frequency, Mutual Information, the χ^2-test, the χ^2-test with Yates' correction, the log-likelihood ratio, the Dice coefficient, and the modified Dice coefficient) were compared.

1. Introduction

1.1 Background and motivation

In the fields of Japanese natural language processing (NLP) and information retrieval (IR), increasing demand for the word indexing of texts has led to extensive use of Japanese morphological analysis (JMA), that is, segmentation and tagging of input character strings. Consequently, methods for (semi-) automatically acquiring candidate terms (see Note 1) for JMA dictionaries are strongly required.

One of the authors has been developing an IR system (Takano et al. 2000: 19–20), and was confronted with the difficulties caused by unregistered terms. The system has a navigation window displaying a graph of the topical terms in the retrieved documents, and the quality of the navigation-window was affected by unregistered terms (words) because they could cause JMA errors resulting in 'junk words' being displayed in the window.

For example, the abbreviation 外為法 of 外国為替管理法 (Foreign Exchange Law) is over-segmented into 外, 為, and 法. These errors affects not only the quality of the window, but also IR precision. Almost all JMA errors are over-segmentation errors and one of the main reasons is that almost every single Chinese character (*kanji*) is registered as a word in a JMA dictionary. Unregistered abbreviations, which are about 20% of unregistered terms, are particularly likely to cause over-segmentation errors.

To reduce the number of the errors and to improve the IR precision, it is necessary to collect such unregistered terms.

1.2 Existing studies

There have been a number of studies on automatically acquiring unregistered terms (term candidates) from the target corpus, both in the field of IR and NLP (see an extensive review by Kageura and Umino (1996: 259–289)). Even limited to NLP domains, a number of methods have been developed for term extraction using syntactic features, pattern matching, and *n*-gram statistics (Bourigault 1992: 977–981; Justeson and Katz 1995: 9–27; Franti and Ananiadou 1996: 83–88; Condamines and Rebeyrolle 1998: 29–35; Bowden et al. 1998: 43–49).

In Japanese-language-oriented NLP studies, thare have also been many studies on term acquisition and information extraction (IE). In the NLP field, JMA research has tackled the detection of unregistered single words (terms) by using rule-based approaches (Yoshimura et al. 1989: 294–301; Park and Kakei 1997: 71–86) and probabilistic approaches (Nagata 1994: 201–207). For extracting general terms, methods based on character *n*-gram statistics (Nagao and Mori 1994: 611–615; Shimohata et al. 1995: 71–78) and methods based on compound noun productivity of a word (Nakagawa and Mori 1998: 64–70) have been proposed. Proper noun extraction (company names, product names, etc.) based on templates (Kitani and Mitamura 1994: 404–413; Matsuo and Kimoto 1995: 1838–1844) have been proposed for IE.

However, we did not directly apply the existing methods because existing JMA approaches do not treat general terms that are sequences of registered words, and other methods (including *n*-gram co-occurrence-based approaches) attain rather poor precision for the automatic construction of a dictionary.

1.3 Our approach

We investigated 1,107 unregistered words (658 different words) in randomly chosen sentences, and found that they consist of place names, person names, company names, organization names, other proper nouns, ordinary nouns (nominal compounds), abbreviations of previously mentioned nouns, and other non-nominal words (see Table 1).

Among these words, place names are the easiest to treat by incorporating a place name dictionary (note that place names are basically a fixed set, which is different from Japanese person names that have a vast variety and are being newly generated) and address templates pre-processor into JMA.

Examining the contexts in which they appear, we noticed that person names, company names, organization names, and abbreviations (50% of all the unregistered words) could be extracted by combining specifically tailored methods (based on pattern matching and several statistical measures) with very high precision and high recall. However, to acquire the rest of nouns (general nouns or nominal compounds, 13% of the total unregistered words), we need to study more about the mathematical foundation of 'unithood' (tendency of a string to be a linguistic unit) and 'termhood' (tendency of a string to be a topic). We thus decided to develop specifically tailored methods for person names, company names, organization names, and abbreviations.

As for person names, we have already proposed an extraction method that uses pattern matching, dictionary lookup, and entropy criteria. The recall and precision of the method are approximately 80% and 99%, respectively (Hisamitsu et al. 1997: 329–334). To acquire other terms (mainly company names, organization names, and abbreviations), we found a rich source of such terms and developed a simple and highly precise method for acquiring them. The objective of this paper is to report both the source and the method.

Tabel 1. Classification of unknown terms in newspaper articles

	% of occurrences (*tokens*)	% of different words (*types*)
place names	9	8
person names	13	14
company names	16	16
organization names	1	1
nominal compounds	13	13
abbreviations	20	16
others	28	32

1.4 Objectives

The primary objective of this paper is to report a rich source of terms that has received little attention.

The source is 'parenthetical expressions' (PEs), pairs of character strings *A* and *B* related to each other with parentheses, as in *A*(*B*), such as 外国為替管理法(外為法), which means the Foreign Exchange Law. We refer to *A* as the *outer term*, and to *B* as the *inner term*. If the inner term and the outer term in a PE are exchangeable, we refer to such a PE as a PET (a pair of exchangeable terms). 外国為替管理法(外為法) is an typical example of a PET. PETs contain a number of important terms (such as company names, organization names, law names and theory names) and their acronyms, abbreviations, synonyms, or other paraphrases. Since providing a list of PETs can assist users of the IR system, the acquisition of PEs is an important task.

One year's worth of newspaper articles (about 145,000 articles) contains around 300,000 PEs, or one PE about every 10 lines. It was estimated that over 5,000 PETs, and over 15,000 company names are contained in such PEs. It is important that PEs can be very easily extracted by using pattern matching (see Note 2).

Another important objective of this paper is to present the extraction method itself. In particular, we report the effectiveness of combining statistical measures with a small set of rules and pattern matching for PET acquisition. After bigram co-occurrence statistics are used to select PET candidates, a set of rules are used to examine the selected PEs and pick up PETs. In order to acquire proper nouns such as company names, entropy criteria is used to find clue terms that are inner terms accompanying the target terms.

As a very important by-product, this paper gives a comparative evaluation of seven statistical measures as a secondary objective (frequency, Mutual

Information, the χ^2-test, the χ^2-test with Yates' correction, the log-likelihood ratio, the Dice coefficient, and the modified Dice coefficient). We used these measures to identify PET candidates, and found significant difference in their ability to identify candidates.

1.5 Outline

Section 2 classifies PEs semantically. Section 3 classifies PEs from a statistical viewpoint and defines our method for acquiring terms from PEs by using a set of rules, bigram statistics, and entropy. Section 3 also reports a quantitative evaluation of the acquired terms for several cases and a comparative evaluation of seven bigram statistics. This paper is summarized in Section 4, and the seven bigram statistics are defined in the appendix.

2. Classification of PEs

2.1 Number of PEs

In the 1992 issues of *Nikkei Shinbun* (about 145,000 articles), there were 292,799 PEs (177,098 different PEs), 25,421 of which appeared at least twice.

2.2 Examples of PEs and classification by their semantics

The following classifies the PEs mentioned above into major categories:

C1: pairs of exchangeable terms (PET)
The outer and inner terms are semantically exchangeable.

- abbreviation
  外国為替管理法(外為法): Foreign Exchange Law [acronym]
  譲渡性預金(CD): Certificate of Deposit (CD) [acronym in a different language]
  朝鮮民主主義人民共和国(北朝鮮): *Democratic People's Republic of Korea* (North Korea) [non acronym abbreviation]
- non abbreviation paraphrase
  短期プライムレート(最優遇貸し出し金利) [two expressions for "prime rate"]

C2: reading

Inner terms written in phonetic characters represent the reading of outer terms.

色丹(しこたん): *Shikotan* [a place name]

C3: supplementary comments

The outer and inner terms are not exchangeable. Major subcategories are:

- COMPANY (CITY)
  日本鋼管(東京): *Nippon Steel* (*Tokyo*)
- PERSON (AGE)
  佐々木一郎(58): *Sasaki, Ichiro* (58)
- PERSON (POSITION)
  エリツィン(大統領): *Yeltsin* (president)

C4: Categorization of articles or Topics

日本鋼管(会社人事): *Nippon Steel* (company personnel affairs)
林健太郎著(読書): Written by *Kentaro Hayashi* (*reading**)
[*This "*reading*" is a column name.]

C5: Others

理由(10): reason (10) [numbering]

A number of useful terms for JMA and/or IR were contained in these PEs, and we extended the targets and aimed at acquiring terms from PETs and PEs of type C2, and terms such as company names from PEs of types C3 and C4.

3. Extraction of useful PEs by combining simple rules and statistical measures

3.1 Difficulty with genuine rule-based approach

The most simple method for acquiring PETs would be to acquire only one-to-one pairs from a corpus. However, this simple method does not work because of two serious problems: there are a number of accidental co-occurrences in PEs and this rule cannot capture ambiguity or notational variants of inner/outer terms.

Examples of ambiguity:

譲渡性預金(CD)	Certificate of Deposit
現金支払機(CD)	Cash Dispenser
コンパクトディスク(CD)	Compact Disc

Examples of notational variants:

先進国首脳会議(G7)	The G7 Summit
先進 7 ヶ国首脳会議(G7)	The G7 Summit

An elaborated method is thus needed. As for PETs acquisition, one possibility is to combine several rules to identify typical PETs as follows:

For a PE *A*(*B*),
If outer term *A* or inner term *B* is written in only alphabetical characters or *katakana* (phonetic characters for loan words),
Then *A*(*B*) is a PET; (R1)
Else if *B* is a *weak substring* of *A*,
Then *A*(*B*) is a PET; (R2)
Else if *B* is written in hiragana (phonetic characters),
Then *B* is a reading of *A*. (R3)

A 'weak substring' is defined as follows:
B is a weak substring of *A* if *B* contains at least 3 of the characters in *A* and more than half of the characters appear in *A* in the same order.

A proper substring is defined as follows:
B is a proper substring of *A* if all the characters in *B* appear in *A* in the same order.

The concept of weak substring captures such abbreviations as 朝鮮民主主義人民共和国(北朝鮮), which means North Korea.

These simple rules work fairly well when applied only to very frequent PEs. However, when they are indiscriminately applied to all PEs, the acquisition precision drastically falls.

For example, because rule R1 only covers character types, it cannot identify the PET in the following example; the rule also identifies other PEs as PETs (in the example below, NKK is a kind of an acronym of a company 日本鋼管):

PE		Frequency
ＮＫＫ(会社人事)	company personnel affairs	11
ＮＫＫ(３)		7
ＮＫＫ(４)		6
ＮＫＫ(日本鋼管)	← PET	3
ＮＫＫ(財務短信)	brief financial report	3
ＮＫＫ(決算数字)	settlement of account	3
ＮＫＫ(格付け)	bond rating	3

In addition, the weak substring condition in rule (R2) results in the incorrect acquisition of a number of accidental co-occurrences.

For company name acquisition, on the other hand, terms such as 会社人事 (corporate personnel affairs) and 財務短信 (brief financial report) are important clues indicating that the corresponding outer terms are company names. However, picking up these inner terms by simply browsing a large number of PEs is too costly and too ad-hoc. We need some assistance that is, statistical measures.

3.2 Statistical classification of PEs

We can use statistical measures for highlighting the previously mentioned two typical types of PEs: the PETs and the PEs each inner terms of which appears with a number of different outer terms.

3.2.1 *Strong-co-occurrence type*

There are pairs of outer and inner terms such that one inner term and another outer term very often co-occur. Naturally, this type of PE corresponds to the PETs and PEs of type C2. For example, ＮＫＫ(日本鋼管) is a typical PET of this type. We measured the strength of the co-occurrence by using bigram statistics for identifying PETs and PEs of type C2. The results using all seven measures are compared later.

3.2.2 *Outer-term-diversity type*

Some inner terms have a variety of outer terms appearing with them. For example, 会社人事 (corporate personnel affairs) is very likely to have a number of corresponding outer terms because there are a number of articles on personnel affairs. One measure for sensitively measuring the diversity is entropy. It has worked very effectively in acquiring clue words (position or profession names for persons) in person-name acquisition (Hisamitsu and Niwa 1997: 329–334).

3.3 Acquisition of PETs

3.3.1 *Filtering PEs by using bigram statistics*

To preliminarily select candidate PEs before applying certain rules, we used a statistical measure to sort the PEs in descending order of the co-occurrence strength between their inner and outer terms.

There are several statistical devices for measuring the co-occurrence strength between two terms. For example, frequency, Mutual Information, and the χ^2-test have been used in a number of studies. However, as Dunning pointed out, the last two measures have a tendency to over-estimate low-frequency bigrams (Dunning 1993: 61–74), and there have been only a few comparative studies of bigram statistics (Kageura 1999:149–166).

We compared the seven bigram statistics mentioned in Section 1.4, and found that the χ^2-test with the Yates' correction, the modified Dice, and the log-likelihood ratio were the most effective for our purpose. We define these seven measures in the Appendix.

Once a statistical measure is selected, the PEs are sorted in descending order of the value given by the measure. The rules are applied to the PEs to which the measure assigns values larger than a threshold value. The PEs are referred to as a 'source domain'. A threshold value was selected heuristically for each measure. For the frequency, the selected threshold value was 3, and the source domain contained 12,000 different PEs (about 3,000 PETs and about 300 PEs of type C2). For the corrected χ^2-value, the threshold value was the value of the maximum value for PEs of frequency 1. The source domain contained 6,366 different PEs (again containing 3,000 PETs and about 300 PEs of type C2). This fact implies that the combination of the corrected χ^2-value and the rules must have higher precision than that of frequency and the rules.

For the log-likelihood ratio, the threshold was defined in the same way which was used for the corrected χ^2-test. For the modified Dice, the threshold was the maximum value for the PEs of frequency 2.

Table 2 shows the number of PETs and PEs of type C2 contained in the top 100, 500, and 1,000 sorted PEs per the seven measures. This table shows the overestimation of low-frequency events when χ^2 and Mutual Information are used. Since the identification of PETs and PEs of type C2 has objective 'correct answers', this table makes it possible to compare the performance of the bigram statistics in a fairly direct way.

Table 2. Number of PETs and PEs of type C2 contained in the top 100, 500, and 1,000 sorted PEs per the seven measures

	1–100	1–500	1–1000
Chi-square with Yates' correction	90	452	807
Modified dice	95	447	832
Log-likelihood ratio	88	418	727
Frequency	81	335	554
Chi-square	16	61	114
Dice	16	61	114
MI	0	1	2

* PEs with the same value are sorted alphabetically. Chi-square and Dice could not be distinguished by using the top 1,000. This also happens in Table 3.

3.3.2 *Combination of rules and bigram statistics*

The rules which we actually used are based on those given in Section 3.1. The major difference is that the ranking of the frequency of a PE and the ranking of the value assigned to the PE by the selected measure are compared to determine a branch of processing. If a former ranking of an PE is lower than a latter ranking of the PE, a 'weak substring condition' is used to identify the PE as a PET. This avoids rejection of abbreviations that satisfy the weak substring condition. In the rules we used M to denote the selected measure.

If outer term A or inner term B is written in only alphabetical characters or *katakana*,
    Then $A(B)$ is a PET.
Else if B is written in hiragana (phonetic characters),
    Then B is a reading of A;
Else if B is contained in the intersection of set $A(*)$ and $*(A)$,
    Then $A(B)$ is a PET;
Else if both A and B are dates (see Note 3),
    Then $A(B)$ is a PET;
Else if $Ord(A(B), \text{frequency}) > Ord(A(B), M)$ and B is a weak substring of A,
    Then $A(B)$ is a PET;
Else if $Ord(A(B), \text{frequency}) \leq Ord(A(B), M)$ and B is a proper substring of A,
    Then $A(B)$ is a PET;
Else reject

$A(*)$ denotes the set of inner terms having A as an outer term, $*(A)$ denotes the set of outer terms having A as an inner term, and $Ord(A(B), M)$ denotes the order of $A(B)$ given by the measure M.

Table 3 shows the accuracy of the identification of PETs and PEs of type C2 from the top 500 PEs in the source domain. The third and the fourth lines show the number of errors of the two types.

Table 4 shows the accuracy of three cases for 200 randomly chosen PEs from the source domain.

From Tables 3 and 4, we conclude that the combination of the corrected χ^2 with the rules worked most effectively for the identification of PETs and PEs of type C2. For example, 3,852 terms were acquired around 98% accuracy when the corrected χ^2 was used.

3.4 Acquiring company names, organization names, and person names

As mentioned above, PEs of the type 'outer-term-diversity' contain target terms, such as company names and organization names. Such PEs have clue inner terms, such as 会社人事 (corporate personnel affairs). Entropy can sharply highlight these clue terms.

For inner term B with outer terms $A_1,\ldots,A_m$ appearing $f_1,\ldots,f_m$ times, respectively, $E(B)$, the outer-term entropy of B, is defined as follows:

$$E(B) = -\sum_{i=1}^{m} \frac{f_i}{F} \log_2 \frac{f_i}{F}, \quad F = \sum_{j=1}^{m} f_{i\bullet} .$$

Sorting the inner terms in descending order by $E(\cdot)$ forces clues to near the top of the ordered list. Table 5 shows the top 10 inner terms (except numbers). Six of the terms in Table 5 are the typical clues to company names, and two are clues to person names. For example, the set of the outer terms of 決算数字 (closing accounts) and the outer terms of 会社人事 contained only company names (3,255 different items). By using the inner term template '本社*' (本社 means the headquarter and * stands for a wild card), which is a generalization of inner term 本社東京 (headquarter, *Tokyo*), 13,205 different company names are acquired with 99.5% precision.

By using 人事 (personnel affairs), which appeared in the top 20, about 1,000 non-private organization names are acquired with 95% accuracy.

Table 3. Number of PETs and PEs of type C2 contained in the top 100, 500, and 1,000 sorted PEs per the seven measures

	correctly identified	correctly rejected	incorrectly rejected	incorrectly identified
Chi-square with Yates' correction	438	46	14	2
Modified dice	434	43	13	10
Log-likelihood ratio	406	72	12	10
Frequency	308	151	27	14
Chi-square	61	344	0	95
Dice	61	344	0	95
MI	1	449	0	50

Table 4. Accuracy of three measures for 200 randomly chosen PEs from the source PEs

	correctly identified	correctly rejected	incorrectly rejected	incorrectly identified
Chi-square with Yates' correction	113	80	5	2
Modified dice	97	79	3	21
Log-likelihood ratio	80	98	3	19

Table 5. Top 10 inner terms with the highest entropy

決算数字; 11.30 (closing accounts)	東京; 9.28 (Tokyo)
会社人事; 10.90 (company personnel affairs)	本社東京; 9.23 (headquarter, Tokyo)
死去;10.82 (died)	有価証券含み損 ; 9.12 (hidden loss of marketable securities)
業績修正・配当異動; 9.89 (correction of business result, change of dividend)	仮称 ; 8.97 (tentative name)
ニューフェイス; 9.58 ("new face" — column name)	読書 ; 8.90 ("books" — column name)

* Numbers are the entropy values. Left column gives the top 1 to 5.

3.5 Coverage estimation

The words acquired by the proposed method cover 67% of unregistered company names and 95% of abbreviations in the sample unregistered words mentioned in Section 1.3 (in other words, 10% and 19% of the sample words, respectively). The person names acquired by our proposed method (Hisamitsu et al. 1997) cover 95% of the person names in the sample words (namely, 10% of the sample words). Therefore, together with place names (10% of the sample words), our proposed methods cover about 50% of the sample unregistered words.

4. Conclusion

We have developed a practical method for collecting a number of important terms (such as company names, organization names, law names, and their abbreviations) from newspaper articles. We found that parenthetical expressions (PEs) were a rich source for acquiring such terms. The method uses a small number of rules, bigram statistics, and entropy, and collected about 17,000 terms with over 97% precision.

Using bigram statistics to select candidate PEs assists the application of the rules to acquire pairs of exchangeable terms which contain a number of target terms. We compared the usefulness of seven statistical measures (Mutual Information, frequency, the χ^2-test, the χ^2-test with Yates' correction, log-likelihood, Dice coefficient, and modified Dice coefficient) and found that the χ^2-test with Yates' correction, the modified Dice coefficient, and log-likelihood were effective for our task.

We also found entropy worked very well to highlight inner PE terms that were important clues for acquiring proper nouns, such as company names, organization names, and person names.

The result of the comparative evaluation of bigram statistics indicates that the χ^2-test with Yates' correction, the modified Dice coefficient, and log-likelihood are preferable in picking up non-incidental co-occurrences in the sense that they do not over estimates low frequent events. Therefore they can be applied to, for example, term extraction methods based on bigram statistics, and improve their accuracies.

Appendix

Here we define the seven bigram statistics. All the statistical measures are calculated based on the following contingency table, in which $n_{ij}(i, j = 1, 2)$ denotes the number of PEs satisfying the corresponding conditions. For example, n_{21} denotes the number of PEs whose outer terms are not A and inner terms are B.

	B	*not B*
A	n_{11}	n_{12}
not A	n_{21}	n_{22}

We define $n_{i\bullet}$ and N as follows:

$$n_{i\bullet} = n_{i1} + n_{i2}, \; n_{\bullet j} = n_{1j} + n_{2j},$$

$$N = \sum_{ij} n_{ij}.$$

Log-likelihood ratio

Dunning pointed out that the log-likelihood ratio is a better measure for treating rare events (Dunning 1993). The idea of the likelihood ratio is based on comparing the maximum values of two likelihood functions derived from different hypotheses. Here we give a different (but equivalent) expression from one given in Dunning (1993):

$$2\sum_{ij} n_{ij}\left(\log_2 \frac{n_{ij}}{N} - \log_2 \frac{n_{i\bullet} n_{\bullet j}}{N^2}\right).$$

Dice (modified Dice) coefficient

These are heuristically obtained measures. The Dice coefficient has been reported not to over-estimate low-frequency bigrams compared to mutual information. The modified Dice coefficient was defined in Kitamura and Matsumoto (1996), and reported to significantly improve the performance of the Dice coefficient:

$$\textit{Dice coefficient} = \frac{2n_{11}}{n_{1\bullet} + n_{\bullet 1}},$$

$$\textit{Modified Dice coefficient} = \log_2 \left(n_{11} \times \frac{2n_{11}}{n_{1\bullet} + n_{\bullet 1}}\right).$$

χ^2 and χ^2 with Yates' correction

χ^2 is defined as follows:

$$\chi^2 = \sum_{ij} \frac{\left(n_{ij} - n_{1\bullet} n_{\bullet 1}/N\right)^2}{n_{1\bullet} n_{\bullet 1}/N} = \frac{N\left(n_{11} n_{22} - n_{12} n_{21}\right)^2}{n_{1\bullet} n_{2\bullet} n_{\bullet 1} n_{\bullet 2}}.$$

The χ^2-test is based on the fact that the binomial distribution Bi(n,p) is well approximated by a normal distribution when $np(1\text{-}p)>5$. This means that the χ^2-test should not be applied to low-frequency events. According to Yates' correction, χ^2 is calculated as follows when one of n_{11}, n_{12}, n_{21}, and n_{22} is smaller than 5:

$$\chi^2 = \frac{N\left(\left|n_{11}n_{22} - n_{12}n_{21}\right| - N/2\right)^2}{n_{1\bullet}n_{2\bullet}n_{\bullet 1}n_{\bullet 2}}.$$

Mutual Information

Mutual Information (precisely, self-mutual information, (Church and Hanks 1990)) is defined as follows:

$$MI = \frac{\left(n_{11} - N/2\right)^2}{n_{1\bullet}n_{2\bullet}n_{\bullet 1}n_{\bullet 2}}.$$

As has been pointed out by others, this measure should not be used to compare the co-occurrence strength of high-frequency and low-frequent events.

Notes

1. In this paper, we use 'term' for simply a word or a word sequence.
2. In this paper we considered only outer terms *A* consisting of *kanji* characters (Chinese characters), *katakana* characters (phonetic characters for loan words), and English letters. This greatly simplifies the extraction of PEs but still covers 99% of our target terms. *A* of *A*(*B*) was extracted as the longest character sequence that satisfies the above condition and precedes *B*.
3. The Japanese language uses both the Christian and Japanese era dates.

References

Bourigault, D. 1992. "Surface Grammatical Analysis for the Extraction of Terminological Noun Phrases." *Proc. of COLING'92*: 977–981.

Bowden, P., Evett, L., and Halstead, P. 1998. "Automatic Acronym Acquisition in a Knowledge Extraction Program." *Proc.of Computerm'98*: 43–49.

Church, K.W., and Hanks, P. 1990. "Word Association Norms, Mutual Information, and Lexicography." *Computational Linguistics* 6(1): 22–29.

Condamines, A. and Rebeyrolle, J. 1998. "CTKB: A Corpus-based approach to a Terminological Knowledge Base", *Proc.of Computerm'98*: 29–35.

Dunning, T. 1993. "Accurate Method for the Statistics of Surprise and Coincidence." *Computational Linguistics* 19(1): 61–74.

Frantzi, K.T., and Ananiadou, S., and Tsujii, J. 1996. "Extracting Terminological Expressions." *Technical Report of SIGNL* 96(27): 83–88.

Hisamitsu, T., Niwa, Y., and Nitta, Y. 1997. "Acquisition of Person Names from Newspaper Articles by Using Lexical Knowledge and Co-occurrence Analysis." *Proc.of NLPRS'97*: 329–334.

Justeson, J.S. and Katz, S.M. 1995. "Technical Terminology: Some Linguistic Properties and an Algorithm in Identification in Text." *Natural Language Engineering* 1(1): 9–27.

Kageura, K. 1999. "Bigram Statistics Revisited: A Comparative Examination of Some Statistical Measures in Morphological Analysis of Japanese Kanji Sequences." *Journal of Quantitative Linguistics* 6(2): 149–166.

Kageura, K. and Umino, B. 1996. "Method of automatic term recognition: A review", *Terminology* 3(2): 259–289.

Kitani, T. and Mitamura, T. 1994. "An Accurate Morphological Analysis and Proper Name Identification for Japanese Text Processing", *Trans.of IPSJ* 35(3): 404–413.

Kitamura, K. and Matsumoto, Y. 1996 "Automatic Extraction of Word Sequence Correspondences in Parallel Corpora." *Proc. of WVLC'96*: 79–87.

Matsuo, H. and Kimoto, H. 1995. "A Content Extraction Method from Japanese Texts Based on Pattern Matching Using Extraction Patterns", *Trans. of IPSJ* 36(8): 1838–1844 (in Japanese)

Nagao, M. and Mori,Y. 1994. "A New Method of N-gram Statistics for Large Number of n and Automatic Extraction of Words and Phrases from Large Text Data of Japanese", *Proc. of COLING'94*: 611–615.

Nagata, M. 1994. "A Stochastic Japanese Morphological Analyzer Using a Forward-DP, Backward-A* N-Best Search Algorithm", *Proc. COLING'94* I: 201–207.

Nakagawa, H. and Mori, T. 1998. "Nested Collocation and Compound Noun For Term Extraction." *Proc.of Computerm'98*: 64–70.

Park, C-J. and Kakei, K. 1997. "Acquisition Method of Unknown Word's Morpheme Dictionary Information Using Word's Juxtapositional Relationships." *Journal of Natural Language Processing* 4(1): 71–86. (in Japanese)

Shimohata, S., Matsuo, T. and Nagata J. 1995. "Extraction of Frozen Patterns from Corpora through Entropy Thresholds." *Technical Report of SIGNL*, 95(110): 71–78. (in Japanese)

Takano, A., Nishioka, S., Niwa, Y., Iwayama, M., Hisamitsu, T., Sakurai, H., and Imaichi, O. 2000. "*DualNAVI* - dual view interface bridges dual guery types," Proc. of RIAO 2000 (3): 19–20.

Yoshimura, K., Takeuchi, M., Tsuda, K. and Shudo, K. 1989. "Morphological Analysis of Japanese Sentences Containing Unknown Words", *Trans. IPSJ* 30: 294–301. (in Japanese)

Chapter 11

Software tools to support the construction of bilingual terminology lexicons*

David A. Hull
Xerox Research Centre Europe

Many problems in terminology translation can be solved by working with existing translated texts. However, large-scale bilingual lexicon building from previously translated documents takes a lot of human effort. This chapter describes an automatic terminology alignment algorithm that can be used as a valuable pre-processing step in the interactive process of lexicon construction. The system can present the human expert with a summary of the plausible translations of high enough quality that it can reduce the number of sentences which need to be read by roughly a factor of five in many cases. When compared to a manually constructed lexicon in a particular case study, the automatic system achieved a precision of 56% and an exact recall of 70%. In addition, more than half the remaining terms can be obtained with minimal edit operations on the extracted text.

1. Introduction

Terminology management is a core component of the translation task. The process of terminology translation consists of two distinct sub-tasks (Reichling 1998). First, the translator must learn what the source language term means. Second, he or she must find the best way to describe this term in the target language. Traditional resources such as bilingual dictionaries, thesauri, and term databases are all crucial to the terminology translation task. However, due to the dynamic and continuing process of term generation, they are never entirely sufficient. Large corpora from the same domain are an important supplemental resource. The classical approach to terminology translation is to find as many instances of the source language term as possible and use them understand the meaning of the term based on its context. The next step is to go to target language corpora from the same domain, search for the same concept, and find the term used to express it. The latter task is much more challenging, because you usually don't know exactly what you are looking for, which means that a lot of background reading may be required. While some of this effort can be distributed if you are translating many terms at the same time, this is still a time-consuming approach to terminology translation and usually not feasible on a large scale.

Fortunately, a great deal of information can be gained by working with existing translations. In many projects, translation service groups have established translation memories[1] that serve as a vital resource for subsequent work in that domain. When working with a translation memory, a search that finds matches for a source language term will also provide the translator with sentences that contain possible translations. Of course, user satisfaction will depend on the quality of the original translation. If the sentence pairs come from multiple independent sources, one can expect to compile a good list of plausible translations. If not sufficient, this information can at least serve as the starting point for a much more restricted search in the target language domain. While this process is more efficient than undirected search, it can still take a long time to develop a complete understanding of how a term is used. For frequent terms, this may involve reading hundreds of sentence pairs. If the terminologist is starting in a new domain and wants to develop a bilingual lexicon from scratch, this represents a daunting challenge.

Recent advances in translation aid software can make the problem of terminology translation much more tractable. The software is designed to help the terminologist find term equivalents in corpora consisting of sentences and their translations. The software has two important components, automatic terminology extraction tools and statistical term alignment algorithms. In this chapter, we focus on the latter task, statistical terminology alignment, by presenting a case study on the problem of bilingual lexicon extraction. We evaluate an existing terminology alignment system by comparing its performance to that of human experts working on the same task, the construction of a bilingual lexicon from a corpus provided by the European Court of Human Rights. While the current evaluation is not directly associated with the work performed by the terminologists, it already demonstrates the strong potential of this technology. In the remaining sections, we describe the terminology alignment algorithms, provide some background on the corpus and the task, and present a quantitative comparison of automatic and manual alignment strategies. In the final commentary, we discuss some preliminary results from a user-oriented evaluation of this technology.

2. Methodology for bilingual lexicon construction

The final goal in this exercise is to take a large collection of sentences and their translations (such as a translation memory) and derive a bilingual terminology lexicon. This process can be broken down into the following basic steps:

1. Source language term recognition
2. Source language term merging and verification
3. Extraction of target language equivalents
4. Target language term merging and verification

The first step consists simply of recognizing and extracting the word sequences that are likely to constitute valid terms in the source language text. Many of these terms will have variants that should be merged and replaced with a single canonical form. It may be necessary to verify that the choice of canonical form is consistent with a previously existing term database. Next, the translation equivalents for each of the terms must be extracted. Once again, there is the issue of variant recognition, normalization, and verification of the chosen canonical form. When there are multiple translations of a source language term, terminologists will check whether any or all are correct and appropriate. At the end of this labor-intensive process, the reward is a high-quality (relative to automatic methods) domain-specific bilingual terminology lexicon.

Traditionally, all the steps in this process have been performed manually. There has been a strong push in recent years towards using automatic term recognition algorithms (Bourigault 1996; Justeson 1995), and these algorithms prove to be very useful when backed up by manual verification procedures. Researchers are also becoming increasingly successful at identifying and normalizing term variants (Jacquemin 1996). Our work has focused on building automatic and semi-automatic terminology alignment algorithms using statistical methods. Recent research has demonstrated that statistical models can be highly successful at aligning words (Brown 1993; Melamed 1998). A number of promising approaches have been developed which can extend existing word alignment algorithms to multi-word terms (Gaussier 1998; Smadja 1995; Wu 1995). Following this work, we have developed an alignment system known as TRINITY, which uses statistical word alignment techniques to automatically construct a bilingual word and phrase lexicon from a collection of translated sentences (Hull 1998).

The TRINITY system has traditionally approached the alignment problem as follows (all steps are automatic):

- **(T1a)** Recognize terms in the source language
- **(T1b)** Recognize terms in the target language
- **(T2)** Perform a statistical word alignment
- **(T3)** Use **(T1)** and **(T2)** to align the extracted terms.

Steps **(T1a)**, **(T1b)**, and **(T2)** are independent and can be performed in parallel. The aligned terms are intended for use in cross-language text retrieval and translation memory systems. While this version of TRINITY can also support the task of interactive bilingual lexicon construction, the traditional fully automatic model is not ideal for the task. As part of this study, we have adapted the TRINITY system to make it more suitable for lexicon construction, and it will eventually be integrated into a software support system for machine assisted terminology management and translation. Step **(T1)** assumes that both the source and target language texts are of equal quality and accuracy, when in practice one text is usually a translation of the other. It also supposes that high quality language analysis and term extraction tools are available in both languages. Step **(T3)** aligns terms in the source language to terms in the target language. However, source language terms are often translated by a sequence of words which do not define a term in the target language.

Therefore, we have adapted the TRINITY system to support the following user-centered extraction process:

1. Automatic source language recognition of term candidates
2. Manual normalization and verification of source language terms
3. Automatic extraction of target language candidate translations
4. Manual normalization and verification of translations

This process involves several important changes to the TRINITY system. First, terms are not extracted on the target language side at all. Rather the source language term and the statistical word alignment are used to identify a sequence of words in the target language which is likely to contain the translation. There is no specific term to term alignment step. It is up to the terminologist to validate and/or correct the translation. We begin by describing the statistical word alignment algorithm used by the TRINITY system.

3. Statistical terminology alignment

Statistical word alignment algorithms take advantage of common regular co-occurrence patterns between source and target language words to establish links between occurrences of these words in individual sentence pairs. The TRINITY system is based on probabilistic translation model developed by (Hiemstra 1996). The Hiemstra model uses a variant of the EM algorithm to iteratively estimate a word translation probability matrix. This means that each source language word is represented by a vector of target language words weighted by their translation probability and vice-versa. The matrix is sparse, since each individual term has a relatively limited number of likely translations. The TRINITY system takes this translation probability matrix and uses a greedy algorithm to estimate the most likely word alignment for each sentence in the collection.

3.1 Hiemstra alignment model

The Hiemstra model represents each sentence pair by a simple two-way table. The rows correspond to source language words, the columns correspond to target language words, and the cells of the table define the expected frequency with which the words in the corresponding row and column are aligned. The row and column sums (or marginal totals) are simply the number of times the given terms occur in the sentence. The cell values (or expected alignment frequencies) are initially unknown and must be estimated. This can be done using a well-known algorithm in statistics, the Iterative Proportional Fitting Procedure (IPFP). The IPFP is traditionally used to estimate missing cells in a contingency table. Given an initial estimate of the table values, it iteratively renormalizes the cell counts by the ratio of the observed and estimated marginal sums until the estimated sums have converged to their observed values. More precisely, the k'th iteration of the matrix n_{ij} proceeds as follows (Hiemstra 1996):

$$n_{ij}^{(k,1)} = n_{ij}^{(k-1,2)} * m_{i.}/n_{i.}^{(k-1,2)}$$
$$n_{ij}^{(k,2)} = n_{ij}^{(k,1)} * m_{.j}/n_{.j}^{(k,1)}$$

where $n_{i.}$ and $n_{.j}$ are the current values for the row and column marginals, and $m_{i.}$ and $m_{.j}$ are the original row and column term frequencies.

The Hiemstra algorithm consists of a preliminary stage where the word co-occurrence counts are initialized, followed by multiple iterations of an approximation to the Expectation Maximization algorithm (McLachlan 1997). In the initial step, the expected alignment count for each pair of words is set to their co-occurrence frequency over the sentence collection. Then, a two-way table is created for each sentence pair, the cell values are set to the global expected alignment counts, and the IPFP is applied to this table. The table elements after convergence of the IPFP are accumulated to produce a new global expected alignment count. The last two steps are repeated for a fixed number of iterations or until some convergence criterion has been satisfied. Assume $C^i_{n,[jk]} = C^i_n(s_j \leftrightarrow t_k)$ is the expected count at iteration i of the alignment between source term s_j and target term t_k in sentence pair S_n, and I is an indicator function (1 if condition is true, 0 otherwise). Then the algorithm is:

1. $C^0_{[jk]} = \Sigma^N_{n=1} I(s_j \in S_n) \times I(t_k \in S_n)$
2. For each s_j and t_k in sentence pair S_n, $n = 1 \ldots N$:
   - $C^i_{n,[jk]} = C^i_{[jk]}$
   - $C^i_{n,[jk]} \rightarrow \text{IPFP} \rightarrow C^{i+1}_{n,[jk]}$
3. $C^{i+1}_{[jk]} = \Sigma^N_{n=1} C^{i+1}_{n,[jk]}$
4. If $i = T_n$ or $\max(j,k)\,|C^{i+1}_{[jk]} - C^i_{[jk]}| < T_d$ end, else (2)

T_n is the maximum number of iterations and T_d is the threshold of convergence. In practice, we have had good success with $T_n = 10$ and $T_d = 0$. From the global counts, we can derive bi-directional translation probability estimates in the following manner:

- $P(s_j \rightarrow t_k) = C(s_j \Leftrightarrow t_k)/\Sigma_m C(s_j \Leftrightarrow t_m)$
- $P(t_k \rightarrow s_j) = C(s_j \Leftrightarrow t_k)/\Sigma_i C(s_i \Leftrightarrow t_k)$

The Hiemstra algorithm has several important properties which should be described in more detail. The IPFP assumes that the row and column marginals add up to the same value, which is equivalent to requiring that the sentences be the same length. Hiemstra addresses this problem by adding a sufficient number of NULL tokens to the shorter sentence to equalize the length. The IPFP also enforces a one-to-one alignment constraint on the word pairs, meaning that it is not possible for two or more tokens in the source language to align to one token in the target language or vice-versa. Therefore, the search space of possible alignments is highly restricted and many real translation patterns cannot be accurately modeled. However, a reduced search space has important advantages, as it allows the system to align rare tokens with a much higher degree of accuracy than would otherwise be possible. Some of the errors caused by the restrictive model can be recovered in subsequent steps when multi-word terms are aligned.

3.2 From translation probabilities to aligned tokens

One could derive the alignment of word tokens within each sentence directly from the cells of the two-way table after the IPFP has converged. However, we find that it is more effective to rely instead on the global translation probability matrix. Given a bi-directional matrix of translation probabilities, the most likely word alignment for a given sentence can be approximated using a simple greedy algorithm (similar to the one suggested by (Melamed 1998), but applied to each sentence individually):

1. Define score: $S_{jk} = P(s_j \rightarrow t_k) * P(t_k \rightarrow s_j) * P(o_{jk})$
2. Sort pairs in descending order of their score: $S^1 \ldots S^n$
3. For S^i_{jk}, $i = 1 \ldots n$
   - If $S^i_{jk} < T$, go to (4)
   - If both s_j and t_k are not aligned already, align them
4. Remaining unaligned s_j and t_k are aligned to NULL

Condition (3) enforces the one-to-one alignment constraint. When the threshold falls below a constant *T*, word alignment is stopped, since many word pairs with low scores are not correctly aligned. The threshold *T* can be adjusted to reflect the relative importance of accuracy and coverage. A high value of *T* results in proportionally fewer alignments, but these alignments are more likely to be correct. The term $P(o_{jk})$ is an offset probability which reflects the relative likelihood that a term in position *j* aligns to a term in position *k*. These terms are estimated in a fashion similar to the offset probabilities used by (Dagan 1993) to make IBM Model 2 more robust (Brown 1993).

While the one-to-one alignment assumption limits the ability of the model to capture all possible translation patterns, there are important advantages to this approach. It significantly reduces the search space for rare terms, which are difficult for statistical algorithms to handle, and makes their correct alignment more likely. This aspect is particularly important to ensure the robustness of the algorithm on small data sets. Special measures can be taken when one of the two languages has compounding (such as German). In this case, one can either assign compounds a marginal count in the IPFP equal to the number of constituents they contain or perform alignment directly on the constituents.

3.3 From aligned tokens to aligned terms

While the Hiemstra alignment algorithm is fully general and can be applied to all words in the text, we find it more effective to restrict the alignment to open-class or content-bearing words (i.e. nouns, adjectives, verbs, and adverbs). It is relatively rare for closed-class or function words to be correctly translated by content words and vice-versa. Spurious alignments of this type are one of the most common errors in the algorithm, so dropping these words substantially reduces the error rate. Of course, one could go ahead and match function words to each other separately, but this information is rarely helpful for the terminology alignment process. In addition, both the source and target text are lemmatized[2] prior to alignment. Lemmatization is optional but it increases the power of the statistical alignment algorithm by reducing the number of word types. The algorithm assigns a link from each content word token in the source language to a target language content word token or the NULL token. Next, the system exploits these links to identify the most appropriate target language equivalent for each source language terminology unit.

The terminology alignment algorithm used in these experiments relies on three basic assumptions. First, the source language term is sacred, meaning that it cannot be extended, truncated, or modified in any way. The source language terms have been verified by the terminologist and therefore should be considered as core units of meaning, whether or not they appear to be the most appropriate units of translation. Second, the target language translation should be a consecutive sequence of tokens. Since a domain expert will verify the target language output, it is important that the target text string be coherent and readable. Given that the algorithms are based on a shallow language analysis, it is difficult to remove terms from the middle of the text string in an effective manner even if the correct translation is not a consecutive sequence of words. Third, returning a text string that is too long is better than returning one that is too short. If the extracted target string contains the correct translation, it is relatively easy for the domain expert to clean it up. If the target string is missing key terms, the expert will probably decide to go back and read the full source and target sentence to find the appropriate translation.

We present a simple summary of the terminology alignment algorithm, beginning with a few basic definitions. One word is aligned to another with high confidence if the same two words are aligned to each other in three or more different sentences, medium confidence if two sentences, low confidence if one sentence. The **target string boundaries** are the first and last target language token aligned to tokens in the source language term. Any target language content word within the target string boundaries that is not aligned to a content word in the source language term is called an **intervening word**. For each instance of the source language term in the sentence collection:

(1) Split the source language term into content words
(2) Find the target language alignment of each word in (1)
(3) Define the **target string boundaries** and check for **intervening words.**
This leads to one of the following four conditions:
- (a) There are no intervening words.
- (b) All intervening words align to NULL
- (c) All intervening words are aligned with low or medium confidence
- (d) One or more intervening word(s) is/are aligned with high confidence

(4) If (3d) continue with (5), else skip to (6)
(5) Set all low confidence alignments of words in the source language term to NULL and return to (3). If no such alignments exists, do the same for medium confidence alignments.
(6) If at least one source language word aligns to NULL, continue with (7), else skip to (8)
(7a) Find the nearest content word in the target language that precedes the lower target string boundary by fewer than four words.
(7b) Find the nearest content word in the target language that follows the upper target string boundary by fewer than four words.
(7c) If either of the words found in (7a) and (7b) align to NULL, expand the target string boundary to include these words
(8) Return the target language string defined by the target string boundaries.

Collect all target strings that align to the same source language string and eliminate duplicates. There is the option to retain the counts of each target language string and order the strings by count.

To summarize, the algorithm begins by taking the target language string bounded by the word alignment. If the string defines is single coherent text unit, it is kept unchanged. Otherwise, the system looks for alignments with low confidence which are the most likely to be incorrect. Any such alignments are deleted and the process is repeated until there is a single coherent text string without intervening words that align elsewhere, if possible. Step (7) is included to favor over-generation of the target string. If a source language term aligns to NULL, it is possible that the correct word alignment was missed, and the algorithm tries to compensate for this by extending the boundary of the target language string. The term translations might well be more accurate if the target string boundaries were adjusted to reflect estimated term boundaries in the target language. This is how the traditional TRINITY term alignment system works (Hull 1998). However, the advantage of this approach is that it requires no linguistic tools other than a word tokenizer for the target language, which substantially increases the language coverage of the system. In addition, it often happens that the translation of the source language terms spans term boundaries in the target language. The approach presented here gives us the ability to capture these cases.

4. Case study: The European Court of Human Rights

In this section, we provide some background material on a related project whose goal is to manually construct a bilingual lexicon with the help of some new software tools. As part of a project financed by the French Ministry of Research and Higher Education,[3] a group of computational linguists and legal terminologists have been working together to build a bilingual lexicon from a set of documents produced by the European Court of Human Rights in Strasbourg. This work represents a collaboration between Christine Chodkiewicz and John Humbley, legal terminologists from the Centre de Terminologie et de Néologie (CTN) du Laboratoire de Linguistique Informatique de Villetaneuse, and Didier Bourigault, a computational linguist from l'Equipe de Recherche en Syntaxe et Sémantique de Toulouse. The goal of the project is to test the performance of the LEXTER terminology extraction system (Bourigault 1996) and a new interface for term validation when used by professional terminologists and to demonstrate the feasibility of the lexicon construction task. Bourigault et al. have written a more complete report on this project, and the following background material has been borrowed from this report (Bourigault 1999).

The European Court of Human Rights is responsible for legal decisions concerning the European Convention for the Protection of Human Rights, which came into force in 1953. There are roughly 40 states which have signed the Convention, and these states have agreed to refer specific cases concerning human rights to the European Court and respect its jurisdiction in this area. From 1959 to 1997, there have been 10 revisions to the protocol of the Convention and the Court has issued roughly 800 judgements (600 of which date from the last seven years of this period). These judgements are transcribed, like the Convention and its protocols, in English and French. The two languages are transcribed at the same time, so it is not possible to distinguish a source and a target text. The corpus, consisting of the Convention, its protocols, and the judgements, covers a specialized legal domain.

In the documents, each sentence in one language corresponds almost exactly to a sentence in the other language. A careful reading of the texts reveals a number of inconsistencies in terminology use, with many terms in each language having more than one valid translation. The names of institutions, such as the Austrian Supreme Court, are translated in an extremely variable fashion from one judgement to another. This is an issue of great concern to the translators of the Court. The goal of this work is to shed light on the specificity and richness of the vocabulary used by the Court and eventually, with its help, to normalize the terminology to the extent possible. This project fits in nicely with the widely recognized need for a functional, up to date bilingual lexicon for this domain.

The project consists of the following steps. First, the original documents are cleaned up, tagged, and formatted. These steps include sentence boundary recognition and the alignment of each sentence with its translation in the other language. Next, the LEXTER system is used to automatically extract terminology from the French documents. The term candidates are then presented to the terminologists using a hypertext interface for validation. For each candidate term, the terminologist has access to all the sentences in the corpus which contain it. Once a term has been validated, the terminologist proceeds to extract its translation in the aligned English sentence.

Roughly 60% of the terms extracted by LEXTER are retained, but of the remaining 40%, only a small fraction are the result of an error in the system. The rest of the rejected terms are valid noun phrases that aren't specially relevant to this particular legal domain. Note that 57% of the terms with frequency one are retained, and these comprise 36% of the total number of retained terms. One would expect that these terms will be particularly challenging for statistical terminology alignment algorithms. During the terminological work, it quickly became apparent that multiple translations are very frequent. Around 26% of the French terms have more than one translation and 17% of the French terms of frequency two have two different English equivalents! The figures are in the same order of magnitude from English to French. (Humbley 1999) provide an analysis of the results from the point of view of translation theory in the legal domain.

5. Evaluating automatic terminology alignment

The collaborators in the lexicon construction project kindly agreed to make their data available to us for a comparative study. The eventual goal is to adapt TRINITY to serve as an interactive software support tool during the actual process of lexicon building. Unfortunately, we arrived too late to play that role in this project. Instead, we are left with the option of using the manually constructed lexicon as a gold standard and measuring how well TRINITY can duplicate it. With this goal in mind, we start with the same base set of terms generated by LEXTER and validated by the terminologist, and replace the manual extraction of English term translations with the automatic output of TRINITY, obtained by following the alignment process described in Section 3.

We begin with the following data files: the sentence-aligned corpus, a list of all the terms extracted by LEXTER and their positions in the corpus, and the final bilingual lexicon constructed by the legal terminologists. We do not have a mapping between the lexicon entries and the sentence pair(s) from which they were extracted. We apply TRINITY to generate a word alignment between the texts and find approximate translations for all the terms extracted by LEXTER. This list is then filtered against the validated bilingual lexicon and the differences are recorded. For the initial results shown in Table 1, a case-insensitive exact string match on the English side of the corpus is performed. Since both methods start with the same set of validated French terms there is no difference on the French language side.

Table 1. Comparing the performance of TRINITY to a manually generated lexicon

Total number of entries	4192
Entries matched exactly	2951
Entries not found	1241
Alternative entries	2336

Precision = 2951/(2951 + 2336) = 56%
Recall = 2951/4192 = 70%

TRINITY obtains a precision of 56% and a recall of 70% relative to the baseline standard. This level of performance is quite good already, and it is important to realize that exact string match is a very strict criterion. In fact, the terminologists often modify the term as it appears in the text before inserting it in the lexicon. For these cases, it is impossible for TRINITY to match the baseline standard exactly. This normalization is not consistent, in the sense that sometimes a plural is converted to a singular and sometimes vice-versa. While these different changes are all perfectly valid from the point of view of the term in question, it is not possible to perform the same normalization automatically, because the system lacks the appropriate background language knowledge. This is much the same reason why 100% accurate automatic terminology extraction is an unachievable goal. Many of the alternative entries come from the same sentences as the lexicon entries that were not found, but since we don't have a map between the official lexicon entries and the corpus, it is not easy to match them up directly.

Table 2. Categorization of differences between TRINITY and the manually generated lexicon

Category		#	%
Alternative translation		103	21
Not correct and not salvageable			
Incomplete translation	67		
Incorrect translation	44		
No translation found by TRINITY	32		
Partially correct translation	28		
Unclear error	14		
Missing negation	2		
Total		187	37
Basically correct and salvageable			
Morphological variant	76		
Missing/inserted function words	20		
Inserted modifier	18		
NULL vs. no translation	2		
Total		116	23
Not correct but salvageable			
String contains correct translation	80		
Matched to wrong instance of the English word	14		
Total		94	19
Total sample size		500	100

To get a better picture of the differences between the TRINITY output and the baseline standard, it is important to perform an in-depth failure analysis. We have begun this process by sampling 500 of the 2336 alternative entries and comparing them to entries in the lexicon. The results of this analysis are summarized in Table 2. The samples have been broken down into four general categories: alternative translations (21%), correct and salvageable (23%), incorrect but salvageable (19%), and incorrect and not salvageable (37%). By salvageable, we mean that the terminologist can derive the correct term from the returned text with minor editing. Each of the latter three groups can be divided into more specific categories.

The majority of alternative translations were probably viewed and rejected by the terminologists, so it is unlikely that this subset would contribute a lot of new entries to the lexicon. Here are some examples (the first entry is from the lexicon, the others are the alternative translations):

circumstances de l'espèce	circumstances of the case events in this case facts of the case
frontière	frontiers boundaries border

A large number of the alternative entries come from single-word terms, which are much more likely to have synonyms.

Entries that are correct and salvageable are of four different types: morphological variants (**défaut de paiement → fails to pay, failed to pay, failure to pay**), missing/inserted function words (**défaut de paiement → default on payment, default of payment, default of the payment**), inserted modifiers (**circonstances de l'espèce → circumstances of the [present] case**), and NULL vs. no translation. The final case simply reflects a difference in notation. The terminologists use the phrase no translation to indicate when a term is not translated while TRINITY uses NULL. Incorrect but salvageable entries are of two different types: over-generation and matching to the wrong instance of a word. Over-generation means that the extracted English string contains extra words which do not belong in the translation (e.g. **intérêt au taux légal → [entitled to] statutory interest**). Matching to the wrong instance of a word means that the same word occurs more than once in the English sentence and TRINITY aligns to the wrong token (e.g. **Grande Chambre → Chamber and the Grand [Chamber]**).

We distinguish six different types of incorrect and unsalvageable entries. An incomplete translation means that one or more English words in the correct translation were missed. A partially correct translation means that at least one word was aligned correctly and at least one word was aligned incorrectly. The difference between partially correct and incomplete is that incomplete entries have no incorrect alignments. An incorrect translation means that the selected English word is completely different from the correct entry. An example of a missing negation is: **absence de violation → violation** instead of **no violation.** In addition, there are cases where the correct translation exists in the text and TRINITY is unable to find it. Some of these omissions are due to sentence alignment errors. Finally, there are a few cases where it is unclear exactly what went wrong or that are hard to classify because they involve many different types of errors.

In order to get a better picture of the performance of the TRINITY system, we propose a more generous definition of recall which includes all entries which have been defined as salvageable. In order to compute the new recall estimate, we must take the information from our sample and extrapolate to the full data set. This means that of the 2336 alternative entries, roughly 481 are alternative translations, 981 are salvageable, and 874 are not salvageable. Ignoring the alternative entries, which don't contribute to the recall with respect to the existing lexicon, the fraction of salvageable entries is roughly 981/(874+981) = 53%. Since this fraction is based on sampling, there is some error associated with it. From sample theory, the 95% confidence interval for the probability that an entry is salvageable is (Barnett 1974, p.42):

$$p \pm 1.96\sqrt{\frac{(1-n/N)*p*(1-p)}{n-1}}$$

In this case p = 0.53, the sample size n = 500, and the population size N = 2336. Therefore, the 95% confidence interval is 53% ± 4%. If we apply this fraction to the 1241 entries not found in the lexicon, we find that there are 656 ± 48 salvageable entries. This gives us an adjusted recall of (2951+656)/4192 = 86% ± 1.2%.

6. Commentary

The results from this comparative evaluation suggest that 70% of the lexicon entries can be derived automatically and more than half of the remaining entries require only minor edit operations. However, this is only an indirect measure of the value of the system. The true measure of success is the amount of time the terminologist saves by using automatic terminology alignment as a preprocessing step. The amount of time saved can only be measured by carefully controlled user experiments that compare productivity with and without the alignment tool. A nice example of this is the report on the Termight system, built by (Dagan 1997). They report that using Termight, AT&T terminologists could more than double their productivity for the task of monolingual terminology extraction.

It is difficult to determine how the recall/precision measures presented in this chapter relate to user productivity. There are three ways in which automatic terminology alignment saves time. First, it reduces the need to search through the target sentence for the desired translation and cuts down on human alignment errors. However, in many cases, the expert will still want to verify the automatically generated alignment by reading the target sentence, so the time savings from this aspect may not be large. Second, it naturally summarizes the translations in a way that makes it easy for the expert to recognize translation variants. Finally, it merges multiple copies of the same translation into a single entry. While none of these steps on their own may seem that significant, it is important to consider the power of having all of them working in conjunction.

Consider the term **détention provisoire**, which occurs 115 times in the corpus. The statistical terminology alignment algorithm returns the following summary:

47	detention on remand	1	remanding in custody
26	detention pending trial	1	remand the accused in custody
19	pre-trial detention	1	remand custody
11	NULL	1	detention [X]
2	remanded in custody	1	detained pending trial
2	remand dentention	1	detained on remand
1	remanding the applicant in custody	1	applicant's detention [X]

From this information, the expert can quickly recognize the four primary translations and their variants, and scan a few sentences to verify each of them. There remain 11 sentences where an alignment was not found and two cases where the translation may be incomplete (marked with an [X]) and will need to be reviewed. Instead of 115 sentences to read, the expert now has 20–25 to read and in the sentences where an alignment has been found, it can be highlighted in color. This represents a possible savings of 75–80% in the time required to construct this entry in the lexicon. While most terms occur with a much lower frequency, meaning that the potential savings will be proportionally reduced, there are still roughly 100 entries in the lexicon which occur with frequency greater than 100, and these entries represent a majority of the extracted term instances.

This analysis suggests that a large part of the work associated with finding translations for frequent terms lies in reading many different sentences in which a word is translated the same way. One can come up with a quick and dirty way to reduce the workload without using an automatic alignment system. Once the expert has recognized and validated a particular translation, the system could rapidly search through the remaining target language sentences and remove all the ones that contain the same translation. While a simple tool like this could save a lot of human effort, it only addresses the third of the three points given above. This solution also fails to handle cases where the same term occurs more than once with different translations in the same sentence. It may seem like this should be a rare event, but it happens more often than one would expect due to the natural human tendency to avoid repetition.

We have conducted some preliminary user-oriented experiments to measure the benefit of using the TRINITY system. Initial results suggest that when combined with a specially designed user interface, TRINITY reduces the time required to construct a bilingual lexicon by 33%, estimating conservatively, when compared to working only with a bilingual concordance. Of course, the time saved for a given term depends on its frequency and the number of translation alternatives, so this number is only a rough approximation. Perhaps more importantly, the user found the task much more rewarding when working with the TRINITY system, because it allowed her to breeze through the easy examples and spend much more time working on the hard (and more interesting) cases. TRINITY can also be used in interactive mode by translators who wish to look up a single term. In this application, most people don't scan more than a few sentence pairs. If the term is relatively common (or the corpus is large), and the type of translation they are looking for is rare, it is likely that they will miss it. With TRINITY, there is a much better chance that they will find it, or at least know where to look.

There are several important properties of the TRINITY term alignment system which have not been mentioned previously. The system can easily and flexibly incorporate word and terminology dictionaries into the translation process. Word-to-word translations are stored in a database of prior counts for the word alignment algorithm. These counts work exactly the same as corpus co-occurrence counts, except that they remain fixed during the iterative updating process. The relative importance of dictionary entries can be set by adjusting these counts. For example, each entry of a domain specific dictionary could be given a weight of five counts, while general language dictionary entries might only receive a weight of one count. Counts could also be adjusted to reflect ambiguity and preferences in translation. The counts introduce a helpful bias into the word alignment process without forcing the system to choose the alignments suggested by the dictionary. A multi-word terminology dictionary can be used during the term alignment process. If the source language term exists in the dictionary and its translation overlaps with the target string boundary, then the boundary will be adjusted to reflect the known correct translation. The system also supports incremental updating. The word alignment from a previous sentence collection can be stored in a fixed database of co-occurrence counts, just as is done with dictionary entries.

Nonetheless, the TRINITY term alignment algorithm can still be improved in many ways. A large number of errors arise from the fact that the algorithm is strongly oriented towards a one-to-one alignment between source and target words. We are working on ways to relax this assumption. Being statistical in nature, the algorithm also works best with large amounts of data. In the current study, there are 12,130 aligned sentences. The performance of the system degrades as that number is reduced. We have had reasonable success in the past with corpora containing as few as 1000 sentence pairs. It is unclear whether the results would still be usable if only a few hundred sentence pairs were available.

While more accurate measures of the benefit of automatic terminology alignment software for lexicon construction will have to await the completion of more serious user studies, the potential of the technology is clear. By compactly summarizing the set of possible translations, these systems may well be able to reduce the human expert's workload by as much as 80% for frequent terms. The comparative study presented in this chapter demonstrates that the TRINITY system can retrieve 75–80% (70% exact + 5–10% correct but requiring small changes by the expert) of the entries in the manually generated lexicon with only a small amount of overhead and find near matches for another 5–10%. We recognize that the task described here is easier than the full terminology alignment problem because this experiment was set up so that there was complete agreement between the human experts and the system on the source language lexicon. We anticipate that statistical terminology alignment tools will eventually become a core component of all translation aid software systems.

Notes

* I am very grateful to Didier Bourigault, Christine Chodkiewicz, and John Humbley for giving advice and making their experimental results available to me for this project. I take full responsibility for any misinterpretations of their work that may appear in this document.

1. A Translation Memory is a searchable database of sentences and their translations.
2. The process of lemmatization converts a word to its morphological root form.
3. Le Ministère francais de la Recherche et de l'Enseignement Supérieur.

References

Barnett, V. (1974). Elements of Sampling Theory, Edward Arnold.

Bishop, Y., Fienberg, S., and Holland, P. (1975). Discrete Multivariate Analysis, MIT Press.

Bourigault, D., Chodkiewicz, C., and Humbley, J. (1999). Construction d'un Lexique Bilingue des Droits de l'Homme à partir de l'Analyse Automatique d'un Corpus Aligné, Terminologies Nouvelles, 19:70–77.

Bourigault, D., Gonzalez-Mulliez, I., and Gros, C. (1996). LEXTER: A Natural Language Tool for Terminology Extraction, in Proc. of the 7th International Congress of EURALEX.

Brown, P., Pietra, S.D., Pietra, V.D. and Mercer, R. (1993). The Mathematics of Statistical Machine Translation: Parameter Estimation, Computational Linguistics 19(2):263–311.

Dagan, I. and Church, K. (1997). Termight: Coordinating humans and machines in bilingual terminology acquisition, Machine Translation, 12(1–2):89–108.

Dagan, I., Church, K.W., and Gale, W.A. (1993). Robust Bilingual Word Alignment for Machine-Aided Translation, in Proc. of the Workshop on Very Large Corpora: Academic and Industrial Perspectives.

Gaussier, E. (1998). Flow Network Models for Bilingual Lexicon Construction from Parallel Corpora, in Proc. of COLING/ACL, Vol.1, pp.444–450.

Hiemstra, D. (1996). Using Statistical Methods to Create a Bilingual Dictionary, Master's thesis, Universiteit Twente.

Hull, D.A. (1998). A Practical Approach to Terminology Alignment, in Proc. of the First Workshop on Computational Terminology: COLING-ACL'98, pp. 1–7.

Humbley, J., Chodkiewicz, C., and Bourigault, D. (1999). Using Lexter to Establish a Glossary of Human Rights, in Proc. of the Conference on Terminology and Knowledge Engineering (TKE'99).

Jacquemin, C. (1996). What is the Tree that we see through the Window: A Linguistic Approach to Windowing and Term Variation, Information Processing and Management 32(4), 445–458.

Justeson, J. and Katz, S. (1995). Technical Terminology: some Linguistic Properties and an Algorithm for Identification in Text, Natural Language Engineering, 1(1), pp.9–27.

McLachlan, G. and Krishnan, T. (1997). The EM Algorithm and Extensions, Wiley.

Melamed, I. D. (1998). Word-to-Word Models of Translational Equivalence, Technical Report IRCS Technical Report #98–08, University of Pennsylvania.
Reichling, A. (1998). Le contexte du Projet Terminologie, Terminologie et Traduction 1:167–171.
Smadja, F., McKeown, K. R. and Hatzivassiloglou, V. (1996). Translating collocations for bilingual lexicons: A statistical approach, Computational Linguistics, 22(1), pp.1–38.
Wu, D. (1995). Grammarless Extraction of Phrasal Examples from Parallel Texts, in Proc. of the Sixth International Conference on Theoretical and Methodological Issues in Machine Translation.

Chapter 12

Determining semantic equivalence of terms in information retrieval

An approach based on context distance and morphology

Hongyan Jing and Evelyne Tzoukermann
Columbia University / Bell Laboratories — Lucent Technologies

An important issue in Information Retrieval is determining the semantic equivalence between terms in a query and terms in a document. We propose an approach based on context distance and morphology. Context distance is a measure we use to assess the closeness of word meanings. This context distance model compares the similarity of the contexts where a word appears, using the local document information and the global lexical co-occurrence information derived from the entire set of documents to be retrieved. We integrate this context distance model with morphological analysis in determining semantic equivalence of terms so that the two operations can enhance each other. Using the standard vector-space model, we evaluated the proposed method on a subset of TREC-4 corpus (AP88 and AP90 collection, 158,240 documents, 49 queries). Results show that this method improves the 11-point average precision by 8.6%.

1. Introduction

Information Retrieval (IR) typically measures the relevance of documents to a query based on word similarity. An important issue in word similarity comparison is the equivalence between terms in a query and terms in a document. The standard assumption is that a word, whenever it appears in the same written form, no matter in a query or a document, always carries the same semantic meaning and is considered the same term. Stemming and word sense based retrieval modify this standard assumption in two opposite directions. Stemming, as a recall enhancing engine, reduces morphological variants to the same root. On the one hand, stemming builds more links between words and as a result, retrieves more related documents; on the other hand, it can also build links between irrelevant words. In contrast, sense-based retrieval is a precision enhancing procedure; it links words based on their semantics. The problem we address in this paper is integrating these two opposite approaches so that they can enhance each other. As the result of the integration, more links are added between morphologically related words in a query and documents, and meanwhile, false links between morphologically relevant but semantically irrelevant words are avoided.

We present a context distance and morphology based strategy. The context distance model aims to tackle word polysemy problem in retrieval so that we can correlate words based on their meanings rather than surface forms. A linguistically principled morphological analyzer is used to replace a traditional stemmer (Porter 1980; Lovins 1968). The context distance model and the morphological processing are integrated in the retrieval stage for determining the semantic equivalence between words in a query and words in documents. The experiments on a sub-collection of TREC-4 corpus show an improvement of 8.6% on the 11-point average precision by the proposed method.

In Section 2, we discuss related work in stemming and sense-based retrieval and analyze the problems in traditional techniques. In Section 3, we present the proposed approach, describing the context distance model and its integration with morphology. We also describe how global corpus information and local document information is used in the proposed approach. In the following section, we describe the experiment on TREC corpus and present case studies. Finally, we conclude by discussing future work.

2. Discussion on stemming and sense-based retrieval

Our work of integrating context distances and morphology is related to the research on stemming and sense-based retrieval. In this section, we discuss related work in the two areas and analyze why the integration of the two methods improves retrieval. We also analyze some drawbacks in the current approaches and discuss how the proposed method tries to overcome these problems.

2.1 Stemming

Stemming conflates morphologically related words to the same root, either by a traditional stemmer such as Porter's (Porter 1980) or Lovins's (Lovins 1968), or by a linguistically based morphological analyzer. Different studies showed inconsistent results of the effect of using stemmers. Harman (1991) showed that stemming provides no improvement over no-stemming at all, and different stemming algorithms make no difference either; Krovetz (1993) showed that stemming does help, and that the improvement is between 1.3% to 45.3% for different test collections and stemmers; a more recent large-scale analysis by Hull (1996) concluded that "some form of stemming is almost always beneficial, but the average absolute improvement due to stemming is small, ranging from 1 to 3%."

Two useful observations have been made in these studies. First, although the overall improvement of stemming seems insignificant, all experiments showed that it does greatly help certain individual queries; however, degradation in other queries may cancel out such improvement in overall results (Hull 1996; Krovetz 1993). This implies that correlating morphologically related words could be potentially very useful, if we can somehow distinguish the cases in which it helps and in which it degrades, and therefore apply stemming only to positive cases.

The second observation is that, although stemmers are applied to words, semantic correlations exist only between particular meanings of morphological variants (Krovetz 1993; Church 1995). For example, given the sentence *The waiter served us dinner*, it would be better to link the word *served* with the word *server* in the sentence *The server brought us the food*, but not the word *server* in the sentence *Client-Server architecture is promising.*

This second observation partially explains to us why the phenomena in the first observation happened. Traditional stemmers strip words without considering the specific words and the specific senses of the words involved. In some cases, queries are retrieved with more accuracy because the morphological variants happen to be also semantically related. In other cases, queries are retrieved with less accuracy because the morphological variants are not semantically related, thus stemming introduces noises in the statistical count. Since the semantic relatedness of morphological variants depends on the specific corpus studied, this might be one of the reasons why different studies showed very inconsistent results.

This analysis leads us to think that if we can integrate traditional stemming with a sense-based retrieval strategy, we may achieve a better result than the case when either method is used alone. This is the reason why we pursued the proposed approach. Corpus-based stemming (Xu and Croft 1998) in some way is in the same direction, in that words are stemmed based on their correlations in the corpus rather than considering only their word forms.

2.2 Sense-based retrieval

The role of word sense disambiguation in information retrieval has been studied by several researchers. Krovetz and Croft (1992) showed that sense disambiguation does not result in as much improvement in the top ranked documents, when we have moderate length queries and documents. The reason is that word collocation has partially reduced word ambiguities in the top ranked documents. Voorhees (1993) showed that a simple word disambiguation technique based on taxonomic relations is not sufficient for retrieval; it unfortunately caused a decrease in performance. Schütze and Pedersen (1995) demonstrated that their clustering-based disambiguation model can effectively improve the retrieval performance by 7% and 14% on average. The work on Latent Semantic Indexing (Deerwester et al. 1990) also uses semantic structures to improve terms found in the queries.

We believe that the kind of sense disambiguation we need for retrieval is different from the general sense disambiguation task as studied in many previous work in Natural Language Processing (Yarowsky 1992; McRoy 1992; Ng and Lee 1996). The fundamental reason is that the underlying assumptions of traditional sense disambiguation do not fit for retrieval applications. There are two underlying assumptions of traditional sense disambiguation: fixed number of senses per word, and one sense per occurrence. As explained below, we believe these assumptions have detrimental effects for retrieval.

2.2.1 *Fixed number of senses per word*

Traditional sense disambiguation uses predefined word senses as standards. The senses usually come from a static, pre-compiled lexicon such as WordNet or LDOCE (Longman Dictionary Of Contemporary English). A word is assumed to have a fixed number of senses as defined in the lexicon. This is problematic in two ways. First, a word in a collection could be used in a sense not covered by the lexicon. For example, *Java* is only listed in the sense of *coffee* in WordNet, while its meaning as a programming language which is frequently used in computer science related articles is missing. In this case, a disambiguation program dooms to fail even before it starts. Second, a word tends to be invoked only in one or a few specific meanings in a particular domain. A large percent of word senses predefined in a lexicon might not be used at all. Considering all predefined senses not only consumes resources but also complicates the disambiguation task by raising the chances of making wrong decisions. A corpus based approach is more useful for unrestricted text retrieval since it avoids the above two problems.

2.2.2 *One sense per occurrence*

The most damage to retrieval, however, comes from the second assumption of traditional disambiguation: one sense per occurrence. For the same word, different lexicons may provide different number of senses. The corresponding relations between the senses defined in different lexicons for the same word are not clear. One sense in lexicon A may correspond to two senses in lexicon B, or it may correspond to part of sense (a) and part of sense (b) in lexicon B. This shows that the distinctions between senses are not absolute. Two different senses of a word may be semantically distinctive, as *bank* in the sense of river bank and *bank* in the sense of a financial institution. They could also be very semantically close. For example, the verb *train* has 10 senses in WordNet, and the first two senses are defined as follows:

Sense 1: train, develop, prepare, make prepared, educate
(definition: prepare for a future task or career
example: The hospital trains the new doctors.)
Sense 2: train, prepare
(definition: undergo training or instruction
example: He is training to be a doctor.)

A semantic lexicon like WordNet makes important semantic distinctions; some of which may be more finely grained than needed for IR. For IR purposes, it would be better to relate the two senses rather than considering them as distinctive and losing such links. While for the case of *bank*, we do need to separate the two senses.

The above examples indicate that the sense distinctions predefined in a lexicon are not suitable for IR. Kilgarriff (1993) rightfully argued that word senses should be decided by the special task involved. Prior studies which have reported improvements (Schütze and Pedersen 1995; Schütze 1998) also abandoned the notion of predefined word senses but decided senses based on the corpus.

Our context distance model uses the same strategy. We abandon predefined word senses but represent senses using context vectors, based on the actual usage of the word in a document. We do not assume absolute sense distinctions but compute the relative distance, based on corpus information. Through these measures, we avoid the problems with traditional sense-based retrieval.

3. The retrieval model based on context distance and morphology

In our proposed approach, a word is assumed to have a dominant meaning in a document (Gale et al. 1992; Yarowsky 1992). We represent this meaning in the form of a context vector. The semantic closeness of two words is indicated by the distance between their context vectors. The distance is computed using a model based on global lexical co-occurrence information.

3.1 The context vector

We encode the semantic meaning of a word in a document using a context vector. The context vector in our model is based on all the occurrences of the same word in the document and the assumption is that a word has a dominant meaning through the document. This is in contrast to the context vector model used in Schütze and Pedersen (1995) and Schütze (1998), where the context vector represents the context of a single occurrence of a word in the document.

To compute the context vector for a target word, all candidate words which can possibly be included in the context vector are first collected. This is accomplished by extracting all the words which appear at least once in the local contexts of the target word in the document. In the experiment, a window of 10 words (five words on either side of the target word) is considered as local context. Then a weight is assigned to each collected word based on the following formula: $Fr(I|T)/Fr(T)$, the frequency of the word I appearing in the window with the target word T divided by the term frequency of the target word. The purpose of this step is to measure the importance of each collected candidate word in the context of the target word. If there are more than 10 candidate words, the final context vector for the target word includes 10 candidate words with the highest weights. In the case of a tie score, a context word with a higher term frequency is selected. If these are less than 10 words in the candidate list, as in the case of short queries, all candidate words are included in the context vector. Therefore, the size of the vector is 10 or less. The context vector is then normalized. As a result, each of the words in the context vector will acquire a weight between 0 and 1. The more frequently a word co-occurs with the target word in the local contexts, the larger the weight.

We show below the context vector for the word *bank* from a sample document (AP881231–0128 in the TREC corpus):

Target word: bank
Context vector :{savings(0.44) federal(0.44) million(0.44) loan(0.33) company(0.22) farmington(0.22) board(0.22) agreed(0.22) billion(0.22) nationwide(0.22)}

In this example, the target word *bank* appears 9 times in the document. The words *savings*, *federal*, and *million* have a higher weight than others in the context vector since they appear 4 times in the local contexts of the target word, while most of the other words occur 2 times. The words in the context vector are important for distinguishing the semantic meaning of the target word. For example, the words *(savings, million, loan,….)* help to disambiguate the target word *bank* as the financial *bank* rather than the river *bank*. The weight associated with each word in the context vector indicates the importance of the word in the context vector.

3.2 The distance between context vectors

The computation of context distance is based on the relevance between words in context vectors. To measure the relevance between two given words, we rely on their co-occurrence information in the corpus. The corpus we used for this computation is the TREC AP88 collection (79,919 documents, 0.24 GB). We use a measure called *corpus relevance* to represent the relevance between two words. The corpus relevance of two words is pre-computed before retrieval, as shown in the following:

$$R(I_1\ I_2) = \frac{DF(I_1\ I_2)}{DF(I_1) + DF(I_2) - DF(I_1\ I_2)}$$

that is, the number of documents containing both words divided by the number of documents containing at least one of the two words. *DF* here represents document frequency and *R* is the corpus relevance. The purpose is to use co-occurrence information in the corpus to measure the relevance between two words. The corpus relevance between two words is a value between 0 and 1. A value of 1 indicates that two words always occur in the same documents in the corpus; a value of 0 indicates they never occur in the same document. Table 1 shows some sample word pairs with high corpus relevance scores and also some sample pairs with low corpus relevance scores.

Table 1. Sample word pairs and their corpus relevance

Word pairs	Corpus relevance
gaza, palestinians	0.600
nyse, dow	0.571
composite, dow	0.537
wheat, grain	0.443
south, year	0.117
food, told	0.052
miles, people	0.051

We consider this corpus relevance score as an indication of relatedness between two words. Words that are more related tend to have a high corpus relevance score, for example, *NYSE* and *Dow*. This information from the corpus analysis provides us with useful word correlations which may not even be present in lexicons.

The distance between two context vectors is computed in two steps. First, we determine the corresponding relations between words in two context vectors. Suppose context vector CV_1 consists of 10 words: $A_1, \ldots, A_{10}$, and context vector CV_2 consists of 10 words: $B_1, \ldots, B_{10}$, we look up the pre-computed corpus relevance value and find the corpus relevance for every pair (A_i, B_j), for $i, j = 1 \ldots 10$. We then sort the 100 corpus relevance values in descending order. The selection of the corresponding pairs starts from the pair with the highest corpus relevance and each word is matched only once. When this step is finished, each word in one context vector will be matched to a word in the other context vector. We represent this matching as $A_i \rightarrow B_{m(i)}$, where $m(i)$ means the match of i, for $i = 1..10$. For example, if A_1 is matched to B_3, then $i = 1$, $m(i) = 3$.

In the second step, we compute the distance between the two context vectors based on the matching in the first step and the pre-computed corpus relevance. If we represent the two context vectors as:

$$CV_1 = \{ A_1(W_{1,1}), \ldots, A_{10}(W_{1,10}) \}$$
$$CV_2 = \{ B_1(W_{2,1}), \ldots, B_{10}(W_{2,10}) \}$$

where A_1 to A_{10} and B_1 to B_{10} are the 10 words in the two context vectors respectively, $W_{i,j}$ is the weight for the *j*-th word in the *i*-th vector. Suppose A_i is paired with $B_{m(i)}$ in the first step, the context distance is computed as follows:

$$Dist\ (CV_1, CV_2) = \Sigma_{i=1..10}\ (R\ (A_i, B_{m(i)}) \times W_{1,i} \times W_{2,m(i)})$$

where $R(A_i, B_{m(i)})$ means the corpus relevance of A_i and $B_{m(i)}$. The computed context distance is a value between 0 and 1. The higher the value, the closer the two contexts vectors. We then compute the *average distance* between two context vectors by dividing the computed distance with the vector size, which is 10 in this case.

If CV_1 or CV_2 has less than 10 elements, the computation is basically similar to the above process except that the vector size equals to the minimal of CV_1 size and CV_2 size rather than the standard size of 10. The average distance is computed by dividing the computed distance with the actual vector size.

There are several reasons why we designed this model to compute the distance between context vectors. First of all, we observed that the semantic closeness of two contexts is not always demonstrated by the presence of the same words, but often by the presence of related words. For example, the word *bank* may occur with the word *money* in one context, and with the word *loan* in the other. If we can capture the close relatedness of *money* and *loan*, we can deduce that *bank* probably has similar meanings in the two occurrences. A model which relies on exact word repetition will fail in this case since it will miss the relations between *money* and *loan.* The kind of lexical relations that exist between the words such as *money* and *loan* or *eat* and *fork* is often not present in existing lexicons. However, lexical co-occurrence information to some degree indicates such correlations. The co-occurrence information has been successfully used for sense disambiguation and query expansion (Schütze and Pedersen 1995; Schütze 1998; Li and Abe 1998; Buckley et al. 1994).

The method we proposed is somewhat similar to the work in (Schütze and Pedersen 1995; Schütze 1998) in that both use context vectors to represent word meanings and both use global corpus and local document information. The significant differences are that while their approach still assigns a *sense* to each word occurrence, we only compute the relative distances. In this sense, we do not assume absolute sense distinctions as they do. While they build context vectors for each occurrence of a word in the document, we compute a context vector for all the occurrences of a word in a document. Their clustering model is also very different from our way of computing context distances.

3.3 Integrating context distance with morphology

Relating morphological variants enhances recall while sense based retrieval improves precision. To make the best of the two, we integrate the semantic-based context distance model with morphological information. For a word in a query, we not only compare it with the same word form in the document, but also with the other morphologically related words in the document. If the context vectors of two morphologically related words are close enough, then the two related words will be equated. This brings us the benefit of a stemmer but avoids the problem of over-generalizing.

Morphological relations are extracted from the CELEX (CELEX, 1995) lexical database. Inflectional variants were acquired from the CELEX English morphology lexicon for words directly, and derivational variants were extracted from the CELEX English morphology lexicon for lemmas by grouping words with the same lemma in a derivational family. A total of 52,447 words (not including inflected forms) were grouped into 17,963 derivational families. A sample derivational family is *(adjust, adjustment, adjuster,...)* or *(private, privacy, privateer, privatize, privatization,...)*.

3.4 The retrieval algorithm

The system consists of the preparation stage and the retrieval stage. In the preparation stage, we build the morphological databases, pre-compute context vectors, and pre-compute corpus relevance. In the retrieval stage, the documents and the queries are first indexed as usual. Before computing the similarity of two documents using a traditional vector model as in SMART system (Buckley et al. 1994), we compute the context distances between a word in a query and its morphologically related words in a document, using the algorithm we have introduced above. If the context vector of the word in the query is close enough to that of its morphologically related word in the document, the two words will be considered equivalent; otherwise, they will be considered different even if they have the same word form. We show some examples in the next section. If the context vector for the word in the query has a very small size, as in the case of short queries, the query word is considered equivalent to its morphologically related words in the document regardless of the context distance between them, since the context vectors have too few words to reliably indicate the meaning of the query word. The algorithm is summarized as follows:

Preparation:

Step 1: Build morphological databases using the CELEX database.
Step 2: Compute context vectors for words in a document.
Step 3: Compute lexical co-occurrences in the corpus and corpus relevance values for each word pair in the corpus.
Step 4: Index the corpus.

Retrieval:

Step 5: For each query and each document:
5.1 Compute the average context distance between the context vector of a word in the query and those of its morphological variants in the document
5.2 If ((the average context distance > the distance threshold) or (the size of the vector is too small))
then
consider the two words as the same term
else
consider the two words as different terms
5.3 Compute the similarity of the query and the document.

4. Experiments and results

We tested the proposed approach on a sub-collection of TREC-4 corpus. The documents we used are the AP88 and AP90 newswire, consisting of 158,240 documents (0.49GB). We used 49 queries of TREC-4 (query numbers 202–250). Retrieval is based on the standard vector similarity model using SMART from Cornell University (Version 11.0) (Buckley et al. 1994). We used the augmented term frequency and inverse document frequency weighting (augmented *tf.idf*) for computing document vectors.

There is one parameter to adjust in the proposed approach: the threshold of context distance for relating one word with the other. We used 15% of documents as training set for adjusting this context distance threshold parameter. We then retrieve on the whole collection. To compare with different approaches, we also performed the same retrieval task using only SMART system. We did two runs: one without stemming and one with stemming. The stemmer used in the second experiment is Triestem, which is provided by SMART and is a modified version of Lovins's stemmer (Lovins 1968).

Compared with the result using stemming, the proposed method achieved an improvement of 8.6% on average precision for 11 points of recall (from an average precision of 0.186 to an average of 0.202). Compared with the no-stemming baseline, the proposed method achieved an improvement of 31.2% on average precision. Table 2 shows the detailed results. Figure 1 shows the results in a graph format.

Table 2. The evaluation result

Recall	Precision			
	No-stem	Stem	New method	
0.00	0.419	0.466	0.489	
0.10	0.282	0.306	0.333	
0.20	0.224	0.256	0.279	
0.30	0.183	0.226	0.244	
0.40	0.162	0.193	0.212	
0.50	0.135	0.169	0.179	
0.60	0.107	0.146	0.156	
0.70	0.080	0.122	0.129	
0.80	0.050	0.081	0.106	
0.90	0.029	0.052	0.064	
1.00	0.013	0.024	0.035	
Average	0.154	0.186	0.202	(8.6%)

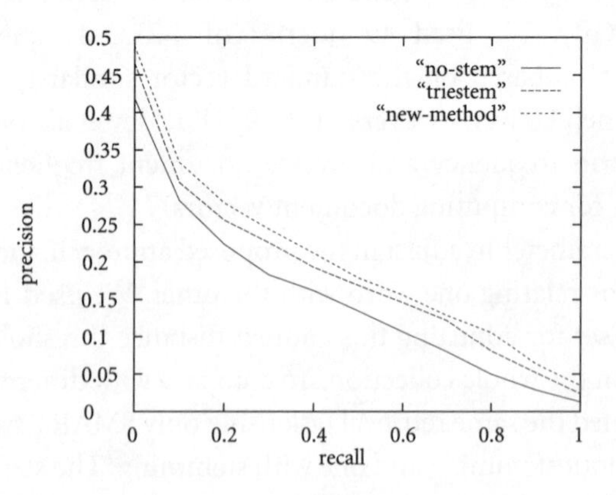

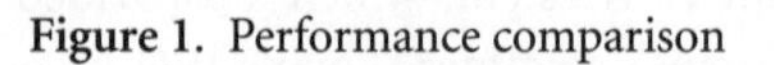
Figure 1. Performance comparison

We also analyzed the performance for individual queries. First, we compared the proposed method and the traditional stemmer with respect to their influence on individual queries. By looking at the results of the two runs on SMART, we can see that traditional stemming using a stemmer like Triestem greatly improved the overall performance in this experiment, from 0.154 average precision to 0.186. Although applying traditional stemming greatly improved the overall performance, it also decreased the performance of a number of queries: 15 out of 49 queries (31%) had a decrease in performance after the traditional stemming was used. Our context distance and morphology based model, in contrast, resulted in performance decrease on only 7 queries, half of the number compared to traditional stemming, while improving the overall performance. We also found that the proposed method is more likely to outperform traditional stemming for longer queries.

Compared to the standard retrieval procedure by SMART, the new approach takes up more space by storing context vectors and corpus relevance values. It also takes more time due to three additional actions: the pre-computing of context vectors, the pre-computing of corpus relevance, and the computing of context distance during retrieval. Hopefully, the problems with time and space can be alleviated by more efficient data storing and computing. The investigation of this issue is in our future work.

To examine whether the computed distance between context vectors provides useful results, we studied a random set of cases. The program correctly identified the semantic closeness between the following two context vectors (the two context vectors have a distance of 0.03012 – the relative large value means they are close):

bank : { savings(0.44) federal(0.44) million(0.44) loan(0.33) company(0.22) farmington(0.22) board(0.22) agreed(0.22) billion(0.22) nationwide(0.22) }

banks : { fdic(0.56) depression(0.42) number(0.28) failed(0.28) post(0.28) fund(0.28) year(0.28) fslic(0.28) loan(0.14) deposits(0.14) }

Note that the two contexts have only one overlapping word. A vector model solely based on word similarities will fail to find the high relevance between the above two context vectors, while our context distance model does capture such relatedness.

The program also correctly identified the non-relatedness of the following two context vectors (the context vectors have a distance of 0.0002 — the small value means that they are not related):

bank: { savings(0.44) federal(0.44) million(0.44) loan(0.33) company(0.22) farmington(0.22) board(0.22) agreed(0.22) billion(0.22) nationwide(0.22) }

bank: { west(0.45) gaza(0.45) strip(0.45) state(0.22) boasted(0.22) called(0.22) hailed(0.22) israeli(0.22) plo(0.22) occupied(0.22) }

5. Conclusion and future work

We have described a new method for determining semantic equivalence of terms in Information Retrieval. The new method integrates the ideas behind traditional stemming and the sense-based retrieval strategy, and tries to make these two seemingly opposite operations enhance each other. We tested the new technique on a sub-collection of TREC-4 corpora and the results showed a measurable improvement.

The context distance model is a sense-based retrieval strategy. Not assuming static sense distinction from an existing lexicon, the model uses the contexts where a word appears to determine its meaning, relying on both local document information and global corpus information .

In the future, we plan to explore alternative ways to compute the distance between context vectors, better ways to use the context distance in determining word similarity in retrieval, and methods for improving the speed of the system. Additionally, we will study how the proposed context distance model can be used for other applications.

Notes

We thank Dr. Judith Klavans and Dr. Christian Jacquemin for the helpful discussions and constructive comments.

References

Buckley, C., Salton, G., Allan, J. and Singhal, A. 1994. "Automatic query expansion using SMART: TREC-3." In *Proceedings of the Third Text Retrieval Conference (TREC-3)*, Gaithersburg, Maryland.

CELEX. 1995. *The CELEX Lexical Database — Dutch, English, German.* CD-ROM. Center for Lexical Information, Max Planck Institute for Psycholinguistics, Nijmegen.

Church, K.W. 1995. "One term or two?." In *Proceedings of the Eighteenth Annual International ACM SIGIR Conference on Research and Development in Information Retrieval (SIGIR '95)*, pages 310–318, Seattle, Washington, USA.

Deerwester, S., Dumais, S.T., Furnas, G., Landauer, T.K. and Harshman, R. 1990. "Indexing by latent semantic analysis." *Journal of the American Society for Information Science* 41(6):391–407.

Gale, A.W., Church, K.W. and Yarowsky, D. 1992. "One sense per discourse." In *Proceedings of the Fourth DARPA Speech and Natural Language Workshop.*

Harman, D. 1991. "How effective is suffixing? ". *Journal of the American Society for Information Science* 42(1): 7–15.

Hull, D.A. 1996. "Stemming algorithms: A case study for detailed evaluation." *Journal of the American Society for Information Science* 47(1):70–84.

Kilgariff, A. 1993. "Dictionary word sentence distinctions: An enquiry into their nature." *Computers and the Humanities* 26:365–387.

Krovetz, R. and Croft, W.B. 1992. "Lexical ambiguity and information retrieval." ACM Transactions on Information Systems 10(2):115–141.

Krovetz, R. 1993. "Viewing morphology as an inference process." In *Proceedings of the Sixteenth Annual International ACM SIGIR Conference on Research and Development in Information Retrieval (SIGIR '93)*, 191–203, Pittsburg, PA.

Li, H. and Abe, A. 1998. "Word clustering and disambiguation based on co-occurrence data." In *Proceedings of the 36th Annual Meeting of the Association for Computational Linguistics and the 17th International Conference on Computational Linguistics (COLING-ACL '98)*, 749–755, Montréal, Canada.

Lovins, J.B. 1968. "Development of a stemming algorithm." *Translation and Computational Linguistics* 11(1): 22–31.

McRoy, S. 1992. "Using multiple knowledge sources for word sense discrimination." *Computational Linguistics* 18(1):1–30.

Ng, H.T. and Lee, H.B. 1996. "Integrating multiple knowledge sources to disambiguate word sense: An exemplar-based approach." In *Proceedings of the 34th Annual Meeting of the Association for Computational Linguistics(ACL '96)*, 40–47, Santa Cruz, CA.

Porter, M.F. 1980. "An algorithm for suffix stripping." *Program* 14:130–137.

Schütze, H. and Pedersen, J.O. 1995. "Information Retrieval based on word senses." In *Symposium on Document Analysis and Information Retrieval (SDAIR)*, Las Vegas, NV, USA.

Schütze, H. 1998. "Automatic word sense discrimination." *Computational Linguistics* 24(1):97–123.

Voorhees, M. E. 1993. "Using WordNet to disambiguate words senses for text retrieval." In *Proceedings of the Sixteenth Annual International ACM SIGIR Conference on Research and Development in Information Retrieval (SIGIR '93)*, 171–180, Pittsburg, PA.

Xu, J. and Croft, W. B. 1998. "Corpus-based stemming using cooccurrence of word variants." *ACM Transactions on Information Systems* 16(1): 61–81

Yarowsky, D. 1992. "Word sense disambiguation using statistical models of Roget's thesaurus categories trained on a large corpus." In *Proceedings of the Fifteenth International Conference on Computational Linguistics (COLING '92)*, Nantes, France.

Chapter 13

Term extraction using a similarity-based approach

Diana Maynard and Sophia Ananiadou
University of Sheffield / University of Salford

Traditional methods of multi-word term extraction have used hybrid methods combining linguistic and statistical information. The linguistic part of these applications is often underexploited and consists of very shallow knowledge in the form of a simple syntactic filter. In most cases no interpretation of terms is undertaken and recognition does not involve distinguishing between different senses of terms, although ambiguity can be a serious problem for applications such as ontology building and machine translation. The approach described uses both statistical and linguistic information, combining syntax and semantics to identify, rank and disambiguate terms. We describe a new thesaurus-based similarity measure, which uses semantic information to calculate the importance of different parts of the context in relation to the term. Results show that making use of semantic information is beneficial for both theoretical and practical aspects of terminology.

1. Introduction

In recent years there has been a growing need for advances in the establishment and management of terminological resources. The vast quantities of new electronic material both cause this problem and enable it to be resolved. In particular, new terms are constantly emerging and undergoing changes in meaning. Although it was once possible to carry out tasks such as term recognition and ontology creation manually, automatic or at least semi-automatic approaches are now required.

The increasing availability of suitable electronic texts has enabled corpus-based methods to be widely used in areas of terminology such as term recognition, but attention has been largely focused on statistical methods involving little or no understanding of terminology. Although relatively successful in practical terms, they contribute few theoretical insights. While some approaches have been of a more linguistic nature, those which involve anything more than very shallow knowledge tend to be restricted to a narrow field and are not portable to new domains.

In this paper we present a two-tiered approach to the extraction of multi-word terms. The underlying layer is corpus-based and is largely statistical, whilst the top layer exploits semantic information found both in the context and in an exterior lexical resource. This not only enables candidate terms to be identified and ranked in order of termhood, but also disambiguation to be carried out, thereby allowing different meanings of terms to be ranked individually.

2. Fundamental principles

2.1 Terms and concepts

It is well known that the correct association of term and concept is important for machine translation (Dubuc and Lauriston 1997), but this is also true for almost any application of computational linguistics involving specialised languages. Translation of technical texts involves finding a suitable equivalence between the source language (SL) term and the target language (TL) term. In order to establish this, equivalence between the SL and TL concepts must first be found. For machine translation, the problem generally lies even deeper, since the SL and TL concepts may not have a direct correspondence. So although translation appears to be simply a matter of establishing a direct term-term correspondence, it is not always quite so simple. Cognitive issues also have to be considered: a concept is not fixed in stone but can vary according to the viewpoint of an individual or a group of people. So establishing the correspondence between SL and TL concepts is not always straightforward.

Whilst we are not aiming to perform machine translation in this work, the same principles apply. We must have some comprehension of the relationship between term and concept in order to understand term variation and ambiguity, both of which are crucial to the theoretical study of terminology and to its practical applications. In order to perform term disambiguation, we need to relate different occurrences of a term to different concepts, and in order to be able to account for term variation, we need to be able to relate different linguistic realisations of a term to one concept. This is virtually impossible unless we already have a clear idea of what these concepts are.

2.2 Contexts

The overall picture cannot be completed without mentioning the linguistic contexts we are investigating. They can be seen as related primarily either to terms or to concepts (Dubuc and Lauriston 1997). The psychological viewpoint sees them as being related to concepts, in that the context serves to position the concept within a particular subject field. Because we view contexts as being the key to understanding a term, we consider that it is the meaning of the term (and thereby the concept) rather than its linguistic realisation which is most relevant to the context. The alternative approach views the context from a more structural position, regarding the context as a source of collocational information and syntactic structures. In this case, the context is linked to the term itself rather than to its underlying meaning. Although contexts do certainly serve this purpose, we consider this to be an incidental rather than a primary function. Because we regard contexts from a semantic rather than a syntactic viewpoint, we adopt an approach that considers the context in relation to the concept rather than to the term. According to this approach, we see the concept as a *bridge* between context and term. Since we aim to illuminate the relationships not only between text and concept but also between concept and term, clearly an understanding of concepts is also vital.

2.3 Approaches to term recognition

Approaches to term recognition really require an in-depth understanding of the nature of terms, and thereby "not only contribute to the applications of computational linguistics but also to the theoretical foundations of terminology" (Kageura and Umino 1996). Some comprehension of the behaviour of terms is thus crucial to any successful approach to automatic methods of term recognition and disambiguation.

Methods of automatic term recognition involving purely linguistic information have been fairly limited. They fall into two main categories: those which use extrinsic information and those which use intrinsic information. The types of information used tend to be syntactic for the former, e.g. LEXTER (Bourigault 1992), and syntactic or morphological for the latter, e.g. (Ananiadou 1988).

More recently, approaches to ATR have veered towards using both statistical and linguistic information (Daille et al. 1994), (Justeson and Katz 1995), (Frantzi 1998). Generally the main part of the algorithm is the statistical part, but shallow linguistic information is incorporated in the form of a syntactic filter which only permits certain combinations of syntactic categories to be considered as candidate terms. Little use has been made of semantic information for the purpose of term recognition, largely because, in contrast to morphological and syntactic information, it is hard both to identify and to manipulate.

2.4 Extracting semantic information

On the other hand, semantic information has been used fairly extensively for other purposes such as knowledge acquisition and word sense disambiguation. Because they are not used specifically for terminology, these methods tend to use general language dictionaries or thesauri. One common method is to compare the content of the dictionary definition of a word with the words in the surrounding context. Lesk (1986) used an online dictionary to calculate the overlap between dictionary definitions of word senses, Smeaton and Quigley (1996) calculated word-word similarity between related words in a thesaurus, while Yarowsky (1992) captured the meanings of word senses from semantic categories in Roget's Thesaurus.

The application of these methods to word sense disambiguation has been largely successful. There are, however, two main reasons why they are not entirely suitable for our work. Firstly, they are used for word sense rather than term sense disambiguation. Secondly, they are designed to deal with general rather than domain-specific language. Technical terms are not covered sufficiently in any general language dictionary or thesaurus, and we propose that they really require a more specialised source of information.

An alternative approach to the acquisition of semantic information involves the use of a disambiguated corpus for training. Riloff and Lehnert (1992) developed an algorithm to derive relevancy cues from training texts, which they used for information extraction. Soderland et al. (1995) also developed a system to identify concepts in a text, by means of linguistic features which reliably identified the conceptual content of a phrase. Grefenstette (1994) adopted a hybrid, knowledge-poor approach to the automatic extraction of semantic information from large corpora, using only syntactic information. The advantage of these techniques is that they require no dictionary or thesaurus and provide information specific to the corpus. However, they do require suitable large-scale corpora.

2.5 Term sense disambiguation

In many ways, term sense disambiguation is similar to the problem of word sense disambiguation, but it differs in two main aspects. Firstly, terms are domain-specific, which means that general language resources and techniques may not be appropriate. Secondly, the majority of technical terms consist of more than one word (the average length of English NP terms is approximately 1.91 words, depending on the type of corpus). The ambiguity of multiword terms is generally not caused by different senses of the individual components of the term, but by different senses of the term as a whole. The different meanings of the term may be linked to different domains, but they may equally be present within a specific domain. Although domain-specific text is likely to contain the meanings of a term related to that domain, it does not rule out the possibility of the general meaning of that term being used as well. For example, in biochemistry, the term *complement* is used to refer to a component of blood serum, but it might equally be found in a medical text with its general meaning. Similarly, the term *drug* found in a medical text could refer to either an illegal substance or simply to a kind of medicine. Because of these differences, techniques applied to word sense disambiguation are not always appropriate for term sense disambiguation.

3. Contextual information

3.1 NC-value method

Our approach is built on a method for automatic term recognition called NC-Value (Frantzi and Ananiadou 1999). This uses a mixture of statistical and linguistic information to rank candidate terms. We make use of the contextual information already acquired to incorporate deeper forms of linguistic knowledge, thereby improving the recognition and also performing disambiguation of terms, so that different senses of a term are distinguished and individually ranked. In Frantzi's approach, potential terms are first extracted from a corpus and ranked using the C-value method (Frantzi and Ananiadou 1999) based on frequency of occurrence and term length. Contextual information is then incorporated into the algorithm, in the form of weights based on the statistical characteristics of the context words.

Context words are composed of any nouns, adjectives and verbs in a fixed-size context window, either preceding or following a potential term. The context words are extracted and assigned a weight based on how frequently they appear with terms, and these weights are combined to produce a *context factor* for each term. The NC-value combines the C-value with this context factor to produce a re-ranking of the list of terms:

$$NCvalue(a) = 0.8 * Cvalue(a) + 0.2 * CF(a)$$

where
a is the candidate term,
Cvalue(a) is the C-value for the candidate term,
CF(a) is the context factor for the candidate term.

If a candidate string is not found as a nested string, the C-Value is calculated from its total frequency and length. If it is found as nested, the C-Value is calculated from its total frequency, length, frequency as a nested string, and the number of longer candidate terms it appears in.

3.2 Identifying relevant contextual information

It is widely recognised among terminologists that linguistic contexts provide a rich and valuable source of information. The problem lies in identifying those parts of the context which are actually relevant. Although a domain-specific corpus is used, it is clear that not all parts of the context are equally useful. Traditionally, a KWIC index is used to find a window of words surrounding candidate terms, but these contexts then have to be manually investigated — a time-consuming and laborious process.

The linguistic knowledge used in the NC-Value approach is very limited, since it is only the syntactic category of the context word which is taken into account. It considers neither any differences that might exist between the categories, nor the position in which the context word occurs with respect to the term. For example, it might be the case that nouns are more useful than verbs in predicting termhood, or that verbs preceding a term are more useful indicators than verbs following a term.

Another factor which plays an important role is that of the *meaning* of the context words. We propose two new indicators of termhood:

- context words which are themselves terms (which we call *context terms*)
- context words which are closely related in meaning to their co-occurring terms.

Our claim is that if a context word has some contribution towards the determination of a term, there should be some significant correspondence between the meaning of that context word and the meaning of the term. In other words, there should be some identifiable semantic relation between the two, which can be used to make a contribution towards the correct identification and comprehension of a term. The following two sections describe how this is achieved. The two indicators of termhood proposed above are incorporated using weights. Firstly, context terms are assigned a weight dependent on how frequently they occur with the candidate term. Secondly, a semantic weight is allocated to each candidate term based on its similarity with all its context terms.

3.3 Context term weight

The first parameter we consider is the status of the context word. If it is a term, we predict that it is more likely to be significant than a non-term, in other words, that terms are better indicators of other terms. This stems from the fact that terms do not tend to occur singly or randomly, but in groups, particularly in domain-specific texts (Maynard and Ananiadou 1998a).

Since we do not know in advance which context words are terms, this step can only be undertaken once we have a preliminary list of candidate terms. For this we use the top of the list of terms extracted by the C-value approach, since this should contain the "best" terms (or, at least, those which behave in the most term-like fashion). A context term weight (CT) is assigned to each candidate term based on how frequently it appears with a context term. It is formally described as follows:

$$\mathrm{CT}(a)=\Sigma_{d\in T_a} f_a(d)$$

where
a is the candidate term,
T_a is the set of context terms of a,
d is a word from T_a,
$f_a(d)$ is the frequency of d as a context term of a.

4. A thesaurus-based similarity measure

Using a million-word corpus of eye pathology records, candidate terms are extracted using the NC-value method, along with context windows of 5 words either side of the term. Each context word and term is then tagged with its semantic type, using information provided by the UMLS Metathesaurus. Generalisations can then be made about these semantic types and the relations between them. The context words are divided into terms and non-terms. Context terms will automatically receive a higher weighting, since they are predicted to have a stronger association with other terms than context words have.

4.1 Semantic information in UMLS

The UMLS (Unified Medical Language System) (UMLS 1997) is a set of knowledge sources containing information about medical terminology, organised in a hierarchical structure. Not only does it provide a classification system for the terms, but it also contains morphological, syntactic and semantic information. The Semantic Network contains additional information about the relations between the semantic classes to which the terms are assigned.

Each term and context term is tagged with its semantic type from the UMLS Metathesaurus. For example, the term *actinic keratosis* will be tagged with the semantic type *acquired abnormality*. Relational information about the semantic types is also available. This information is generic rather than specific, i.e. details are provided about classes of terms rather than about individual terms, and do not necessarily hold for every member of that class. For example, a relationship exists between the semantic classes of *disease or syndrome* and *acquired abnormality* such that the former is a *result_of* the latter. This does not imply that any disease is the result of any acquired abnormality, but simply that there is a general relationship of this kind between the two classes, such that diseases or syndromes can be the result of acquired abnormalities.

4.2 Calculating similarity in the UMLS semantic network

The similarity between context term and candidate term is measured using the UMLS Semantic Network, which is a hierarchy of semantic types. Our approach is modelled on techniques used in Example-Based Machine Translation (EBMT) (Zhao 1996), (Sumita and Iida 1991). EBMT aims to select the most similar example for a given problem, by defining a set of relevant examples and comparing them with the problem in terms of context and configuration. Most of these comparison methods involve using some kind of semantic distance measure, based on the relative positions of the two items within a hierarchical network.

In its simplest form, similarity is measured by edge-counting — the shorter the distance between the words, the greater their similarity. The Most Specific Common Abstraction (MSCA) method (Kolodner 1993) involves tracing the respective paths of the two words back up the hierarchy until a common ancestor is found, and then measuring the average distance from node to this point (the MSCA). The shorter the distance to the MSCA, the more similar the two words. The position of the MSCA within the hierarchy can also be used to measure similarity (Zhao 1996), (Sumita, and Iida 1991). The lower down in the hierarchy the MSCA, the more specific it is and therefore the more information is shared by the two concepts, thus making them more similar. We combine these two ideas by defining two weights as follows:

- **positional weight**: the vertical position of the nodes within the hierarchy, measured by the combined number of nodes belonging to each word
- **commonality weight**: essentially the horizontal distance between the two nodes, measured by the number of shared common ancestors multiplied by the number of words (usually two).

The nodes in the Semantic Network are coded such that the number of digits in the code represents the (inclusive) number of leaves descended from the root to that node, as shown in Figure 1. Similarity between two nodes is calculated by dividing the commonality weight by the positional weight to produce a figure between 0 and 1, 1 being the case where the two nodes are identical, and 0 being the case where there is no common ancestor (which would only occur if there were no unique root node in the hierarchy).

$sim(w1, w2) = com(w1, w2)/pos(w1, w2)$

where
$com(w1, w2)$ is the commonality weight of word 1 and word 2
$pos(w1, w2)$ is the positional weight of word 1 and word 2.

As an example, the similarity between *plant* (node TA111) and *fungus* (node TA112) would be calculated as follows:

com (TA111, TA112) = 4 common ancestors (*T* + *TA* + *TA1* + *TA11*) * 2 words = **8**

pos (TA111,TA112) = 5 nodes (*T* + *TA* + *TA1* + *TA11* + *TA111*) + 5 nodes (*T* + *TA* + *TA1* + *TA11* + *TA112*) = **10**

sim (TA111,TA112) = com/pos = 8/10 = **0.8**

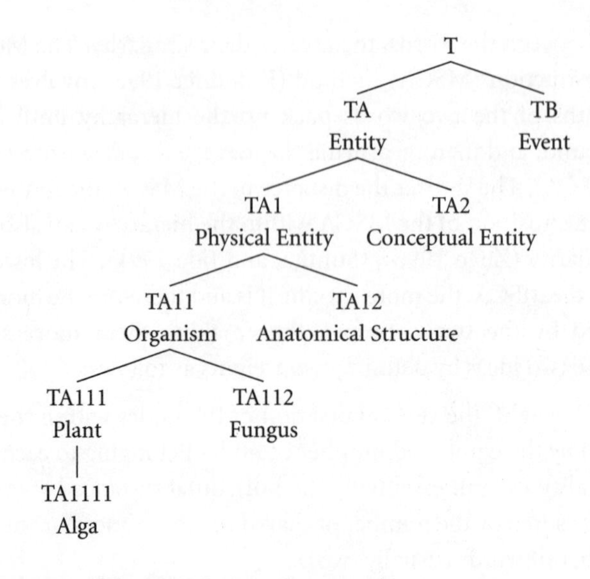

Figure 1. Fragment of the UMLS semantic network

It becomes clear that the further down in the hierarchy the two items are, the greater their similarity, which is intuitive since they are more specific. It is also intuitive that the greater the horizontal and/or vertical distance between words in the network, the less similar they are.

5. Results and evaluation

5.1 Incorporating the weights

The measure described in the previous section calculates the similarity between each term and the "significant" context words it occurs with, i.e. the context terms. The similarity weight is then combined with the context term weight to form a Context Weight for each candidate term. The Context Weight is then combined with the original NC-Value to form the SNC-Value, which gives a new ranking for the candidate terms.

$$CW(a) = \Sigma_{b \in C_a} f_a(b) * weight(b) + \Sigma_{d \in T_a} f_a(d) * sim(d,a)$$

where
a is the candidate term,
C_a is the set of context words of a,
b is a word from C_a,
$f_a(b)$ is the frequency of b as a context word of a,
$weight(b)$ is the weight of b as a context word,
T_a is the set of context terms of a,
d is a word from T_a,
$f_a(d)$ is the frequency of d as a context term of a,
$sim(d,a)$ is the similarity weight of d occurring with a.

5.2 Disambiguation of terms

The semantic weight is calculated separately for each occurrence of a term, rather than just once for each term. This enables a distinction to be made between different usages of a term, even within a single corpus. If a term is ambiguous, it will usually have more than one semantic type, and therefore different semantic weights can be calculated for different meanings of a term. Intuition, followed by experimentation, showed that the meaning of a term with the highest semantic weight was most frequently the correct one in the context (Maynard and Ananiadou 1998b). This also helps validate our theory that terms occur with semantically related context words.

5.3 Evaluation of the context term weight

To evaluate the effectiveness of the context term weight, we performed an experiment to compare the frequency of occurrence of each context term with terms and with non-terms. For each context term (in all its occurrences), we counted the number of terms and non-terms it appeared with. The results depicted in Table 1 show that 90% of context terms appear more frequently with a term than with a non-term, and only 4% appear less frequently. The figure in the second column indicates not the total number of co-occurrences, but the number of context terms occurring in the proportion indicated by the first column (more, less or equally frequently with terms, as opposed to non-terms). Another property of context terms should be that if they appear more frequently with terms at the top of the list than terms at the bottom of the list (i.e. they occur more often with "better" terms), then they are better indicators. We therefore conducted an experiment to see how often context terms appeared

Table 1. Occurrences of context terms with terms and non-terms

Occurrence	No. of context terms	Percentage
More frequent with term	419	90%
Equally frequent with either	28	6%
more frequent with non-term	17	4%

with terms from each part of the list. The C-value list of terms was again divided into 3 equal sections and the number of occurrences of context terms with terms from each section of the list was calculated. The results depicted in Table 2 confirm overwhelmingly that context terms occur more frequently with terms at the top of the list — 76% of all context terms occurring with terms from the top, and only 9% occurring with terms from the bottom.

Table 2. Occurrences of context terms with terms

List Section	No. of Context Terms	Percentage
Top	31310	76
Middle	6019	15
Bottom	3927	9

5.4 Evaluation of the semantic weight

One of the problems with our method of calculating similarity is that it relies on a pre-existing lexical resource. Whilst this is not a perfect solution, since there are likely to be omissions and possibly errors, there are also inherent problems with other methods such as relying solely on corpus data. Bearing in mind its innate inadequacies, we can nevertheless evaluate the expected theoretical performance of the measure by assuming completeness, and concerning ourselves only with what is covered by the thesaurus.

The semantic weight is based on the premise that the more similar a context term is to the candidate term it occurs with, the better an indicator that context term is. So the higher the total semantic weight for the candidate term, the better the ranking of the term and the better the chance that the candidate term is valid. To test the performance of the semantic weight, we sorted the terms in descending order of their semantic weights and divided the list into three, such that the top third contained the terms with the highest semantic weights, and the bottom third contained those with the lowest. We then calculated the proportion of valid and non-valid terms (as determined by manual assessment) in each section of the list.

The results depicted in Table 3 reveal that in the top third of the list, 76% were terms and 24% were non-terms, whilst in the middle third, 49% were terms and 51% were non-terms. Most of the valid terms are thus contained in the top third and the fewest valid terms are contained in the bottom third. Also, the proportion of terms to non-terms in the top of the list is such that there are more terms than non-terms, whereas in the bottom of the list there are more non-terms than terms. The evaluation therefore demonstrates two things:

- More of the terms with the highest semantic weights are valid, and fewer of those with the lowest semantic weights are valid,
- More valid terms have high semantic weights than non-terms, and more non-terms have lower semantic weights than valid terms.

Table 3. Semantic weights of terms and non-terms

	Term	Non-Term
Top set	76%	24%
Middle set	56%	44%
Bottom set	49%	51%

5.5 Comparison with statistical methods of measuring similarity

Using a pre-defined thesaurus to calculate similarity has the pitfalls that the hierarchy does not always tend to be even, especially when it has been created manually, as in the case of UMLS. So the distance between two nodes may actually reflect differing degrees of similarity, depending on which section of the thesaurus they occur in. Although we take into consideration the vertical position of the nodes, this is to account for the fact that nodes lower in the hierarchy are intuitively more similar, rather than for any discrepancies in the uniformity of the ontology. Various methods of regulating this problem have been proposed, e.g. (Resnik 1995), (Smeaton and Quigley 1996). In almost all similarity measures using thesauri, statistical information is either solely used or at least incorporated into the measure. However, there is no clear evidence to suggest that adding statistical information will significantly improve the measure, where the statistical part is not the primary component, and where a relatively small corpus is used as the basis for frequency information.

The methods which intuitively seem most plausible are based on information content. The information content of a node is related to its probability of occurrence in the corpus. The more frequently it appears, the more likely it is to be important in terms of conveying information, and therefore the higher the weighting it should receive. We performed two experiments to compare such methods with our similarity measure. The first considers the probability of the MSCA of the two terms, whilst the second considers the probability of the nodes of the terms being compared.

The probability of a node is calculated by its frequency in the corpus. Since semantic types do not appear as such in the corpus, this frequency is found by summing the frequencies of all the terms in the corpus belonging to this semantic type. To estimate the probability of a semantic type, we divide its frequency of occurrence by the total frequency of all semantic types occurring in the corpus. This can be described more formally as follows. We define the probability of a term occurring in the corpus as:

$$P(t_j) = f(t_j) / \Sigma_{S \in T} \Sigma_{tj \in Si} f(t_j)$$

where
T is the set of semantic types occurring in the corpus;
S is a semantic type belonging to T;
t_j is a term belonging to a semantic type S;
$f(t_j)$is the frequency of term t_j occurring in the corpus.

The probability of a semantic type occurring can then be defined as:

$$P(S_i) = \Sigma_{tj \in Si} P(t_j)$$

where
S_i is a semantic type;
t_j is a term;
$P(t_j)$ is the probability of t_j occurring in the corpus.

5.5.1 *Experiment 1*

The first experiment involves adding the probability of the MSCA to the similarity value of a term. For each combination of term and context term, the weight of the MSCA is added to the similarity weight to give a new score. The idea stems from the approach of (Smeaton and Quigley 1996) which uses the probability of the MSCA alone to calculate similarity between words. Our rationale for using the probability of the MSCA is that the MSCA is the most significant part of the hierarchy when measuring similarity, because it is the lowest part of the hierarchy (and thus the most informative part) at which the two terms are similar. Below this point, the two terms begin to differ, so any additional information encountered will not be common to both. Thus it should be beneficial to the measurement of similarity to take particular notice of this *lowest informative point* at which the similarity between the two is greatest in terms of information yielded, and thus at this point that the probability should be measured.

5.5.2 *Experiment 2*

It could also be argued that it is the probability of the individual nodes being considered that is most relevant to similarity. If a particular semantic type is statistically important, then this is likely to reflect on all the terms belonging to that semantic type. It could therefore be claimed that two terms which belong to statistically important semantic types have a greater degree of similarity than two terms which do not. Care must be taken, however, to avoid blurring the distinction between the theoretical notion of similarity and its practical usage.

The second experiment involves calculating the probability of the node, to form what we call the information content (IC) weight. So when similarity is calculated between a term and a context term, the IC weight of the node under which each is positioned is added to the similarity weight.

The experiments incorporating the idea of information content into the similarity measure were evaluated by comparing the number of terms and non-terms found in the top, middle, and bottom sections of the list of terms ordered by similarity.

The results, shown in Tables 4 and 5, are remarkably similar, and in fact differ little from the original similarity measurement shown in Table 3 and discussed earlier.

6. Conclusions

As we had originally suggested, neither method was significantly better than the other, nor did either show any real improvement over our original method. This does not necessarily mean that all three methods are equivalent, however.

Table 4. Experiment 1 — Semantic weights of terms and non-terms

	Term	Non-Term
Top set	76%	24%
Middle set	57%	43%
Bottom set	49%	51%

Table 5. Experiment 2 — Semantic weights of terms and non-terms

	Term	Non-Term
Top set	76%	24%
Middle set	59%	41%
Bottom set	48%	52%

Each of the methods does produce different results in that the values attributed to the terms differ, but this has no real impact on the overall performance, i.e. in distinguishing terms from non-terms and ranking them accordingly. The original weight and the first experiment have a similar range of values for the weights, whilst the second experiment has a greater range.

As is often the case, the criteria for evaluation is dependent on the application. The simple experiments described above show that for the purposes of our method of term ranking, any of the three similarity measures is better than none, but that there is very little difference which one is used. For other applications or with different data sets, the choice of measure might be more significant, but our purpose here is to evaluate the measures locally rather than globally, i.e. within the context of our system.

As mentioned earlier, the system could be improved by incorporating other kinds of semantic information into the measure, such as relational information not captured by the similarity measure. Information about context words is not fully exploited, in particular regarding verbs. The similarity measure itself is also lacking in that it fails to account for terms not found in the thesaurus. The results have nevertheless demonstrated the usefulness of incorporating deeper forms of linguistic information for term extraction and for its practical applications.

References

Ananiadou, S. 1988. *Towards a methodology for automatic term recognition.* PhD thesis, University of Manchester, UK.

Bourigault, D. 1992. "Surface grammatical analysis for the extraction of terminological noun phrases." In *Proc. of 14th International Conference on Computational Linguistics*, 977–981. Nantes, France.

Daille, B., Gaussier, E. and Langé, J. 1994. "Towards automatic extraction of monolingual and bilingual terminology." In *Proc. of 15th International Conference on Computational Linguistics*, 515–521. Kyoto, Japan.

Dubuc, R. and Lauriston, A. 1997. "Terms and contexts." In *Handbook of Terminology Management*, Wright, S. and Budin, G. (eds.), 80–87. Amsterdam: John Benjamins.

Frantzi, K.T. 1998. *Automatic Recognition of Multi-Word Terms.* PhD thesis, Manchester Metropolitan University, UK.

Frantzi, K.T. and Ananiadou, S. 1999. "The C-Value/NC-Value domain independent method for multi-word term extraction." In *Journal of Natural Language Processing* 6 (3): 145–179.

Grefenstette, G. 1994. *Explorations in Automatic Thesaurus Discovery.* Boston, MA: Kluwer.

Justeson, J. and Katz, S. 1995. "Technical terminology: some linguistic properties and an algorithm for identification in text." In *Natural Language Engineering* 1: 9–27.

Kageura, K. and Umino, B. 1996. "Methods of automatic term recognition." In *Terminology* 3 (2): 259–289.

Kolodner, J. 1993. *Case-Based Reasoning.* San Mateo, California: Morgan Kaufmann.

Lesk, M. 1986. "Automatic sense disambiguation: how to tell a pine cone from an ice cream cone." In *Proc. of 5th International Conference on Systems Documentation*, 24–26. New York.

Maynard, D.G. and Ananiadou, S. 1998a. "Term Sense Disambiguation Using a Domain-Specific Thesaurus." In *Proc. of 1st International Conference on Language Resources and Evaluation (LREC)*, 681–687. Granada, Spain.

Maynard, D.G. and Ananiadou, S. 1998b. "Acquiring contextual information for term disambiguation." In *Proc. of 1st Workshop on Computational Terminology, Computerm'98*, 86–90. Montreal, Canada.

Resnik, P. 1995. "Disambiguating noun groupings with respect to WordNet senses." In *Natural Language Processing Using Very Large Corpora*, Church, K., Armstrong, S., Isabelle, P., Tzoukermann, E. and Yarowsky, D. (eds.), 77–98. Boston, MA: Kluwer.

Riloff, E. and Lehnert, W. 1992. "Classifying texts using relevancy signatures." *Proc. of 10th National Conference on Artificial Intelligence*, 329–334. *San Jose, CA.*

Smeaton, A. and Quigley, L. 1996. "Experiments on using semantic distances between words in image caption retrieval." In *Proc. of 19th International Conference on Research and Development in Information Retrieval*, 174–180. Zurich, Switzerland.

Soderland, S., Fisher, D., Aseltine, J. and Lehnert, W. 1995. "CRYSTAL: Inducing a conceptual dictionary." In *Proc. of the 14th International Joint Conference on Artificial Intelligence*, 1314–1319. Montreal, Canada.

Sumita, E. and Iida, H. 1991. "Experiments and prospects of example-based machine translation." In *Proc. of 29th Annual Meeting of the Association for Computational Linguistics*, 185–192. Berkeley, California.

UMLS 1997. *UMLS Knowledge Sources.* National Library of Medicine US Dept of Health and Human Services, 8th edition. Bethesda, MD.

Yarowsky, D. 1992. "Word sense disambiguation using statistical models of Roget's categories trained on large corpora." In *Proc. of* 14th International Conference on Computational Linguistics, 454–460. Nantes, France.

Zhao, G. 1996. *Analogical Translator: Experience-Guided Transfer in Machine Translation.* PhD thesis, UMIST, UK.

CHAPTER 14

Extracting knowledge-rich contexts for terminography

A conceptual and methodological framework*

Ingrid Meyer
University of Ottawa

Knowledge-rich contexts express conceptual information for a term. Terminographers need such contexts to construct definitions, and to acquire domain knowledge. This paper summarizes what we have learned about extracting knowledge-rich contexts semi-automatically. First, we define the concept of a knowledge-rich context, its major types and its components. Second, we describe a methodology for developing extraction tools that is based on lexical, grammatical and paralinguistic patterns. Third, we outline the most problematic research issues that must be addressed before semi-automatic knowledge extraction can become a fully mature field.

1. Introduction

By *terminography,* we mean the practical task of producing dictionaries[1] of lexical items that are specific to specialized domains of knowledge. Before they can produce entries for terms, terminographers must carry out three tasks:

- Identification of terms: what *are* the terms that should be described for the domain in question?
- Conceptual analysis of terms: what do these terms *mean*?
- Linguistic analysis of terms: how are the terms *used* in context?

The primary focus of this paper is conceptual analysis. As is well-known in the literature (Cf. Picht and Draskau 1985; Sager 1990; Wüster 1979), conceptual analysis is the cornerstone of terminography. Conceptual analysis essentially involves examining the *characteristics* of the concept designated by the term (Cf. Meyer et al. 1997). Conceptual characteristics, according to a useful distinction often made in the philosophy of language (Cf. Sowa 1984) can be of two types: (1) *attributes*, which hold for the concept in question without involving other concepts specific to the domain (e.g., COLOUR, HEIGHT, WEIGHT), and (2) *relations*, which link the concept to other concepts in the domain (e.g., HYPERONYMY, MERONYMY, CAUSALITY). As a result of analyzing conceptual relations, a high-quality terminology project ultimately aims to illustrate the *network* of concepts underlying the terms of the domain. In traditional term banks and specialized dictionaries, the conceptual network is usually represented implicitly, through the definitions and examples provided to elucidate the meaning of a term. In the more recently developed terminological knowledge base model (Otman 1997), however, networks may be shown explicitly, for example through graphical representations.

Whatever type of terminological repository they are working with, terminographers have at their disposal two basic strategies for acquiring conceptual knowledge. On the one hand, they can interview domain experts personally. On the other hand, they can consult texts written by the experts. The second option is becoming increasingly attractive for conceptual analysis (and for the two other terminology tasks) because of the easy availability of electronic texts (= *corpora*), particularly on the WWW.[2]

Despite the quantities of data that it may contain, a corpus is only as useful as the tools available for extracting this data. When it comes to finding conceptual information in a corpus, conventional extraction tools offer the terminographer one principal feature: the KWIC (key-word-in-context) concordance. A KWIC concordance shows all occurrences of a given term, along with contexts of a fixed length. From this selection of terms-in-context, the terminographer must manually pick out the most *knowledge-rich* contexts, i.e., those which indicate important conceptual characteristics for the search term. When a term occurs hundreds or thousands of times, finding the knowledge-rich contexts is obviously extremely labour-intensive. Hence, a growing number of researchers in computational terminography (as well as information retrieval) are beginning to develop methods and tools for extracting knowledge-rich contexts semi-automatically.

Purpose. The purpose of this paper is to summarize what we have learned about semi-automatic, terminography-oriented knowledge extraction in the few short years that this technology has been feasible. We will draw primarily on the experiences of our own research project (known as COGNITERM),[3] which has investigated the problem from a terminographical as well as an information retrieval perspective in a variety of domains[4] over the last three years, using a knowledge-engineering-based toolset called DocKMan.[5] Our purpose is *not*, however, to promote this or any other particular tool. Rather, we aim to present (1) a very *generic* conceptual and methodological framework for research in semi-automatic knowledge extraction (Sections 2 and 3), and (2) an analysis of what we perceive to be the most problematic research issues in the field (Section 4). We hope that this paper will be useful to researchers who are developing knowledge-extraction tools, as well as to terminographers and other language professionals who are trying to understand the potential and challenges of this new technology.

Organization. The rest of this paper is divided into three sections. Section 2 investigates the concept of a knowledge-rich context (KRC) by providing an analysis of the two main types of KRC. Section 3 presents our methodology for developing a knowledge-extraction tool. Finally, Section 4 discusses the most pressing research problems of the field. Our paper is illustrated with corpus examples[6] for the domain of the environment, for the terms *compost* and *composting*.

2. Anatomy of a knowledge-rich context

The methodology for tool development described in Section 3 is based on the identification of linguistic and paralinguistic patterns underlying KRCs. Since these patterns correspond to certain aspects of KRCs, it is important to understand (1) what we mean by a knowledge-rich context, (2) what principal types of contexts there are, and (3) what the elements of each type are. These three issues are discussed below.

2.1 What is a 'knowledge-rich context'?

By *knowledge-rich context*, we designate a context indicating at least one item of domain knowledge that could be useful for conceptual analysis. In other words, the context should indicate at least one conceptual characteristic, whether it be an attribute or a relation. Because relations are by far the more problematic, this paper will focus on them. The following are examples of knowledge-rich contexts for the term *compost*:

(1) a. Compost: a ready-to-use soil enricher that looks and feels like dark, crumbly soil.
b. Compost is perhaps best defined as organic material deliberately assembled for fast decomposition.
c. Compost is a practical method of recycling organic matter, resulting in improved soil structure and strong, disease-resistant plants.
d. Compost, a dark, nutrient-rich soil conditioner, consists of a small amount of soil along with decomposed or partially decomposed plant residues.
e. Compost is classified as a soil conditioner rather than a fertilizer.

(2) a. Compost enriches topsoil with organic matter and plant nutrients, improves water infiltration, and increases water availability and nutrient retention in sandy soils.
b. Compost contains nutrients, nitrogen, potassium and phosphorus.
c. If the nitrogen proportion is too high, the compost may become too hot, killing the microorganisms.
d. Not all compost is equally effective. For high-quality decomposition it needs a good balance of the basic Four: Greens, Browns, Moisture, Air.

Example-sets 1 and 2 share one common denominator: each example indicates at least one conceptual characteristic, typically a relation. Examples 1a-e all illustrate the relation of HYPERONYMY (generic-specific), in that they provide possible genus terms for *compost* (*soil enricher, organic material, method of recycling, soil conditioner*). Other relations are illustrated as well: MERONYMY (part-whole) in (1d) and (2b–d), and PURPOSE in (1b) (decomposition), (1c) (to improve soil and plants), and (2a) (to enrich topsoil ... improve water infiltration ... etc.). (1a) and (1d) provide ATTRIBUTE information (what compost looks and feels like).

Uses of KRCs. KRCs have three practical uses in the terminographer's working environment: (1) to provide definitions, (2) to provide starting-points for definitions, and (3) to enhance the terminographer's general domain knowledge. Regarding (1), terminographers might use a high-quality KRC *intact* as a definition within a term entry. Regarding (2), terminographers might use lower quality KRCs as *starting points* for a definition. In many working environments, terminographers construct definitions by "piecing together" elements of various KRCs. Regarding (3), a certain amount of domain knowledge is critical for tasks such as identifying synonyms, standardizing terms, establishing equivalences between terms in different languages, etc.

A KRC can comprise just one clause or sentence, or it can span a number of sentences (like 2d). We therefore distinguish between *intra-sentential* and *extra-sentential* KRCs, analogous to Pearson's (1998) *simple* and *complex* defining expositives.[7]

Despite their similarities, example-sets (1) and (2) also differ in significant ways. We have therefore found it useful to classify them, respectively, as two distinct types of KRC: *defining* and *explanatory*.[8] These two types are discussed in turn below.

2.2 Type 1: Defining KRCs

The main common denominator of examples 1a-e above is that they all resemble the classic, Aristotelian definition, which is typically formulated as:

X = Y + differentiating characteristics

This formula has four components. X is the term to be defined, Y is the hypernym, and the differentiating characteristics are those characteristics necessary and sufficient (in the logical sense) to distinguish the concept designated by X from other members of the same class. The left-side of this formula is traditionally called the *definiendum*, while the right side is known as the *definiens*. The "=" sign, the fourth component of the definition, indicates that the definiendum and definiens should be substitutable for each other in any context, without changing the meaning of the context.

Consistent with this formula, contexts (1a–e) all "attempt" to indicate the important conceptual relation of HYPERONYMY. We say "attempt" because the genus term in 1c is illogical, classifying an object (*compost*) as a type of method. Also consistent with the classic definition, contexts (1a–d) (but not e) provide a variety of conceptual characteristics for the concept of *compost*. 1a and d provide ATTRIBUTES, while 1b and c both tell us something about the PURPOSE of *compost*.

Clearly, (1a–e) are far from being "perfect" examples of an Aristotelian definition. Aside from the illogical hypernym in (1c), the hedge *perhaps* in (1b) is atypical of formal definitions, and it is questionable whether any of the examples contains necessary and sufficient characteristics in the logical sense. Most critically, sentence (1e) contains *no* differentiating characteristics at all.

All these problems are typical of defining KRCs that one finds in "real-life" texts, as opposed to linguists' constructed examples or lexicographers' dictionary entries. There are two reasons why we accept such imperfect defining contexts as valid output from a knowledge-extraction tool. The first reason relates to the three potential *uses* of KRCs we noted earlier. While an imperfect KRC cannot be used *intact* as a definition, it can be used as a *starting point* for a definition, and can also enhance the terminographer's general domain knowledge.

The second reason for accepting imperfect definitions is that this is what terminographers have always been forced to do, even when corpora were paper-based. As terminographers know all too well, high-quality definitions are the exception rather than the rule in most of the corpora they work with. While experts may be extremely knowledgeable in their domains, they are not necessarily good definition writers (or, for that matter, good writers in the broadest sense). Terminographers are therefore trained to distinguish between high- and low-quality definitions, and to make necessary adjustments for the latter.

2.2.1 *Types of defining KRCs: Dictionary vs. naturally occurring*

Example 1a is different from the others in that it is presented as a dictionary entry would be, with the "=" slot implicit in the separation between definiendum and definiens, rather than being lexicalized by a phrase like *is a* (1c) or *is defined as* (1b). Because of its dictionary style, we call this type of context a *dictionary defining KRC*. In contrast, we term examples such as (1b–e), which occur naturally in running text without being marked in any particular way, as *naturally occurring defining KRCs*. Dictionary defining contexts are, by far, the more infrequent type. They may be placed outside the main body of the text (e.g., at the end) in some textbooks and other didactic material, and often at the start of the body of the text when authors wish to define their basic concepts before beginning. Furthermore, they are generally of higher quality than naturally occurring defining contexts. Since dictionary defining contexts are marked typographically (Cf. Pearson 1998: 162), it is important to establish a special class for them if they are to be adequately handled by extraction tools.

2.2.2 *Elements of a defining KRC*

As mentioned earlier, defining contexts conform to the classic definition formula, namely "X=Y + differentiating characteristics". While the standard "textbook" examples of definitions provided by linguists and lexicographers may appear straightforward, the examples one finds in "real" running text tend to deviate in numerous ways from the standard formula. A variety of deviations that may occur, in particular those which have an impact on extraction tools, are discussed below (a broader and more detailed study can be found in Pearson 1998).

"X". While the formula shows the X (i.e., the term) on the left, in reality it may occur on the right, or at least after the term, as in:

(3) … a humus-rich soil amendment known as compost.

Furthermore, and extremely problematic for knowledge-extraction tools, the term may be replaced by a pronoun or a phrase in an anaphoric reference. In running texts, it is also common to replace a term by a generic term (especially in cases of multi-word noun phrases) or by another type of term variant (Cf. Daille et al. 1996).

"=". As example-set (1) illustrates, the "=" can be lexicalized in phrases such as *is defined as*, *is a*, *is classified as*, etc. Such phrases are an obvious type of pattern that knowledge-extraction tools can use for the HYPERONYMY relation. However, the "=" can sometimes be expressed through punctuation, as in the appositive structure found in example (1d). In the following example, HYPERONYMY is indicated through dashes:

(4) Adequate levels of organic matter — compost or humus — are essential…

Punctuation may also be involved in dictionary defining contexts (e.g., the ":" in (1a)). In many cases the "=" is implicit in text structure (e.g., the X taking the form of a heading, the Y found on the next line).

"Y" This slot contains a genus for the "X". As illustrated in examples (1a–e), the genus term may vary from one author to another. A common reason for this is the author's point of view, as has been discussed in the literature on conceptual multidimensionality (Bowker 1995). The term *composting*, for example, can be discussed from the point of view of waste management (recycling), or from the point of view of soil enhancement. Examples (6a)–(6b) illustrate the first viewpoint, while examples (5a)–(5b) illustrate the second. Example (7) gives both viewpoints simultaneously, resulting in two fillers for the "Y" slot.

(5) a. Composting is a biological decay process which converts organic wastes into a crumbly, sweet smelling earth-like substance.
b. Composting is the controlled biological degradation of organic material.

(6) a. … the EPA classifies composting as a form of recycling.
b. … composting is one of the easiest of all recycling techniques…

(7) Composting is the natural process of decomposition and recycling of organic material into a humus-rich soil amendment known as compost.

The terminology literature stresses that definitions should contain the *closest* genus, i.e., the genus immediately above the concept in its generic-specific hierarchy. For example, a *colour laser printer* should ideally be defined as a type of *laser printer*, and not simply as a *printer*. In real texts, however, it is common to find generic terms that are too broad (e.g., *vermicompost* defined as a type of *soil conditioner* instead of a type of *compost*).

Differentiating characteristics. According to the Aristotelian formula, the differentiae come after the Y. As illustrated in example-set (1), however, they may also precede the Y, particularly in the case of attributes ((1a): ready-to-use, (1d): dark). In some cases, even relations can be expressed adjectivally, as in (1d), where nutrient-rich (illustrating MERONYMY, i.e., "containing nutrients") modifies soil conditioner.

We noted earlier that HYPERONYMY is associated with a number of recurrent patterns. The same applies to other relations expressed by the differentiae. Consider some of our contexts from example-set (1):

(1) c. Compost is a practical method of recycling organic matter, resulting in improved soil structure and strong, disease-resistant plants.
d. Compost, a dark, nutrient-rich soil conditioner, consists of a small amount of soil along with decomposed or partially decomposed plant residues.

In (1c), *resulting in* indicates a CAUSE-EFFECT relationship between *compost* and *soil structure/plants.* In (1d), *consists of* indicates a MERONYMIC relationship (*soil* and *plant residues* described as "parts" of *compost*).

In contrast to the Aristotelian formula, the characteristics found in real texts are typically not necessary and sufficient. Sometimes, a long list of detailed conceptual characteristics follows (and/or precedes) the Y, while other times there is just one or even none at all, as we already noted for example (1e).

It is debatable whether a sentence such as (1e), which provides no conceptual characteristics, should even be classified as a defining context, since it lacks one of the four basic elements of the classic definition formula. For our purposes, we have decided to classify such contexts as defining nevertheless, for the following reason. We have found that in most cases, when a sentence contains only a genus term, some conceptual characteristics will be not far off (for example, in previous or subsequent sentences). In other words, a sentence containing just the hypernym can usually be seen as just one part of an intersentential defining context.

Hedges and modals. The Aristotelian formula makes no explicit provision for two devices that are often used to attenuate the "force" of a defining KRC, namely hedges and modals. Examples (1b) and (8a) below use the hedges *perhaps* and *one way of seeing*, while (8b) uses the modal *can*:

(1) a. Compost is perhaps best defined as organic material deliberately assembled for fast decomposition.

(8) a. One way of seeing composting is as a drying process (through evaporation due to microbially generated heat)…
b. Composting can be defined as a biological decay process which converts organic wastes into a crumbly, sweet smelling earth-like substance.

2.3 Type 2: Explanatory KRCs

Let us reconsider the explanatory contexts shown in example-set (2):

(2) a. Compost enriches topsoil with organic matter and plant nutrients, improves water infiltration, and increases water availability and nutrient retention in sandy soils.
b. Compost contains nutrients, nitrogen, potassium and phosphorus.
c. If the nitrogen proportion is too high, the compost may become too hot, killing the microorganisms.
d. Not all compost is equally effective. For high-quality decomposition it needs a good balance of the basic Four: Greens, Browns, Moisture, Air.

As all these examples illustrate, explanatory contexts differ from defining ones in that they lack a hypernym. In other words, the "Y" element of the Aristotelian formula is missing. Without a "Y", the formula no longer has a true "=" component either: the right-hand side of the formula is not intended to be "substitutable" for the left-hand side. Because there is no Y, the characteristics are not intended to have the full "differentiating" function of a high-quality definition. We therefore represent explanatory contexts as follows:

$X \supset$ characteristics

As there is no genus, the Y has been dropped. In its logical sense, the "$\supset$" means "implies" in the strict sense of "must have". We use it in a looser sense to mean that the concept designated by X either "must have" or "typically has" one or several conceptual characteristics (note, we have removed the qualifier *differentiating*).

Why would terminographers be interested in contexts which, lacking hypernyms, do not closely resemble definitions? The reasons are the same ones we discussed for imperfect defining contexts: explanatory contexts can perhaps serve as starting points for definitions, and at the very least, they enhance the terminographer's general domain knowledge.

Let us examine the elements of an explanatory context in terms of its "sides", the missing hypernym, and the characteristics.

"*Sides*". The notion of a "left-hand side" or "right-hand side" can be as evident as it is for defining contexts (e.g., (2a, b)). On the other hand, it may disappear almost completely, as in (2c, d).

Absence of hypernym. Why is there no hypernym? Pearson (1998: 157) offers a number of reasons:

- The hypernym may have been specified previously in the context (i.e., the explanatory context may be part of an inter-sentential defining context).
- A full definition may have been given previously, and the explanatory context is intended to enhance that definition by providing more characteristics.
- The term may be so high up in the conceptual hierarchy that the hypernym is intuitively obvious. This applied to some degree to our example term *composting*, which most people would intuitively know is some kind of process.

To these reasons we would add a few more:

- A writer may consider a hypernym to be obvious in the case of a compound, e.g., that *composting* is a hypernym of *vermicomposting* and *cold composting.*
- The importance of the HYPERONYMY relation may vary from one domain to the next. In medical texts, for example, writers may be more likely to specify key relations (e.g., SYMPTOMS, TREATMENT) of a particular disease X than to specify that X is a kind of disease.
- Certain types of words, as has been pointed out by numerous lexical semanticists, do not lend themselves well to definition by HYPERONYMY. This is well-known for verbs and adjectives (Fellbaum 1990; Gross and Miller 1990), and has also been pointed out for some classes of nouns (Miller 1990).
- In some cases, a genus may be appropriate, but is not provided by the writer due to poor writing skills. Although linguists have argued that defining is to some degree an innate linguistic skill, all writers do not master it equally well.

Characteristics. We saw earlier that defining contexts may express certain conceptual relations through typical lexical patterns. The same is true for explanatory contexts (with the exception, of course, of HYPERONYMY). (2b,c), for example, indicate MERONYMIC relations through the words *contains* and *proportion.*

3. A methodology for developing knowledge-extraction tools

In this section, we shall examine a number of methodological issues in developing terminography-oriented knowledge-extraction tools. We discuss the way a terminographer would use such tools (3.1), the concept of a *knowledge pattern*, which underlies the design of such tools (3.2), and the process of integrating knowledge patterns into the tools (3.3).

3.1 Knowledge-extraction tools and the terminographer

For the purposes of this paper, we shall assume a *term-oriented* approach to the use of knowledge-extraction tools (another approach is discussed in Section 5). In other words, we assume that the terminographer uses the knowledge-extraction tool once he/she has already identified the terms to be described for the domain (using some type of term extraction tool, Cf. Kageura and Umino 1996). According to this scenario, the terminographer has a term in mind, and asks the system to search the corpus for those contexts that indicate a particular conceptual relation for this term. For example, "find me functions for the term *compost*". The system would provide a KWIC display of these contexts, allowing the user to manipulate the output in ways that have become standard in modern concordance tools (e.g., context expansion, sorting, etc.).

It would be up to the terminographer to specify which relation he/she was interested in (assuming, of course, that the system has been programmed to handle that relation). When the terminographer is just beginning to study a term, he/she might start with HYPERONYMY, since this corresponds to definitional contexts. In other words, as well as getting the hypernym, the terminographer would normally also get some other relations via the differentiating characteristics. As research progresses, or if defining contexts are scarce, the terminographer might want to get explanatory contexts by querying for additional relations.

It must be stressed that today's knowledge-extraction tools are still *semi-automatic*, in the sense that the terminographer must manually filter out the *noise*. By *noise*, we mean contexts that the system "thinks" illustrate the specified conceptual relation, but which really do not. Because of the complexity of natural language, completely noise-free results are not likely to be obtained in the foreseeable future. Nor are they necessary in order for knowledge-extraction tools to be useful to the terminographer. For example, if a term appeared a thousand times in a text, it would take significantly less time to eliminate (manually) 10 instances of noise from 50 candidate KRCs, than to examine all one thousand contexts.

3.2 Underlying approach: Knowledge patterns

Current knowledge-extraction tools (e.g., Ahmad and Fulford 1992; Bowden et al. 1996; Condamines et Rebeyrolle 1998; Davidson et al. 1998) are based on the premise that a given conceptual relation will manifest itself in certain predictable, recurring patterns in text. These patterns, which we term *knowledge patterns*,[9] are entered into the extraction tool. When the user specifies the term and the relation he/she is interested in, the tool searches the corpus for instances of linguistic patterns occurring a specified distance to the left and/or right of the term.

For a knowledge-extraction tool to be able to use these patterns effectively, the programmer needs to specify, for every type of relation that the tool will handle: (1) the patterns themselves, and (2) restrictions on the context in which the pattern appears. These two components are discussed below.

3.2.1 *Types of knowledge pattern*

Knowledge patterns can be of three types, lexical, grammatical, or paralinguistic.

Lexical patterns are the most common type, involving one or more specific lexical items (and sometimes morphological variants). Some of our patterns for HYPERONYMY include "is a", "classified as", "defined as"; for MERONYMY, "its", "is a part of", "contains"; for FUNCTION, "needed for", "serve* as", "designed for"; etc.

Grammatical patterns. These apply to a small number of attributes and relations. The pattern NOUN + VERB (with some verbs excluded), for example, is very productive for indicating the function relation, in addition to the function-related lexical patterns. Various types of ATTRIBUTES may be conveyed through ADJ + NOUN. Obviously, to handle grammatical patterns, the corpus must be at least part-of-speech tagged (we use a shallow parser in our own work).

Paralinguistic patterns. These involve a variety of patterns that are not strictly grammatical or lexical. They include punctuation, as well as various elements of the general structure of a text. The following are examples of the use of punctuation to indicate HYPERONYMY for the term *compost*:

(9) a. compost or humus, a dark, nutrient-rich soil conditioner, …
b. Adequate levels of organic matter — compost or humus — are essential.…

Regarding more general aspects of text structure, we saw in 2.2.1 above that dictionary defining KRCs have very particular structures, for example, placing the term in bold, following it with a colon, placing the definiendum and definiens on separate lines, and so on. In other cases, we have found excellent defining and explanatory KRCs immediately after questions such as:

(10) a. What is compost?
b. What does compost consist of?

3.2.2 *Restrictions on knowledge patterns*

Pattern restrictions should ensure that the pattern does not generate too much noise, but on the other hand, that it does not exclude valid contexts. Consider the types of sentences that might be generated, for example, for HYPERONYMY, by the "be* + ARTICLE" pattern, for the terms *composting* and *compost*, if no restrictions were applied:

(11) a. This approach to composting is a viable method of dealing with animal carcasses.
b. Worm composting is a way of recycling kitchen wastes for apartment dwellers.
c. Compost might be the most popular soil enhancer if it were better publicized.

The first two examples constitute noise in that they refer not to the concept of *composting* in general, but to a particular approach to it in the first, and to a subtype of it in the second. The restrictions on this pattern would therefore need to specify that no kind of modifier (whether phrase or simple noun) may precede the search term. The third example is invalid because of the conditional form of the verb. While using "be" in the pattern allows the plural, which is normally valid (e.g., *worm composters are composters that…*), it unfortunately opens the door to unwanted noise. Our own approach has been to restrict the "BE + ART" pattern to the specific forms "is a", "are an", "is an", "are a", and "are" (the latter only if preceding and following words are nouns and plural).

Another extremely important condition is the size of the search window (i.e., the number of characters/words before and after the search term). If the search window is too small, the system may exclude contexts such as the following, where the search term *vermicomposting* is quite a distance from the pattern "is an":

(12) Vermicomposting, which is also known as worm composting (and means exactly what it says!), is an effective means of decomposing kitchen wastes when space is at a premium.

On the other hand, the wider the search window, the greater the potential for noise. Ultimately, determining the best window size (and all the other restrictions on any given pattern) involves a meticulous analysis of the output for each pattern, as described below.

3.3 Methodology for developing knowledge-extraction tools

Our methodology consists of: (1) identifying an initial set of knowledge patterns for each conceptual relation that the system will handle; (2) analyzing the output in order to identify other patterns that should be added, or restrictions that should be applied to existing patterns; (3) making the required changes in the system; (4) repeating steps 2 and 3 as often as necessary. In short, the process is one of iterative refinement.

3.3.1 *Identifying the knowledge patterns*

We have taken two largely manual approaches to identifying initial sets of knowledge patterns. In some projects, we have simply generated KWIC concordances for a number of search terms, identifying those contexts that contain KRCs, and classifying the KRCs by conceptual relation. Another approach that has had good results was to examine records in a terminological database called TERMIUM.[10] Here, we examined both the definition and context fields of TERMIUM. Both fields contain contexts selected by terminographers from texts in the domain. The goal of both fields is to illustrate the meaning of the concept to the user: the definition field includes contexts resembling a classical Aristotelian definition, while the context field includes explanatory contexts. The advantage of this approach is that most records will contain knowledge patterns, and hence one achieves a good return for the time spent. The disadvantages are (1) the KRCs are typically of high quality, i.e., the best that the terminographer can find in "real text", and hence, they are not totally representative; and (2) since the KRCs are de-contextualized, one does not find a representative sample of paralinguistic patterns.

In principle, a more automatic approach to detecting knowledge patterns would involve starting with a set of terms for which the relations are already known (i.e., hypernyms and hyponyms, wholes and parts, etc.), and programming the system to (1) detect those contexts that present the term sets in close proximity, and (2) analyze the contexts for commonalities, some of which would presumably be knowledge patterns.

3.3.2 *Analyzing the output and refining the patterns*

In our experience, supplying the extraction tool with an initial set of patterns, no matter how meticulously they have been gathered and analyzed, is not the end of the development process. On the contrary, developing a definitive set of patterns and restrictions requires many passes at analyzing the output for noise and silences, as discussed below.

Noise. While any valid pattern is bound to produce some valid contexts (i.e., "hits"), the same pattern may produce noise as well. For each relation, systems developers must study the examples of noise to determine which ones can be corrected through pattern restrictions, and which ones probably cannot. Examples (11a–c) in 3.2.2 above illustrated a number of restrictions that could be applied to the pattern "be* + ARTICLE" to reduce noise. However, even one restricted version of this pattern, "is a", can generate noise such as 14a and 14b, alongside valid hits such as (13):

(13) Compost is a practical method of recycling organic matter and reducing solid waste.

(14) a. Compost is a rich topic for scientific research.
 b. Composting is a traditional idea with a broad new appeal.

These examples raise the question of whether one should attach additional conditions to "is a" to exclude words like *topic* and *idea.* The decision to refine to this level of detail ultimately depends on the project's resources and goals. Regarding the latter, if the goal is to develop a system for just one particular domain and text type, it may be realistic to aim at virtually noise-free output. If, on the other hand, the system is meant to be generic (i.e., useful in a variety of domains and for a variety of text types), we doubt that all possible cases of noise could ever be anticipated for any pattern.

The more polysemous a lexical pattern is (Cf. 4.1.2), the greater its chances of generating noise. Consider the preposition *in.* While *in* indicates many true MERONYMIC contexts (e.g., "If your compost mix is too low in nitrogen…"), it also generates large amounts of noise (e.g., "as temperatures rise in the compost…"). In order to bring the noise for such polysemous patterns to acceptable levels, numerous restrictions may be required (e.g., for "in", restricting the word previous to "high", "low", etc.).

Silences. Silences are KRCs that express a given relation in the corpus, but that are not found by the system. Normally, they are missed due to some lack in the existing knowledge patterns for that relation. Finding silences is a labour-intensive process, since it involves manually analyzing a full KWIC concordance for the search term, and manually identifying all the valid KRCs for the relation in question. Some examples of misses we encountered in our initial work on HYPERONYMY, using the pattern-set "is a", "are an", "is an", "are a", and "are" included:

(15) a. The result is compost or humus, a dark, nutrient-rich soil conditioner.
b. … a humus-rich soil amendment known as compost.

An analysis of silences such as these indicates further patterns one might want to add: the pattern of appositive structure (indicated by commas) in 15a, and the lexical pattern "known as" in (15b).

The trade-off between recall and precision. The process of adding new patterns as a result of analyzing silences raises one significant problem: while every addition to the knowledge patterns should increase the number of hits compared with the preceding pass, it also has the potential to increase the noise. To use standard information retrieval terminology, any gain in *recall* tends to cause a reduction in *precision.*[11] In other words, any addition made to the knowledge patterns should be considered tentative until the subsequent pass confirms that the benefits of increased hits outweigh the disadvantages of increased noise. For example, 2 or 3 additional hits would not justify increasing the noise tenfold.

4. Problematic issues

In principle, the approach to knowledge extraction described above seems extremely appealing. In practice, however, this type of work is far more difficult than we had originally expected. Three substantial difficulties are discussed below, concerning: (1) the nature of knowledge patterns, (2) the nature of conceptual relations, and (3) issues in the evaluation of knowledge-extraction tools.

4.1 The nature of patterns

Knowledge patterns, whether lexical, grammatical, or paralinguistic, are complex in their very nature, and in the way they can be realized in text.

4.1.1 *Unpredictability*

With lexical patterns in particular, one has the sense that one "will never get them all". While certain patterns seem quite logical — e.g., "is a" for HYPERONYMY, "contains" for MERONYMY — others are extremely unpredictable. Consider the word *recolonize* in the following example:

(16) The numbers and types of mesophilic microbes that recolonize compost as it matures …

Out of context, one would never associate *recolonize* with MERONYMY. However, in the above sentence, it does convey the important concept that microbes are a "part" of compost, at least in a very general sense of "part".

4.1.2 *Polysemy*

A given pattern may convey not only one particular conceptual relation, but other relations as well. The lexical pattern "classifi* as", for example, can indicate both a hypernym and a hyponym of the search term:

(6) a. … the EPA classifies composting as a form of recycling
(17) Most of the compost currently being used by the landscape and nursery industries is classified as unrestricted grade.

The first example provides a hypernym (*form of recycling*) for *compost*, while the second provides a hyponym (*unrestricted grade compost* being a type of *compost*). While the two relations involved are closely related in that they are converses of each other, the polysemy of a pattern can also involve less closely related relations,[12] or can occur between relations and attributes. The lexical item "its", for example, is a valuable pattern for the MERONYMIC relation, but of course can also indicate a variety of attributes.

For the terminographer using a knowledge-extraction tool, polysemy of this kind means that the system will return, for a certain type of relation, not only contexts for the specified relation but contexts for other relations as well. While the latter should, strictly speaking, be classified as noise, they are in a sense "good noise" in that they at least give the terminographer a KRC, even if it does not correspond to the specified relation.

More serious are cases where a pattern generates contexts that terminographers would not find useful in any way. Take the lexical pattern "defined as", in an example we saw earlier:

(1) b. Compost is perhaps best defined as organic material deliberately assembled for fast decomposition.

While *define* indicates HYPERONYMY here, in the domain of computing it often means 'to create' or 'to call into existence'. For example, when users create columns in a word-processor, they first define the columns. In this domain, therefore, the system might return many contexts that have no relation to HYPERONYMY, such as the following context taken from a corpus about the programming language, JAVA:

(18) The System Class is defined as final and is composed entirely of static variables and methods.

4.1.3 *Domain-dependency*

It appears that there are a significant number of knowledge patterns that are domain-*in*dependent. However, every domain we have worked on so far seems to have a small number of patterns that are clearly specific to that domain. Regarding lexical patterns, for example, "flavour" can indicate HYPERONYMY in the computing domain, as in "Arity [Prolog] is a flavour of Prolog"; *species* (X is a species of Y) is typical of the biological sciences; *shade* (Maroon is a shade of red) is used to indicate HYPERONYMY for colour terms; etc.

In our work on the medical domain, which focussed on problems of childbirth, we found numerous knowledge patterns for CAUSALITY that are clearly specific to medical writing. The CAUSALITY patterns that we had found in the composting domain included such predictable structures as *X causes Y, X results in Y, Y results from X*, etc. In our medical corpus, however, we encountered patterns involving lexical items such as *risk, exposed to*, and *complication*, as illustrated below:

(19) CVS carries a small risk of miscarriage.

(20) Significant birth defects occur in up to one fourth of babies exposed to this drug.

(21) The major short-term complications of CVS are pregnancy loss and diagnostic error.

4.1.4 *Anaphoric reference*

Our approach to knowledge extraction assumes that the system will search for patterns occurring within a specified distance to the left and/or right of the search term. A major problem with this approach is that in normal writing, the term will not be repeated over and over again, but rather, replaced by pronouns, the generic term, term variants, etc. For example, the following context indicates several functions for compost, but they would not be found using the pattern "search term + VERB":

(22) Compost should be cultivated by every gardener. This "black gold" improves soil structure, texture and aeration and increases its water-holding capacity. It loosens clay soils and helps sandy soils retain water. Adding it to soils aids in erosion control, promotes soil fertility and stimulates healthy root development in plants.

Clearly, finding inter-sentential KRCs, particularly when they involve anaphora, is a long-term research issue for tool developers, and also complicates tool evaluation, as discussed in 4.3.

4.1.5 *Inherent limitations of patterns*

In some cases, knowledge is expressed in forms of creative writing that do not involve linguistic patterns, or any easily "programmable" paralinguistic ones:

(23) Using this "black gold" on your landscape is like setting up a savings account. The interest you draw from your compost soil bank is healthier plants, reduced water and fertilizer bills, a reduction in pest problems….

A human reader easily sees that this context conveys functional information for compost, but a pattern-based extraction tool cannot. Even in rather technical texts, and certainly in didactic ones, metaphorical usage such as this can abound.

4.2 The nature of conceptual relations

Some conceptual relations appear to be more complex than others. Winston et al. (1987), for example, have argued that MERONYMY involves an extensive taxonomy of part relation types. These different types of MERONYMY, in turn, appear to generate different lexical patterns. For example, when we applied the set of meronymic patterns we had used for *compost* to the term *composting*, the percentage of silences increased dramatically. Since composting designates a process, rather than a concrete object, it has "temporal" rather than "physical" parts. These are designated by patterns such as "X is a stage of Y", "X is a phase of Y", which were not relevant at all for the term *compost.*

As knowledge-extraction technology is applied to other relations, we may find other cases where knowledge patterns are dependent on a particular aspect, or type, of conceptual relation. More troubling, we may find that the existing theories of conceptual relations are inadequate. In our own work, our researchers often disagree on the relation type expressed by a particular context. In the composting corpus, for example, it was not at all obvious what we should accept as indisputable "parts" of compost. While it seemed fairly straightforward that organic materials should be included, we were faced with the problem of whether the organisms living in the compost should actually be considered part of it. While microorganisms directly help in making compost, as do small creatures like worms, it is hard to know exactly where to draw the line — for example, does one include beetles and even mice and rats as parts of compost? Issues such as these underline a need to specify "tighter ways of identifying instances of specific relations" (Bowden et al. 1996: 157).

4.3 Evaluation of knowledge-extraction systems

In evaluating a knowledge-extraction system, one ultimately wants to know how good its recall and precision are. While these calculations may be straightforward in some types of information retrieval, they are highly complex in the case of KRCs. As mentioned above, there exists no consensus among linguists on how many relations there are, and on the precise nature of every relation. This causes problems in determining what constitutes a "hit". Even in cases of relatively uncontroversial relations, for example HYPERONYMY, problems occur when the relation is not "perfectly" expressed in real text. For example, should we count as a hit for HYPERONYMY a case where it is not the immediate hypernym that is used (e.g., the author defines *vermicompost* as a type of *soil conditioner* rather than as a type of *compost*)? Shall we accept examples such as (1c), where *compost* was given the conceptually illogical hypernym *method*?

For accurate recall and precision statistics, one also needs to have an accurate count of the "silences". The method we described for this involved doing a concordance on the search term, and figuring out manually how many instances of the concordance output constituted valid expressions of a given relation. This method, however, assumes that the context includes the search term. Therefore, it misses most cases where the search term is absent, as discussed in 4.1.4. Until natural-language processing handles anaphora perfectly, we shall have to be satisfied with imperfect, KWIC-based statistics of silences.

5. Discussion

In this paper, we have attempted to show that despite a number of problems that still face this nascent technology, semi-automatic knowledge extraction has interesting potential for improving both the quality and quantity of a terminographer's work. As we have seen, automatically extracted KRCs can provide terminographers with a quick source of full definitions, starting-points for definitions, and various kinds of domain knowledge that can assist in the general task of conceptual analysis.

In the future, it would be interesting to explore whether knowledge-extraction tools may be an aid in corpus-*building* as well as corpus-*analysis.* It is well-known in the terminology literature that technical texts correspond to a variety of communicative situations: experts writing for other experts, experts communicating with students of the field, experts or semi-experts writing for the lay public. In our experience, the number of KRCs varies depending on the text type. Predictably, it appears that the bigger the gap between the writer's and the reader's level of domain knowledge, the greater the number of KRCs that will be found. Like lexicographers, terminographers try to build "balanced" corpora (Cf. Meyer and Mackintosh 1996), and one way to achieve balance is to ensure that the corpus texts represent a range of communicative situations. Knowledge-extraction tools are a possible way of assessing (based on the proportion of KRCs) what type of communicative situation a given text corresponds to, and hence, may be an adjunct to other corpus-building tools.

As knowledge-extraction tools develop, it will also be interesting to explore ways of using them that go beyond the *term*-oriented approach we have described here. In principle, the underlying concept of knowledge patterns also allows for a conceptual, *relation*-oriented approach, i.e., with the terminographer asking the system to show all term-sets that are linked by relation X. For example, the HYPERONYMY relation would generate a skeletal generic-specific hierarchy, probably an excellent starting-point for a terminographer just beginning to explore a new domain.

These are just some of the possibilities that can be explored now that terminography-oriented knowledge-extraction tools are starting to become mature. We hope that this paper — by clarifying exactly what these tools should detect in a corpus, by describing the methodology for developing the tools, and by analyzing the hard research problems of the field — will be seen as a useful step towards bringing this technology closer to every terminographer's workstation.

Notes

* This research has been funded by the Social Sciences and Humanities Research Council of Canada (SSHRC), the National Sciences and Engineering Research Council (NSERC), and Nortel, Inc. Douglas Skuce and Judy Kavanagh are primarily responsible for developing the DocKMan knowledge-extraction system on which this research is based. Laura Davidson and Kristen Mackintosh contributed to various aspects of corpus development and data analysis.

1. Terminological dictionaries can be of various types, including published dictionaries, term banks, and glossaries (i.e., lists of equivalents for different languages).

2. Ideally, both strategies are recommended. Experts do not always write clearly, and in our experience, there have always been some concepts for which clarification by the expert directly was useful.

3. Established in 1990, this project investigates a variety of issues in *terminography-oriented concept analysis.*
Cf. http://aix1.uottawa.ca/~imeyer/research.htm.

4. This paper focuses on an environmental domain. For examples from the medical domain, Cf. Meyer et al. 1999.

5. For more details on DocKMan, Cf. Skuce and Kavanagh 1999.

6. This 500,000-word corpus was taken from the WWW, and consists mainly of texts written by experts or semi-experts for laypeople. In other words, the texts are highly explanatory. The terms *compost* and *composting* each occurred about 1000 times in the corpus, making semi-automatic knowledge extraction clearly useful in this case.

7. Our concept of a KRC is analogous to Pearson's (1998) *defining expositive.*

8. We recognize that this classification is somewhat simplistic, and does not cover *all* contexts that might be useful to the terminographer. However, we feel that it covers by far the majority. For a much more detailed overview of various authors' classifications of definition-like contexts, Cf. Pearson 1998.

9. These patterns have been designated by various terms in English, depending on the researcher: *formulae* (Lyons 1977); *diagnostic frames* or *test frames* (Cruse 1986); *frames* (Winston et al. 1987); *definitional metalanguage* and *defining expositives* (Pearson 1996); *knowledge probes* (Ahmad and Fulford 1992).

10. The official termbank of the Government of Canada, available on CD-ROM, containing over a million records in English, French and Spanish.

11. *Recall* and *precision* are key information retrieval concepts. *Recall*=hits ÷ (hits + silences). *Precision*=hits ÷ (hits + noise). Explained simply, when we want to know the recall for a particular search, we are really asking: "Out of all the relevant sentences in the corpus, how many did our search actually retrieve?". When we want to know the precision for a particular search, we are really asking: "Out of all the sentences that were extracted during this search, how many were hits?".

12. More examples, from our work in the medical domain, can be found in Meyer et al. 1999, Section 3.2.2.

References

Ahmad, K. and Fulford, H. 1992. "Knowledge Processing: 4. Semantic Relations and their Use in Elaborating Terminology." (Computing Sciences Report CS-92–07). Guildford: University of Surrey.

Bowden, P.R., Halstead, P. and Rose, T.G. 1996. "Extracting Conceptual Knowledge From Text Using Explicit Relation Markers." In *Advances in Knowledge Acquisition.* Proceedings of the 9th European Knowledge Acquisition Workshop, EKAW'96, Nottingham, United Kingdom, May 1996. N. Shadbolt, K. O'Hara and G. Schreiber (eds), 147–162.

Bowker, L. 1995. A Multidimensional Approach to Classification in Terminology: Working Within a Computational Framework. PhD thesis, Centre for Computational Linguistics, University of Manchester Institute of Science and Technology.

Condamines, A. and Rebeyrolle J. 1998. "CTKB: A Corpus-based Approach to a Terminological Knowledge Base." In *Computerm '98: First Workshop on Computational Terminology.* Proceedings of the workshop, COLING-ACL'98, Montreal, Canada, August 1998. D. Bourigault, C. Jacquemin, and M.-C. L'Homme (eds), 29–35. Montreal: Université de Montréal.

Cruse, D. 1986. *Lexical Semantics.* Cambridge: Cambridge University Press.

Daille, B., Habert, B., Jacquemin, C. and Royauté, J. 1996. "Empirical Observations of Term Variations and Principles for their Description." *Terminology* 3(2): 197–258.

Davidson, L., Kavanagh, J., Mackintosh, K., Meyer, I., and Skuce, D. 1998. "Semi-automatic Extraction of Knowledge-Rich Contexts from Corpora." In *Computerm '98: First Workshop on Computational Terminology*, Proceedings of the workshop, COLING-ACL'98, Montreal, Canada, August 1998. D. Bourigault, C. Jacquemin, and M.-C. L'Homme (eds), 50–56. Montreal: Université de Montréal.

Fellbaum, C. 1990. "English Verbs as a Semantic Net." *International Journal of Lexicography* 3(4): 278–301.

Gross, D. and Miller, K.J. 1990. "Adjectives in WordNet." *International Journal of Lexicography* 3(4): 265–277.

Kageura, K. and Umino, B. 1996. "Methods of Automatic Term Recognition: A Review." *Terminology* 3(2): 259–290.

Kavanagh, J. 1995. The Text Analyzer: A Tool for Extracting Knowledge from Text. Unpublished MSc Thesis. Department of Computer Science, University of Ottawa, Ottawa, Canada.

http://www.csi.uottawa.ca/~kavanagh/Thesis/thesisAbstract.html

Lyons, J. 1977. *Semantics: Volume 1.* Cambridge: Cambridge University Press.

Meyer, I. and Mackintosh, K. 1996. "The Corpus from a Terminographer's Viewpoint." *International Journal of Corpus Linguistics* 1(2): 257–258.

Meyer, I., Eck, K. and Skuce, D. 1997. "Systematic Concept Analysis within a Knowledge-Based Approach to Terminology." In *Handbook of Terminology Management, Vol. 1*, S.E. Wright and G. Budin (eds), 98–118. Amsterdam/Philadelphia: John Benjamins.

Meyer, I., Mackintosh, K., Barrière, C., and Morgan, T. 1999. "Conceptual Sampling for Terminographical Corpus Analysis." *Proceedings of the Fifth International Congress on Terminology and Knowledge Engineering (TKE'99)*, 256–267.

Miller, G.A. 1990. "Nouns in WordNet: A Lexical Inheritance System." *International Journal of Lexicography* 3(4): 245–264.

Otman, G. 1997. "Les bases de connaissances terminologiques: les banques de terminologie de seconde génération." *META* 42(2): 244–256.

Pearson, J. 1998. *Terms in Context.* Amsterdam/Philadelphia: John Benjamins.

Pearson, J. 1996. "The Expression of Definitions in Specialised Texts: A Corpus-based Analysis." In Euralex'96 Proceedings, Part II. Papers submitted to the Seventh Euralex International Congress on Lexicography in Göteborg, Sweden, Gellarstam et al. (eds), 817–824. Göteborg: Göteborg University, Department of Swedish.

Picht, H. and Draskau J. 1985. *Terminology: An Introduction.* Guildford: University of Surrey.

Sager, J. 1990. *A Practical Course in Terminology Processing.* Amsterdam/Philadelphia: John Benjamins.

Skuce, D. and Kavanagh, J. 1999. "A Document-Oriented Knowledge Management System." *Proceedings of the Fifth International Congress on Terminology and Knowledge Engineering (TKE'99)*, 320–329.

Sowa, J.F. 1984. *Conceptual Structures: Information Processing in Mind and Machine.* Reading, Mass.: Addison-Wesley.

Winston, M.E., Chaffin, R. and Herrmann, D. 1987. "A Taxonomy of Part-Whole Relations." *Cognitive Science* 11(4): 417–444.

Wüster, E. 1979. *Einfhhrung in die allgemeine Terminologielehre und Terminologische Lexicographie.* Schriftenreihe der Technischen Universität Wien. Wien/New York: Springer Verlag.

Chapter 15

Experimental evaluation of ranking and selection methods in term extraction

Hiroshi Nakagawa
The University of Tokyo

An automatic term extraction system consists of a term candidate extraction subsystem, a ranking subsystem and a selection subsystem. In this paper, we experimentally evaluate two ranking methods and two selection methods. As for ranking, a dichotomy of unithood and termhood is a key notion. We evaluate these two notions experimentally by comparing *Imp* based ranking method that is based directly on termhood and C-value based method that is indirectly based on both termhood and unithood. As for selection, we compare the simple threshold method with the window method that we propose. We did the experimental evaluation with several Japanese technical manuals. The result does not show much difference in recall and precision. The small difference between the extracted terms by these two ranking methods depends upon their ranking mechanism *per se*.

1. Introduction

As widely known, automatic term extraction is definitely useful in various areas including (1) Automatic index extraction from a volume of text, (2) Terminology extraction from one academic field, and (3) Keywords extraction from documents for IR purposes. Especially (1) and (2) have so far been done manually and cost too much. Therefore, an automatic term extraction technology would be great help for these purposes. Kageura and Umino (1996: 259–289) refer to two essential aspects of the nature of terms, namely unithood and termhood.

Unithood refers to the degree of strength or stability of syntagmatic combinations or collocations. For instance, a word has very solid unithood. Other linguistic units having strong unithood are compound words, collocations, and so forth.

Termhood refers to the degree that a linguistic unit is related to domain-specific concepts. Termhood is usually calculated based on term frequency and bias of frequency (so called Inverse Document Frequency). Even though these calculations give a good approximation of termhood, still they do not directly reflect termhood because these calculations are based on superficial statistics.

According to these two aspects, we have a dichotomy of term extraction methods, namely term extraction based on unithood and that based on termhood. Obviously, terms that have high termhood should be extracted as terms. However, to directly measure termhood of the given term candidate is extremely difficult because only the writer of a document knows which terms are important terms. Many researchers have tried to work out the way to approximate termhood by some score that is often calculated based on unithood so far. Therefore, the question we would like to ask is how directly the given extracting method measures termhood even though it is based on unithood. The accompanying question is what characteristics the terms extracted by each method have. In fact, they are tough questions to answer theoretically. The best thing we can do at this moment is to compare experimentally the performance of several term extraction methods. Since it is still difficult to compare many methods, in this paper, we compare only two methods: C-value based method (Frantzi and Ananiadou 1996: 41–46) and *Imp* based method (Nakagawa 1997: 598–611).

2. Overview of a term extraction system

A term extraction system, in general, consists of three subsystems, namely (1) candidate extraction, (2) ranking, and (3) selection, as shown in Figure 1.
Texts

In the following, we sketch each of these three subsystems along with the previous works.

Term candidates extraction subsystem

There are two major types of term candidates in terms of linguistic structure. One is an N-gram of characters. The other is a word. Much work has been done on character based N-gram, especially in some Asian languages like Japanese (Fujii and Croft 1993: 237–246) and Chinese (Lam et al. 1997: 68–80). Since all of these aim at extracting terms for information retrieval, character based N-

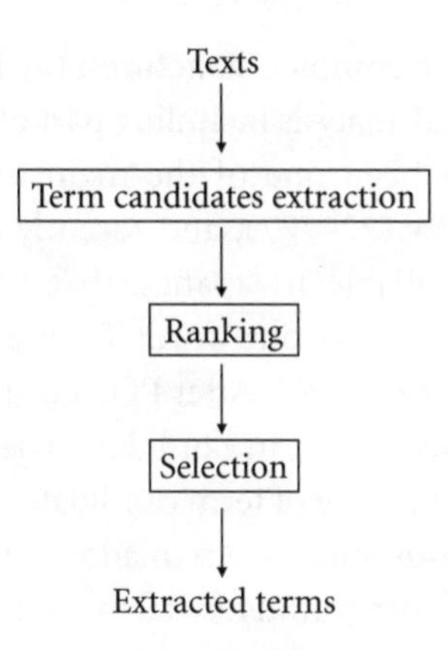

Figure 1. Structure of term extraction system

grams give us enough quality as keywords for IR. However, for non-IR purposes like (1) and (2) above, character based N-grams are not suitable because back of the book indexes or terminologies of one academic field are not superficial sequences of characters but are words bearing semantically coherent information. Therefore, in this paper, we concentrate on terms based on words.

Term candidates that consist of words are nouns or compound nouns. To extract promising term candidates of compound noun and at the same time to exclude undesirable strings such as *is a* or *of the*, the most frequently used method is to filter out the words being members of the stop-list. In these days, more complex structures like noun phrases, collocations consisting of nouns, verbs, prepositions, determiners, and so on, become focused on (Smadja and McKeown 1990: 252–259; Frantzi and Ananiadou 1996: 41–46; Zhai and Evans 1996: 17–23; Hisamitsu and Nitta 1996: 550–555; Shimohata et al. 1997: 476–481). All of these are good term candidates in a document or a specific domain because all of them have a strong unithood. Needless to say, but as for complex terms like compound words or collocations, we have the following basic assumption:

Assumption *Complex terms are to be made of existing simple terms.*

A structure of complex term is another important factor for automatic term extraction. It is expressed syntactically or semantically. As a syntactic structure, dependency structures that are the results of noun phrase parsing are focused on in many works. Of course, we need heuristics or statistics to select plausible dependency structures (Zhai and Evans 1996: 17–23).

Since we focus on these complex structures, the first thing to extract term candidates is morphological analysis including part of speech (POS) tagging. In English, POS tagging has been one of the main issues in natural language processing, i.e. (Brill 1994a: 722–727), and recently high quality POS taggers such as (Brill 1994b) are available. In Japanese that is an agglutinative language, morphological analysis segments out words from a sentence, and does POS tagging, too (Matsumoto et al. 1996). After POS tagging, the complex structure mentioned above is extracted as a term candidate. The previous works proposed many promising ways for this type of term candidate extraction. Zhai and Evans (1996: 17–23) focus on noun phrases. Ananiadou (1994: 1034–1038) proposes the way to extract word compounds as terms. Hisamitsu and Nitta (1996: 550–555) and Nakagawa (1997: 598–611) concentrate their efforts on compound nouns. Smadja and McKeown (1990: 252–259), Daille et al. (1994: 515–521), Frantzi and Ananiadou (1996: 41–46) and Shimohata et al. (1997: 476–481) try to treat more general structures like collocations.

Ranking subsystem

In order to extract domain specific terms from term candidates extracted in Term Candidates Extraction subsystem, we have to rank them according to their termhood. This ranking has been developed as keyword weighting like *tf.idf* which is widely used in IR. As written in (Kageura and Umino 1996: 259–289), the frequency information about a word, like *tf.idf*, is an approximation of termhood. Obviously, a notion of termhood implies a semantic weight. Then, the basic idea is that frequency information about a word is probably reflected from the semantic importance of the word. Bilingual co-occurrences, namely alignments in bilingual corpus, are used to catch semantic importance of words (Daille et al. 1994: 515–521). However, from the viewpoint of term extraction, ranking methods based on unithood are also intensively studied. For instance, various kinds of statistic information about words co-occurrences which are used to extract promising term candidates that are in the form of collocation (Smadja and McKeown 1990: 252–259; Frantzi and Ananiadou (1996: 41–46); Shimohata et al. (1997: 476–481), are of this type. Among them, C-value (Frantzi and Ananiadou 1996: 41–46), entropy (Shimohata et al. 1997: 476–481), and Mutual Information (Church and Hanks 1990: 22–29) are promising.

Selection subsystem

As for the selection from ranked candidates, we find a very general scheme such as likelihood test (Dunning 1993: 62–74). However, we do not find much work that directly treats a term selection process. At the first glance, a selection by the predetermined threshold is, seemingly, simple and powerful. However, the real problem is the way to determine the threshold that works equally well on unseen documents. Since the method using a simple threshold is not the only method, it is a challenging problem to find another promising selection method.

Target of this paper

In this paper, we report on our experimental results of two automatic term extraction methods. Roughly speaking, "term" means an open compound (Smadja and McKeown 1990: 252–259), which is defined as an uninterrupted sequence of words. One extraction method we focus on here is C-value based term extraction (Frantzi and Ananiadou 1996: 41–46). The other method we focus on here is based on a certain kind of statistics about compound word formation (Nakagawa 1997: 598–611). Both methods propose the way to rank collocations or compound words according to the importance of each of them. Once all of the term candidates are ranked, then we need a method to select real terms from those ranked candidates. In our experiments, we use a simple threshold selection method and a window method that is introduced later in this paper. Finally we compare and evaluate the results of every combination of these two ranking methods and these two selection methods.

3. Ranking methods

3.1 C–value based method

One of the famous approaches based on statistics about linguistic structure is the ranking method based on C-value (Frantzi and Ananiadou 1996: 41–46). They recently updated the definition of C-value and introduced NC-value that is the combination of C-value and the context factor (Frantzi and Ananiadou 1999: 145–179). Of course, the new C-value or NC-value might show the better performance. But we adopt the method described by (Frantzi and Ananiaodu

1996:41–46) because the original C-value reflects their original intention. Their term extraction system first extracts all candidates of collocation. Then, it uses the measure they call **C–value** defined by the following formula:

$$\text{C}-\text{value}(a) = (\text{length}(a)-1)\times \text{freq}(a) \quad a \text{ is not nested} \tag{111}$$

$$\text{C}-\text{value}(a) = (\text{length}(a)-1)\times \left(\text{freq}(a) - \frac{\text{t}(a)}{\text{c}(a)}\right) \quad \text{otherwise} \tag{2}$$

where a is a collocation, freq(a) is the frequency of occurrence of a in the corpus, t(a) is the number of occurrence of candidates of collocation that contain a, and c(a) is number of the distinct candidates of collocations that contain a. First of all, C-value(a) primarily depends on freq(a) which means how frequently a is used. Thus, if a is a multi-word collocation, C-value shows how stable the collocation a is used. In this sense, C-value(a) indicates unithood of a. But, in fact, things are more complicated. For instance, the collocation "Wall Street" seems to be ranked high in the corpus about finance and business. However, if "Wall Street" almost always appears as a part of "Wall Street Journal" in the corpus, the latter should be ranked higher and the former should be ranked much lower. C-value implements this idea. Precisely speaking, the greater the number of distinct extracted candidate terms that contain a string a, the bigger the C-value of a is. Note that the range of C-value is still confined between the frequency of occurrence of a and zero. Since this characteristic reflects how the writers treat a to some extent, C-value is regarded to indicate termhood as well. Consequently, C-value indicates the combination of unithood and termhood. Thus, henceforth, we regard C-value based term extraction method as a method indirectly based on both unithood and termhood.

3.2 Compound noun based statistics

Obviously, the relation between simple terms and complex terms in which they are included is very important. To my knowledge, this relation has not been paid enough attention so far. Nakagawa (1997:598–611) shows a new direction that focuses on the method to use this relation. Here we focus on compound nouns among various types of complex terms. In technical documents, the majority of domain specific terms are complex terms, more precisely compound nouns. In spite of huge number of technical terms being compound nouns, relatively small number of simple nouns contribute to make these compound nouns. Considering this fact, we propose a new scoring method that measures the importance of each simple noun. This scoring method for a simple noun measures how many distinct compound nouns contain the simple noun as their parts in a given document or a set of documents. *Pre* (simple word) and *Post* (simple word) are introduced for this purpose, and defined as follows.

Definition 1

In the given text corpus, *Pre(N)*, where *N* is a noun appearing in the corpus, is the number of distinct nouns that *N* adjoins and make compound nouns with *N*, and *Post(N)* is the number of distinct nouns that adjoin *N* and make compound nouns with *N*.

The key point of this definition is that *Pre(N)* and *Post(N)* do not count the number of total occurrences of words that are adjacent to *N*, but the number of distinct words that adjoin *N* or *N* adjoins. It means that *Pre(N)* and *Post(N)* do not measure surface statistics of compound nouns containing *N*, but do measure how the writer of the technical document interprets *N* and uses it in the document. If a certain word, say *W*, expresses the key concept of the system that the document describes, the writer of the document must use *W* not only many times but also in various ways that include forming and using many compound nouns that contain *W*. This kind of usage really reflects the termhood of that word. In this sense, *Pre* and *Post* very directly measure termhood. Figure 2 shows an example of *Pre* and *Post*.

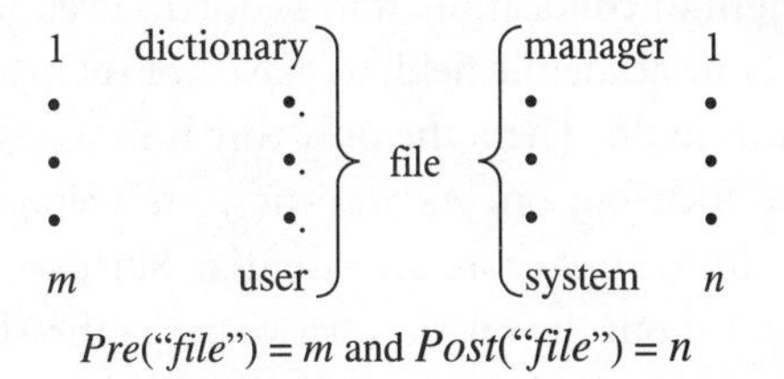

Figure 2. An example of *Pre* and *Post*

Next, we extend this scoring method to cover compound nouns. For the given compound noun $N_1N_2....N_k$ where N_is are simple nouns, the scores of importance of $N_1N_2....N_k$, which is called $Imp(N_1N_2....N_k)$, would be defined, for instance, in the following ways.

$$Imp_1(N_1N_2....N_k) = \prod_{i=1}^{k}((Pre(N_i)+1)\times(Post(N_i)+1)) \tag{3}$$

$$Imp_2(N_1N_2....N_k) = \left(\prod_{i=1}^{k}((Pre(N_i)+1)(Post(N_i)+1))\right)^{\frac{1}{2k}} \tag{4}$$

$Imp_1(N)$ directly depends on the length of compound noun *N*. $Imp_2(N)$ is normalized by the length of *N*, and does not depend on the length of *N*.

4. Term selection subsystem

We have already explained ranking methods in Figure 1 in the previous section. Then, in the whole system of term extraction depicted by Figure 1, we need to define a selection process, which selects real terms from ranked candidates. As a selection process, we think of two methods: the simple threshold method and the window method.

4.1 Simple threshold method

It is easy to use a predetermined threshold about the score, like C-value or *Imp*, on ranked candidates to select real terms. Namely, the candidate terms whose C-value or *Imp* score are over that threshold are selected as the real terms and other candidates are abandoned. This selection method is quite simple, but the real difficulty we face in this type of selection is the way to determine the optimum threshold. We do not have a solid theory to determine the threshold which works equally well for various documents at this moment, because each document has distinct characteristics in text length, number of vocabularies, distribution of length of collocation, and so forth. Even in the case where we treat documents of one academic field, we have not yet had any theoretical way to determine the threshold. Then, the only way is to use statistics over a set of documents we are focusing on. As statistics, an average μ and a standard deviation σ of C-value or *Imp* score are essential. Since we have not yet known any thing theoretical about the relation between the threshold th, μ, σ and the contents of documents, the easiest way to determine the threshold th with μ and σ is given by the following formula:

$$th = a \cdot \mu + b \cdot \sigma \qquad (5)$$

where constants a and b are determined to give the best threshold th in terms of recall and precision. Actually, the best a and b depend on individual document. But, if μ and σ express enough amount of information about the given document, we can expect that a and b that are optimized for one document or a set of documents work equally well for other documents. In fact, the best a and b are not heavily different for five Japanese software manuals we use for our experiment.

4.2 Window method

The simple threshold method described in the previous section uses the global statistics like μ and σ but does not use local statistics at all. Then, we focus on the statistical value within the window on ranked candidates as local statistics. In this method, which we call *window method* henceforth, a window with a certain width is moving from the position of the highest ranked term candidate down to the position of the lowest ranked term candidate. For instance, a window of width = 3 is depicted in Figure 3.

Imp_2	compound NP
19.90	dictionary
17.18	morph dictionary
14.83	morph
13.52	morph dic. file
13.25	morph concentration
12.90	dic. file

Figure 3. Window with width = 3

A position of the window is characterized by the largest value of *Imp* or C-value of the term candidate within the window. For instance, in Figure 3, the window's position corresponds to 17.18. Now we use some statistical values we obtain from the contents of window along with the window moving downwards, to decide whether the nouns in the window is selected as a real term or not. Among several kinds of statistical value, we pay our attention to the real term ratio in the window, RTR in short, which is defined as follows.

$$\mathrm{RTR} = \frac{\#(\text{real term in the window})}{\text{window width}} \qquad (6)$$

where $\#X$ means the number of members in the set denoted by X.

The reason why we pay our attention to RTR is that RTR is, in fact, high in the windows of high *Imp* value. Moreover, the number of real terms increases as the length of document increases. In addition, a number of distinct simple nouns and compound nouns in the text also increases as the document becomes longer. Therefore, RTR is likely to be less dependent on the length of document.

We also pay attention to the compound noun ratio in a window, CNR in short, defined as follows.

$$\text{CNR} = \frac{\#(\text{compound noun in the window})}{\text{window width}} \tag{7}$$

The reason why we pay attention to CNR is that the majority of real terms in technical documents are usually compound nouns in the Japanese technical documents we investigated. By considering the nature of RTR and CNR, we reach the following expectation: In the window whose corresponding *Imp* value is high, the majority of simple and compound nouns within the window are real terms, and at the same time, the majority of them are compound nouns, too. Therefore, we expect high relevance between them. In Table 1, we show the correlation coefficients between RTR and CNR for Imp_1 and Imp_2 of five Japanese technical manuals shown in Table 2.

Table 1. Correlation Coefficients between RTR and CNR in a case of a window of width = 5

Manual	Coefficient	
	Imp_1	Imp_2
JUMAN	.753	.682
SAX	.628	.591
EGG	.808	.788
HV-F93	.737	.705
Play-Station	.738	.692

Since almost all correlation coefficients between CNR and RTR are higher than 0.6, they are high enough to use CNR value instead of *Imp* values themselves for selection by the given threshold. And from the value of these coefficients, we confirm that among simple and compound nouns having high *Imp* values, the majority of terms are compound nouns. Therefore, what we have to do is to find an optimum, or at least a sub-optimum, threshold of CNR to select the real terms. In the selection process, the term candidate that is located at the center of the window is selected as a real term if CNR of the window is larger than the pre-determined threshold; otherwise that candidate is not selected.

5. Experiments

As described previously, we focus here on two ranking methods and two selection methods described in the previous sections, respectively. Then, we made experiments for every combination of ranking method and selection method, namely (1) *Imp* + simple threshold (*Imp+Sth*), (2) *Imp* + window method (*Imp+Win*), (3) C-value + simple threshold (*Cval+Sth*), and (4) C-value + window method (*Cval+Win*) . In the rest of this section, we compare the results of these combinations and evaluate these combinations.

Now we explain the details of our experiment. We use five technical manuals written in Japanese shown in Table 2.

Table 2. Manuals written in Japanese used for this research

Manual	Number of sentences	Size (KB)	Number of real terms
JUMAN(software) Morphological analyzer	436	31	106
SAX(software) Parser	433	28	207
EGG(software) Kana-Kanji converter	628	30	108
Home use VCR Mitsubishi HV-F93	1461	69	259
Video Game Machine SONY Play-Station	131	7	39

Terms that are to be extracted, namely real terms are extracted manually in the following way. Three people who use or know well these softwares or hardwares extract manually real terms which, they think, are important to understand and/or characterize the contents of those five manuals. Term Candidates Extraction process shown in Figure 1 is done as follows. Firstly the morphological analyzer JUMAN segments out words from the sentence, and assigns each word a POS tag. Secondly every noun sequence that may contain Japanese particle NO ("of" in English) is extracted as a term candidate. Using both of these term candidates and the real terms above mentioned, we evaluate the previously described combinations, namely *Imp+Sth*, *Imp+Win*, *Cval+Sth*, and *Cval+Win*, by recall, precision and F-measure.

As for *Imp* function, we compare Imp_1 and Imp_2, and finally select Imp_2 because it gives the better performance in terms of F-measure:

$$F = \frac{(1+\beta^2) \times Precision \times Recall}{\beta^2 \times Precision + Recall} \tag{8}$$

where β indicates how much a user is interested in recall as precision. We choose 1.0 as the value of β in our experiment.

As described earlier, our window method has two parameters, which is to say CNR threshold and window width. We tune a CNR threshold and a window width to optimize F-measure. We choose the following four window widths, namely 5, 10, 20 and 30. Then we apply the following 19 CNR thresholds, namely 0.05, 0.1, 0.15, 0.2, …, and 0.95 for each of those four window widths. Considering the results we get with all the combinations of window width and CNR threshold, we select the combination of the window size and the CNR threshold that gives the best F-measure.

As for the simple threshold method, on the other hand, for the simplicity of threshold selection, we fix $a=1$ and tune b in the previously described formula of threshold:

$$th = a \cdot \mu + b \cdot \sigma \tag{9}$$

to minimize F-measure.

In (Frantzi and Ananiadou 1996:41–46), C-value is calculated for word n-grams where n≥2. Here, we decide to use a C-value of uni-gram to rank every n-gram based on C-value in order to compare *Imp* based method with C-value based method. To apply C-value to uni-gram, we change the definition of C-value into the following:

$$\mathrm{C-value}(a) = \mathrm{length}(a) \times \left(\mathrm{freq}(a) - \frac{\mathrm{t}(a)}{\mathrm{c}(a)} \right) \tag{10}$$

Under these experimental conditions, we apply our window method and the simple threshold method to two groups of candidates that are ranked based on *Imp* and C-value, respectively.

We show the results of term extraction of four cases, that is to say *Imp+Win, Cval+Win, Imp+Sth* and *Cval+Sth,* in Table 3, 4, 5 and 6, respectively. They are the best ones in terms of F-measure. Each table shows the parameters of the selection subsystem such as *b*, window width and the threshold of CNR (Th-CNR), precision (P), recall (R) and F-measure(F) that correspond to the case which gives the best F-measure for each of these five manuals.

As indicated in Tables 3, 4, 5 and 6, *Imp+Win* shows the best F-measure.

Table 3. The results of *Imp+Win*

Manual	Window width	Th-CNR	R	P	F
JUMAN	20	0.6	0.491	0.658	0.562
SAX	30	0.1	0.507	0.507	0.507
EGG	30	0.6	0.472	0.405	0.436
HV-F93	5	0.3	0.602	0.495	0.544
Play-Station	20	0.4	0.615	0.5	0.552
Average			0.537	0.513	0.520

Table 4. The results of *Imp+Sth*

Manual	*b*	R	P	F
JUMAN	−0.3	0.519	0.509	0.514
SAX	−0.75	0.541	0.5	0.520
EGG	−0.2	0.556	0.345	0.427
HV-F93	−0.7	0.629	0.452	0.526
Play-Station	−0.95	0.615	0.5	0.552
Average		0.572	0.461	0.508

Table 5. The results of *Cval+Win*

Manual	Window width	Th-CNR	R	P	F
JUMAN	05	0.35	0.319	0.708	0.44
SAX	20	0.2	0.691	0.464	0.555
EGG	5	0.35	0.741	0.273	0.399
HV-F93	20	0.4	0.741	0.339	0.465
Play-Station	10	0.3	0.667	0.413	0.509
Average			0.631	0.439	0.474

Table 6. The results of *Cval+Sth*

Manual	*b*	R	P	F
JUMAN	0.1	0.425	0.584	0.492
SAX	−0.6	0.696	0.45	0.546
EGG	−0.2	0.556	0.345	0.427
HV-F93	−0.7	0.629	0.452	0.526
Play-Station	−0.95	0.615	0.5	0.552
Average		0.572	0.461	0.508

Moreover, *Imp* based methods outperform C-value based methods, whichever selection subsystem is employed.

In actual applications, we have to deal with unseen documents. That means that we could not use the optimized parameters described in Tables 3, 4, 5 and 6. To estimate the performance of proposed systems for unseen documents, we use the average values of the parameters, and show the results in Tables 7, 8, 9 and 10. The general tendency is almost the same as the best F-measure cases shown in Tables 3, 4, 5 and 6 where P, R, and F stand for Precision, Recall and F-measure, respectively. Precisely speaking, *Imp* based methods outperform C-value based methods. The degradations of F-measure are less than 5% in every case except for *Cval+Sth* whose degradation is 9.6%. This means that all of these combinations are expected to work well for unseen documents, at least, for technical manuals.

For more precise comparison among four combinations, we show recall-precision relations of *Imp+Win*, *Imp+Sth*, *Cval+Win* and *Cval+Sth* for each of these five manuals in Figures 4, 5, 6, 7 and 8, respectively.

In these figures, the window width is 30 and the threshold of CNR, which corresponds to Th-CNR in Tables 3 through 10, varies from 0.1 to 0.9 in the window method, and the parameter *b* of simple threshold method varies from -3 to +3. As you know from these figures, *Imp* based methods are superior to C-value based methods. However, the difference between *Imp* based methods and *Cval+Sth* is not significant in JUMAN, SAX, and EGG. *Cval+Sth* is far worse than *Imp* based methods in HV-F93 manual and Play-Station manual. *Cval+Win* is far worse than other three methods in all manuals. We will describe the reason for these phenomena later on. In brief, *Imp* based ranking method that is directly based on termhood slightly outperforms C-value based ranking method that is indirectly based on both of unithood and termhood. It is needless to say that these experimental results could not be generalized. The best ranking method could depend on many factors including language, academic area, size of corpus, etc.

Next, we are going to focus on extracted terms themselves for each ranking method. As an example, we show the terms extracted from the manual of JUMAN (Japanese morphological analyzer software). We show the terms extracted by both of Imp_2 + Window Method and C-value + Window Method, the terms extracted exclusively by Imp_2 + Window Method, and the terms extracted exclusively by C-value + Window Method in the following. Since the document itself is written in Japanese, the extracted terms are also Japanese. For the convenience of nonnative readers, we show the English translations of these, too.

Table 7. The results of *Imp+Win* (Window width = 22, CNR = 0.376)

Manual	R	P	F
JUMAN	0.443	0.580	0.503
SAX	0.372	0.583	0.454
EGG	0.481	0.374	0.421
HV-F93	0.521	0.491	0.506
Play-Station	0.487	0.559	0.521
Average	0.460	0.512	0.481

Table 8. The results of *Imp+Sth* ($b = -0.58$)

Manual	R	P	F
JUMAN	0.639	0.280	0.390
SAX	0.598	0.468	0.525
EGG	0.585	0.383	0.463
HV-F93	0.564	0.524	0.543
Play-Station	0.488	0.526	0.506
Average	0.575	0.436	0.485

Table 9. The results of *Cval+Win* (window width = 12, CNR = 0.32)

Manual	R	P	F
JUMAN	0.769	0.251	0.378
SAX	0.726	0.334	0.457
EGG	0.726	0.291	0.415
HV-F93	0.718	0.424	0.533
Play-Station	0.594	0.475	0.528
Average	0.707	0.355	0.462

Table 10. The results of *Cval+Sth* ($b = -0.35$)

Manual	R	P	F
JUMAN	0.670	0.311	0.425
SAX	0.478	0.518	0.497
EGG	0.722	0.263	0.385
HV-F93	0.483	0.398	0.436
Play-Station	0.359	0.378	0.368
Average	0.542	0.374	0.422

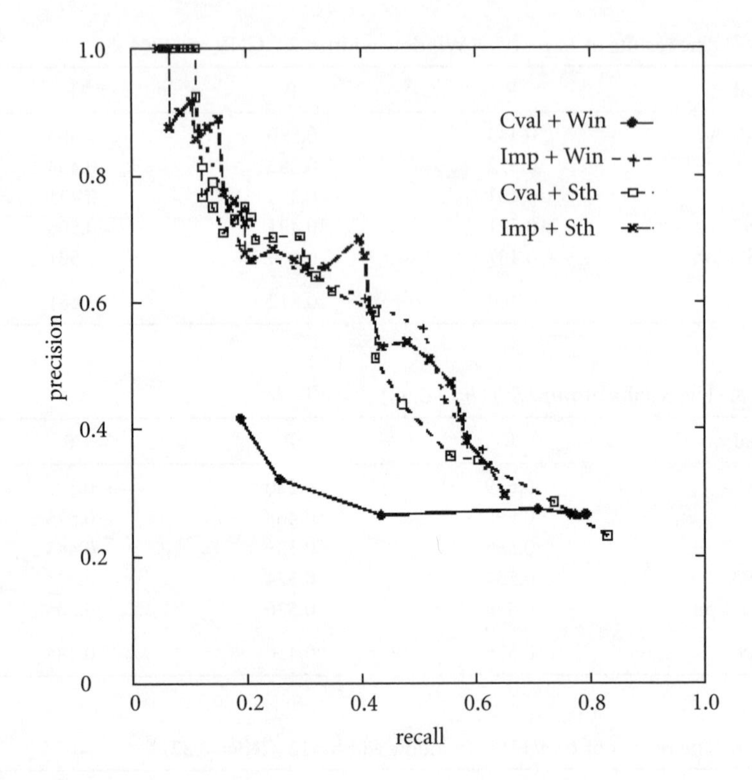

Figure 4. Recall-Precisions for JUMAN

Parts of terms extracted from a Japanese manual by both of *Imp*$_2$ based and C-value based ranking methods

C Ban (C version)/JUMAN sisutemu (JUMAN system)/Prolog Ban (Prolog version)/Gurahu Kouzou (graph structure)/Kosuto (cost)/Kosuto Keisan (cost calculation)/Kosuto Haba (cost band width)/Sisutemu Zisho (system dictionary)/Sisutemu Hyoujun Zisho (system standard dictionary)/Sisutemu Hyoujun BUnpou (system standard grammar)/Yuuza Zisho (user dictionary)/ Imi Zisho (semantic dictionary)/Kakutyousi (extension)/Katuyou (inflection)/ Katuyou Kankei Zisho (inflection relation dictionary)/Kstuyou-kei Mei /(inflection name) Katuyou Zisho (inflection dictionary)/Keitaiso (morphology)/Keitaiso Kosuto (morphology cost)/Keitaiso Kaiseki (morphological analysis)/keitaiso Kaiseki Puroguramu (morphological analysis program)/

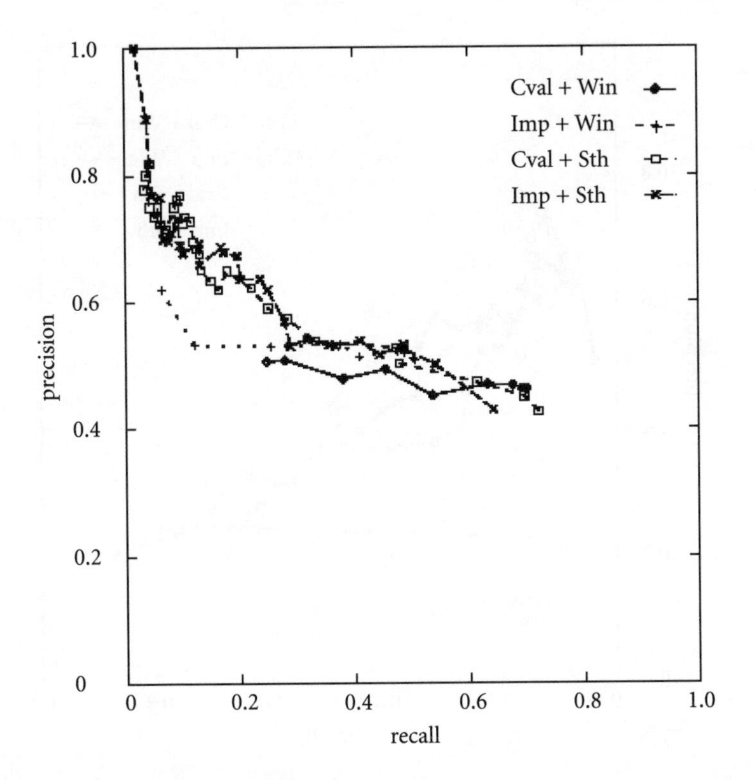

Figure 5. Recall-Precisions for SAX

Keitaiso Kouzou (morphological structure)/keitaiso Zisho (morphology dictionary)/Keitaiso Zisho Fairu (morphology dictionary file)/Keitaiso Jouhou (morphology information)/Keitai Hinshi (morph part of speech)/Keitai Hinsi Bunrui Zisho (morph part of speech classification dictionary)/Keitai Hinshi Mei (morph part of speech name)/Midasigo (entry word)/Go (word)/.......

Total number of extracted terms is 53.

Terms exclusively extracted by *Imp*$_2$ based ranking method

.jumanrc Fairu (.jumanrc file)/Entori (entry)/Opushon Teigi (option definition)/Gurahu (graph)/Hasshu Teeburu (hashing table)/Katuyoukei (inflection form)/Kihonkei (root form)/Gobi (suffix)/Hyousou (surface)/Henkan (transformation)/

Total number of extracted terms is 10.

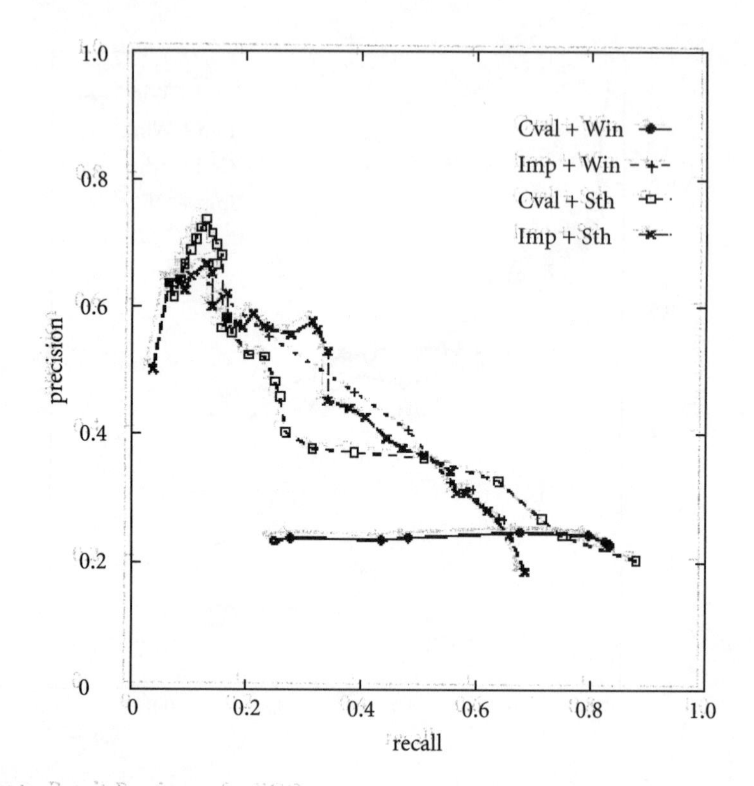

Figure 6. Recall-Precisions for EGG

Terms exclusively extracted by C-value ranking method

Opushon Teigi Fairu (optional definition file)/Keitaiso Bunpou (morphology grammar)/Kousetu Jouhou (postfix information)/Kouzou (structure)/ Soku-Jou (lattice like)/ Takubo Bunpou (Takubo grammar)/ Rensetu Kanousei (connection possibility)/

Total number of extracted terms is 7.

At the first glance the majority of terms, 75.7%(=53/70), are extracted by both of C-value based ranking method and *Imp* based ranking method. This means that these two ranking methods based on different concepts, say directly based on termhood and indirectly based on both termhood and unithood, actually give very similar results. It is too early to say, but unithood and termhood has strong correlation in terms of ranking candidates of terms, which are collocations or

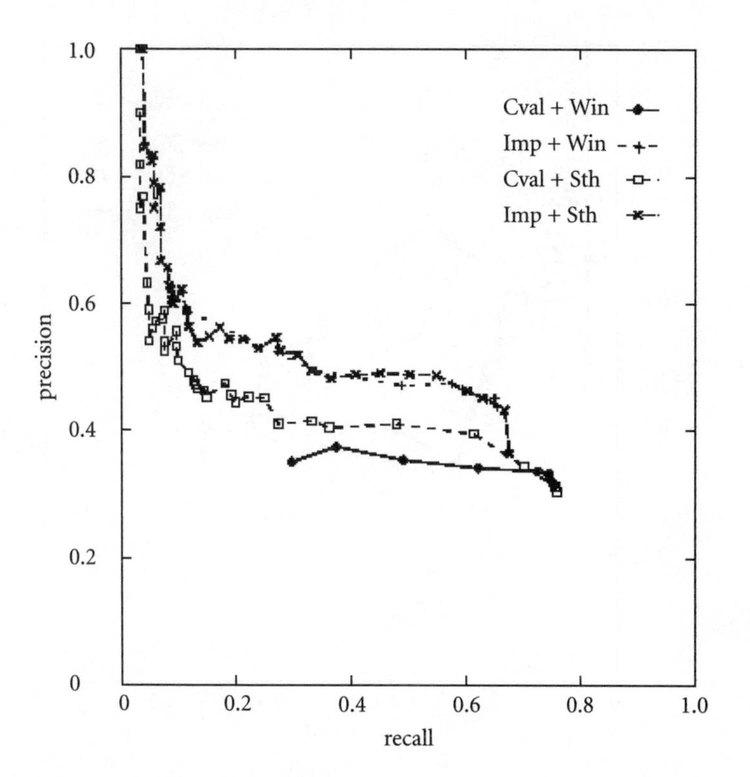

Figure 7. Recall-Precisions for HV-F93

compound nouns. The theoretical background of this correlation is, at this moment, an open problem.

Focusing on the actual mechanism of these two methods, it is much more important to investigate the terms exclusively extracted by each ranking method. Six out of seven terms extracted exclusively by C-value based ranking are collocations, in other words, compound nouns in this case. It is a reasonable result because C-value is originally developed to rank not simple nouns but collocations. We forced to change its original definition in order to score simple nouns. We once again write our new definition of C-value here:

$$\mathrm{C-value}(a) = \mathrm{length}(a) \times \left(\mathrm{freq}(a) - \frac{\mathrm{t}(a)}{\mathrm{c}(a)} \right) \tag{11}$$

From this formula, it is known that a simple noun, which is a part of many compound nouns, gets a high score of $(\mathrm{freq}(a) - \mathrm{t}(a)/\mathrm{c}(a))$ of (11). However, since its length is 1, it does not have a high score when compared to longer compound nouns. A simple noun that is not a part of many compound nouns

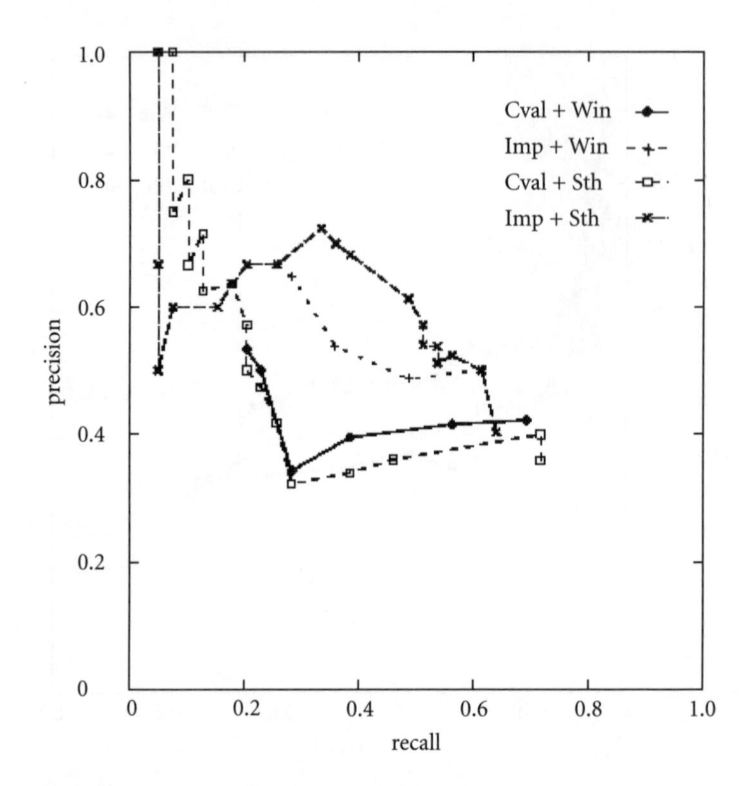

Figure 8. Recall — Precision for Play-Station

obviously does not have a high score by the definition of C-value. This is the reason why C-value based ranking does favor longer collocations, in other words it does favor compound nouns. On the contrary, seven out of ten terms extracted by Imp_2 based ranking are simple nouns. *Imp* is calculated with *Pre(N)* and *Post(N)*, which express how important the simple noun *N* is. Especially for compound nouns, Imp_2 does not depend on the length of a compound noun by its definition. Therefore, simple nouns are treated as equally well as longer compound nouns. This is the reason why Imp_2 based ranking method favors a simple noun more than C-value based ranking method does. In brief, whether simple nouns are preferred to compound nouns or not does not depends on the dichotomy of unithood and termhood, but on whether a scoring method treats simple nouns and compound nouns equally or not. In this sense, it is said that *Imp* based ranking method has high flexibility because it has many variations for the definition of *Imp* that is defined with *Pre* and *Post*. To conclude this section, we answer the pending questions, namely (1) why *Cval+Win* is the worst, and (2) why *Cval+Sth* is as equally bad as *Cval+Win* especially for HV-F93 and Play-Station manuals. We answer the first question at first. Since C-value is low for simple nouns in general, there remain quite a few of simple nouns that are to be selected in low C-value area. Moreover, in that low C-value area, there remain very few compound nouns. Then, in that area, if we put high threshold of CNR, we fail to select many terms that are simple nouns. On the contrary, if we put low threshold of CNR, we end up with picking up many non-real terms, because the majority of candidates in that low C-value area are not real terms. In short, the algorithm of the window method does not work well in low C-value area. Next we answer the second question. The users of these two equipments, HV-F93 and Play-Station, are not engineers but ordinary people. Consequently, many of important terms are simple nouns. Thus, C-value based method may fail to give high score to the real terms that are simple nouns.

6. Conclusions

We have first explained a dichotomy of unithood and termhood. We explain C-value based method which is a ranking method indirectly based on both of termhood and unithood. Then, we explained the ranking method that uses statistics of compound noun structure, called *Imp* that is directly based on termhood. We also explain the simple threshold method and the window method that are used to select real terms among ranked term candidates. We experimentally estimate *Imp* based method and C-value based method for Japanese technical manuals. Both are showing the almost same result in precision, recall and F-measure. But the sets of terms extracted by two methods are little bit different. In this sense, how directly an extraction method is based on termhood is not unique characteristics of term extraction, and still there remain many linguistic features from the viewpoint of term extraction.

We are now conducting the experiment of term extraction from English documents. A term extraction process for English documents is basically the same as the Japanese case described above. The difference is in the term candidate extraction subsystem. In English document cases, at first we apply the input document a part of speech tagger such as (Brill 1994b) to assign a part of speech tag to each morpheme. In Japanese case, a compound noun is a consecutive sequence of nouns, which may include particle NO ("of" in English) between nouns. However, terms in English often take a pattern of adjective + noun, noun + preposition + noun, etc as well as a noun sequence. So, we need a linguistic filter to pick up those patterns exclusively. To apply a stop-list is also necessary to exclude words that are not suitable components of terms of the target domain. The easiest way, which we actually try to use, to apply *Imp* function to texts is to pick up sequences of words that are not interrupted by any word in the stop-list. We have already applied *Imp* function based term extraction method to uninterrupted words sequences to small English corpus. The result seems to be not bad, but to evaluate our method by processing much larger corpus is our future problem. Seeking better definition of *Imp* function experimentally and comparison of other different term extraction methods using larger scale corpora are also our future problems.

References

Ananiadou, S. 1994. "A methodology for automatic term recognition." In *Proceedings of 15th International Conference on Computational Linguistics*, 1034-1038.

Brill, E. 1994a. "Some advances in transformation-based part-of-speech tagging." In *Proceedings of 11th National Conference on Artificial Intelligence*, 722–727.

Brill, E. 1994b. "Supervised part of speech tagger." *http://www.cs.jhu.edu/~brill/.*

Church, K.W. and Hanks, P. 1990. "Word association norms, mutual information, and lexicography" *Computational Linguistics*, 16(1): 22–29.

Daille, B., G.aussier, E. and Lange, J.M. 1994. "Towards automatic extraction of monolingual and bilingual terminology." In *Proceedings of 15th International Conference on Computational Linguistics*, 515–521.

Dunning, T. 1993. " Accurate methods for the statistics of surprise and coincidence."*Computational Linguistics*, 19(1): 62–74.

Frantzi, T.K. and Ananiadou, S. 1996. "Extracting nested collocations." In *16th Proceedings of 15th International Conference on Computational Linguistics*, 41–46.

Frantzi, T.K. and Ananiadou, S. 1999. "The c-value/nc-value method for atr." *Journal of Natural Language Processing*, 6(3): 145–179.

Fujii, H. and Croft, W.B. 1993. "A comparison of indexing techniques for Japanese text retrieval." In *Proceedings of 16th International Conference on Research and Development in Information Retrieval*, 237–246.

Hisamitsu, T. and Nitta, Y. 1996. "Analysis of Japanese compound nouns by direct text scanning." In *16th Proceedings of 15th International Conference on Computational Linguistics*, 550–555.

Kageura, K. and Umino, B. 1996. "Methods of automatic term recognition: a review." *Terminology*, 3(2): 259–289.

Lam, W., Wong, C.Y. and Wong, K.F. 1997. "Performance evaluation of character, word and n-gram-based indexing for Chinese text retrieval." In *Proceedings of the Second International Workshop on Information Retrieval With Asian Languages*, 68–80.

Matsumoto, Y., Kurohashi, S., Yamaji, O., Taeki, H. and Nagao, M. 1996. *Instruction Manual of Japanese Morphological Analyzer JUMAN3.1*. Nagao Lab. at Kyoto University.

Nakagawa, H. 1997. "Extraction of index words from manuals." In *Conference Proceedings of Computer-Assisted Information Searching on Internet*, 598–611.

Shimohata, S., Sugio, T. and Nagata, J. 1997. "Retrieving collocations by co-occurrences and word order constraints." In *Proceedings of 35th Annual Meetings of the Association for Computational Linguistics*, 476–481.

Smadja, F.A. and Mckeown, K.R. 1990. "Automatically extracting and representing collocations for language generation." In *Proceedings of the 28th Annual Meetings of the Association for Computational Linguistics*, 252–259.

Zhai, C. and Evans, D.A. 1996. "Noun-phrase analysis in unrestricted text for information retrieval." In *Proceedings of 34th Annual Meetings of the Association for Computational Linguistics*, 17–23.

Chapter 16

Corpus-based extension of a terminological semantic lexicon*

A. Nazarenko, P. Zweigenbaum, B. Habert and J. Bouaud
LIPN — UPRES-A 7030 & Université Paris 13 (Nazarenko)
DIAM — AP-HP & Université Paris 6 (Zweigenbaum, Bouaud)
LIMSI & EA 370 Université Paris 10 (Habert)

This paper addresses the problem of extending and tuning a terminological semantic lexicon to new domains and corpora. We argue that by relying on both a sublanguage corpus and a core semantic lexicon, it is possible to give an adequate description of the words that occur in the corpus. Our tuning method explores the corpus and gathers words that are likely to have similar meanings on the basis of their dependency relationships in the corpus. The aim of the present work is to assess the potential for classifying words based on the semantic categories of "neighbors". The tagging procedure is tested and parameterized on a rather small French corpus dealing with coronary diseases (85,000 word units). This method is systematically evaluated by creating and categorizing artificial unknown words. Although word semantic categorization cannot be fully automated, the results show that our tagging procedure is a valuable help to account for new words and new word uses in a sublanguage.

1. Introduction

In medical information processing, medical nomenclatures and thesauri (Cimino 1996) are being used extensively, from classifying patient data for statistical purposes to decision-support (Musen and van Bemmel 1997). However, the constant changes in techniques and approaches prevent these fundamental resources from ever being complete. Moreover, variations in terminology can be observed for a given specialty in different places. There is therefore a constant endeavor to tune vocabularies and terminologies to account for new words and new word uses.

Controlled terminologies help to record and access medical information. Semantic lexica, which associate (syntactic and) semantic categories to words, are necessary as well. They help to match controlled terms to the expressions that actually occur in corpora, for instance via synonymy relationships between heads or modifiers, or via semantic pattern-matching (McCray et al. 1994; Naulleau 1998). This contributes to terminology construction and update, by allowing the acquisition of terms from corpora and their linkage with existing controlled terms (Nelson et al. 1998). This also facilitates terminology usage, for instance in document indexing or in a controlled language setting, since it helps identify the suitable controlled terms for an initial expression (Sneiderman et al. 1996).

Here we address the problem of extending a semantic lexicon for a given sublanguage. We use an existing terminology as a "seed", as it offers categories which correspond more tightly to the salient notions and relations in the domain than a general semantic lexicon such as *WordNet* (Fellbaum 1998). We argue that by relying on both a corpus and a core semantic lexicon based on a terminology, it is possible to tune, to extend, and to adjust this lexicon to give an adequate description of the words that occur in the corpus.

We rely on a method which explores a sublanguage corpus and gathers words that are likely to have similar meanings. We derive a set of *a priori* semantic classes from a terminology for this sublanguage. We then propose a method to assign a semantically unknown word to the class that contains the words that are most similar to it on the basis of their observed behavior in the corpus.

Till now, we have tested on single words instead of multi-word terms, and with a small set of domain-specific, high-level classes rather than with a multi-level hierarchy. These constraints allow us to test the method more easily. But we claim as well that such coarse-grained categories are more relevant to semantic retrieval than finer ones.[1] The aim of the present work is to assess the potential for classifying words based on the semantic categories of "neighbors" identified through normalized syntactic distributional properties: their dependency relationships in the corpus.

The remainder of this section presents our experimental setting. Section 2 describes our general approach to lexicon tuning: we rely both on corpora and lexical resources. Section 3 presents our tuning method which complements and adjusts an existing lexicon with respect to a corpus. It is based on the propagation of semantic tags in ZELLIG graphs. The first results called for a systematic evaluation, which is described in Section 4 and which helped to parameterize our method. Results are reported in Section 5. The last sections discuss the results (6) and the potential applications (7) of this work.

1.1 The MENELAS corpus

These experiments were carried out on a French corpus which was initially designed for the European project MENELAS (Zweigenbaum 1994), devised for the development of a system for analyzing medical reports. The MENELAS corpus gathers texts dealing with coronary diseases (patient discharge summaries, discharge letters and a handbook on coronary angiography). It is a rather small corpus (85,000 word units) as compared to the very large corpora which are sometimes required to test NLP techniques. However, this size is typical of the available technical corpora, which are often too small for statistical methods and nevertheless too large for manual analysis.

1.2 The SNOMED terminology

The experiments also made use of an existing terminological resource: the "Systematized Nomenclature of Human and Veterinary Medicine", version 3, also called "SNOMED International" (Côté et al. 1993). SNOMED is a multi-axial, hierarchical terminology with 11 high-level "axes": Topography (T), Morphology (M), Function (F), Living Organisms (L), Chemicals, Drugs, and Biological Products (C), Physical Agents, Activities, and Forces (A), Occupations (J), Social Context (S), Diseases/Diagnoses (D), Procedures (P), and General Linkages/Modifiers (G). There is a French translation for a subset of this terminology, the Microglossary for Pathology (12,500 terms) (Côté 1996). SNOMED is one of the medical terminologies with the best coverage of clinical terms (Chute et al. 1996). We have chosen it as a compromise between clinical coverage and availability in French. We limited the richness of the SNOMED hierarchy to its 11 high-level categories without considering their subcategories. This choice was a compromise between the size of the tagset and the reliability of the tagging, to which we return below (see Section 2.3).
As test material for our method, we created a semantic lexicon where each relevant word in the MENELAS corpus is assigned one or more of these categories. This lexicon totals 1,902 lemmas.[2] It can be seen as a simplified version of a subset of the terminology relevant for the corpus, with only single-word terms.[3]

1.3 Tuning the SNOMED lexicon to the MENELAS corpus

In previous work (Habert et al. 1996), we explained how ZELLIG discovers similarities between words according to the contexts they share within a given domain. The present work attempts to show that this corpus-based knowledge (similarities) and a semantic lexicon (obtained from SNOMED) can be combined to tune this lexicon to the domain of coronary diseases as described in the MENELAS corpus. The similarities between words help to tag words that are unknown to the semantic lexicon and to detect ill-tagged words. The tagset consists of the high-level SNOMED axes used as general semantic categories. Through systematic experiments, the present work attempts at quantifying the extent to which this process succeeds in proposing a correct category for a given word of the corpus as several parameters of the method are submitted to variation.

2. A corpus- and knowledge-based approach

2.1 The need for semantic knowledge

Many attempts have been made to infer semantic categories from corpora using purely endogenous methods, i.e., using no semantic knowledge apart from the one driven from the corpus itself. Using the syntactic distribution of words in a corpus, as obtained by a parser, to group words into semantic classes, has already been the subject of past research (Hirschman et al. 1975). The increased availability of large corpora as well as of robust NLP techniques and tools has revived this type of work. As noted in (Grefenstette 1994), one can usually distinguish three steps in discovering semantic affinities between words:

> First-order techniques examine the local context of a word attempting to discover what can co-occur with that word within that context. Second-order techniques derive a context for each term and compare these contexts to discover similar words or terms. Third-order techniques compare lists of similar words or terms and group them along semantic axes.

After cooccurrence and similarity relations, third-order techniques aim at bringing out equivalence distributions between words, that is to say, at building semantic classes.

However, no coherent and interpretable semantic classes can be built on purely endogeneous grounds. Some of the classes obtained by Bensch and

Savitch (1995) or McMahon and Smith (1996) seem to be semantically sound at first sight but one must adjust their boundaries and check their consistency to turn them into actual categories. A similar conclusion can be drawn for the similarity subgraphs of (Habert et al. 1996).

Some external source of knowledge is therefore required to name semantic classes, either human interpretation (as in (Faure and Nedellec 1998) which presents the construction of word classes as an interactive process) or a preexisting lexical resource.

2.2 Specialized *vs.* general-purpose lexical resources

General lexical resources such as ordinary language dictionaries or thesauri are often used. Many works have exploited *WordNet*, *Roget's Thesaurus* or traditional, albeit machine-readable, dictionaries for word sense disambiguation on newspaper corpora for instance. These lexical resources have also been exploited for more technical corpora. In sublanguages, words often have very specific and unusual meanings; polysemy does exist but it is often limited. (Basili et al. 1997; Basili et al. 1998) propose a corpus-based method to adapt *WordNet* or *LDOCE* to a sublanguage: all non-attested word senses are eliminated; on the other hand, if there is corpus evidence of an unknown word use, a corresponding new sense is added. Hamon et al. (1998) exploit the French dictionary *Le Robert* to identify synonymous pairs in the list of terms of a document. Although it is often assumed that general lexical resources are of no use for the processing of technical texts, these first experiments have shown that this approach is relevant as soon as lexical information is controlled by corpus attestations.

As far as technical corpora are concerned, one usually looks for specialized lexical sources, if there are some (Morin 1998; Hamon et al. 1999). However, adequate lexical knowledge sources are seldom available. From one experiment to another, the domains are always slightly different. Charlet et al. (1996) underline that knowledge bases depend on the task they have been designed for. This is equally true for lexical knowledge bases. Moreover, in a technical domain such as medicine where terminological uses change with place and time, terminologies are quickly out-of-date.

Our approach is close to the works based on specialized lexical sources as we make use of similar lexical information. However, our aim is closer to Basili's. We argue that specialized resources, as well as more general ones, need to be updated for each specific application (domain and task). Our approach is similar to that of Basili et al. (1997), even if our tuning method differs from theirs.

2.3 Few general semantic categories

For our tuning procedure, we deliberately took a small set of general semantic tags as in (Basili et al. 1993). As explained in the introduction, we worked with the 11 high-level categories (Topography, Morphology, Function, Living Organisms…) of the SNOMED terminology.

Basili et al. (1993) argue that a set of a dozen tags is a good starting point to perform manual word sense disambiguation. A refined tagset would increase the contrast between expert judgements. Choosing a tag is also less costly if the tagset is smaller. In our case, the tagging procedure relies on a vote among the categories of similar words. Increasing the tagset would spread out semantic information for a given word. (Agirre and Rigau 1996) came to a similar conclusion while exploiting *WordNet* for word sense disambiguation: instead of relying on the small, numerous and always questionable synsets, they rather take the "general categories" represented by *WordNet* files. More recent work by Basili et al. (1997) also relies on these general *WordNet* categories.
As will be shown below, starting with general categories still gives clues for further subcategorization.

3. A tuning method based on word dependency similarities

Our reference corpus is first processed with the ZELLIG suite of tools (Habert et al. 1996) which builds a similarity graph of the corpus words (actually, lemmas). The graph nodes are the words: two words are connected if they are considered similar. These words are tagged according to the top SNOMED categories. The graph is then used to tag unknown words or to detect erroneous tags.

3.1 Building a similarity graph of the corpus

ZELLIG follows the above mentioned three-step process to discover similarities between words within a given domain according to the contexts they share (Nazarenko et al. 1997). It relies on normalized syntactic noun phrases (NPs) as local contexts for the first-order step. It uses parse trees retrieved by noun phrase extractors (in the present experiment, LEXTER (Bourigault 1993)). It leaves as such the attachments produced by the parser.[4] ZELLIG automatically reduces the numerous and complex noun phrases provided by LEXTER to elementary dependency trees, which more readily exhibit the fundamental binary relations between content words (Harris 1991).

A first step consists in rewriting these parse trees so as to get normalized binary trees: each level associates a head with either an argument or an adjunct. This normalization process facilitates the extraction of dependency relationships. The second step consists in extracting elementary dependency trees, in which a head (in this case a noun) is modified by another content word (a noun, possibly with a preposition or an adjective).[5] For instance, from the parse tree for "*signe périphérique de décompensation cardiaque*" (Figure 1), ZELLIG yields the set of elementary trees of Figure 2. Note that this normalization process simplifies the contexts, reduces their diversity and increases their number: from one complex parsed context for *décompensation*, the normalization produces two elementary contexts (trees *a* and *c*).

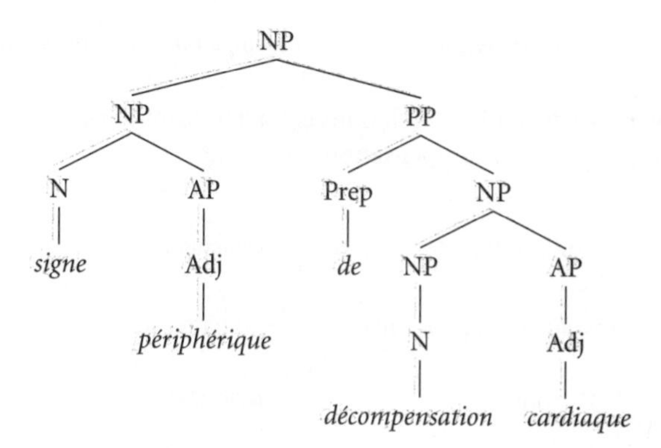

Figure 1. Complete parse tree for "signe périphérique de décompensation cardiaque"

Second-order affinities show which words share the same contexts. For instance, the following words can replace *signe* in tree *b*: *récidive* (1 occurrence), *épisode* (2 occurrences), etc. All these words can occur in the same context: a N P N tree, whose second noun is *décompensation* and whose preposition is *de*.

A graph is computed by ZELLIG to exhibit salient similarities. The words constitute the nodes. An edge corresponds to a certain amount of shared contexts, according to a given measure and a chosen threshold, which vary in the following experiments. Figure 3 shows the immediate edges around the word *artère* and brings out the words that are similar to *artère* at threshold 9.

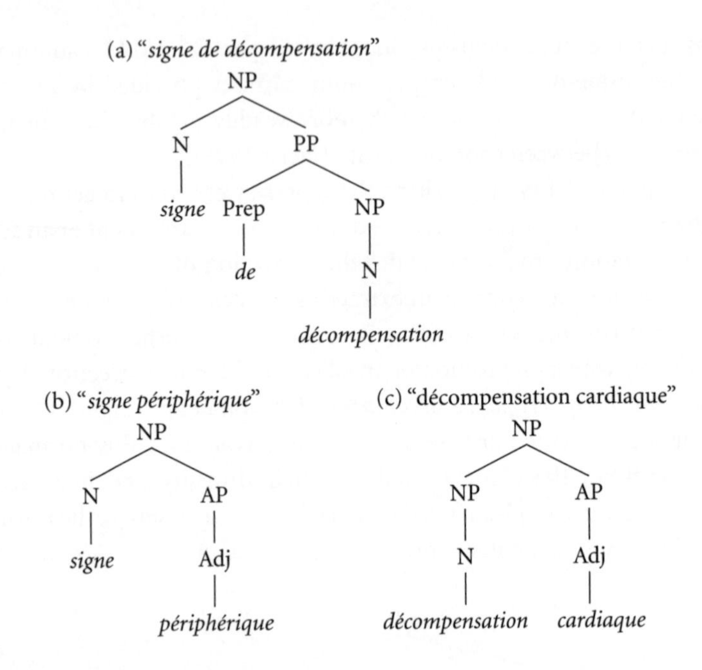

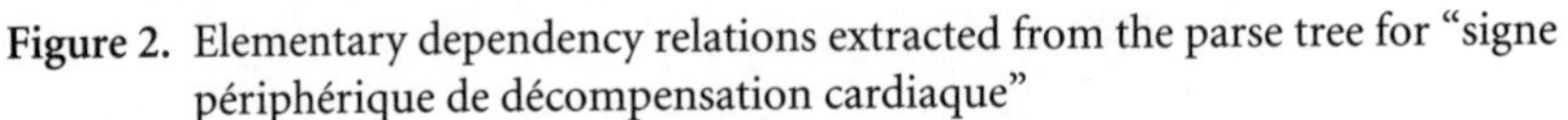

Figure 2. Elementary dependency relations extracted from the parse tree for "signe périphérique de décompensation cardiaque"

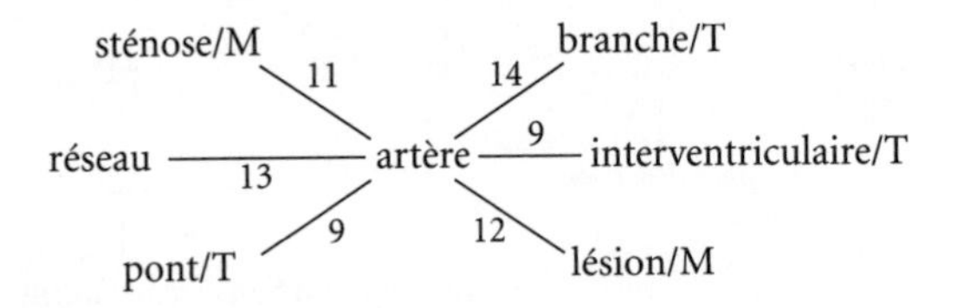

Figure 3. Edges around the word artère

For this experiment, the similarity measure is CTXT (see Section 4.2.). Each edge is labeled with the number of context types shared by the two words it links. In this example, the words which share less than 9 contexts with *artère* are not considered similar to it and do not appear. On Figure 3, SNOMED categories (/T, /M) have been added (projected) to nodes, as explained below (Section 3.2.).

As a third-order technique, ZELLIG first computes the strongly connected components (the sub-graphs in which there is a path between every pair of distinct nodes) and the k-cliques (the sub-graphs in which there is an edge between each node and *every other node* of the graph). These are the most relevant parts of the graph on topological grounds. The underlying intuition is

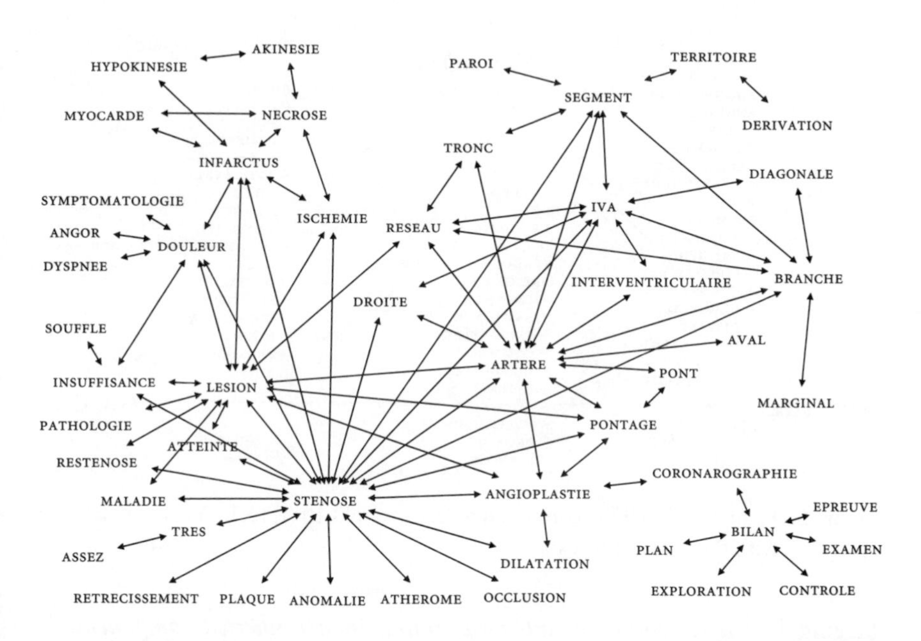

Figure 4. Example of a connected component computed with threshold 10 (CTXT). Edges are labelled with the shared contexts

that a connected component relates neighboring words with semantic intersections and that the cliques tend to isolate sets of synonyms, of antonyms or scalar groups of words. Examples of a connected component and a clique are presented on figures 4 and 5. Figure 5 shows on each edge the contexts shared by the two nodes that it links. For the sake of clarity, these contexts have been removed from the edges in Figure 4.

The connected components are further used in the tagging method described below.

3.2 Tuning a lexicon

The ZELLIG graph represents a map of the corpus words which can be confronted to an existing categorization in order to complete, correct, specialize and update it.

For instance, as explained in the introduction, the SNOMED Microglossary (Côté 1996) only covers a part of the corpus lemmas. Our tagging method therefore starts with a categorization of only a part of these lemmas. The SNOMED categories of known words are projected on the ZELLIG graph nodes. The unknown words are initially untagged. We chose the following

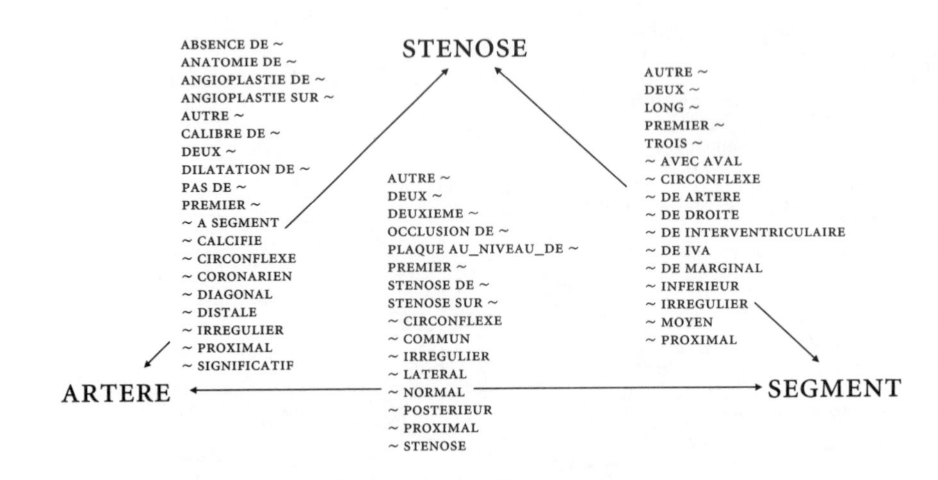

Figure 5. Example of a clique computed with threshold 10 (CTXT). Edges are labelled with the shared contexts

tagging heuristic: *given an untagged lemma in a connected component, its semantic category is chosen by majority (according to a given voting procedure, see Section 4.4) of those of its neighbors.* The categories are thus propagated through the edges from the already tagged lemmas (known words) to the untagged ones (unknown words). As a trivial case, untagged lemmas in a homogeneous connected component get the semantic category of the rest of the component. In contrast, some lemmas may remain untagged if there is no majority among their neighboring tags. The same propagation process also brings out tagging inconsistencies if a word has a tag which contradicts those of its neighbors.

3.3 First experiment

In a first experiment (Nazarenko et al. 1997), we only categorized 937 lemmas (those that were present in the original MENELAS semantic lexicon). We then projected these categories on the lemmas at the nodes of the connected components and of the cliques obtained at thresholds 5 and 10.

On the connected component of Figure 6, many lemmas can be tagged according to the SNOMED nomenclature and a few ones (*e.g.*, `apical` or `artériel`) are unknown. Giving unknown words the category which has the majority among their neighbors assigns category G to `/apical`, `/postéro-inférieur`, `/distale` and `/récent` (unanimously for the first 3, 2 against 1 for `/récent`), and this choice is correct according to our knowledge of the domain; `/artériel` obtains a tie with 1 against 1 (`G/gauche` `T/coronarien`), and therefore does not get tagged. Considering a set of 143 lemmas (corresponding to all the connected components but the largest) and starting with 87 already tagged lemmas, this heuristic tagged 46 of them and left untagged 10 lemmas unknown to SNOMED. 38/46 taggings were consistent with our knowledge of the domain, 4 were erroneous, and 4 raised a doubt which required to go back to the corpus.

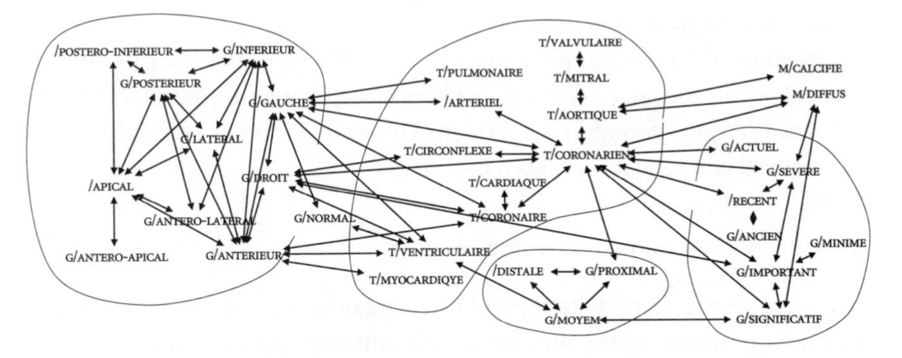

Figure 6. Grouping lemmas with same SNOMED category in a connected component. Categorized lemmas are preceded with a tag. This connected component is computed with threshold 5.

4. Evaluating the tuning method through systematic experiments

To assess the performance of the method, we carried out systematic experiments and we evaluated the tagging results as several parameters of the method were submitted to variation.

4.1 Creating artificial unknown words

In the preceding experiment, it was difficult to give a proper evaluation of the method for two reasons. The first one is that words unknown to SNOMED in the ZELLIG graphs computed at the preceding thresholds for the MENELAS corpus are not very numerous (the problem of sample size). The second one is that it is sometimes difficult to determine which would be *the* proper tag for a given word (the problem of reference) since there is no gold standard for the problem.

Following a traditional evaluation procedure (cf. for instance (Grefenstette 1994) for the creation of artificial synonyms), we artificially created unknown words, *i.e.*, words known to SNOMED but for which we removed the SNOMED tags, and tried to have their tags automatically guessed. We also varied the threshold, so that more words were involved. We consequently extended our test semantic lexicon to cover these lemmas. This resulted in an experimental sample of 1,902 lemmas, whereas the first one only contained 57 (actually) unknown words. We consider that a tag guessed by our method is correct if it corresponds to the one in our reference lexicon.

We then had a procedure examine each word in turn, assuming its category was unknown, guessing it from its neighbors, and comparing the guess with the reference category found in the lexicon. This evaluation protocol helps to test the method and tune its various parameters.

4.2 Computing a similarity value

In our first experiments with the ZELLIG suite of tools, we considered that two words were similar if the number of the different contexts they shared was above a given threshold. A context in which a word occurs more often may be considered stronger than one with only a few occurrences, so that two words that often occur in a given common context may be deemed more similar than two words that only occur once each in that context. This is what the CTXO measure takes into account. Besides, words that occur with many non-shared contexts may be considered less similar than words that only occur in shared contexts. The jaccard measure below can be used to model this behavior.[6]

Each word W_i occurs in a set of different contexts $\{ctx_i^k\}$, each with a number of occurrences $|ctx_i^k|$. Given a word W_i and a potential neighbor W_j, we compute a similarity $sim\text{-}X_{ij}$ between W_i and W_j. We used as sim-X_{ij}:

- their number of shared context types:
  $sim\text{-}CTXT_{ij} = |\{ctx_i^k\} \cap \{ctx_j^k\}|$
  (this is the initial similarity measure we used (Habert et al. 1996));
- the frequency of their shared context types:
  $sim\text{-}CTXO_{ij} = \sum_{k \in \{ctx_i^k\} \cap \{ctx_j^k\}} \min(|ctx_i^k|, |ctx_j^k|)$;
- a Jaccard measure (Saporta 1990) equivalent to the Dice coefficient (Dice 1945) frequently used in information retrieval (Salton and McGill 1983; Frakes and Baeza-Yates 1992) over context types:

$$sim\text{-}JACCARD_{ij} = \frac{sim\text{-}CTXT_{ij}}{|\{ctx_i^k\} \cup \{ctx_j^k\}|}.$$

JACCARD is the only of the three to be a normalized similarity index. It normalizes the number of shared context types by the total number of context types of W_i and W_j, so that words which are used in exactly the same contexts are favored over words which occur not only in many shared contexts (*sim*-CTXT$_{ij}$), but also in many distinct contexts.

Polysemous words are multiply tagged on graph nodes. As a crude method to take all these tags into account, a polysemous word votes once for each of its categories.

Table 1 shows the similarity values for *décompensation*, *palpitation* and *insuffisance.*

Table 1. Similarities of "décompensation", "palpitation", "insuffisance"

arête	CTXT	CTXO	JACCARD
décompensation, palpitation	2	2	0.25
décompensation, insuffisance	2	6	0.04
palpitation, insuffisance	3	3	0.05

4.3 Pruning the graph

Given a similarity measure, we then prune each couple of words whose similarity falls below a given threshold.

Depending on the chosen threshold, two words may appear similar or not. The pruning modifies the topology of ZELLIG graphs: when the threshold is raised, the number of edges decreases, leading to smaller connected components. Figure 7 shows how raising the threshold and changing the similarity measure affect the subgraph of *décompensation*, *palpitation* and *insuffisance* and thus the whole tuning method.

As there was no *a priori* reason for choosing one pruning threshold or another, we examined a relevant series of thresholds for each kind of measure: {1 2 … 19} for CTXT, {1 2 3 4 5 10 15 20} for CTXO, and {.00 .02 .04 .06 .10 .20 .30 .40 .50 .60} for JACCARD.

4.4 Ranking the categories of the immediate neighbors

Given a word W_i in the pruned graph, we have each of its immediate neighbors vote for its category, as found in the lexicon. We tested two vote aggregation methods:

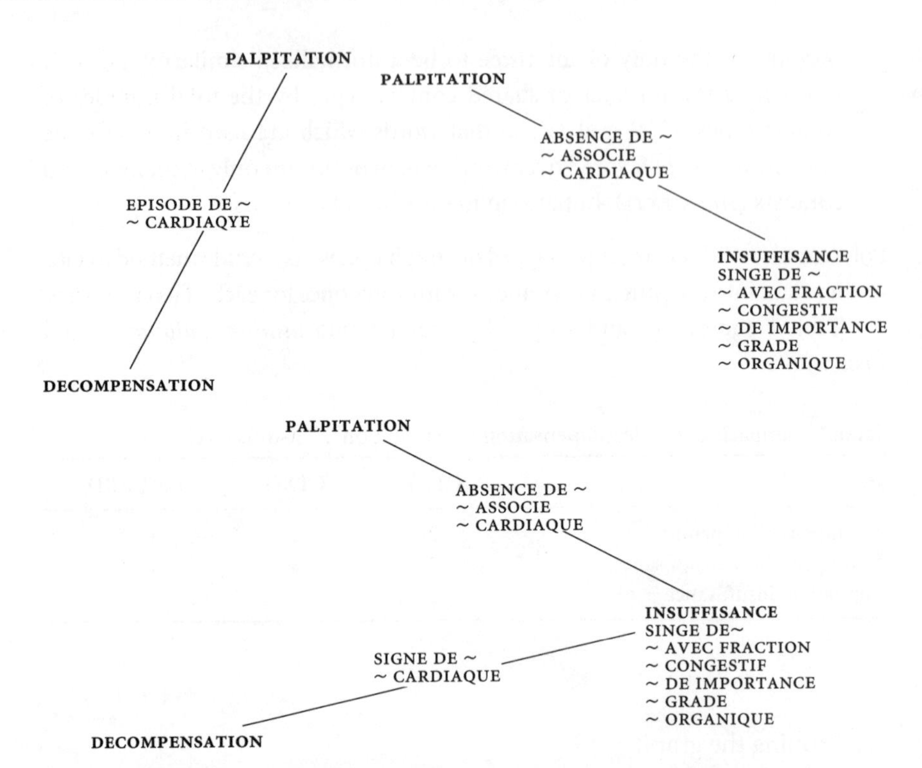

Figure 7. Alterations to the subgraph of "décompensation", "palpitation" and "insuffisance" due to similarity measure variations (for similar thresholds)

- each vote is counted as one (unweighted);
- the vote of each neighbor W_j is weighted by its similarity $sim\text{-}X_{ij}$ with word W_i.

The first voting procedure takes the graph as a Boolean similarity matrix whereas the second one takes similarity distances into account.

Votes for the same category are summed, and categories are ranked according to their cumulated votes. The top-ranked category is assumed to be the category of the word W_i. For instance, on Figure 3, two categories compete for the tagging of *artère*. Taking W_i= *artère*, in the weighted aggregation scheme, gives the following two scores:

- $\sum_{\text{cat}(j)=T} sim\text{-}CTXT_{ij} = 45$,
- $\sum_{\text{cat}(j)=M} sim\text{-}CTXT_{ij} = 23$,

so that category T (Topography) is ranked first and M (Morphology) is ranked second. T is actually the correct SNOMED tag for *artère*.

5. Results

Table 2 shows how many units were computed at each step of the method. LEXTER extracted 6,896 NPs in which 10,832 elementary trees were identified. Elementary trees mostly cover noun dependency constructs, so that some words (342, *i.e.*, 15%) were left out at this stage. The resulting 21,664 contexts include 2,073 nouns, adjectives, proper nouns and past participles, plus 11 prepositions (0.5%, used as links in the contexts). Focusing on the 40,427 triples {shared context, $word_1$ $word_2$} again eliminates 204 lemmas (10%) that only occur in idiosyncratic contexts. In total, 23% of the NP lemmas did not reach the graph. Once on the graph, lemmas were tagged according to the lexicon. This lexicon happened to lack 149 of the lemmas, so that the corresponding nodes were removed from the graph, which caused a few more nodes to become disconnected from the rest of the graph. 158 lemmas (8.5%) were lost at that stage, which resulted in a total diminution of 715 lemmas (29.5%) starting from the initial NP contents. The maximal recall the tagging step may obtain in this setting is thus 70.5%.

Table 2. Numbers of units at different processing stages (T=threshold)

(a) Number of noun phrases and contexts					(b) Number of nodes (lemmas in graph)		
Unit	Unit		Lemmas		Unit	Lemmas	
	occ.	types	occ.	types		T=1 (none)	T=2 (CTXT)
Noun phrase	6,896	4,566	2,4023	2,426			
Elementary tree	10,832	4,925	2,5012	2,084	Node	1,869	712
Context	21,664	3,590	2,1664	2,073	Not in lexicon	149	
Shared context	40,427	1,513		1,869	Connected tagged node	1,711	672

Given a word, our procedure ranks the categories of the neighbors, from most to least salient. The correct category for the word may get ranked first (rank 1), which is the desirable situation. It may also be ranked second, third, etc., or may not be present at all in the neighbors. There may also be a tie between the first and following categories.

We examine the distribution of ranks among the words of the graph obtained at the various thresholds for each measure (CTXT, CTXO, JACCARD) and with each ranking method (unweighted, weighted), both as a percentage of the total number of words in the graph (relative) and as an absolute number of words. The percentage of rank 1, which is the ratio of the number of correctly categorized words (rank 1) over the total number of words considered at that threshold, corresponds to the categorization *precision*. *Recall* is computed as the absolute number of rank 1 words over the total number of words in the corpus noun phrases (*i.e.*, 2,426 words). Table 3 provides precision and recall figures for the six combinations of similarity and weighting choices and for the main thresholds.

Table 3. Precision and recall figures for the different parameters (T = threshold)

T	CTXT				T	CTXO				T	JACCARD			
	unweighted		weighted			unweighted		weighted			unweighted		weighted	
	pre	rec	pre	rec		pre	rec	pre	rec		pre	rec	pre	rec
1	45.8	32.3	51.3	36.2	**1**	45.8	32.3	53.0	37.3	**0.00**	45.8	32.3	51.7	36.4
2	49.5	13.7	56.0	15.5	**2**	48.0	16.6	57.1	19.8	**0.02**	46.5	32.6	51.7	36.4
3	55.7	8.5	65.1	9.9	**3**	51.2	12.4	59.6	14.4	**0.04**	47.4	32.8	52.6	36.4
4	56.7	5.1	66.8	6.0	**4**	50.8	9.1	63.4	11.3	**0.06**	47.7	32.6	52.3	35.7
5	60.4	3.8	69.5	4.4	**5**	48.9	7.3	61.6	9.2	**0.10**	46.6	30.3	51.2	33.3
6	60.5	2.7	67.0	3.0	**7**	47.3	5.1	62.2	6.7	**0.15**	45.7	25.6	50.2	28.2
7	57.5	1.9	68.8	2.3	**10**	51.4	3.7	58.9	4.2	**0.20**	44.4	22.6	49.1	25.0
8	66.1	1.5	75.0	1.7	**15**	44.7	1.9	55.3	2.3	**0.30**	43.4	16.0	47.1	17.3
9	70.5	1.3	75.0	1.4	**20**	47.8	1.4	55.1	1.6	**0.40**	44.6	12.7	45.9	13.0
10	64.1	1.0	69.2	1.1	…					**0.50**	43.6	11.9	45.0	12.3
11	55.2	0.7	65.5	0.8						**0.60**	43.4	6.8	43.4	6.8
12	47.8	0.5	56.5	0.5						…				
13	33.3	0.2	44.4	0.3										
…														

6. Discussion

6.1 Variation of precision and recall with parameter settings

Weighting increases clearly (by 5 to 10%) both precision and recall for all methods and at most thresholds. The semantic category conductivity of ZELLIG graph edges — that is, they allow the possible propagation of a semantic category to a word from its neighbors — is thus proportional to their similarity strengths.

Precision varies with the **threshold** for CTXT: it rises from 46/51% (depending on whether weighting is on/off) at threshold 1 to an optimum of 70/75% at thresholds 8–9, and then decreases. CTXO displays slightly less variation, while JACCARD is remarkably stable around 44–47/49–52% at thresholds 0.00–0.20 and keeps a 43% precision at the maximum threshold.

Recall, obviously, quickly decreases with the **threshold** for CTXT and slightly less for CTXO, while the decrease for JACCARD is much slower.

In summary, weighting seems to be beneficial in all cases, as in any of the studies of similarity and clustering performed over the past 50 years. Maximum recall requires to use a low threshold for all methods (except for JACCARD, but using a higher threshold does not increase precision in that case). At low thresholds, the three methods do not display really different precision scores.

We are thus facing the traditional trade-off between precision and recall: the higher the threshold the more reliable the assigned categories. It could improve the method to assign categories to graphs of decreasing thresholds and to assign reliability measures to these assigned categories.

It is interesting to observe that, with CTXT, which displays rather better precision with some non-minimal thresholds, the assigned categories are fairly stable when the threshold is decreased. 93.5% of the correct categories found at threshold 9 (unweighted) are also found at threshold 8. 100% and 77.7% of the correct categories found at thresholds 6 and 3 respectively can also be found with a lower threshold. Only 10% of the words that are correctly categorized with a threshold higher than 2 are not correctly categorized with the graph of threshold 2. This leads us to favor recall over precision.

On the whole, among the 2,426 words in the SNOMED corpus reduced to NPs, 1,711 (70.5%) appear in the threshold 1 CTXT graph, the missing words being words with such a specific use that they share no context with any other word. At threshold 2, 672 (27.6%) words remain. Among these 672 words, 49.6% automatically receive a correct category through the unweighted scheme. If one considers that only 602 words can actually be categorized (70 should not be categorized because of a tie), we end up with a 55.3% precision. This global percentage is encouraging if one considers that randomly choosing a category among a set of 11 categories would yield a score of 9%. However, asssigning G to all words gives a better baseline precision of 301/672 or 44.8%.

6.2 Variation of precision and recall with SNOMED categories

In fact, the quality of the categorization procedure varies with the SNOMED category, ranging from 14.3% for L (Living Organisms) to 65.4% for G (General Linkages/Modifiers)[7] as is shown on Table 4.

Table 4. Results per SNOMED category (CTXT, unweighted, threshold 2)

Category	# of words	Correctly categorized		
		Local continuity tagging		Probabilistic tagging (baseline)
		Nb	%	%
Physical agents, activities, and forces (A)	12	2	16.7	1.8
Chemicals, drugs, and biological products (C)	8	3	37.5	1.2
Diseases/diagnoses (D)	24	4	16.7	3.6
Function (F)	110	61	55.4	16.4
General linkages/modifiers (G)	301	197	65.4	44.8
Living organisms (L)	7	1	14.3	1
Morphology (M)	58	10	17.2	8.6
Procedures (P)	63	22	34.9	9.4
Social context (S)	2	0	0	0.3
Topography (T)	87	33	37.9	12.9
Occupations (J)	0	0	0	0
Overall	672	333	49.6	44.8

Table 4 shows that the categorization precision is roughly correlated with the number of words in each category, the largest categories G (General Linkages/Modifiers) and F (Function) obtaining the highest precision. This is a known property of memory-based reasoning systems (Berry and Gordon 1997).

Assigning a probability to each category according to its frequency gives a better baseline than random choice for comparison. Table 4 shows that, for all categories, the actual categorization precision is clearly higher than the probability score.

On the contrary, the categorization results are not correlated with the density of the graph. A word can be correctly or incorrectly categorized independently of the number of neighbors it has in the graph. Therefore nothing prevents the categorization of words that have specific uses and share contexts with a single word, provided there is at least one shared context.

Our categorization procedure could also help humans to structure the larger categories into smaller ones. The vote brings out the major category, *i.e.*, the most salient category among neighbors, but may also bring out a minor category, the second most salient one. For instance, among the G-categorized words (General Linkages/Modifiers), one can contrast the G_T (G + topography) and G_P (G + procedure) subgroups:

1. G_T `antérieur antéro-apical apical collateral minime significatif sévère …`
2. G_P `actuel année immediat jour mois possibilité réalisation réapparition …`

   which may prove relevant for further subcategorization.

6.3 Limitations

The analysis of erroneous categories brings out the major cases of categorization ambiguity (apart from the words which can belong to several categories — we do not focus on these polysemy phenomena). The general category G is responsible for a large number of errors, especially for the modifiers: adjectives *ischémique* and *systolique* and nouns such as *mouvement,* which can be viewed as a "support noun", all get categorized as G whereas they generally correspond to SNOMED functions (F). In these cases, purely syntactic similarities seem to be stronger than semantic characteristics. However, the much larger representation of the G category in the lexicon also increases the probability for each lemma to have G neighbors (Berry and Gordon 1997). Note that Hirschman et al. (1975) carefully set apart words with specific syntactic behaviors so that their clustering method could work properly.

We mention three limitations in these experiments. First, we used semantic categories originally suited for terms in the SNOMED nomenclature. When we built our single-word test lexicon with these categories, it was easier to manually categorize words that occur as term heads in the SNOMED Microglossary than those that only occur as modifiers: many of the latter were therefore categorized in the G category (general linkages and modifiers). As a result, term heads are generally better categorized than the other components, whose semantic roles heavily depend on the noun they modify. This mainly affects precision.

Secondly, the noun phrase extractor whose output was normalized by ZELLIG, in this experiment LEXTER, filters its results: it only yields phrases which can function as terms. The syntactic pattern and the semantic classes of the components must be compatible with such a role. For instance, *sténose serrée à la fin du tronc commun* is filtered out, as the complex preposition *à la fin du* does not occur in terms. This only affects recall.

Last, the morpho-syntactic tagger used by LEXTER is not error-free. Tagging errors imply erroneous attachments and phrases, which affect both precision and recall.

7. Perspectives

7.1 Further experimentation

We noted above that whereas weighting was useful, using a threshold was not really desirable, and that the different similarity measures tested do not bring drastic changes at low thresholds.

In the reported experiments, the graphs are first built, then pruned and finally categorized according to the SNOMED axes. However, SNOMED categories could be incorporated at earlier steps, into either the graph pruning or the graph building processes. In the first case, once the graph is built, the contexts are categorized. Similarity could therefore be no longer based on context types or occurrences but on categorized context types or occurrences. In the second case, context categorization would be done before the graph is built and would thus modify the graph topology itself by highly increasing the edge number. Categorizing the contexts is a generalization process (Grishman and Sterling 1994) that decreases the contextual diversity and modifies the resulting similarities. Incorporating semantic categories at earlier steps would further normalize the dependency contexts.

7.2 Terminology tuning and updating

This categorization method, originally developed for tuning an incomplete nomenclature for a given technical corpus, can have various other applications. It could be used to progressively enrich a nomenclature from incoming texts, *i.e.* to incorporate the texts produced by one or several hospitals or departments on a monthly, weekly or daily basis. Actually, our procedure can even categorize some hapaxes: it can work at low thresholds since the categorization of a word does not require it to have a large number of neighbors. Even if only few unknown words appear in each group of texts, we argue that an automatic categorization process is necessary. Manual categorization is not only costly, it is also not fully reliable. In a technical domain where terminology is changing according to place and/or time, it may be difficult to manually identify the category of an unknown word which could be a deceptive cognate or to detect the new uses of an already known word.

A different kind of application would consist in enriching the nomenclature itself. Categorizing unknown words extends its coverage and we have seen how the voting results can help to subcategorize a general category such as the

SNOMED G axis. However, such an application requires that our method be tested on larger corpora.

7.3 Semantic categorization

This tagging procedure produces a semantic categorization of the words in the corpus. Such a categorization is useful both for terminological applications (control and structuration of terminologies, term definition, etc.) and for NLP ones (syntactic disambiguation, acquisition of selectional patterns, acquisition of extraction patterns, etc.).

This process is designed to aid human terminological work. It cannot be fully automated but we have shown that, starting with few general semantic categories and a core lexicon which are available for many domains or which can be built for a specific purpose (Basili et al. 1993), the tagging procedure can help extend and refine the initial lexicon.

8. Conclusion

We presented a method for tuning a terminological semantic lexicon to new domains and corpora. The reported experiment aims at tuning a semantic lexicon derived from the SNOMED medical nomenclature to the MENELAS corpus. The method is based on the ZELLIG suite of tools and exploits local continuity in graphs of dependency-based similarities. A tagging procedure is designed that propagates semantic tags through the graph edges from known words to unknown ones.

Systematic experiments of categorizing artificial unknown words have been carried out. They help evaluate the whole tuning method. In the context of our experiment, the tagging procedure consists in choosing one tag among 11. The results are fairly good (almost 50% precision) compared with a baseline tagging choosing the most probable tag (44.8%) but they do not allow an automatic tagging. Syntactic dependencies are interesting clues for semantic categorization but tagging inconsistencies call for human analysis. For instance, if a semantic constraint is violated, *i.e.* if the tag of a word is inconsistent with those of its neighbors, one cannot guess from the corpus alone whether this is due to an initially erroneous tag or to an ellipsis. Our method is therefore designed as an aid for terminological building and updating.

Result comparison has shown that thresholding the similarity graphs is useless and that a normalized similarity measure does no better than more trivial ones, at least on a small corpus. ZELLIG graphs are thus used as a Boolean similarity matrix where two lemmas are connected if they share at least one context. Weighting only benefits the voting procedure: it gives better results for the propagation of semantic categories. However, we have shown that the voting can be performed even for words which have only few neighbors.

These results have important consequences for the terminological applications of our method as it can be applied to small corpora and help to categorize infrequent words.

Notes

* We thank Dr. R.A. Côté for graciously providing us a copy of the French version of the SNOMED Microglossary for Pathology.

1. For instance, the refinements of *WordNet* synsets lead to difficulties when there are used in query extension (Voorhees 1998).

2. A lemma subsumes the morphological variants of a word. For instance, the masculine singular form is chosen for an adjective: *marginal* is the lemma for *marginal, marginale, marginaux,* and *marginales.*

3. Some of these single-word terms existed as is in the Microglossary; other words occurred in multi-word terms of SNOMED; and some did not occur at all in the SNOMED Microglossary. The latter two kinds of words were categorized manually to build this test semantic lexicon.

4. LEXTER uses non ambiguous contexts in order to choose between competing attachments. For instance, in the parse tree for *signe périphérique de décompensation cardiaque* (Figure 1), *cardiaque* is attached to *décompensation* and not to *signe* because *décompensation cardiaque* is found in the corpus and *signe cardiaque* is not.

5. Two techniques were used successively. The first technique consists in "undoing" the rules which have been applied to derive the parse tree and to check after each simplification phase whether the current result exhibits an elementary dependency between content words. The second technique uses underspecified tree descriptions as an approximate tree matching device (Vijay-Shanker 1992).

6. All the context types do not necessarily have the same significance. Let us consider for example two contexts of *artère, type d'artère* (*a*) and *diamètre de l'artère* (*b*). The second one is far more semantically informative than the first one which is a kind of complex determiner. *b* is therefore more discriminating for word similarity measures. These linguistic properties may vary from one corpus to another. They are difficult to formalize and to take into account as such. They are regularly approximated quantitatively, however, for example in information retrieval systems.

7. Category S (Social Context), for which no correct category was found, does not have a significant size; the 12 J words (Occupations) in our corpus happened to all be hapaxes — that is words occurring only once — with specific contexts.

References

Agirre, E. and Rigau, G. 1996. "Word sense disambiguation using conceptual density." In *Proceedings of the 4th Workshop on Very Large Corpora (Coling'96)*. Copenhague.

Basili, R., Della Rocca, M. and Pazienza, M.T. 1997. "Contextual Word Sense Tunig and Disambiguation." *Applied Artificial Intelligence* 11:235–262.

Basili, R., Pazienza, M.T., Stevenson, M., Velardi, P., Vindigni, M. and Wilks, Y. 1999. "An empirical approach to lexical tuning." In *Proceedings of the Workshop on Adaptating Lexical and Corpus Ressources to Sublanguages and Applications (First International Conference on Language Resources and Evaluation)*. Grenada.

Basili, R., Pazienza, M.T., Stevenson, M. and Velardi, P. 1993. "Acquisition of selectional patterns in sublanguages." *Machine Translation* 8:175–201.

Bensch, P.A. and Savitch, W.J. 1995. "An occurrence-based model of word categorization." *Annals of Mathematics and Artificial Intelligence* 14:1–16.

Berry, M.J.A. and Gordon, G.S. 1997. *Data Mining: for marketing, sales, and customer support*. Chichester: John Wiley and sons.

Bourigault, D. 1993. "An endogenous corpus-based method for structural noun phrase disambiguation." In *Proceedings of the 6th European Chapter of the Association for Computational Linguistics*.

Charlet, J., Bachimont, B., Bouaud, J. and Zweigenbaum, P. 1996. "Ontologie et réutilisabilité: expérience et discussion." In *Acquisition et Ingénierie des connaissances: tendances actuelles*, N. Aussenac-Gilles, P. Laublet and C. Reynaud (eds) 69–87. Toulouse: Cépaduès-Editions.

Chute, C.G., Cohn, S.P., Campbell, K.E., Oliver, D.E. and Campbell, J.R. 1996. "The content coverage of clinical classifications." *Journal of the American Medical Informatics Association* 3 (3):224–233.

Cimino, J.J. 1996. Coding systems in health care. In *Yearbook of Medical Informatics '95: The Computer-based Patient Record*, J.H. van Bemmel and A.T. McCray (eds) 71–85. Stuttgart: Schattauer.

Côté, R.A., Rothwell, D.J., Palotay, J.L., Beckett, R.S. and Brochu, L. (eds) 1993. *The Systematised Nomenclature of Human and Veterinary Medicine:* SNOMED *International*. Northfield: College of American Pathologists.

Côté, R.A. 1996. *Répertoire d'anatomopathologie de la* SNOMED *internationale, v3.4*. Sherbrooke, Québec: Université de Sherbrooke.

Dice, L.R. 1945. "Measures of the amount of ecologic associations between species", *Journal of Ecology* 1945.

Faure, D. and Nédellec, C. 1998. "A corpus-based conceptual clustering method for verb frames and ontology acquisition." In *Proceedings of the Workshop on Adaptating Lexical and Corpus Resources to Sublanguages and Applications (First International Conference on Language Resources and Evaluation)*, P. Velardi (ed) 5–12. Granada.

Fellbaum, C. (ed) 1998. *WordNet: an electronic lexical database* [Language, Speech and Communication], Cambridge, MA: The MIT Press.

Frakes, W.B. and Baeza-Yates, R. (eds) 1992. *Information Retrieval: Data structures and Algorithms.* Upper Saddle River, NJ: Prentice Hall.

Grefenstette, G. 1994. "Corpus-derived first, second and third order affinities." In *Proceedings of EURALEX*, Amsterdam.

Grishman, R. and Sterling, J. 1994. "Generalizing automatically generated selectional patterns." In *Proceedings of the 15th International Conférence on Computational Linguistics (Coling'94)* 742–747. Kyoto.

Habert, B., Naulleau, E. and Nazarenko, A. 1996. "Symbolic word clustering for medium-size corpora." In *Proceedings of the 16th International Conference on Computational Linguistics (Coling'96)*, J.I. Tsujii (ed), 490–495. Copenhagen.

Hamon, T., Garcia, D., and Nazarenko, A. 1999. "Détection de liens de synonymie: complémentarité des ressources générales et spécialisées." *Terminologie Nouvelle* (to appear).

Hamon, T., Nazarenko, A. and Gros, C. 1998. "A step towards the detection of semantic variants of terms in technical documents." In *Proceedings of the 18th International Conference on Computational Linguistics (Coling'98)* 498–504, Montréal.

Harris, Z.S. 1991. *A theory of language and information: A mathematical approach.* Oxford: Oxford University Press.

Hirschman, L., Grishman, R. and Sager, N. 1975. "Grammatically-based automatic word class formation." *Information Processing & Management* 11:39–57.

McMahon, J.G. and Smith, F.J. 1996. "Improving statistical language model performance with automatically generated word hierarchies." *Computational Linguistics* 22 (2):217–247.

McCray, A.T., Srinivasan, S. and Browne,A.C. 1994. "Lexical methods for managing variation in biomedical terminologies." In *Proceedings of the 18th Annual SCAMC* 235–239, Washington: Mc Graw Hill.

Morin, E. 1998. "Prométhée, un outil d'aide à l'acquisition de relations sémantiques entre termes." In *Actes de la cinquième conférence annuelle sur le Traitement Automatique des Langues Naturelles (TALN'98)* 172–181, Paris.

Musen, M.A. and van Bemmel, J.H. 1997. *Handbook of Medical Informatics.* Springer-Verlag.

Naulleau, E. 1998. *Apprentissage et filtrage syntactico-sémantique de syntagmes nominaux pertinents pour la recherche documentaire.* Doctorat en informatique, Université Paris XIII, Villetaneuse.

Nazarenko, A., Zweigenbaum, P., Bouaud, J. and Habert, B. 1997. "Corpus-based identification and refinement of semantic classes." *Journal of the American Medical Informatics Association* 4 (suppl):585–589.

Nelson, S.J., Kuhn, T., Radzinski, D., Sherertz, D.D., Tuttle, M.S. and Spena, R. 1998. "Creating a thesaurus from text: A 'bottom-up' approach to organizing medical knowledge." *Journal of the American Medical Informatics Association* 5 (suppl): 1046.

Salton, G. and McGill, M.J. 1983. *Introduction to Modern Information Retrieval.* New-York: McGraw-Hill.

Saporta, G. 1990. *Probabilités, analyse des données et statistique.* Paris: Technip.

Sneiderman, C.A., Rindflesch, T.C. and Aronson,A.R. 1996. "Finding the findings: identification of findings in medical literature using restricted natural language processing." In *Proceedings of the AMIA Annual Fall Symposium*, J.J. Cimino (ed) 239–243. Washington DC.

Vijay-Shanker, K. 1992. "Using descriptions of trees in a Tree Adjoining Grammar." *Computational Linguistics* 18 (4):482–516.

Voorhees, E.M. 1998. "Using *WordNet* for text retrieval." *WordNet: an electronic lexical database*, In C. Fellbaum (ed) [Language, Speech and Communication] 285–303. Cambridge, MA: The MIT Press.

Zweigenbaum, P. and Consortium MENELAS 1994. "MENELAS: an access system for medical records using natural language." *Computer Methods and Programs in Biomedicine* 45:117–120.

Chapter 17

Term extraction for automatic abstracting*

Michael P. Oakes and Chris. D. Paice
Lancaster University

In this paper we describe term extraction from full length journal articles in the domain of crop husbandry for the purpose of producing abstracts automatically. Initially, candidate terms are extracted which occur in one of a number of fixed lexical environments, as found by a system of contextual templates which assigns a semantic role indicator to each candidate term.

Candidate terms which can be lexically validated — that is, whose constituent words and structure conform to a simple grammar for their assigned role — receive an enhanced weight. The grammar for lexical validation was derived from a training corpus of 50 journal articles. Selected terms may be used to generate a short abstract which indicates the subject matter of the paper.

We also describe a method for compiling a list of sequences which indicate the statistical findings of an experiment, in particular the interrelationships between terms. Such word sequences, when extracted and appended to an indicative abstract, will produce an informative abstract which describes specific research findings in addition to the subject matter of the paper.

1. Introduction and background

Concept-based abstracting (CBA) uses a shallow processing approach to instantiate a semantic frame containing the most important concepts discussed in a source text. Each slot in the frame is associated with a particular semantic role, and is denoted by a role indicator. A simple output template is used to convert an instantiated frame into a short textual abstract.

In this paper, we outline the application of the CBA approach to papers in the field of crop husbandry, using the following semantic roles: crop species (SPEC), cultivar (CV), high level property (HLP), low level property (LLP), chemical agent (AGENT), pest or disease (PEST), influence (INF), location (LOC), soil (SOIL) and year (WHEN). The property HLP here refers to a broad property of a crop species or cultivar — often “growth rate” or “yield”. A low-level property, LLP, is some quantity such as “root length” which may be measured in the course of an experiment. Its value may be taken as an indicator of an HLP, but it is not in itself the final objective.

The CBA method uses a set of *contextual templates* against which the source text is compared. These are designed to match the text at points of high information content, where inferences can be made about which concepts most truly reflect the content of the document. They consist of alternating *literals* and *fillers*, where a literal is a whole-word string which must match some segment of the source text exactly, and a filler is any sequence of words occurring between literals. Wherever a template matches, it triggers the extraction of a filler string from the source text, which is assigned to a relevant role indicator.

As an example, the template “spring ? was sown” would match the phrase “spring barley was sown”. Here, “spring” and “was sown” are literals, while the symbol “?” matches the filler string “barley”. The role associated with the “?” symbol might be SPEC (crop species), and thus the filler “barley” would be assigned to SPEC. This provides evidence that a main crop species described in the text is barley.

After the text has been scanned, a list of several filler strings may be associated with each role, one for each template match. Some of these strings will be inappropriate, or will contain extraneous words which need to be ignored. Thus, from each list of extracted filler strings, one or more substrings need to be selected as relevant terms for that role. To this end, a set of whole-word substrings is generated, containing sequences of from one up to (say) four words. The substrings may be weighted, since some templates are more reliable than others. If any substring appears more than once, the weight associated with each instance is combined. The most highly weighted substrings found in this way are taken as terms for the given role.

The output of our template matching program is a list for each role of the most likely candidates for that role, arranged in decreasing order of (a) total weight, (b) length in words and (c) number of occurrences in the set of candidates. A sample extract of the output, showing the three most highly weighted candidate strings for the role of influence (INF), is shown in Figure 1.

In previous experiments (Paice and Jones 1993; Jones 1995), domain-specific templates were created manually. Oakes and Paice (1999) describe a method for generating the templates automatically. In this paper, we will discuss how the process of identifying the most suitable candidate string or strings for each role can be enhanced by the use of *lexical validation*, whereby

INF			
weight	*length*	*occurrences*	*21 string*
11.81	1	18	temperature
5.48	2	7	leaf canopy
4.25	1	5	photoperiod

Figure 1. Sample output from the template matching program

any candidate filler string (or substring) which is composed of words from a given vocabulary combined according to an approved grammar is preferred to any candidate string which does not conform to this vocabulary and grammar.

From a set of instantiated roles, an output template based on Liddy's (1991) abstract structure can be used to generate a textual abstract (Jones and Paice 1992). This produces an 'indicative' abstract, which indicates to the reader the subject matter of the paper. In the hope of also capturing some 'informative' material, i.e., the actual research findings of the paper, Jones (1995) looked for sentences containing 'indicator constructs' such as "Our results indicate that...". In this paper we describe our approach to the problem of extracting fuller information about results by identifying phrases such as "A had a significant effect on B", revealing the relationship between variables A and B, namely that A is an independent variable and B is a dependent variable.

An output template based on a design by Jones and Paice (1992) is shown in Figure 2. This works by replacing each role identifier (such as PEST) by the chosen string (such as "potato tuber moth"), where available. Each text segment is output in sequence, excepting those containing uninstantiated role identifiers, which are ignored. The segments labelled 1 to 8 are used to generate the indicative abstract, whereas item 9 refers to additional extracted material, containing indicator constructs, which give information about results.

The general method of using templates for automatic abstracting, though developed independently, has many similarities with the information extraction approach which has been explored by the MUC projects (ARPA 1995). The use of contextual expressions for extracting conceptual relationships has been reported recently by a number of workers — e.g., Bowden (1999), and Condamines and Rebeyrolle, elsewhere in this volume.

The various term extraction requirements of the concept-based abstracting approach illustrate four basic techniques for term extraction:

1. This paper studies the effect of AGENT on the HLP of SPEC

....*OR*

This paper studies the effect of INF on the HLP of SPEC

2. when it is infested by PEST.
3. An experiment was undertaken
4. in WHEN
5. using cultivars CV
6. [in, at] LOC,
7. where the soil was SOIL.
8. The HLP [is, are] measured by analysing the LLP.
9. RESULTS: CORRELATIONS.

Figure 2. Abstract template based on Jones and Paice (1992)

1. Traditional methods using existing sources such as thesauri, or performing word and phrase frequency analyses with domain-specific corpora (Salton 1968; Kelledy and Smeaton 1997).

2. Identification of terms by examination of consistencies in their immediate context. This method is analogous to the Cloze test in language testing (see, for example, Tribble and Jones 1990), where the subject is asked to supply words or phrases which would fit meaningfully into blanked-out portions of text. All words or phrases fitting into a single blank space will be of a single (usually grammatical) category.

3. Identification of terms by examination of their internal structure. Phrases in documents useful as content identifiers may be found using statistical measures of the strength of association between text words. For example, Gale, Church, Hanks and Hindle (1991) use mutual information to identify word collocations in text. Alternatively phrases might be identified by syntactic analysis methods that describe the word-class sequences which are permissible in candidates for phrase extraction. Researchers who have employed this approach include Klingbiel (1975), Maeda, Momouchi and Sawamura (1980) and Ruge, Schwartz and Warner (1991). A combined approach using both statistical and syntactic criteria has been developed by Gaussier and Langé (1994) and Daille (1995). Strategies for annotating text according to the semantic categories of the constituent words are reviewed by Wilson and Thomas (1997). In this paper we propose rules for the combination of role-indicating words and phrases, such that any word sequence conforming to this lexical validation grammar is accepted as a domain-compatible technical term.

4. Classification of terms by recognition of the relationships between them. A hierarchy of predicates describing the rhetorical structure of abstracts and the interrelationships between variables has been produced by Rama and Srinivasan (1993).

The structure of the remainder of the paper is as follows: In Section 2 the method of production of the lexical validation grammar is described, while in Section 3 we explain how lexical validation is used for the selection of the most promising technical terms. In Section 4 we describe the construction of a set of contextual templates for extracting informative, statistics-related statements from a text. Section 5 explains how our approach to term extraction and abstracting can be adapted quite easily to a fresh domain.

2. Producing the lexical validation grammar

2.1 Compilation of the grammar-creation thesaurus

Our grammar-creation thesaurus was constructed using a training corpus of 50 electronically stored journal articles in the domain of crop husbandry (about 105,000 words), compiled by Jones (1995). The process began by compiling a list of all words in the training corpus with a frequency of 5 or more which could be classified under one of the original 10 roles (see above). Unfamiliar terms were categorised by examining their contexts in the training corpus using a concordancing program.

The original thesaurus was augmented as follows: All non-stoplisted words in the training corpus with a frequency of 30 or more were assigned to a role, with a new role being created if a word did not fit conveniently into one of the original 10 roles and could not be confidently stoplisted. No new roles were formed to accommodate words with a frequency of less than 30, but all words with a frequency of 5 or more were examined to see if they could fit into an existing role (including roles newly created for words with a frequently over 30). The additional roles created for single words are listed in Figure 3.

All words fitting into one of these new roles with a frequency of 5 or more were added to the grammar-creation thesaurus. A repeated sequence detection program was used to generate all sequences of length 2 to 5 words occurring 5 times or more in the training corpus, and which did not start or end with a stop word. The threshold frequencies were arbitrary, but represent a reasonable balance between high thresholds with a small number of thesaurus entries, and lower thresholds yielding a larger thesaurus but requiring much more manual scrutiny to find sparsely occurring examples.

PART	(part, e.g. "leaf", including adjectives such as "foliar");
MEAS	(measure e.g. "length");
UNIT	(units e.g. "days");
TEMP	(time-related words, e.g. "diurnal" or "spring");
LLP-STAG	(stages of the plant life-cycle not directly under the experimenter's control e.g. "inflorescence" or "death");
INF-STAG	(stages of the plant life cycle determined by the experimenter, e.g. "ploughing" or "cropping");
NUM	(numerics, e.g. "6", or "thousand");
ENDO	(a subset of AGENT, being chemicals which can also act as natural nutrients or endogenous compounds, such as "water" or "potassium").

Figure 3. Additional roles for single words

The grammar-creation thesaurus was then further augmented by adding all 'meaningful' high frequency multi-word units (MWUs) or phrases found in the training corpus. The MWUs deemed meaningful were those which could be manually assigned to one of the 10 original role identifiers. Other MWUs marked for further reference were statistics-related phrases, denoted "*ST", the significance of which in the generation of informative abstracts will be discussed in Section 4. The five most frequently occurring items of length 2 to 5 words taken from the manually annotated word sequence frequency lists are shown in Figure 4. The first item in each line shows either the relevant role identifier, or "*ST" to denote a statistics related phrase, or "REJ" to denote a word sequence which was rejected because it neither constituted a term nor was related to the statistical findings of an experiment. The second item indicates the frequency of the sequence, and the third item is the actual sequence.

Some of the entries in the grammar-creation thesaurus, including both selected MWUs and single words, are shown in Figure 5. The whole grammar-creation thesaurus contains 1466 terms. The format of the entries in the thesaurus is

specific term |ROLE|.

*ST	8	all treatments gave a significant
*ST	8	treatments gave a significant increase
INF	7	combined seed and foliar treatment
*ST	7	correlation of yield with kernel
REJ	7	seed and foliar treatment ethirimol
LLP	26	number of spikes meter-2
*ST	17	direct correlation of yield
*ST	13	significant increase in yield
REJ	10	shown in Table 1
REJ	10	yield with the number
LLP	32	number of spikes
INF	28	soil water potential
REJ	21	during grain fill
*ST	20	analysis of variance
LLP	19	median emergence time
HLP	87	grain yield
LLP	69	root growth
REJ	59	dry matter
LLP	56	dry weight
SPEC	46	winter wheat

Figure 4. Sections from the annotated high frequency MWU lists

Combined seed and foliar treatment |INF|
seed and foliar treatment |INF|
changes in tuber volume |LLP|
number of spikes meter-2 |LLP|
total leaf dry mass |LLP|
leaf dry mass |LLP|
potato tuber moth |PEST|
citrus and avocado |SPEC|
hordeum vulgare L |SPEC|
Tridemorph spray |AGENT|
Maris Piper |CV|
tuber volume |LLP|
grain yields |HLP|
planting date |INF|
morphine concentration |LLP|
coastal plain |LOC|
stem nematode |PEST|
silt loam |SOIL|

winter wheat |SPEC|
sugar beet |SPEC|
dry mass |LLP|

tridemorph |AGENT|
Simmonds |CV|
morphine |ENDO|
sugar |ENDO|
yields |HLP|
drought |INF|
planting |INF-STAG|
greenhouse |LAB|
exudation |LLP|
Inflorescence |LLP-STAG|
Tasmania |LOC|
volume |MEAS|
2 |NUM|
grain |PART|

tuber |PART|
seed |PART|
stem |PART|
foliar |PART|
nematode |PEST|
geese |PEST|
moth |PEST|
loam |SOIL|
silt |SOIL|
wheat |SPEC|
citrus |SPEC|
potato |SPEC|
avocado |SPEC|
winter |TEMP|
metre-2 |UNIT|
1991 |WHEN|

Figure 5. Sample entries in the grammar-creation thesaurus

2.2 Generation of grammar rules

A string replacement program was then used to convert the grammar-creation thesaurus into a set of rules for the lexical validation of candidate terms. Each MWU in the grammar-creation thesaurus was compared with all MWUs consisting of fewer words and single terms in the grammar-creation thesaurus. Whenever the shorter entry was an exact substring of the longer entry, that element of the longer MWU was replaced by the role identifier of the shorter term. Only whole-word matches were considered in this substitution process. Each original MWU with matching substrings substituted by the relevant role identifier would then constitute a grammar rule for the lexical validation and/or interpretation of candidate terms. For example, the two-word entry

tridemorph spray |AGENT|

meaning "tridemorph spray is an agent" was matched against all single-word terms in the grammar-creation thesaurus. A match was found with the entry

tridemorph |AGENT|

meaning "tridemorph is an agent". Substitution of the matching substring "tridemorph" in the longer term with the role identifier of that substring ("AGENT") yielded the grammar rule

[AGENT] spray=[AGENT]

meaning "any agent spray is an agent". This grammar rule could, for example, be used to validate the candidate term "fungicide spray". If there is an entry in the thesaurus for the single term "fungicide", and its role is AGENT, then the string "fungicide spray" will be accepted as a valid term by the grammar, and given the interpretation "AGENT". Consider also the four-word entry in the grammar creation thesaurus

number of spikes meter-2 |LLP|.

This was matched against all the items in the grammar-creation thesaurus consisting of up to three words. Matching substrings were found in the rules:

number of spikes |LLP|
meter-2 |UNIT|

Substitution of the substrings by their role identifiers yielded the grammar rule

[LLP] [UNIT] = [LLP]

meaning that any low level property followed by mathematical units also describes a low level property. Each MWU was matched against the list of shorter terms in order of decreasing length of the shorter terms. Thus "number" was not replaced by "MEAS", even though the thesaurus contained the entry

number |MEAS|.

A small number of grammar rules were discounted, such as

MH [NUM] = [CV].

This was derived from

MH 383 |CV|

where it was clear that the original string represents a 'primitive' concept, which should be regarded in its entirety rather than in decomposed form. Instead, the original strings were kept in the rule set. Another example of such a primitive concept was "sugar beet" (SPEC), even if "sugar" (ENDO) was also in the grammar-creation thesaurus. Other primitive concepts such as "coastal plain" (LOC) remained in their original form because none of their constituent substrings were found in the thesaurus.

The generated lexical validation rules were then collated. The resulting list was alphabetically sorted to bring entries identical on the left hand side (LHS) together, enabling one to check for duplication and consistency, in particular instances where the same LHS of a rule was found to have more than one contradictory interpretation. For example, the following sequences are interpreted as LLP if the chemical represented by ENDO is acting as an endogenous compound, but as INF if the chemical is acting as an externally applied agent:

[ENDO] concentrations = [INF]
[ENDO] concentrations = [LLP]
[ENDO] content = [INF]
[ENDO] content = [LLP]
[ENDO] levels = [INF]
[ENDO] levels = [LLP]

The existence of alternative interpretations of grammar rules does not prevent their being used for lexical validation. If both forms of the rule appear in a lexical validation grammar, then candidate substrings for a given role which match the LHS of the rule will be accepted if either form of the rule has the same interpretation as the role.

The part of the lexical validation grammar generated from the sample section of the grammar-creation thesaurus of Figure 5 is shown in Figure 6.

Combined [INF] = |INF|
[PART] and [PART]
treatment = |INF|
changes in [LLP] = |LLP|
[LLP] [UNIT] = |LLP|
total [LLP] = |LLP|
[PART] [LLP] = |LLP|
[SPEC] [PART] [PEST] = |PEST|
[SPEC] and [SPEC] = |SPEC|
hordeum vulgare L = |SPEC|
[AGENT] spray = |AGENT
Maris Piper = |CV|
[PART] [MEAS] = |LLP|
[PART] [HLP] = |HLP|
[INF-STAG] date = |INF|
[ENDO] concentration = |LLP|
coastal plain = |LOC|
[PART] [PEST] = |PEST|
[SOIL] [SOIL] = |SOIL|

[TEMP] [SPEC] = |SPEC|
sugar beet = |SPEC|
dry mass = |LLP|
number of spikes = |LLP|

tridemorph = |AGENT|
Simmonds = |CV|
morphine = |ENDO|
sugar = |ENDO|
yields = |HLP|
drought = |INF|
planting = |INF-STAG|
greenhouse = |LAB|
exudation = |LLP|
Inflorescence = |LLP-STAG|
Tasmania = |LOC|
Volume = |MEAS|
2 = |NUM|

foliar = |PART|
grain = |PART|
tuber = |PART|
seed = |PART|
stem = |PART|
moth = |PEST|
nematode = |PEST|
geese = |PEST|
silt = |SOIL|
loam = |SOIL|
potato = |SPEC|
wheat = |SPEC|
citrus = |SPEC|
avocado = |SPEC|
Winter = |TEMP|
Metre-2 = |UNIT|
1991 = |WHEN|

Figure 6. Sample entries in the lexical validation grammar

3. Use of lexical validation in template matching

An extra procedure was added to the template matching program to increase the weight any candidate string which conformed with the lexical-validation grammar and which had the desired interpretation. Sample output from the template matching program after all candidate substrings for the role of SPEC (crop species) have been compared with the entries in the lexical validation grammar is shown in Figure 7. The entries in each row, reading from left to right, are the weight for the candidate substring, its length in words, the number of occurrences found by the templates and the substring itself. The two terms "spring beans" and "beans" have both been successfully validated by the grammar, and assigned an additional weight of 10. For "spring beans", the relevant components of the grammar are

[TEMP][SPEC] = [SPEC]
spring = [TEMP]
beans = [SPEC].

weight	length	occurrences	string
10.02	2	1	spring beans
10.00	1	1	beans
0.09	1	2	vegetative
0.04	2	1	producing vegetative
0.00	1	1	harvest
0.00	1	1	spring

Figure 7. Sample output from template matching program with incorporation of lexical validation (role indicator = SPEC)

Although the grammar contains an entry for "harvest", this is associated with the role indicator INF-STAG, not SPEC as required here. Hence, the candidate string "harvest" receives a zero weight. Similarly "spring" in the thesaurus has the role TEMP, so this term is also zero weighted. The words "vegetative" and "producing " do not appear in the thesaurus, and so the two middle entries in the table retain their initial small weights.

The addition of 10 to the weight for a lexically validated term, and the assigning of zero for a term which has the wrong role indicator, are quite arbitrary. An alternative would be to multiply the 'raw' weight by some factor so as to increase the weight for a validated term, or decrease it if the role indicator is wrong.

The advantage of recognising candidate terms by means of a grammar rather than using a thesaurus of literal strings is that fewer grammar rules than thesaurus entries will be required, in order to recognise all the terms in the thesaurus. The grammar will also be able to recognise a large number of additional terms not present in the thesaurus. For example, consider the grammar rule

[PART] [LLP] = LLP

which states that a low level property associated with a particular part of a plant should be accepted as a low level property. The lexical validation grammar contains 49 different plant parts and 36 different low level properties, so the rule in question requires $49+36+1=86$ separate entries in the grammar. However, these 86 entries represent $49\times36=1764$ potential terms (the cartesian product of each possible low level property paired with each possible plant part). In contrast, the grammar-building thesaurus from which the grammar rule was derived had just 42 actual examples of literals describing a low level property associated with a part of a plant.

Many of the word combinations recognised by the grammar will have been unanticipated by the thesaurus builder. Of course, some of the combinations included by the grammar, although syntactically acceptable, would not be semantically feasible. For example, the left hand component [PART][LLP] would allow the term "root photosynthesis", even though the root of a plant is not normally responsible for photosynthesis. However, such unfeasible combinations would be very unlikely to occur in a genuine scientific text.

3.1 Empirical evaluation

The effectiveness of the lexical validation grammar was measured empirically using the information retrieval measures of recall and precision. In each case the list of role fillers output by the abstracting system for 20 different documents taken from the *Australian Journal of Experimental Agriculture* was compared against the ideal list of role fillers for the same 20 documents, as selected and agreed by both of the present authors.

Strict recall and precision were based on the number of occasions the automatically selected role filler matched the human-selected filler exactly; permissive recall and precision also took into account the number of times the machine-selected filler was either a substring or a superstring of the human-selected filler string. The strict measures represent the success of the system at selecting exactly the right terms, whereas the permissive measures reflect its success at detecting where in a text a concept is mentioned.

The evaluations were performed first without lexical validation (*no LV*), and then again when the weights for the candidate strings were doubled if the candidate strings were lexically validated (*LV*). Sample results for a set of manually produced templates are shown in Table 1.

These results show a modest improvement in performance resulting from the incorporation of lexical validation. The results overall are not particularly

Table 1. Effect of lexical validation

	no LV	LV
Strict recall	14.8%	17.5%
Permissive recall	28.6%	32.4%
Strict precision	11.0%	14.0%
Permissive precision	21.1%	25.9%

pleasing, but the methods used are amenable to further adjustment and optimisation. Results for a much larger collection of crop studies papers, and for a collection in a different domain, will be reported in a later paper.

4. Extraction of statistics-related expressions

In Sections 2 and 3 we described methods for automatically extracting the ten categories of term necessary to fulfil the indicative function of abstracts automatically produced by the method of Jones and Paice (1992). However, if our automatically generated abstracts are also to perform an informative function, we must be able to infer additional information about the relationships between terms, particularly those found in the Results and Conclusions sections which report the statistical findings of an experiment. In this section we describe our method for identifying sequences of text in which dependent and independent variables, and statistical terminology, are interrelated. The idea is that such text sequences (or the sentences containing them) should be extracted and used to fill Part 9 of the output template shown in Figure 2.

As a first step, the training corpus was annotated using the lexical validation grammar, so that all specific concepts mentioned (e.g., "tridemorph spray") were replaced by their corresponding role indicators (e.g., "AGENT"). Then the repeated sequence detection program (see Section 2.1) was used to examine all word sequences of length 2 to 5 words occurring 5 times or more in the annotated corpus. It was noticed that in the more common sequences many terms describing variables were accompanied by magnitudes, either static magnitudes describing the extent of a variable, or dynamic magnitudes describing some change in the variable. It seemed likely that magnitude terms would be very useful for characterising results-related sentences.

The most frequent of the magnitude expressions found were as follows:

a. "Static" magnitudes, denoted "Q":
average; high; highest; *levels; low; lower; maximum; *mean; mean; median; *potential; proportion of; proportional; range of; *rates; rates of; relative; spread of; total; uniformity of; *values.

b. "Dynamic" magnitudes, denoted "DQ":
decrease in; decreased; *decreased; differ in; *differences; differences in; *fall; fall in; falling; *increase; increase in; increased; *increased; increased the; *increases; increases in; *increment; *losses; reduced; reducing the; reduction in; *reductions; reductions in; *removal; *was decreased; *was greater; *was increased; *was reduced; variation in.

Magnitudes marked with * occur after the variable, whereas the others occur before the variable.

The six most common combinations of a magnitude and a variable are shown in Table 2. All magnitudes or quantity words occurring in the grammar-annotated training corpus were substituted by their relevant codes (Q or DQ). The repeated sequence detection program was used again, this time to find all sequences of length 2 to 12 words with a frequency of at least 5 in the corpus. Examples of such sequences are shown below:

direct correlation of HLP with the LLP
INF gave a significant DQ HLP
AGENT gave a significant DQ HLP
LLP DQ from NUM to NUM UNIT
significant INF treatment interaction.

Table 2. Most frequent combinations of a magnitude and a variable

Frequency	Code	Example
123	DQ LLP	decrease in leaf dry mass
120	Q LLP	average morphine concentration
90	Q INF	high rainfall
80	DQ HLP	variation in yield
55	Q LLP-STAG	high inflorescence
50	LLP DQ	tuber volume was increased

A subjective decision was taken as to which of these sequences were relevant to the statistical findings of an experiment, and how they might be combined with each other to produce meaningful phrases. A set of rules was created manually to describe the syntactic structure of most of the high frequency statistics-related phrases. This set of rules is shown in Figure 8. In order to make this set of rules more widely applicable or domain-independent than the lexical validation grammar, the resulting phrases are described in terms of independent and dependent variables, denoted IV and DV respectively. VAR denotes a variable which may be either dependent or independent.

In the domain of crop protection, the independent variable could be AGENT, ENDO, LLP, LLP-STAG or PEST while the dependent variable could be ENDO, INF, INF-STAG, LLP, LLP-STAG or PEST. The reason LLP, LLP-STAG and PEST can fall into either category is that they can act as intermediate variables. For example, in the same experiment an agent can affect a pest (making PES a dependent variable), while the effect on the pest will have an effect on the growth or yield of the crop, making PEST an independent variable. Similarly, a chemical categorised as ENDO could be externally applied, making it an independent variable, or it may be produced by the plant in response to an outside influence, making it a dependent variable. Two high frequency statistical terms, not informative on their own, which could not readily be included in the rule set as part of complete phrases were "analysis of variance" and "linear regression". For the purpose of creating informative abstracts, it might be possible to extract the entire sentence whenever these terms are encountered in the Results or Conclusions sections of a scientific article.

This work is still in progress, and results will be reported later.

5. Changing the domain

In order to transport the CBA system to domains other than crop protection, it is necessary to determine a new set of roles to describe the new domain, and to create a thesaurus where specific instances of each generic role are listed. This can be done by examining a selection of original papers in the new domain, and generating phrase frequency lists for that domain; use of a word manipulation tool such as WordSmith (Scott 1996) is most useful here. The new roles are the generic categories of the non-stoplisted high and mid-frequency phrases. In a technical domain, a pre-existing domain lexicon may be adapted, or a domain expert may need to be used, to produce the thesaurus of roles and instances. Grefenstette (1994) describes SEXTANT, a system for automatic thesaurus generation, but some domain knowledge is still required to interpret the automatically derived word categories.

(no) (direct) correlation of VAR with VAR;
IV gave [a,no] significant DV ;
DV from NUM to NUM UNIT ;
there was [a,no] significant effect of IV on DV;
DV by NUM per cent;
IV was important in contributing to DV;
IV gave [a,no] ([highly,statistically]) DV;
IV did not affect DV;
(no) significant VAR VAR interaction;
DV due to IV was (not) significant at p [<,=] NUM;
VAR [with,by] VAR was (not) significant at p [<,=] NUM;
VAR was associated with VAR;
IV significantly affected the DV;
IV did not significantly affect the DV;
(no) significant effect of IV on DV;
IV had [a,no] ([highly,statistically]) significant effect on DV;
(no) ([direct, significant, negative]) [correlation$, association$, relationship$, differences$, interaction$] between VAR and VAR;
VAR and VAR were ([highly, significantly, slightly, not]) correlated;
VAR and VAR were linearly related;
IV was more effective than IV;
VAR more rapidly than VAR;
VAR was more sensitive than VAR.

VAR=(the) ([Q,DQ]) ([Q,DQ]) VAR ([Q,DQ]) ([Q,DQ]);
VAR=VAR and VAR;
DV=DV and DV;
IV=IV and IV.

[,] denotes alternatives; () denotes optional components; $ shows that either singular or plural forms are acceptable.

Figure 8. Rules for typical phrases describing statistical findings of an experiment

Once the set of roles and the thesaurus have been prepared, templates can be generated automatically (Oakes and Paice 1999). The lexical validation grammar is produced from the thesaurus by a domain independent substring substitution process (see Section 2.2 above).

The knowledge engineering effort required for our system to transfer domains is much less that that required for other automated abstracting systems which employ a training corpus. The CRYSTAL system of Soderland et al.

(1995) and the CIRCUS system of Riloff and Lehnert (1994) both require that the entire training corpus should not only be parsed according to syntactic structure, but every domain related term should be manually tagged according to its semantic meaning by domain experts. We were able to adapt our system to the domain of computational linguistics in about three person-weeks (this work will be described in a later publication).

Using a grammar to recognise candidate terms, rather than a thesaurus of literal strings, enables potentially more compound terms to be recognised by fewer rules. This is a general advantage of using semantic categories rather than precoordinated terms, as illustrated by the SNOMED multiaxial nomenclature (Lussier, Rothwell and Cote 1998).

Note

* The project 'A Concept-Based Method for Automatic Abstracting' was funded by the Library and Information Commission (formerly the British Library Research and Innovation Centre) under award number LIC/RE/011.

References

ARPA. 1995, Advanced Research Projects Agency. Proceedings of the Sixth Message Understanding Conference (MUC-6), Morgan Kaufmann, San Francisco, CA.

Bowden, P.R. (1999) *Automated Knowledge Extraction from Text.* PhD thesis, The Nottingham Trent University, Nottingham, England.

Daille B. (1995) *Combined Approach for Terminology Extraction: Lexical Studies and Linguistic Filtering.* UCREL Technical Papers, 5, Department of Linguistics, University of Lancaster, England.

Gale W.A., Church K.W., Hanks P. and Hindle D. (1991) *Using Statistics in Lexical Analysis.* In Zernik U. (ed.), "Lexical Acquisition: Exploiting On-Line Resources to Build a Lexicon", Lawrence Erlbaum Associates, Hillsdale, NJ, 115–164.

Gaussier E. and Langé J-M. (1994) *Some Methods for the Extraction of Bilingual Terminology.* In Jones D. (ed.), Proceedings of the International Conference on New Methods in Language Processing (NeMLaP), UMIST, Manchester, England, 242–247.

Grefenstette G. (1994) *Explorations in Automatic Thesaurus Discovery,* Kluwer International Series in Engineering and Computer Science 278, Boston / Dordrecht / London.

Jones, P.A. (1995) *Automatic Abstracting and Indexing of Technical Documents: An Approach Based on Concept Selection.* Ph.D. Thesis, Department of Computing, Lancaster University, England.

Jones P. A. and Paice C. D. (1992) *A 'Select and Generate' Approach to Automatic Abstracting.* In McEnery A. and Paice C. D. (eds.), 14th British Computer Society Information Retrieval Colloquium, Workshops in Computing, Springer-Verlag, London, 141–154 .

Kelledy F. and Smeaton A. F. (1997) *Automatic Phrase Recognition and Extraction from Text.* In Furner J. and Harper D. J. (eds.), Proceedings of the 19th Annual British Computer Society Information Retrieval Specialist Group (BCS-IRSG) Colloquium, Robert Gordon University, Aberdeen, Scotland.

Klingbiel P. H. (1975) *Phrase Structure Rewrite Systems in Information Retrieval* Information Processing and Management 11(2), 113–126.

Liddy E. D. (1991) *The Discourse-Level Structure of Empirical Abstracts.* Information Processing and Management, 27(1), 55–81.

Lussier Y. A., Rothwell D. J. and Cote R. A. (1998) *The SNOMED model: A Knowledge Source for the Controlled Terminology of the Computerised Patient Record.* Methods of Information in Medicine, 37(2), 161–164.

Maeda T., Momouchi Y. and Sawamura H. (1980) *An Automatic Method for Extracting Significant Phrases in Scientific or Technical Documents.* Information Processing and Management, 16(3), 119–127.

Oakes M. P. and Paice C. D. (1999) *Automatic Generation of Templates for Automatic Abstracting.* Proceedings of the 21st British Computer Society Information Retrieval Specialist Group Colloquium (IRSG '99), University of Strathclyde, Scotland, http://www.ewic.org.uk/ewic/workshop/list.cfm.

Paice C. D. and Jones P. A. (1993) *The Identification of Important Concepts in Highly Structured Technical Papers.* In Korfhage R., Rasmussen E. and Willett, P (eds.), Proceedings of the 16th International ACM-SIGIR Conference, Pittsburgh, PA, USA, 69–77.

Rama D. V. and Srinivasan P. (1993) *An Investigation of Content Representation Using Text Grammars.* ACM Transactions on Information Systems 11(1), 51–75.

Riloff E. and Lehnert W. (1994) *Information Extraction as a Basis for High-Precision Text Classification,* ACM Transactions on Information Systems 12(3), 296–335.

Ruge G. Schwarz C. and Warner A. J. (1991) *Effectiveness and Efficiency in Natural Language Processing for Large Amounts of Text.* Journal of the American Society for Information Science, 42(6), 450–456.

Salton G. (1968) *Automatic Information Organization and Retrieval.* McGraw-Hill, New York.

Scott, M. (1996) *WordSmith Tools Manual.* Oxford University Press.

Soderland S., Fisher D., Aseltine J. and Lehnert W. (1995) *CRYSTAL: Inducing a Conceptual Dictionary,* Proceedings of the 14th International Joint Conference on Artificial Intelligence, Montreal (part 2), 1314–1319.

Tribble C. and Jones G. (1990) *Concordances in the Classroom.* Longman, Harlow.

Wilson A. and Thomas J. (1997) *Semantic Annotation.* In "Corpus Annotation", Garside R., Leech G. and McEnery A. (eds.), Longman, London & NY, 53–65.

About the contributors

Akiko Aizawa received a Ph.D. in Electrical Engineering from the University of Tokyo in 1990. She is an Associate Professor at the National Institute of Informatics, Japan. Her research interests include Mathematical Analysis of Textual Data, Knowledge Discovery, and Evolutionary Computation.

Sophia Ananiadou received her Ph.D. in Computational Linguistics at UMIST (Manchester, G.B.). She is a Senior Lecturer at the Department of Computer Science of the University of Salford as well as a Senior Research Fellow at the Department of Language Engineering of UMIST (University of Manchester Institute of Science and Technology) She has a background in Linguistics, Computational Linguistics, and Computer Science. Her areas of specialization are Terminology, Machine Translation, Morphology, Sublanguages, and Corpus Processing.

Peter Anick's applied research at Digital Equipment Corporation spanned expert systems, natural language interfaces, machine-aided translation, and intelligent information retrieval. His PhD thesis from Brandeis University applied corpus linguistic techniques to the problem of generating terminological feedback for iterative information retrieval. He currently works at search engine company AltaVista, where he continues to explore ways to exploit linguistic knowledge for improving on-line search.

Jacques Bouaud received a Ph.D. degree in Biomathematics from the University of Paris 7 in 1989. Since 1988, he has been a member of the artificial intelligence and medicine team of "Service d'Informatique Médicale/Direction des Systèmes d'Information/Assistance publique — Hôpitaux de Paris" where he is involved in R&D activities. His main interests focus on Knowledge Engineering and Knowledge Dissemination in the medical context.

Didier Bourigault is a researcher at the CNRS-ERSS (Toulouse, France). For his Ph.D. thesis, he developed a terminology extraction software product in collaboration with the French Electricity Board and the Ecole des Hautes Etudes en Sciences Sociales. He participated in major conferences for Computational Linguistics and knowledge engineering (EACL, COLING, KAW). He helped create and spearhead the TIA group, a French research group on Computational Terminology and Knowledge Engineering. He works as a consultant in the field of Language Engineering and Computational Terminology.

Teresa Cabré Castellví holds a Ph.D. in Romance Philology from the University of Barcelona (1977), and is currently Professor of Linguistics and Terminology at the Universitat Pompeu Fabra as well as a member of the Institute of Catalan Studies, the most important scholarly society in Catalonia. Her research interests include general and Catalan lexicology, lexicography, theoretical and applied terminology, and she has done much work in establishing and developing applied linguistics. She was the director of the Catalan Center for Terminology, TERMCAT (1985–88), and she set up the Catalan Language Service at the University of Barcelona (1989–93). She has been one of the forces behind the Reference Center for Language Engineering as a part of the government-sponsored Research Plan for Catalonia.

Chun-Liang Chen received his Master's degree in Computer Science from the National Taiwan University in 1999. He is currently working with an Internet startup company. His research interests include Information Retrieval and Natural Language Processing.

Lee-Feng Chien received his Ph.D. in Computer Science from the National Taiwan University in 1991. Since 1993 he has joined in the Institute of Information Science, Academia Sinica, and is currently an associate research fellow as well as the PI of the institute's Information Retrieval Program. He is also an adjunct professor in the Information Management Department, National Taiwan University. Dr. Chien's research interests include Information Retrieval, Spoken Language Processing, and Natural Language Processing.

James J. Cimino, M.D. is an Associate Professor of Medical Informatics and Medicine at Columbia University, where he divides his time between medical informatics research, teaching, patient care, and system development. His principle areas of research are the development of knowledge-based controlled medical terminologies and the use of the World Wide Web to integrate on-line information resources with electronic medical records.

Anne Condamines successfully completed her Ph.D. in Linguistics at Toulouse II in 1990. Since 1993, she has been a full-time researcher at the CNRS within ERSS, Toulouse II, France. She is project-leader for the ERSS group 'Semantics and Corpus'. In 1993, she launched with Didier Bourigault a research group funded by the Ministry for Research on the theme 'Terminology and AI' which brings together terminologists, linguists and computer scientists. In 1994, she was awarded a national prize by the CNRS and its partners for her achievements in bridging the gap between theoretical research in language-engineering and its industrial applications.

Beatrice Daille is an Assistant professor at the Computer Science Department of the University of Nantes, France. She is also the head of the Natural Language Processing (NLP) research team of the Computing Institute of Nantes (IRIN). She trained first in Mathematics and Computer Science, then specialized in Computational Linguistics, and has been working in this field since 1989. She in particularly interested in practical natural language processing systems for information access and text mining.

Rosa Estopà Bagot holds a Ph.D. in Applied Linguistic from the Pompeu Fabra University (1999). She is currently a teaching assistant at the Pompeu Fabra University. She is a member of IULA and IULATErm. Her research interests include Lexicology, Neology, and Applied Terminology. In her thesis, she proposes a multifunctional terminology extractor.

Eric Gaussier holds a degree in Applied Mathematics from Ecole Centrale Paris and a Ph.D. in Computer Science from University Paris 7. He is currently working at XRCE (Xerox Research Centre Europe) as a Computational Linguist. His main research focuses on the Linguistic Analysis of Documents for Information Access, including Monolingual and Bilingual Terminology Extraction, (cross-language) Information Retrieval, and Machine Learning Techniques for Linguistic Knowledge Acquisition and Processing.

Benoît Habert has a background both in linguistics (lexical statistics and discourse analysis) and computer science (inheritance mechanisms for NLP). Lectures in semantics at Nanterre University (Paris X). His current research fields are automatic semantic category acquisition on the one hand and inductive text typology on the other hand.

Thierry Hamon is a Ph.D. student in Computer Science at the Laboratoire d'Informatique de Paris-Nord (Institut Galilée, Universite Paris-Nord, France). His research interests include Computer Science, Natural Language Processing, Corpus Linguistics, and Terminology.

Toru Hisamitsu has an M.A. in Mathematics (1986) from the University of Tokyo and a Ph.D. in Information Science (2000) from the University of Tokyo. He is Senior Research Scientist at the Central Research Laboratory, Hitachi. Ltd. (Japan). His main research interests are Japanese morphological analysis, quantitative approaches to lexical semantics, and their application to the user-interface for large scale information access.

David A. Hull is a Research Scientist at the Xerox Research Centre Europe in Grenoble, France. He received his Ph.D. in statistics from Stanford University in 1994 for a dissertation on applying statistical learning algorithms to text routing and filtering. He is active in the fields of information retrieval and computational linguistics. His current research interests include text filtering, cross-language text retrieval, and the statistical terminology alignment from parallel bilingual corpora.

Christian Jacquemin is a Professor in Computer Science at the University of Paris 11 and a researcher at the CNRS-LIMSI laboratory. He received his PhD from University of Paris 7. His work is focused on automatic term and variant recognition through shallow transformational NLP techniques. He has developped a tool called Fastr available for research purposes at http://www.limsi.fr/Individu/jacquemi/.

Hongyan Jing is a Ph.D. candidate in the Computer Science Department of Columbia University (New York). Her dissertation is on automatic text summarization. Her other interests include Information Retrieval, Digital Libraries, and Robust Natural Language Processing Techniques.

Kyo Kageura, Ph.D., is an Associate Professor at the National Institute of Informatics, Japan. His main research interest is integrating linguistic, conceptual and quantitative approaches to modeling term formation and terminological growth. He is also interested in terminological applications, such as automatic thesaurus construction.

Marie-Claude L'Homme is an Associate Professor at the Department of Linguistics and Translation of the University of Montreal (Canada). She has a background in Translation, Terminology, and Linguistics. She is specialized in terminology, and computational terminology. Her current research focuses on the implementation of formal semantic models in computational terminology applications.

Diana Maynard is a Research Associate in the Dept. of Computer Science at the University of Sheffield, UK, where she is working in the area of Information Extraction. She is currently completing a Ph.D. in Automatic Term Recognition at Manchester Metropolitan University, UK. She has a B.Sc. in Computational Linguistics & French from UMIST, Manchester, and an M.Sc. in Cognitive Science from Manchester University.

Ingrid Meyer is an Associate Professor at the School of Translation and Interpretation, University of Ottawa, Canada. Her principal areas of terminological specialization are computational terminology, conceptual aspects of terminology, and relations between terms and general-language words.

Hiroshi Nakagawa is a Professor at the Digital Library Division of the Information Technology Center (University of Tokyo, Japan). He is specialized in Computational Linguistics, Information Retrieval, Natural Language Processing, Japanese syntax, semantics and pragmatics, Automatic Term Recognition.

Adeline Nazarenko (Ph.D. in computer Science) is Maitre de Conférences at the Computer Science department, Paris-Nord University. She is member of the LIPN (Laboratoire d'Informatique de Paris-Nord). He is specialized in Computational Linguistics and Corpus Semantics, and she is currently working on knowledge acquisition from textual data.

Yoshiki Niwa has a Ph.D. in Mathematics (1986) from the University of Tokyo. He is a Senior Research Scientist at the Central Research Laboratory, Hitachi. Ltd. (Japan). His main research interest is in the quantitative approaches to lexical semantics and its application to the user-interface for large scale information access.

Michael P. Oakes. has a B.Sc. in Biochemistry (Sheffield), an M.Sc. in Audiology (Salford), an M.Sc. in Computing (Bradford), and a Ph.D. in Computer Science (Liverpool). He is currently a Research Associate at the Natural Language Processing Group (Department of Computer Science, University of Sheffield, England). His fields of specialization are Information Retrieval, Bilingual Text Alignment, and Information Extraction. He also published a book entitled *Statistics for Corpus Linguistics*, Edinburgh University Press, 1998.

Chris Paice is a Lecturer at the Computing Department of Lancaster University, (England). He has been interested in automatic abstracting for more than 20 years, with a paper on the 'indicator phrase' method presented at the BCS/ACM symposium at St. John's College, Cambridge in June 1980. Since then, he has undertaken a succession of projects on automatic abstracting, some in collaboration with colleagues at UMIST. Other areas of research interest include: information retrieval models, stemming algorithms, and retrieval and navigation in long texts.

Josette Rebeyrolle is a Ph.D. student in Linguistics at the University of Toulouse II. Her research interests include Lexical Semantics, Corpus Linguistics, and Terminology.

Evelyne Tzoukermann, after completing her Ph.D. at the University of Paris, obtained a Fulbright fellowship and pursued a post-doctoral year at Brown University. She spent two years at IBM Watson Research Center as a visiting scientist and is now at Bell Labs, Lucent Technologies. Her research interests include computational linguistics, information retrieval, and text-to-speech synthesis.

Jordi Vivaldi Palatresi is an Electronic Engineer who has been working on Natural Language Processing since 1987. He started working in machine translation, then moved to his current position at the Institute for Applied Linguistics where he is working mainly in corpus compilation and processing. His current research interest is term detection.

Pierre Zweigenbaum graduated from École Polytechnique and from ENST. He received a Ph.D. in Computer Science and the "Habilitation à diriger des Recherches". He has been since 1984 in the Department of Medical Informatics of Assistance Publique — Hôpitaux deParis. His work has focussed on NLP in Medicine, from syntax to knowledge representation. He was coordinator of the European project MENELAS, and team leader in two other European projects (NLPAD and DOME) on medical language processing.

Subject Index

In the series NATURAL LANGUAGE PROCESSING (NLP) the following titles have been published thus far, or are scheduled for publication:

1. BUNT, Harry and William BLACK (eds.): *Abduction, Belief and Context in Dialogue. Studies in computational pragmatics.* 2000.
2. BOURIGAULT, Didier, Christian JACQUEMIN and Marie-Claude L'HOMME (eds.): *Recent Advances in Computational Terminology.* 2001.
3. MANI, Inderjeet: *Automatic Summarization.* n.y.p.